'Some serious solutions to some very serious problems. Inspiring, readable and so great to feel that, in Gordon Brown, there's a proper, big-brained adult in the room.'
David Schneider, actor and writer

'Particularly important and shown in the pages of this book is Gordon Brown's commitment to international cooperation and the role of international institutions.'
Ban Ki-moon, Former Secretary-General of the United Nations

'Gordon Brown draws on his unparalleled experience to show us how international cooperation is the only way to solve the challenges of our societies, economies and environment. Every chapter is brimming with ideas and insight – and will leave you feeling inspired to change the world.'
Baroness Minouche Shafik, Director of the London School of Economics and author of *What We Owe Each Other: A New Social Contract*

'In the face of so many assaults on the truth that all countries depend on each other, it has never been more vital to fight back and assert the imperative of finding global answers to global problems. Gordon Brown does so with passion, clarity and an invigorating combination of urgency with thoughtfulness, of alarm about the threats with confidence that we can indeed meet them. This is a book that will galvanise and give heart to the struggle for a sustainable, just and peaceful future.'
Fintan O'Toole, author

'Gordon Brown highlights the global challenges our generation must meet and makes the case for the global cooperation we urgently need.'
Graça Machel, Founder, Graça Machel Trust

'I've seen the great work Gordon Brown has done on financing education in the world's poorest countries. Now that he turns his mind to other pressing global issues to find solutions that could bring genuine change to the world, I'm going to pay attention. I'm going to read. And hope.'
Jo Nesbø, author

'Gordon Brown's wisdom, integrity and passion make him an essential voice for us all to heed, and to give us hope, in these unchartered times.'
David Tennant, actor

'Gordon Brown is one of the last grown-up, truly committed politicians dedicated to public service, putting those he served needs before his own – always. With this book he helps us envisage a brighter future towards which we can all make a contribution and as ever, Brown seeks to steer us towards a better world shaped by our better selves.'
Arabella Weir, actor and comedian

SEVEN WAYS TO CHANGE THE WORLD

How to Fix the Most Pressing Problems We Face

GORDON BROWN

**SIMON &
SCHUSTER**

London · New York · Sydney · Toronto · New Delhi

First published in Great Britain by Simon & Schuster UK Ltd, 2021

Copyright © Gordon Brown, 2021

The right of Gordon Brown to be identified as the author
of this work has been asserted in accordance with
the Copyright, Designs and Patents Act, 1988.

3 5 7 9 10 8 6 4 2

Simon & Schuster UK Ltd
1st Floor
222 Gray's Inn Road
London WC1X 8HB

www.simonandschuster.co.uk
www.simonandschuster.com.au
www.simonandschuster.co.in

Simon & Schuster Australia, Sydney
Simon & Schuster India, New Delhi

The author and publishers have made all reasonable efforts
to contact copyright-holders for permission, and apologise
for any omissions or errors in the form of credits given.
Corrections may be made to future printings.

A CIP catalogue record for this book
is available from the British Library

Hardback ISBN: 978-1-3985-0361-8
eBook ISBN: 978-1-3985-0362-5

Typeset in Perpetua by M Rules
Printed and bound by CPI Group (UK) Ltd, Croydon, CR0 4YY

MIX
Paper from
responsible sources
FSC® C020471
FSC
www.fsc.org

To my brothers John and Andrew.

*All Gordon Brown's proceeds from this book will
go to the Jennifer Brown Research Laboratory
and Theirworld children's charity.*

CONTENTS

PREFACE

Why have hundreds of thousands of lives been needlessly lost during the pandemic through a lack of equipment, medicine and vaccines?

Why does a sword of Damocles hang over the global economy, which is under constant threat of financial crises and suffering pitifully low growth?

Why, despite the genius of the world's best scientists, are we struggling to halt climate change?

Why, in 2021, are there still 260 million school-age boys and girls who will not be in education even after the pandemic is finally over?

Why are our promises to end extreme poverty and avoidable infant and maternal mortality being betrayed?

Why can't we collect taxes from some of the world's wealthiest people and companies, instead of standing by as they hide their fortunes in tax havens?

And why is there a new nuclear arms race under way, with half a dozen countries threatening to become nuclear-weapon powers?

None of these questions is easy to answer and to do so involves an intensive search for information and complex judgements – but they all have one characteristic in common: they are global problems that need global solutions. None can be resolved by one country, organisation or leader on their own. None can be solved without a degree of cooperation between nations.

But for the most part, this does not happen, and when it does, it is insufficient. There is a mismatch between the global nature of the problems we face and our capacity – or willingness – to resolve them as a global community. Instead, we continue to work within a predominantly national framework.

The result is that families go hungry, children go uneducated, men and women go without work, taxes that could fund our public services are not paid, our environment deteriorates, people die of disease, and nuclear weapons with the power to destroy our entire planet grow in number, with proliferation and escalation an ever-present threat.

Nothing has brought this home to me more than the avoidable waste of human lives as a result of our collective failure to prevent, control and overcome the COVID-19 pandemic. We were ill-prepared for the onslaught of the virus not because we lacked expert doctors, scientists or academics, nor because there was no manufacturing capacity to produce the treatments and cures, but because over many years we have failed to get our act together: no early warning systems worth their name; no adequate exchange of information between countries; no proper monitoring; no obligations on states to take remedial action; no sufficiently large reserves of drugs or even protective equipment; and no agreement on how we share the burden of paying for what we desperately need from ventilators to vaccines. And so this book started with a set of questions that I felt that, after more than forty years in public life, I needed to investigate and try to answer. I wanted to understand why, in the face of such glaring need, national governments seemed so ineffective and international institutions seemed so powerless to act. And what, through practical measures, we could do about this state of affairs.

How we organise ourselves as an international community is not an abstract question to be dealt with only by diplomats and lawyers, it is of immediate and pressing relevance to all of us. Even as vaccination protects lives from the effects of the disease, we still face a common virus and a common recession. As I write, each country is having its own domestic debate on recovery and what we do next; unsurprisingly, there are common themes that emerge, and instead of debates in America that are America-centric, in Europe that are Euro-centric and in Asia that are Asia-centric it makes sense to consider whether problems common to us all call for similar responses and shared solutions. I want to bring leaders to an understanding that they need to think global.

Seven Ways to Change the World is thus an inquiry into what I also call the world's 'ungoverned spaces'. This term has traditionally meant the unsafe, lawless zones in failing and fragile states where private warlords, bandits, pirates, terrorist insurgents, arms traders, illicit drug dealers and black marketers hold sway. Governance in such areas is notoriously difficult, with the public will disregarded and the public good tarnished by private actors merely out for their own gain. But I am not talking about these places; the ungoverned spaces I have in mind are alarmingly much vaster, if still sharing in certain traits. They encompass the entire global environment – polluted oceans, desiccated forests and fast-expanding deserts. They span the global financial system as tax havens, offshore financial centres and illicit flows of money facilitate the looting of public coffers by the world's least needy. And they include the world's thermonuclear safety regime, ever more technologically sophisticated but also ever more vulnerable to accidents and manipulation.

Like their traditional counterparts, these ungoverned spaces are all lacking effective governance in the name of the public good. To clean up these areas, we need to turn well-meaning but currently underperforming international institutions into effective swords for justice. The recent pandemic has highlighted this. Despite all the efforts of the WHO and the many brilliant medics and scientists around the world, much of global health is an ungoverned space. Too often it is a case of 'everyone for himself or herself', rather than recognising that we are all in this together. As a result thousands have died who, with proper care, could and should have lived.

We can debate whether the virus was avoidable: what is clear is that the unimaginable human loss was avoidable. This became a man-made disaster. Similarly, poverty, pollution and nuclear proliferation are avoidable ailments. And as I reflected on these preventable problems and what we could do to solve them, I realised that the underlying failure was the yawning gap between our need to cooperate and our willingness to do so. The case for international cooperation had to be made.

In this book, I identify what I consider to be the seven most challenging global problems. I start with global health but range widely to include: global financial instability; climate change and environmental damage; the barriers to education and opportunity; the humanitarian crisis and global poverty; global inequality and one of its biggest manifestations, the continued use of global tax havens; and nuclear proliferation. These are problems that require global responses and cannot be fully addressed without cross-border cooperation.

There are, of course, other challenges of a global nature, many now emerging in the field of advanced technology, not least in the rules governing cybersecurity, artificial intelligence, the Internet and globalisation's digital networks. In areas like cybercrime, there is still no global oversight body, even when, as Professor Ian Goldin points out in his book *The Butterfly Defect*, 'a single computer virus, such as WannaCry or NotPetya – whether produced by organised state agencies or lone-wolf individuals – can spread globally and cause billions of dollars of damage within days'. What we do to address challenges like these would require another book by writers more expert than me, but I will touch upon possible ways forward in the context of the China–USA relationship, when I look at what can be done to avert a future of 'one world, two systems'.

In spring 2020, just as the scale of the common threat became obvious, President Trump withdrew critical American funding from the World Health Organization, the one forum that unites medics, scientists and policy makers across the world. Saddened by this and the global response to the crisis and impatient to see things change, I started to write about the need for cooperation. Now, as I complete this book, Trump's successor, in a few weeks of clear vision and active politics, has inaugurated what may become a new era of partnership and international cooperation. And if this book can offer some ideas that can shape such a future it will have served its purpose.

President John F. Kennedy – a good man in a crisis, whether in command of a wrecked motor torpedo boat in the Pacific War or managing the challenges of the Cuban Missile Crisis with calm resolve and agility – was fond of saying: 'The Chinese use two brush strokes to write the word "crisis". One brush stroke stands for danger; the other for opportunity. In a crisis, be aware of the danger – but recognise the opportunity.' The seven crises I highlight present us with the chance to think of changes we can make which, if enacted, would address some of the most pressing challenges felt across continents. These seven actions are not going to be seven new wonders of the world but they are practical advances that can make a difference to millions of lives.

PART ONE

Learning From Our Past

INTRODUCTION

In late 2019 an invisible virus, thought to have surfaced from a wet market in a huge industrial Chinese city, spread round the world in fewer than eighty days. COVID-19 has already done more damage than any economic downturn or military conflict in recent history. At time of writing, in spring 2021, COVID-19 has infected more than 127 million people – more than any epidemic since the Spanish flu of 1918–19. This microscopic parasite, 10,000 times smaller than a grain of salt, has caused more deaths – in excess of 3 million – than any war in the West since 1945. And it has wrought more financial havoc, disrupted more trade, killed off more jobs, led to more lost production and caused more company closures than any modern recession.

COVID-19 has not only attacked our human bodies and shattered our economic fabric, it has also undermined the cultural and social foundations of our lives. As individuals, we have come face to face with our own vulnerability and mortality. Each of us has been sharply reminded of the sheer precariousness of life and the fundamental fragility of the human condition. And the pandemic has called into question much of what we know about disease, technology, economics and human behaviour, to the extent that our pre-COVID-19 world is simply no more. Across the board, well-established paradigms about the role of individuals, markets and states have been challenged and long-held assumptions about the nature of the social contract, the openness of our societies, the responsibilities of governments, the reach of the state and even the very idea of progress have been called into question. All these issues require investigation. In this book, we will interrogate our prevailing ideas, ideologies and institutions and ask why they proved so inadequate in their response to the challenge of COVID-19; and how we can now take the crisis as an opportunity to create a better world.

As unprecedented as what has been variously called the Great Lockdown and the Great Virus Crisis has been, it has shone a new light on age-old problems: oppressive poverty; the unequal distribution of opportunities; and what the economist J. K. Galbraith referred to sixty years ago as the contrast between public squalor and private wealth – the inequalities and divisions that arise from the way our economy is run, our resources are allocated and our environment is managed.[1]

It has accelerated changes already in train, not least the flight from the physical to the virtual. Even before the pandemic, a profound transition was already under way, taking us from the old, industrial, workplace-based economy to the more recent information and technology revolution – The Fourth Industrial Revolution – and on to an as-yet undetermined future. So, even when the pandemic is over, it is unlikely there will be a return to 'business as usual'. Indeed, the very idea of a 'normality' is now little more than a fiction, and in no sense a guide to the future in a world continuously reshaped by radical uncertainty.

For the crisis is also forcing onto the agenda new ways of thinking that may otherwise have taken years to emerge; what was previously unimaginable suddenly becomes imaginable, making it possible to begin discerning more clearly what is wrong and what needs to be reconsidered and reset. And, slowly, more and more of us are coming to realise that there is an underlying problem that goes beyond the way we deal with one virus: namely, our failure as an international community to organise ourselves and to prevent and manage crises that affect us all. Quite simply, in order to address global problems that need global solutions, we have to find better ways of working together.

At the start of 2020, we were slow to understand that a pandemic knows no boundaries and has no respect for political frontiers, and that if a pandemic crosses borders, so must the response. But in 2020 people and states still stuck rigidly to a system of national rules, borders and frontiers – which the virus did not. As a result, nation after nation lost control of the spread while our international institutions failed to command sufficient support or authority to coordinate successful interventions. All countries faced the same virus (which soon demonstrated its intrinsic capacity to produce new variants) and the same economic recession, required the same medical supplies in response and needed prompt and explicit cooperation to get the virus under control, starting with a mutually beneficial exchange of information. And yet in nations across the world governments failed to draw the logical conclusion: that to protect ourselves locally, we had to act globally.

A year on, political leaders have yet to act on the knowledge that we will not be able to finally eliminate the disease in each of our own countries until it is fully eradicated in all countries. They have failed to conclude that we have no alternative but to act together. And it is only when one stands back to reflect on the scale of the disaster – the hundreds of thousands of avoidable deaths and countless avoidable hospitalisations – that one can begin to truly understand the colossal scale and impact of our failure to work together to protect lives; the yawning gap between the need for cooperation and our failure to deliver it; and the underlying crisis of our international order.

Now, with COVID-19 still raging across the planet, we must confront this failure. Because while the virus stands out as the most obvious example, the truth is that every single one of the key challenges facing humanity today, many of which threaten to destroy our way of life and the planet with it, requires a similar internationally coordinated response. A view of the world made up of competing nations and empires, each of them self-contained and ploughing their lone furrows, had outlived its relevance in the last century, never mind this one. It is a simple fact that in a world that has become increasingly interconnected and globalised, the seven challenges discussed in this book – from pandemics and pollution to nuclear proliferation and poverty – cannot be fully addressed without cross-border cooperation.

Yet, as the pandemic has shown, the tragedy – both in lives lost and the trillions squandered in lost economic activity – is that we still, too often, see a resolution to these challenges primarily through a nationalist lens, to be solved within the confines of the nation state acting on its own. As the popularity of nationalist slogans like 'America First', 'China First', 'Russia First' and 'India First' remind us, much of the world retains a nationalist mindset, often dances to jingoistic tunes and can all too easily march under chauvinistic and sometimes xenophobic banners. Instead of uniting people in a common cause, the 'my country first and only' zealots subdivide the human species into exclusive tribes structured around 'insiders' ('us') and 'outsiders' ('them'), and when nationalist passions blind us to the possible benefits of international cooperation like this, the inevitable consequence is that global problems remain unaddressed.

But we cannot respond by wishing away the inevitable tension between, on the one hand, the realities of global interdependence and the pressures of global economic integration and, on the other, the instinct to retain one's national sovereignty and to bring decision-making closer to home. In no way do I seek to abandon the nation state and offer the utopian impossibility of some global government. But the practical task before us is to end the mind-set which sees the competing rights of national sovereignty and international cooperation as a zero-sum game, and to dispel the notion that any gains enjoyed by one country will always come at the expense of another. We can, and must, do better than that.

In summary, the challenge of our times is to reconcile the demands of globalisation, sovereignty and democracy, and achieve an optimal balance between the responsibilities borne by our international institutions and by nation states. Whether the challenge is battling a pandemic, tackling the looming threat of climate change, or preventing a new nuclear arms race, it can no longer be ignored or held over to another day. Instead, we are called upon to act with what Martin Luther King Jr called 'the fierce urgency of now'. Indeed, as King also observed, 'In this unfolding conundrum of life and history, there *is* such a thing as being too late.'[2]

Some might argue that it is already too late. More than sixty years ago, Albert Schweitzer, the renowned Nobel Prize-winning doctor, warned us that 'man has lost the capacity to foresee and to forestall. He will end by destroying the Earth.'[3] Similarly, the reason given by the inventor and space entrepreneur Elon Musk for his breathless rush to fly a spaceship to the moon and then Mars is not his curiosity or competitive desire to be the first there. Nor is it a natural instinct to explore the unknown and 'go where humankind has never gone before'. And nor is it a longing to bequeath a scientific discovery or even – as was famously cited by George Mallory as his explanation for persevering in his ultimately fatal efforts to scale Mount Everest – 'because it's there'.[4] Musk's quest is born not of that positivity or optimism, but rather of fear and pessimism: to insure against our planet's possible destruction, he says, we need to become a multi-planet species. Earth has seen five extinctions, he tells us, and, while we may be able to develop the technology to shield the planet if an asteroid hits, it is important to get a self-sustaining base on Mars in the event of a climate disaster or a nuclear war. Mars is 'far enough away from Earth that it's more likely to survive than a moon base', he explained. 'If there's a third world war, we want to make sure there's enough of a seed of human civilisation somewhere else to bring it back and shorten the length of the dark ages.'[5]

That fatalism was shared by the late Stephen Hawking, who – to improve the chance of human survival from planet-wide events, such as global thermonuclear war – consistently argued for the colonisation of other planets within the solar system. Only a few years before he died, he prophesied that humanity faces two options: either we colonise space within the next 200 years or we face the prospect of extinction.

Hawking and Musk paint quite apocalyptic visions of our planet's fragile future, specifically – in their eyes – due to climate change and the potential for nuclear war. I reject this pessimism. But I accept that the future of our planet *is* fragile and that it is not science fiction to believe that the world could be laid low in a number of ways, even going beyond climate change or radioactive fallout as a result of open nuclear conflict. The planet could be disrupted by a financial crash even more devastating than that of 2008–09; it could be disrupted by the mass exodus of millions of people fleeing from war, poverty, lack of opportunity or global warming; or it could be disrupted by our failure to address glaring injustices and unacceptable inequalities.

In this sense, the pandemic has not just been a crisis in its own right, but also a salutary warning of what may be to come. It tells us that we are as unprepared as an international community to face these challenges as we were for 9/11 or for the global financial crisis or for climate change itself. And it warns us that, if we do nothing to alleviate environmental issues, financial challenges, poverty, inequality and ignorance, we will split asunder. But, if we *can* address these issues – and if we do so this decade – I believe that it is not too late to turn things around. However, in order to do so, we will need to work together.

Global problems need global solutions

I remember being asked during the 2009 financial crisis how I would sum up what I had learned from the storm that engulfed us. 'It's the economy, stupid – isn't it?' I was asked, as many repeated back to me the oft-quoted Bill Clinton campaign slogan. 'No,' I said, 'what I have learned is that global problems need global solutions.' Even then, it was clear that, in our ever-more interdependent world, we would not achieve success by working in isolation; we would have to come together to deal with global problems that we cannot not solve on our own. And, in this crisis, I have learned something more: there are such things as global public goods, like a good climate and a healthy, disease-free environment, that we all need, so it makes sense for all countries to work together to make sure we all have them.

But yet, running almost parallel, nationalism has been on the rise. We have found that the nation state – which has, for centuries, been able to command outsized political loyalty and exercise coercive power – is resurgent as the only real centre of political gravity. And we see it not only in the UK's rejection of the EU, or in China's national security law repressing free speech in Hong Kong, or in the Russian president's opportunism and aggression both at home and abroad, but in almost every region of the world. In India's revocation of the special status of Kashmir; in Ethiopia's internal war and its fight with Egypt and Sudan over the damming of the Nile; in the Iran–Saudi and Qatar–UAE conflicts; in Turkey's military aggression in the Middle East; in the Nagorno-Karabakh conflict pursued by Azerbaijan.

But there has been no greater demonstration of the damage nationalism does than the protectionism that has characterised the nativist responses to the pandemic: national leaders desperately trying to corner the global market in vaccines, with no thought for others, and refusing to supply their neighbours with essential drugs, protective medical equipment and vaccines themselves, even when they have a surplus that exceeds what they can use. At the very time they have been needed most, international institutions like the World Health Organization (WHO) and the United Nations (UN) have been bypassed and undermined, with cross-border cooperation set aside in favour of go-it-alone responses.

For years, we have prided ourselves in the development of global supply chains for goods like medical equipment and in the circuits of mutual dependence these supply chains created. So important did they become, in fact, that they were dubbed 'solidarity chains' as testament to the inability of anyone anywhere to opt out of the world. But, during 2020, they were at breaking point, their disarray providing a sharp corrective to all those who assumed that progress would inevitably produce an open, not closed, world of trade and commerce.

We can, however, take heart from the willing international collaboration that, in defiance of populist nationalists, emerged across the world of medicine in response to COVID-19. Scientists and projects that could have been competing against each other commercially actually united in an altruistic communal response to a global threat. In one triumphant week in November 2020, three international groups of researchers and three multinational companies, all of which had been engaged in non-stop rounds of laboratory research and field tests and trials, announced a vaccine breakthrough after only eight months of intensive work. This success alone should be a rebuke to those who challenge science and threaten to undermine reason as the basis for decision-making. The new vaccines draw on collegiate work by scientists across Europe, the US and Asia. Nothing better sums up the interdependent nature of our economy than a US company employing scientists from Turkey to create a vaccine in laboratories in Germany, with many of the doses to be manufactured in India. The speed at which new cures and new solutions have been explored and discovered through this cross-border collaboration shows that we have the technological capacity on a global scale to confront the challenges we face and that decent-minded people of different nationalities are keen to cooperate across borders to find solutions.

So we have to address the mismatch between this current medical and scientific cooperation and a lingering failure on the part of our political leaders to come together to ensure this happens quickly and universally. Seemingly unanswerable scientific breakthroughs – those that could, for example, vaccinate the entire world or decarbonise the planet – are at risk of being torpedoed by powerful vested interests. Or sidelined by bureaucratic indifference. Or undermined by weak and incompetent political leaders. Or sabotaged by geopolitical rivalries and by nations clinging to old-fashioned and absolutist views of national sovereignty – or by hostility to new thinking.

'The difficulty lies not so much in developing new ideas as in escaping from old ones,' the renowned economist John Maynard Keynes concluded. As a result, the multilateral cooperation that is necessary to deal with a global problem does not happen and the very real tensions between economic and environmental priorities and between the developed and developing world go unresolved. Perhaps no one could have anticipated how unequal to the task of chaos prevention world leaders would have been in 2020, but their failures are a salutary reminder that the best ideas can be rendered worthless by bad political decisions.

These and other global problems seem more intractable today because we trade, travel, holiday, study and invest across borders at a rate and at a level far greater than ever before.[7] We can communicate instantaneously and continuously with anyone in almost any part of the world and it is said that we live in a world that is not only interdependent, but also, in some respects, fused together. Until COVID-19 hit, more and more goods and services were being exchanged in global supply chains. This means that we are not just more economically integrated and interconnected; we are dependent on each other in a way we have never been before. The openness of our economies creates great opportunities, but it also makes us more vulnerable. Borders have become more porous to everything from infectious diseases and drugs to illegal immigration and terrorists, so disruptions that start in one part of the world, like a pandemic, can quickly affect all parts of the world.

In the past thirty years, cross-border trade has risen from 20 per cent of all world economic activity to 35 per cent.[8] In the pre-COVID-19 period, 4 billion flights were made by aeroplane every year, following a 100 per cent increase in air travel in just one decade.[9] Geographical mobility is now so common that 260 million people have migrated from the country of their birth, including 100 million from developing countries to the developed world. A few years ago, fewer than 2 million students studied away from their home country; before the virus hit, that number was predicted to treble to 6 million.[10] Such intermingling of individuals from different backgrounds, cultures and traditions – often leading to intermarriage – means that, in almost every country, with perhaps Japan and parts of Eastern Europe being the only advanced-economy exceptions, largely homogeneous communities are increasingly becoming heterogeneous ones.

This opening up has profound economic effects. The first, pre-1914 era of globalisation happened under the umbrella of the British Empire and the Gold Standard. It ended in the First World War and in decades of protectionism. The post-1945 world order, agreed at the Bretton Woods Conference in July 1944, again freed up trade, but not the movement of capital, other than within local and national financial markets. It is the much more intensive globalisation of the past thirty years that has brought not just free trade, but also free capital flows – what some call the trans-nationalisation of capital.

But such is the scale of our openness as an economy that, when things go wrong in one place, trouble can be transmitted to almost every place – farther, faster and deeper than ever. Interlocking systems, each with their own feedback loops, can break down in ways that, as with COVID-19, can cause chaos we cannot foresee. Instability anywhere can become a threat to stability everywhere. 'We created globalised networks because they could make us more efficient and productive and our lives more convenient,' explained Gautam Mukunda, the author of *Indispensable: When Leaders Really Matter.* 'But, when you steadily remove their buffers, backup capacities and surge protectors in pursuit of short-term efficiency or just greed, you ensure that these systems are not only less resistant to shocks, but that we spread those shocks everywhere.'[11]

So it is clear that if we want all the benefits that flow from an open economy, we need to discover far better ways of cooperating across borders and think afresh about what kind of world we seek. It is a rethink that has to resolve our central paradox: as the world is increasingly being pushed together by economics and technology, it is being pulled apart by culture and ideology.

There is a huge disconnect between where we are physically – more interconnected, more interdependent, more integrated than ever before – and where we are geopolitically – tribal, protectionist and disconnected. Economic integration is a fact, but, in its wake, social disintegration is a threat. It may seem obvious that we are all facing similar challenges and that, if COVID-19 is everyone's problem, so are climate change, the risk of nuclear weapons, and global poverty and inequality. But, in a new century, when the case for global cooperation and solidarity to address these shared problems may seem to be growing stronger, we run up against this opposite cultural trend favouring isolationism and the growth of anti-immigrant populist nationalist movements inciting xenophobia. The danger of this is that – as allegorised by Pascal Lamy, former director-general of the World Trade Organization (WTO) and a supporter of European unity – 'nations will be solids, the European Union will become liquid and the globe gaseous'.[12]

The truth is that, if we are to overcome these challenges, globalisation and the opening up of greater economic competition between nations will have to be complemented by new manifestations of cooperation and by greater social solidarity across national borders. At the very least, we have to achieve what has been missing in the response to the pandemic: a mutual understanding that there are problems that are not just common to us all and shared universally, but are also truly global – in the sense that they affect us all directly – and cannot be resolved without us working together.

We are at a 'hinge' or 'threshold' moment when much of the old is being exposed and then discredited and discarded. And the fault lines that have been exposed cut across almost every aspect of our economic lives. People who have seen how one disaster – a pandemic – can change our lives now see another disaster – climate change – in the same light. The shift from coal and oil is a good example of how change is on the agenda; few now doubt that we are at the beginning of the fossil fuel sell-off. By the end of it, coal will have become history and oil, now reaching and perhaps passing its peak, will fade. The hope is that we are entering a new era of climate protection, but, as with other areas I will discuss later, we are still in a zone of unpredictability betwixt the end of one era and the beginning of an as-yet unknown one. As the Italian philosopher and revolutionary Antonio Gramsci said of 1918: the old order is dying, but the new order is struggling to be born; our leaders still unable to let go of the past and yet to prove they have a clear idea of what it means when they talk of building a better future.[13]

In the essays that follow, I will look at seven of the biggest challenges our world faces and sketch out positive proposals for resolving them. Aware of the entrenched interests that might frustrate progressive change, I will also examine how barriers to progress can be overcome. But, first, I must set out the recent changes in the way we see the world that have been ushered in and accelerated by COVID-19.

I

THE 'BC' WORLD

Every generation faces its own apocalyptic moments and COVID-19 will define the twenty-first century in the same way the assassination of Archduke Franz Ferdinand, Nazi fascism and the fall of the Berlin Wall became fundamental benchmarks of the twentieth century. Indeed, COVID-19 has already overtaken 9/11 and the global financial crisis as the event that has done most to shape our still-young century. Just as it is foolhardy to make accurate predictions about future weather when you are caught in the middle of a snowstorm, it is difficult to make accurate predictions about our post-pandemic future, but February 2020 now seems like prehistory.

For COVID-19 has brought to the surface failings in our institutions. It has also challenged established ideas about progress and it has raised questions that now require addressing: questions about how much control we have over nature and our environment; questions about the openness of our societies, the responsibilities of states to their citizens for their health, welfare and security, as well as fairness of these arrangements; and questions about whether we cooperate well enough across borders. Many of these were issues that we thought we had resolved in the aftermath of the Second World War, with new forms of social protection established within countries, ranging from healthcare to welfare, and with international institutions founded to deal with cross-border cooperation. But COVID-19 has revealed just how fragile these structures were, so, in order to understand why our world is failing, we need to take a look at our pre-COVID-19 world and at how inadequate it has been found to be when faced with life-and-death challenges.

Our relationship with nature

BC – before COVID-19 – we assumed that, instead of nature controlling humans, humans would increasingly control nature. Despite the obvious facts and scientists' warnings, we convinced ourselves that we were masters of our universe and that we had taken full charge of the natural world around us. But we are now discovering just how much our lives – be it the opportunities we have or the vicissitudes we face – are determined by nature, over which we, as human beings faced with pandemics and climate change, have been losing control. COVID-19 has made us acknowledge that there is much about disease, climate and nature that we still do not understand.

It has also made us appreciate that our continued and ever more intensive exploitation of the planet is outpacing its capacity to regenerate. For, while we may not control nature the way we expected, we have changed nature in ways that are worrisome. It is for these reasons that we now talk of the Anthropocene – the epoch in which our own actions and the choices we make as human beings will, from now on, determine the future of almost every species on the planet and the fate of the planet itself. COVID-19, climate change and our collective failure to deal with both are, as one academic study put it, 'diseases of the Anthropocene'.[1]

Individual and community

BC – before COVID-19 – we put the rights of the individual on a pedestal at the expense of obligations to our wider community, despite the fact that we are all members of families and groups shaped by our cultures and histories and thus we are all embedded in a larger whole. The balance had swung away from the collectivism of the post-war years to a new individualism that manifested itself in many forms – libertarianism, self-interest, the rejection of deference, suspicion of authority, the erosion of trust, the exhaustion of social capital and, more generally, a tendency to think not so much of what is best for the community or the public good, but rather what is best for ourselves. At the turn of the century, one major academic study described people as 'bowling alone'.[2] By 2020, millions were alone – and not even bowling.

But being physically isolated in 2020 has, it seems, made us more aware of the benefits of contact and communication. We have discovered that we depend on each other more than we thought and that we value what is rooted and close-to-home more than the distantly networked. Being alone and celebrating the freedom to be ourselves within a culture that elevates personal autonomy now seems less attractive than a culture that encourages cooperation and commends reciprocity and generosity. Western discussions surrounding the celebration of Christmas 2020 brought this home: for most families, the burning issue was not what presents they gave or received but how they could come together.

By indicating that we prefer to cultivate and embed a sense of community over hyper-individualism, we may now be able to answer the anti-communitarian rhetoric that became widespread from the 1980s and say that there is indeed 'such a thing as society'.[3] For millions have found that, just as we cannot feel at ease living a life of spiritual meaninglessness, we cannot feel comfortable living in a world in which the rights and responsibilities of citizenship are not distributed according to morally acceptable standards that we can all subscribe to and which bind us together.

Risk or security

BC – before COVID-19 – our world had also become, in the late sociologist Ulrich Beck's words, 'a risk society'. It was more interconnected, integrated and interdependent than ever before, but also ever more dependent on a highly specialised division of labour in supply chains that criss-crossed continents.[4] This made us increasingly vulnerable to a range of uncertainties and dangers – from disease and terrorism to economic disruption and job insecurity – that inevitably flow from an open, mobile and rapidly changing global economy.

Of course, during periods of economic growth, individuals will tend to take on and pile up ever-greater amounts of risk, not least debt, without protecting or insuring against a possible reversal of fortunes. To obtain the levels of income they aspire to and to keep their taxes low – or, in many cases, simply because there was no other option – many of our fellow citizens (notably gig-economy and zero-hours-contract workers, the self-employed and start-up entrepreneurs) have been prepared to – or forced to – live with such risk at the expense of adequate protection against unemployment, adequate financial provision for old age or even adequate health cover. At the same time, a 'winner takes all' mentality took root and glossed over the downside risks of things going wrong, wiping from our collective memory what we knew of the pain experienced by those who were not 'winners'. One of the consequences of the pandemic is the increased need for protection and a willingness to accept digital forms of control that, up until recently, many had opposed.

Now we are all having to assess what level of uncertainty we are prepared to live with and what price we are willing to pay for our safety and security. Europe has always been more risk-averse than the US, and most of the rest of the world has offered far less social protection than Europe. But during 2020, according to *The Economist*, the world saw the launch of 1,600 new crisis-induced social protection programmes – and a discernible shift from the traditional means-tested, insurance-based payments to universal benefits that have included direct cash hand-outs to whole populations in the US, Japan, Hong Kong, Singapore and in parts of South Korea and to significant sections from Brazil to Togo.[5] With what has been the biggest expansion of welfare states in living memory has come a renewed appreciation of the role of the state in pooling and underwriting risks and there is growing support for the kind of citizens' national income for all tried out in Finland. Future governments will almost certainly be expected to do more to minimise risks and maximise security when faced with ageing populations and more disruption, from climate change to technological innovation, and everywhere the social contracts that bind our societies together will have to be rewritten. If we do not do so social divisions will grow and with it political dissent. But in recent months governments have not just got into the habit of underpinning the incomes of their citizens but underpinning their entire economies, thus altering the role of the state.

The changing responsibilities of the state

BC – before COVID-19 – the West had become more than a market economy and more like a market society, to the extent that even citizenship, body parts and designer children could be bought at a price. This market fundamentalism grew deep roots with profound impacts: public amenities withered as we classified public spending less as a productive, life-enhancing investment and more as a state pile-up of liability.

Today, the West is paying a heavy price for poor infrastructure and underfunded public healthcare systems, and the rest of the world is counting the cost of never having such systems. We may have talked a great deal about personal and social responsibility, but, in our daily lives, we tended to act as consumers rather than citizens and to opt for the material freedoms that markets offer rather than choosing to be active members of a society with shared obligations to each other.

But, since the outbreak of COVID-19, I hear few people saying 'markets know best' or repeating the famous words of neoliberal fundamentalists: 'You cannot buck the market.'[6] Indeed, the state has come to be seen as indispensable, not just as the lender of last resort, but also the insurer, provider and, for many, employer of last resort. Even in 2021, as the virus recedes, financial markets everywhere are being underwritten by national governments. State purchases of high-risk junk bonds are the nearest we can get to the public underwriting of losses from betting and gaming. But, to keep the financial markets moving forward in the midst of the recession, such bonds are being bought up by central banks. Financial rewards remain privatised, but financial risk has been nationalised – something that will reshape the balance between markets and state well into the future.

Future governments will almost certainly be expected to take a much more proactive role in ensuring that societies have the resilience to overcome crises from wherever they come. Citizens who have been counting the cost – in lost lives – for underfinanced health and poor social protection systems have also tolerated far greater intrusion into their private lives, not least the tracking, tracing and surveillance that have been deemed necessary to control the pandemic. Big questions about the future role of the state cannot be ignored and people are asking whether understandable demands for more effective protection against disease – and the need for more interventionist governments to deliver this – play into the hands of those who seek authoritarian uses of, and controls over, technology.

Many are asking whether, in future, the urgent need for action in a crisis will drown out concerns about restrictions on individual freedoms. Though beyond the remit of this book, one question that has been also been raised by the crisis, and that matters to the many millions who value individual freedom and fear the encroachment of something akin to an Orwellian state, is: can we show that technology can empower citizens without over-empowering big tech or the state? And, moreover, is it possible to avoid the imposition of surveillance regimes, the loss of liberty and the consequent erosion of trust between rulers and the ruled?

It is right to worry about the excessive power of the world's high-tech giants that now have both the algorithms and, between them, a near-monopoly control to dictate how we communicate digitally, and to ask whether democracy and this new kind of capitalism are compatible. A debate is clearly needed about how much of the marketplace that is under the control of these private empires should properly be considered the work of regulated utilities.

But we should already be ready to answer those who seize upon random statistics to claim that totalitarian governments have proved more effective in dealing with the pandemic than allegedly dysfunctional democracies. For, to draw a proper comparison, we would have to look beyond how many or how few have caught COVID-19 and ask a variety of other questions. What has been done to prevent disease – vaccination, for example? What protection is on offer against loss of employment and the growth of poverty? What is the reach and scale of social safety nets? Which countries are prepared to spend public resources on healthcare and how much? How equitably is healthcare distributed? What long-term guarantees of support do citizens have when things go wrong? We will find, I believe, that, measured by any of these metrics, social democracies do better.

New patterns of inequality

BC – before COVID-19 – we were becoming more divided, unequal societies. Indeed, over a period of fewer than fifty years, we have moved from a world in which 60 per cent of the benefits of our economic activity accrued to labour to a world in which

60 per cent of economic output now ends up in the hands of those with capital – those who own stocks, shares and property.[7] For a long time now, the increased financial returns individuals enjoyed from investing in the stock market and real estate have exceeded the returns from undertaking waged employment. The 'unconventional' support given by central banks in 2020 and 2021, which underpinned financial markets and stock exchanges, has accentuated this divide in favour of those who own shares and capital.

Before the crisis, the pre-pandemic world was seeing a further long-term shift, again starting in the West, from an economy whose labour force – once divided between manual and non-manual workers – has become even more rigidly polarised between the education-rich (those with higher education qualifications and who can command high incomes) and the education-poor. Sadly, millions of the education-poor – including those in manual occupations, like labouring and construction, and those in non-manual occupations, such as call centre staff – have few recognised skills and their work is undervalued. Their share of the world's income has continued to fall and they have little or no savings or wealth to their name.

And yet, during COVID-19, we have had to recognise our dependence on the very people who have been the lowest paid, least secure and least appreciated members of our national workforces – the hospital workers, the social care assistants, the delivery drivers, the supermarket staff – all of whom have provided the basic but essential services necessary to keep both our economy and our public services running. They are workers who have been deemed 'semi-skilled' or 'unskilled', but whose contributions and hands-on abilities have been indispensable.

And so there is a growing awareness, true of both high-income and low-income countries, of what people see as the mounting scale of inequalities. Inter-country inequalities may be narrowing a little as countries like China start to catch up with the West and a substantial middle class emerges in Asia. But, in both West and

East, intra-country inequalities have been rising, with a growing gap between the education-poor wage earner and the education-rich capital holder.[8] It is a trend that will continue to intensify as long as the monetary policies pursued by the world's central banks continue raising stock market valuations and protecting those who already have capital over those who depend on a weekly wage and we do too little to compensate the lower-income families and children who have lost out.

And as the justified complaints from the left-out and the left-behind grow, COVID-19, and its aftermath, will force the issues of inequality onto every country's agenda. It will require a renegotiation of the social contract and a greater recognition of the responsibilities all of us owe to the poorest citizens among us – not least the value we place on the contribution of personal service workers, upon whom we have recently relied so much.

Eventually, each country will, of course, find its own way forward as it rebalances the relationships between individuals and communities, between markets and states, between risk and security, between freedom and control, between the very rich and the rest, and between humans and nature.

But what of the global challenges we all share in common and what of the relations between nations as we seek to address these challenges? For there is an overarching consideration – perhaps the greatest long-term one thrown up by COVID-19 – that is the principal subject of this book: how well (or badly) we will manage our increasingly interconnected world and hence the fate of globalisation.

Nationalism and internationalism

BC – before COVID-19 – we tolerated, and even indulged, a stand-off between globalists and nationalists without admitting that 'spill-overs' or contagion from nation to nation could include not only climate change, nuclear proliferation and

financial instability, but also the spread of disease across borders. Most of us felt it was of little consequence to our daily
lives that movements like 'America First' and 'my tribe first'
had descended into 'America First and Only' and 'my tribe first
and only' or that they were sabotaging attempts at international
cooperation.

Yet the challenges posed by nationalism present themselves in
many forms. Why so little cooperation when meeting a pandemic
affecting us all? Is nationalism now the driving force of international relations? Is the post-1945 era of international cooperation
at an end? What has happened to the rules-based international
order? Is multilateralism itself dead? Is 'America First' et al. the
world's only way forward? Are we about to enter a new cold war?
Are we moving to a future of 'one world, two systems'?

And these are not academic issues. In the chapters that follow,
I will look at pandemics, pollution, poverty and nuclear proliferation – problems that require an urgent global response and
solution. All should be on the world's agenda today. None can be
fully solved by one nation acting on its own; these problems can
only be addressed if we work together as a global community.
And it is neither inevitable nor preordained that we can even
solve these problems – it will demand human agency. So, sooner
rather than later, we, as the citizens of the world, will have to
come together. This is not to propose a post-national future but
simply to recognise the both the opportunity and responsibility
to make the most of our interconnected world.

This is, of course, not the first time we have come face to face with
our global interdependence. In 1947, after the Second World War,
when Secretary of State George Marshall announced the US's ambitious plan to come to the aid of the rest of the world, he explained
that his efforts were 'directed not against any country or doctrine,
but against hunger, poverty, desperation and chaos' – problems
that still remain to be fully addressed.[9] He might have expected
that, at some point, we would come up against a killer pandemic.

But he might not have anticipated that, just as the whole world was brought to its knees by COVID-19, so, too, could much of our planet be made uninhabitable in our lifetimes by floods, droughts and storms.

Those with some grasp of post-Second World War history who have seen what has happened to our global order in that time will appreciate the complexities of forging international solutions to otherwise intractable world problems. These difficulties we examine in detail here, for perhaps the best way to explain the difficulties that face our world in the 2020s is to recap briefly on how much the world has changed since 1945 and to do so decade by decade.

In the wake of the Second World War, the US was by far the world's dominant power. Its economy was transformed in scale and it had acquired – not absentmindedly – an empire consisting of numerous far-flung military bases and a range of client dictatorships. While undefeated in war, the UK was broken in peacetime. Much of Europe was cowed by defeat and physical destruction. The economic might of the US came to the aid of Western Europe in the form of the Marshall Plan. The Soviet Union refused to participate and forbade its Eastern European communist puppet satellites from participating. Western Europe, vivified, quickly thrived and, over the decades that followed, communism left Eastern Europe far behind. Eventually, communism failed. Even the East Germans couldn't make it work.

In these heady post-war years, Dean Acheson, the US secretary of state, talked of being 'present at the creation' of a rules-based international order that was emerging in the form of new international institutions: the United Nations (UN), the World Bank, the International Monetary Fund (IMF), the World Health Organization (WHO) and what became the World Trade Organization (WTO).[10] 'We have learned to be citizens of the world,' President Franklin D. Roosevelt declared. 'We are members of the human community.'[11] 'What a great day this can be in history,' proclaimed his successor, President Harry Truman, at the international summit on 26 June 1945 when the founding charter of the UN was signed. Countries had put aside their differences – 'in one unshakable unity of determination – to find a way to end wars'.[12]

But, over the twenty years that followed, which were largely dominated by the Cold War, this brave new (post-war) world was eroded in a much more complex, international, political context. The once-mighty Soviet Union began its long decline towards the expensively armed, paranoid and disruptive Russia of the present day. As US power grew, the various post-war international institutions came to look less like the *efficient* part of the global decision-making system and more like its *dignified* part.

Just as the Marshall Plan – not the World Bank – had become the instrument of economic reconstruction and development in the 1940s, the NATO Security Council – not the UN – became the major guarantor of security from the 1950s. Over time, a number of US-led and Western-dominated institutions began to overshadow more inclusive institutions like the UN. Quickly, it became clear that this was no longer a world in which global problems were going to be solved by the global institutions set up for such a purpose. The rules-based world order Acheson had lauded was declining and, in the course of doing so, acquired a lip-service title: the Washington Consensus. The US, it seemed, was happy to lead the world, but the world that it imagined looked more like an extension of the US.

The Washington Consensus had little to say about tackling climate change, inequality or poverty, hence its increasing irrelevance to the current challenges we confront. Moreover, in its complacency about the stability of the world economy it led, it did not offer a global early warning system to head off financial crises like Russia's in 1997, Asia's in 1998 and the dot-com bubble of 2002 (although the third of these did wonders for the sales of J. K. Galbraith's 1955 book *The Great Crash, 1929*, as did similar subsequent high-tech boondoggles).[13] The markets, it seemed, had learned little and had forgotten most of it.

The Washington Consensus limped on and increasingly meant that all nations would, or should, pursue neoliberal economic policies: the liberalisation of trade; the privatisation of industry; the deregulation of competition; and an obsessive conviction about the importance of controlling inflation, which led, in turn, to public spending cuts in order to pay for tax cuts.

While the financial system was built on the US's ability to underpin global prosperity, nation after nation found that the price of any internationally agreed assistance was high – in both economic and political terms. Marketed by the World Bank as 'structural reform' and later rebranded 'sustainable development', it is, in fact, now better known as 'austerity'.

By the time President Donald Trump assumed power in 2017, the Washington Consensus was no longer supported even in Washington. In its place, in the US and widely elsewhere, came defensive nationalism, with nation after nation imposing tariffs, closing borders, demonising immigrants and imagining external enemies that did not exist. These policies and tendencies have, at various times, served to prop up everything from authoritarianism to dictatorships and systematic kleptocratic corruption that has increased inequality.

For years, in a unipolar era, the US had preferred to act multi-laterally. In a multipolar age, though, it was acting unilaterally and often to the detriment of its own interests. 'The future does not belong to globalists,' Trump told the UN General Assembly the year before COVID-19 struck. 'The future belongs to patriots.'[14]

But, as an ultra-nationalist, populist and capriciously solipsistic leader, self-defining as a uniquely gifted dealmaker, Trump serially failed in all his major initiatives. His conviction that 'tariff wars are easy to start and easy to win' has proved costly, mainly in the US. Obamacare lives and North Korea flaunts its nuclear weaponry. His authoritarian ex-friends Kim Jong-un and Vladimir Putin eventually discarded him as unreliable. And, in the Capitol itself, he lost the House of Representatives and shed much of his formerly devoted support as a result of his disastrous handling of the COVID-19 emergency. His 'America First' agenda, which saw the US depart from its own recent internationalist history, had stymied the Paris climate change agreement, the Iran nuclear accord, the Intermediate-Range Nuclear Treaty, and the work of the WHO and many other UN agencies.

All this has happened – Trump's arrival and his departure – within a new context of aggressive populist nationalism on a global level: 'America First' and similar movements in other countries have created a paradoxical and likely unsustainable global coalition of anti-globalists. Yet too many of our leaders will continue to see the world as Trump did, in terms of a struggle between us and them – a zero-sum game in which, if one country benefits, another loses, with no sense of the bigger win for everyone if we all work together.

The idea of individual self-isolation is now commonplace thanks to the pandemic, but national self-isolation has also taken off. The pandemic has prompted what Henry Kissinger, former US secretary of state, called 'an anachronism, a revival of the walled city in an age when prosperity depends on global trade and movement of people'.[15] Nationalism has gone international, but its go-it-alone approach cannot solve global problems.

Among these many unpredictable, interactive and interdependent variables, there stands out – in the terminology of Donald Rumsfeld, former US secretary of defence – a notable and potentially high-risk 'known unknown': that of a China–US 'two-system' world.

With the Washington Consensus defunct, neither nationalism nor the China–US 'two-system' world offers us a way forward to successfully address climate change, financial volatility, global poverty or inequality, as I will show in my two final chapters.

With borders closing, supply chains fracturing and 'vaccine nationalism' remaining on the agenda, many still want to roll back globalisation and thus limit any one nation's exposure to the vulnerabilities of interdependence.

It comes down to how governments will now respond – and I write with some experience of trying to bring people together to tackle a global emergency. We knew in 2009, when there was a global recession as big as any we had experienced since the 1930s, that no one nation, not even the US, could overcome the crisis on its own: the recession could only be solved through global cooperation. What's more, we needed a new international forum sufficiently inclusive to bind East and West together and sufficiently influential to deliver effective economic collaboration. But bringing into being and managing what became the G20 – a group comprising the leaders of the world's nineteen leading economies and the European Union – was itself a case study in the challenges of achieving a global consensus.

The G7 – the US, Germany, France, the UK, Italy, Canada and Japan – was generally content with its exclusive economic club. It had met regularly since the 1970s and, before 2008, was regarded as the leading forum for economic cooperation. But times had changed: if we were to fashion a globally coordinated response, we needed China, India, the oil states, Latin America and Africa – all suffering because of the crisis – to come to the table. In the words of George Canning, a previous UK foreign secretary and prime minister, we had to summon 'the New World into existence to redress the balance of the Old'.[16]

In creating the G20, we had to not only overcome US scepticism and G7 reluctance, but also reconcile French pressure to broaden the terms of reference – to include, for example, tax and the environment – with Chinese pressure to restrict them. Then came the dispute over membership. Such was the scramble among smaller countries for an invitation to join that, while we retained the name 'G20 leaders group', twenty-three leaders attended the 2008 Washington summit and twenty-four the 2009 London summit.

Despite our differences, we all realised that, if we did not stand together, we would fall separately. We made the unanimous commitment to shared objectives, supported by a bedrock of practical measures, including a coordinated fiscal and monetary stimulus to underpin the global economy with $1 trillion of grants, loans and guarantees. These helped to restore confidence where previously there had been none.

Almost as quickly as the global consensus was achieved, however, it started to dissipate. The UK and others wanted to agree an ambitious 'global compact' under which each country took responsibility to reach a shared global growth objective: returning the world economy to 4 per cent growth. In the end, all that could be agreed was a short-term fiscal stimulus. Worried about subordinating the control of inflation to a push for growth, Germany would not agree medium- or long-term growth targets. And, while we tried to persuade the G20 that, in a low interest rate environment, running a deficit for a number of years was not a problem, even if the long-term debt rose in the short term, the summit of November 2010 ditched the fiscal stimulus and, with varying levels of retrenchment, embraced national programmes of austerity. As a result, the West, especially Europe, entered a low-growth decade.

At my prompting, the G20 had appointed the widely respected economist Manmohan Singh, then-prime minister of India, with a remit to examine the reforms that needed to be made to international institutions in order to make them fit for purpose in an age that was no longer shaped by local and national flows and exchanges, but rather by global flows of people, capital, goods and services. But, sadly, because all our time was spent fire-fighting the increasing retreat into national silos and the politics of austerity, little came of it.

There had been but one brief shining moment when

cooperation was preferred to isolationism, but all too quickly the G20 nations began adopting go-it-alone policies, which included fiscal retrenchment and protectionism. We found a fundamental mismatch still existed between the global nature of our shared challenges and the primarily national approach within which we have since organised ourselves to confront them.

Facing change

'Not everything that is faced can be changed,' wrote James Baldwin, 'but nothing can be changed until it is faced.'[17] And it can be done. In his memoir *Deep Thinking*, world chess genius Garry Kasparov says, 'I remain an optimist, if only because I've never found much advantage in the alternatives.'[18] But, even in a decade already chastened by a pandemic and a global economic crisis, I remain positive in my belief that, despite the many obstacles in our way, we will find a path to regeneration via a new era of global order. Yes, there is a crisis of globalisation, but we are beginning to see the means through which it might be resolved. Crises create opportunities, as we have noted, and having two crises at once, one medical and the other economic, might even be seen as giving greater grounds for hope. Historically – as historian Margaret MacMillan has pointed out – the worst of times may presage the best, as what she calls the 'rivers of history' change direction.[19] The Black Death nearly destroyed England's agricultural workforce, but, in its aftermath, employment terms changed from servitude to waged labour. New economic eras tend to arrive after a shock to the system, as do new systems of thought. The Great Plague of 1665 helped bring about the end of an ecclesiastical-based world, since previously devout citizens found they were not able to pray their way out of the calamity, so instead started looking to a science-based world for solutions. In France, a bad harvest in 1788 coincided with increasing concerns about the regime of King Louis XVI, prompting a surge in progressive thinking and an invitation to his subjects to submit *cahiers de doléances* (ledgers of complaint).[20] Remarkably, centuries before the world wide web and social media, such thinking circulated widely and discontent progressed to insurrection and then revolution.

In the midst of the Second World War, it was hard to imagine any institutions emerging that would be able to keep the peace for three-quarters of a century. But, as we have seen, the destruction and mass slaughter of the Second World War delivered the astonishing rise – within just a decade – of several remediating international institutions, including the UN, the World Bank, the IMF, the WTO and the WHO. Even the Cuban Missile Crisis – when the world came close to nuclear war – was itself a wake-up call for the US and the Soviet Union to seek better ways of preventing escalation, leading eventually to a non-proliferation treaty. So, in dominating the global agenda, COVID-19 has also created an opportunity for the kind of disruption and upheaval that could spur countries into as radical change as we saw after 1945.

Central to this book's thesis – and demonstrated by what good has come from the crisis – is the idea that responsible international cooperation does not undermine the role of nation states and the patriotic pride that most citizens rightly feel for their country. The message of the chapters that follow is not that we should embrace some abstract concept of global government. We simply cannot afford a rerun of the old arguments between globalists and nationalists: with globalists on the one side, accused of overly idealistic and wholly unrealistic ambitions for a form of world government that fails to acknowledge the strong sense of nationhood we ought to value; and patriots on the other, accused, even when not ideological nationalists, of retreating into national silos as though uninterested in anything that happens beyond their own borders. These propositions and counterpropositions are tired and outdated and they get us nowhere.

We cannot ignore the legal, political and cultural significance of borders and the moral meaning that many ascribe to being part of 'us'. We cannot say national identities are disappearing or that people will not define themselves by reference to 'the other'. But we also cannot ignore the demonstrable, practical benefits of cooperation in dealing with problems that no single nation can solve on its own. Isolation is not an option and the alternatives we face are not restricted to an impersonal globalisation or an aggressive nationalism. Instead, we must find a way in which each of us can take pride in our distinctive national identities while, at the same time, developing some of the qualities associated with being a global citizen.

Leaders must take into account both the legitimate interests of nations and our international duty to manage globalisation well, not poorly. Resisting a return to the old 'normalcy' that failed us, we should seek an improved balance between the national autonomy countries desire, and the international coop-eration we need. This can be best achieved not by focusing on some abstract and unattainable system of global governance, but rather on the immediate priorities for global action that could enhance people's day-to-day lives. We do not seek to usurp or weaken the nation state; our aim is simply to bring nations together via practical, workable solutions that will strengthen societies and bolster security in the face of a series of global challenges that no nation, however big, can conquer on its own. The 'responsible cooperation' I favour and the 'society of states' I advocate are both forms of an enlightened patriot-ism that recognises, and does not undermine but upholds, the rights, identity and character of our individual nations as we seek shared solutions to shared problems. If power is defined not in abstract and unrealistic terms – as a sovereignty that is unlimited, indivisible and accountable to no one – but rather as our ability as a community to shape our destiny, the 'national interest' can often be better expressed in the collective sharing of power, rather than seeking to exercise it over others.

Of course, we may not succeed. For, as I show when discussing the lessons learned from the global financial crisis, while we may be able to win an initial battle (for example, preventing a great recession becoming a depression), we are also capable of losing the peace by failing to deliver the long-term reform necessary (which, in the same example, led to a decade of austerity in Europe).

In 1886, in his old age, Alfred, Lord Tennyson wrote 'Locksley Hall Sixty Years After'. By then the UK poet laureate for over three decades, Tennyson was renowned across the world for the optimism of his famous poem 'Ulysses', which talks of an unremitting, unending mission: 'To strive, to seek, to find, and not to yield.' But, in despair at what Tennyson saw around him, 'Locksley Hall Sixty Years After' talks of the poet's desolation with a world that had not fulfilled his early dreams: 'Chaos, Cosmos! Cosmos, Chaos! Who can tell when all will end?'

In response, William Gladstone – the then-prime minister and, until that point, close friend of Tennyson – took the unusual step for a political leader of writing a riposte submitted to the poetry journal *Nineteenth Century*. In his article, he complained that Tennyson was forgetting and ignoring the enormous social progress that had been achieved during his lifetime – the reduction of poverty, the improvement of factory conditions, the public health reforms to attack cholera and typhoid – and even reminded Tennyson of the hymn to progress the poet himself had written sixty years before, entitled simply 'Locksley Hall'.[21] In that poem, Tennyson had outlined a vision of a world 'parliament of man' and wrote: 'When I dipt into the future far as human eye could see; Saw the Vision of the world and all the wonder that would be.'

These words have stood the test of time in all forms of arts and culture, cited in innumerable speeches and quoted in many books. They were even thought of as so significant to those interested in the future of the planet that they were chosen to appear on the dedication plaque of the USS *Voyager* in the futuristic TV series *Star Trek*.

Tennyson wrote of a world transformed when:

> The war-drum throbb'd no longer, and the battle-flags
>   were furl'd
> In the Parliament of man, the Federation of the world.
> There the common sense of most shall hold a fretful
>   realm in awe,
> And the kindly earth shall slumber, lapt in universal law.

Indeed, he is then so optimistic that he talks of: 'Men, my brothers, men, the workers, ever reaping something new; That which they have done but earnest of the things that they shall do.'

Gladstone was right to say that the poem inspired him; Winston Churchill considered it 'the most wonderful of modern prophecies'; Truman carried the words with him in his wallet wherever he went. Indeed, *The Parliament of Man* was the title chosen by Paul Kennedy in his major history, subtitled *The Past, Present, and Future of the United Nations*.

Churchill was, however, realistic about the barriers to co-operation in his time. In his 1935 article 'Nations on the Loose', in which he warned of the Nazi threat, Churchill wrote:

> [M]any intellectuals believed that, after the horrible carnage and desolation of the Great War, the thoughts of mankind would turn irresistibly to internationalism. They hoped that Tennyson's prophecy of the 'Parliament of man, the Federation of the world' would be fulfilled with the rest of his memorable predictions.

But, he concluded, 'the time is not yet'.[22]

Nearly a century on, we are far more knowledgeable about what goes wrong when we fail to cooperate. I hope we can also be wiser. As I will endeavour to convince you in this book, the time for international cooperation is now. 'Let the great world spin for ever down the ringing grooves of change,' as Tennyson said many years ago.

If, in the nineteenth and twentieth centuries, our technological and scientific progress was not matched by sufficient progress in international relations to prevent world wars or antagonistic power blocs, then the challenge in the twenty-first century is to build, through the cooperation that was too often missing back then, the world the younger Tennyson dreamed of: peaceful, equitable and sustainable.

PART TWO

Challenging Our Present:
Seven Ways to Change the World

PREVENTING PANDEMICS: THE FUTURE OF GLOBAL HEALTH

When COVID-19 – stealthy and unstoppable – spread through-out the world infecting and immiserating millions, our doctors, nurses, scientists, researchers and aid workers responded at speed, with commendable dedication, and to remarkable effect.

Aid organisations came together to protect the vulnerable, care for the sick, and comfort the dying and the bereaved. Medics cooperated across borders to identify and evaluate new treatments. Researchers collaborated to find the source of the outbreak, characterise the virus, and develop vac-cines. Scientists throughout the world freely shared emerging information and evidence of progress. One hastily arranged academic study on lockdowns brought together nine institu-tions across the UK, China and America. The way charities and public health teams responded to the new challenges showed humanity at its best.

In one week in November 2020 an astonishing set of announce-ments heralded a historic breakthrough – the discovery of not just one but three COVID-19 vaccines, making 2020 a significant year in the annals of medical advance.

Within three months, six vaccines had already received emergency use regulatory approval by the World Health Organization (WHO) or equivalent bodies, with a further five, including vaccines from China and Russia, licensed by nation states. With twenty-five different suppliers in nineteen countries supplying 280 different components, the first vaccine to pass approval, known as the Pfizer vaccine, was again a triumph of cooperation. Engineered by a Turkish couple based in Germany, the breakthrough in genetic coding that underpins the vaccine was only possible because of the early sequencing and sharing of the virus's digital code by fellow scientists in China. The emergence of effective mass vaccination has given the world a new reason for working together, and here the case for global cooperation is obvious: cutting the risks of morbidity and mortality, and in doing so reducing the probability of successive mutations.

We will never know how many of COVID-19's 140-plus million victims could have been free of disease, given the right decisions on lockdowns, testing and procurement. But we do know that the world was unprepared. Political leaders were caught off guard. Despite the impassioned leadership of WHO head Dr Tedros, our collective failure to mount a truly collaborative response has been culpable, shameful and lethal on a huge scale.

In future years, historians will reflect on millions of lives needlessly lost. While world science has brought forth understanding and innovation, too often national and international politics broadly failed. We have not done enough to pool and share available resources; coordinate and streamline global production of essential medical equipment; or agree and ensure a sufficient and equitable distribution of supplies from basic masks and surgical gowns to vaccines themselves. Because of our failure to work together and successfully mobilise a stronger and more effective international effort, an outbreak that was first detected in Wuhan, a city of 11 million people (bigger than London) that most of us had never heard of before, is likely to damage lives and livelihoods globally for months and years to come.

Of course, there are variations between countries and within countries in the incidence of infection and death. There are questions too about the response and the effectiveness of welfare, employment and economic support programmes to shield families from poverty. But we have to ask questions about what went wrong not just in individual countries but in our overall response to the crisis. And if we are to learn lessons, we need to look at why, faced with a shared danger, the same virus at roughly the same time, and the same need for equipment, cures and vaccines, the world failed to come together, despite the earnest desire of so many people of goodwill to do so. So in this chapter, I will look at what went right and what went wrong in the global response, and what can be done to equip ourselves better for the future.

Microbes do not recognise national borders, and disease spreads without any recognition of countries, citizens or political systems, and the control of infectious diseases is perhaps the closest thing to an obvious global public good. Eradicating the virus within the borders of Europe and North America will fail unless we eliminate it throughout the developing world, and vice versa, and that of course requires globally coordinated action. This is perhaps the best example of multilateralism being to everyone's advantage, a textbook example of where a global problem requires a global response, so we must ask why it is that our response was so inadequate. I start by highlighting the two disheartening but sadly predictable governmental responses of 2020 that undid so much of the good work of scientists, health professionals and aid workers: the delays that arose for various reasons and inflicted so much damage in the first phase of the disease; and, in the second phase, the regrettable competitive vaccine nationalism that continues to blight and delay potentially transformational international action.

I will highlight what's happening in one country, Somalia, which saw in the late 1970s the completion of one of the greatest success stories in the history of the WHO: the final eradication of smallpox. But today — more than 40 years on — as another virus ravages its population of 16 million, thousands are dying unnecessarily without access to even minimal healthcare, and no significant progress towards an effective vaccination programme: in short, a grim example of our collective failure.

From this and other instances, I will try to identify the nature of the underlying systemic weaknesses that collectively account for our failure to deliver nationally and internationally in the face of the current massive challenges of global public health.

It is commonplace to talk of the difficult choices that countries have to make between meeting their domestic needs and discharging their global responsibilities. But I suggest that we look at this in a different light: too many countries have adopted a too-narrow view of their national interests, and are failing to recognise the full benefits of international cooperation, not to mention the necessity of it.

As I write, the most immediate problem is how to prevent more and more serious variants of the virus emerging and circulating – perhaps more rapidly than the familiar earliest variants – and to recognise that in the absence of vaccination programmes in Africa, Asia and Latin America there will be extreme vulnerability to mass infections and the longer these are left unaddressed the more worrying variants we will see. So the best way to reduce the risks is a global vaccination campaign that is as early, effective and comprehensive as possible. But to achieve that the richer nations need to use their aid budgets to help the poorer countries that are currently unable to protect themselves.

Yes, the richer countries do face a choice between financing their national vaccination programmes and contributing to global provision; and there are critics of international aid development who may tell us that charity begins and ends at home. But crudely counterposing one against the other is, in my view, a grave error: it is too short-sighted, too short-termist, and ultimately self-damaging. No one is safe until everyone is safe.

Pandemics have been a feature of the past and will continue to be in the future. We should be prepared for them, never underestimate them, and be ready to combat them together. The need for cooperation on global health – and the benefits that flow from it – will not disappear once COVID-19 is contained or eradicated. There is a need to continue sharing data, research and experience to learn from each other; pooling and sharing resources to be better prepared; and – most importantly – delivering the more general support now being withheld from poorer countries.

Delayed responses

Over more than twenty years – as a government minister and, more recently, as a special envoy of the secretary-general of the United Nations – I have had the privilege of working with international health experts and networks. I have always considered international cooperation in global health, which starts from the widely admired ethical codes of the medical communities, to be much easier to achieve than in other spheres of public policy, such as the economy and the environment. Contrasting the evolution of international public health cooperation with the prospects for cooperation on economic policy, the late economist Richard N. Cooper argued that 'international consensus about practical knowledge, along with shared objectives, is a necessary condition for close international cooperation'.[1] Thus, whereas economists will tend to disagree on both the objectives and effects of their policies, public health cooperation, he argues, has the benefit of scientific consensus on the causes and treatment of diseases combined with evidential numeracy. Indeed, scientific knowledge and expertise can itself be considered a global public good from which everyone benefits and from the benefits of which no one is excluded. When we can find ways to bring such expertise together, highly regarded and effective international organisations and networks can catalyse progress.

But despite the goodwill of scientists and academics, and despite our mutual vulnerability, the intergovernmental collaboration we need has yet to happen. Professor Scott Barrett, whose book *Why Cooperate?* is an introduction to these themes, argues that self-interest, rather than international cooperation, is 'the main thing that's really driving everything we've seen as regards COVID-19'. He adds: 'It's a mixed picture but I think the main driver of policy and individual behaviour so far, more than anything else, is self-interest'.[2]

Cooperation has to start with effective early warning systems, honest reporting and information exchange if we are to contain an outbreak of an infection in one place before it spreads disease, death and economic impact. We cannot say we were not warned about the likelihood of a pandemic – for some time scientists have been predicting an event such as this and a number of larger states claimed to have contingency plans ready to be triggered. Despite such claims it was obvious that we were ill-prepared.

If nations fail to report diseases in a timely manner, if they fail to exchange information, if they fail to put cooperation before their own narrowly defined national interests, then we have little chance of successfully responding when an outbreak occurs. When SARS surfaced in 2003, China was under no legal obligation to report it. As a result of this oversight, 195 countries, including all WHO member states, agreed in 2005 to detailed binding International Health Regulations ranging from tougher requirements for the reporting of outbreaks to new WHO powers over restrictions on trade and travel. Members of the World Health Organization are now required to notify the organisation of all events that 'may constitute a public health emergency of international concern'.[3] China waited a month before reporting COVID-19 in 2020 – an improvement on the three-month delay in reporting SARS, but an unnecessary month in which the Wuhan ophthalmologist who first described the respiratory syndrome appears to have been silenced by officials, with the lethal local, national and international consequences that inevitably ensued.

The WHO not only relies on national governments to offer information about an outbreak, but also insists on securing their explicit permission before allowing international investigators to learn more details. In Wuhan that took time, to the extent that at the time of writing, a definitive report is still awaited. And while the WHO has the right to recommend travel restrictions it cannot enforce them, and in 2020 most states continued to go their own way. It became increasingly clear that having systems, programmes, expertise and regulations in place counted for little if the WHO has neither the means nor the authority to ensure the reporting and access urgently required in a rapidly growing global emergency.

Individual nations were also slow to take control. Jeremy Farrar, the head of the Wellcome Trust – who spent eighteen years in Vietnam responding to a whole series of outbreaks of infectious disease and therefore speaks with authority – stated that by 20 January 2020, many countries had enough information to know what was coming but did nothing. 'We had no human immunity, no diagnostics, no treatment, and no vaccines. Every country should have acted then.' He went on to say that 'Singapore, China, and South Korea did. Yet most of Europe and North America waited until the middle of March, and that defined the first wave.'[4]

Once a disease takes root, comprehensive testing, tracing and tracking is essential to identify potential carriers to prevent further contagion. To be able to respond to increased morbidity rates, our health services – whether in Australia, Brazil or Kazakhstan – required personal protective equipment, effective medications and life-saving technology such as ventilators. With limited stockpiles, valiant attempts were made to coordinate, at a global level, the increased manufacture, purchase and distribution of equipment but they failed, and instead countries vied with others to secure what limited supply there was.

Such problems persist, and for many years there will remain a global need for diagnostics, for existing and new variants, for sharing equipment, and for exchanging genomic sequencing data worldwide. Take what may seem a simple problem – the supply of the medical oxygen dispensed in hospitals which will almost certainly save more lives in 2021 than vaccines. One in five COVID-19 patients need oxygen but in many developing countries such as India, it is a luxury item, available only to the wealthy through private hospitals. Even pulse oximeters – simple low-cost devices that measure blood oxygen levels – are in short supply. Four out of five children who contract pneumonia, the biggest killer of children in developing countries, never receive the oxygen therapy they need; and while oxygen concentration plants in Africa have doubled in number in the last year and UNICEF and the WHO have procured 2,500 additional oxygen concentrators for Africa, no one can say we have mobilised sufficient resources for investment in the oxygen infrastructure that could transform care and survival outcomes for millions and, in 2021, an India without oxygen supplies paid the heaviest of prices.[5]

And yet there was a chance, at the outset, that the world could work together. The initial impetus was certainly there. At the G20 meeting of world leaders on 26 March 2020, as COVID-19 was advancing, President Trump and fellow G20 leaders agreed measures to enhance the global effort. They agreed 'to close the financing gap in the WHO Strategic Preparedness and Response Plan'.[6] And, when G20 health ministers met a month later, on 24 April, before them was a 52-paragraph draft communiqué highlighting the current inequality in health resources available to different countries and the human suffering the pandemic was causing, and committing all countries to strengthening the WHO's mandate in coordinating the fight against the pandemic. The draft communiqué expressed 'concern about the continuity

and lack of sustainable funding' and urged all donors to contribute to the collective effort, saying, 'It is far more cost-effective
to invest in sustainable financing for country preparedness than
to pay to the costs of responding to outbreaks.'[7]

But as the scale of the pandemic grew, governments retreated
into their national silos, rather than opting to work together.
President Trump – increasingly in 'America First' mode and in
the run-up to an election – blamed both China and the WHO,
and the cracks in this multilateral cooperation began to show,
reducing the strength and resolve of any collective action and
politicising what was agreed. Some countries had ready-made
contingency plans to quickly close their borders and lockdown
their economies. Others, including the US, initially ignored
such plans then instituted bans on travellers from China and
elsewhere, with dubious effectiveness. Borders were closed,
and many countries banned any export of medical equipment,
personal protective equipment and pharmaceuticals. There were
even reports of merchant navies seizing goods in mid ocean.
Dozens of countries created barriers of one kind or another.
National interests collided with global interests and too often
the national interests won out. The virus, as viruses do, found
more and more human hosts, and global cases and deaths
skyrocketed.

Of course, in normal times, the UN Security Council would
leave decision-making on health to other UN bodies, but in
crises – including those in global health – the Council has a
well-established role in responding. But it too failed to reach any
agreement on how to deal with COVID-19. China, which held
the rotating presidency of the Security Council in March 2020,
explained that this 'public health' matter was a national issue that
did not fall within the Security Council's 'geopolitical' ambit.
The US demanded that any resolution must specify the Chinese
origins of COVID-19 – labelled by Trump the 'Wuhan virus' –
along with the SARS epidemic of 2003. China responded, by

accusing the US of 'politicising the outbreak'. In an email to UN missions, China stated, 'The groundless accusations and malicious fabrication from the U.S. aim at shirking its own responsibilities, which severely poisoned the atmosphere of global cooperation in containing the outbreak.'[8]

Twenty years ago, Al Gore, then-US vice president, memorably chaired a Security Council debate on HIV/AIDS in Africa. The Security Council passed Resolution 1308, recognising 'the importance of a coordinated international response to the HIV/AIDS pandemic, given its possible growing impact on social instability and emergency situations'.[9] That prompted Kofi Annan, then-UN secretary-general, to propose the establishment of the Global Fund to Fight AIDS, Tuberculosis and Malaria in 2002. Similarly, the UN Security Council intervened when Ebola hit West Africa in 2014, unanimously agreeing Resolution 2177, designating the Ebola outbreak in West Africa a 'threat to international peace and security' and setting up the UN Mission for Ebola Emergency Response.[10]

So, contrary to claims made by both China and the US, there was nothing to prevent the UN Security Council from playing a coordinating role and living up to its history. But the Security Council could not even agree a bland compromise resolution stating that they supported 'all relevant entities of the United Nations system, including specialized health agencies . . . in the global fight against COVID-19'.[11] The US demanded the deletion of the phrase 'specialized health agencies' and, when others refused to remove it, the resolution fell through. Sadly governments have largely failed to work collectively, to come to each other's aid, and to support each other from the start of this global outbreak.

Vaccine nationalism

If we failed in the first wave to cooperate in dealing with the cause of the disease, nine months later, when we had a chance to redeem ourselves, we also failed to cooperate to end the spread of the disease by doing enough to share the miracle of vaccines.

Sadly, 'vaccine nationalism' (countries going their own way in attempts to corner the market in – and in some cases to hoard – supplies) is not just a temporary response prompted by the shortage of the various vaccines. Despite valiant attempts to make things work, the international coordination of supply and distribution will not be adequate even when millions of vaccines become available.

Global cooperation is needed to secure (1) the scaling up of vaccine production to meet global demand; (2) the negotiation and management of vaccine prices to ensure they are affordable for all nations; (3) the fair allocation of vaccines globally, giving priority to those most at risk and health workers; and (4) the rapid deployment of effective global roll-out procedures that are sufficiently flexible to address emerging hotspots. And, crucially, we need to underpin this with sufficient funding and, in particular, to support those low-income nations that will struggle to launch and sustain whole-population vaccination programmes.

We could be doing so much better. Over more than twenty years, I have seen at first hand how public-spirited scientists, medics and policymakers have built and funded global vaccination programmes that have reduced the incidences of polio, cholera, meningitis, yellow fever and tuberculosis.

When I was finance minister, the UK was one of the first countries to support the Global Fund to Fight AIDS, Tuberculosis and Malaria in 2002 and a number of governments joined us in subsidising new drugs and treatments of benefit to poorer countries. Working with charities, such as the Bill & Melinda Gates Foundation, our government was also in the vanguard of the Global Alliance for Vaccines and Immunization (GAVI), established in 2000 to pay for and distribute life-saving vaccines to the developing world. And I was directly involved in the creation of its financial arm, the International Finance Facility for Immunisation (IFFIm), which has raised $8 billion, and working alongside GAVI, has made possible the immunisation of 800 million children. To their great credit, these initiatives are now estimated to have saved 13 million lives.[12]

And so, joined by GAVI, IFFIm and the Global Fund in eradicating communicable diseases, the WHO no longer has to act alone to fulfil its global health mandate. In 2020 I was expecting to see all these inventive approaches brought to bear in heightened collaboration to deal with the COVID-19 crisis.

At the outset, I marvelled at the international coalitions and alliances that quickly emerged, linking scientists, medics and researchers across the world, and at the speed at which they went to work. To their great credit, a body had been convened by nine of the world's leading health organisations, with the unwieldy name of Access to COVID Tools Accelerator (ACT-A), and its vaccine pillar, COVAX, was set up to accelerate the development, production and equitable access to COVID-19 tests, treatments and vaccines. COVAX has two objectives: to secure vaccines for all economies at affordable prices by benefiting from economies of scale and advanced purchase agreements; and, through what is called Advanced Market Commitments, to fund vaccines for ninety-two lower-income countries which otherwise could not afford them. Its plan is that during 2021 it will have sent 1.2 billion doses to vaccinate the most vulnerable 20 per cent of the populations of poor countries with hopes to secure an additional 600,000 doses by the end of the year.[13]

And it is technically possible. Thanks to all the components now available – the science, technology and manufacturing expertise – vaccine production can be ramped up very quickly across the world. We will need to transfer technology, and later in this chapter I discuss what we might do to make that happen. And we will need to build the infrastructure in the seventy-four countries – more than thirty of which are in Africa – that have no previous experience of adult vaccination programmes for any disease. It will require the kind of mobilisation, never before seen in peacetime, that brings together the proven skills of pharmaceutical and logistics companies, national militaries and health professionals.

Who pays?

We have already overcome the challenges of devising a vaccine; we will overcome the current challenges of limited manufacturing capacity and poor logistics; but yet another obstacle will continue to stand in the path of mass vaccination. The cost of vaccinating the world has been estimated at $30 billion a year to cover research, distribution and the cost of immunising 20 per cent of the developing world, with a further $30 billion required to cover 80 per cent. That is a small price to pay, but no one seems willing to pay it.[14]

And yet we cannot afford *not* to pay it. The longer the pandemic persists, the greater the impact of lockdowns and border closures will be on the world economy. Already, in 2020, COVID-19 has cost $15 trillion in global economic rescue packages, on top of $10 trillion in lost output. The US non-profit RAND Corporation estimates that if the virus remains out of control the global economy will lose upwards of $1.2 trillion a year in GDP.[15] If the richest countries are vaccinated, but the poorest are not, it will cost the world $153 billion a year; yet if the world's poorest nations have equal access to COVID-19 vaccines, the high-income countries will earn a return of nearly $5 for every $1 spent on vaccines. And even this may be an underestimate. Factoring in supply and demand shocks, both domestic and foreign, from continued lockdowns, the International Chamber of Commerce predicts that the global economy could lose far more: up to $9.2 trillion, with about 50 per cent of this falling on advanced economies.[16]

And so the $30 billion or so annual bill for the global vaccine programme is a fraction of the trillions COVID-19 is already costing us. In fact, $30 billion is less than 2 per cent of the cost of President Biden's $1.9 trillion American Recovery Act. It would pay the US to underwrite the first $30 billion *on its own*: not as an act of charity but as a form of self-insurance to protect its own national interests. And if the ten largest global economies shared the cost of mass vaccination, one international consortium of researchers, the Eurasia Group, calculate that they would be at least $500 billion better off by 2025.

But sadly the global vaccination effort is wholly reliant on voluntary contributions and donations and too few have been forthcoming. As we stand at the time of writing in March 2021, the current deficit lies at $22.1 billion for 2021 alone,[17] with $3.1 billion urgently required to support vaccination in lower income countries.

The blunt truth is that under existing funding arrangements there is little chance of inoculating the majority of the population in the poorest nations by next year, or perhaps for many years. A vaccine divide is emerging between rich and poor and decisions are being made that determine who is to live and who is to die. These life-or-death choices should not depend on sending round a begging bowl or on charity alone. And as welcome as the UK and US's recent commitments to COVAX are, it is time to negotiate a fairer system of burden-sharing between nations.

Despite COVAX's best efforts to coordinate a vaccine roll-out, there has, instead, been a free-for-all in vaccine procurement. At least fifty-six separate bilateral deals giving priority of access to the richer nations have been signed to date. Canada, for instance, has ordered five times the number of vaccines required for its population – and it is not an outlier.[18] While around 120 countries have begun administering the vaccine, the majority of vaccines have been administered in high-income nations: ten of the richest nations account for around 80 per cent of the completed 260 million vaccines as of March 2021.[19] In comparison, countries dependent on COVAX will receive their doses far more slowly. As things stand, COVAX plans to deliver the first 237 million doses to 142 nations by May 2021, but as I write, two-thirds of all countries have yet to receive any COVID-19 vaccines.[20]

There are heart-warming examples of corporate and national generosity and this year's G7 will be an occasion to add to this, but in itself it will not be enough. AstraZeneca and Johnson & Johnson are producing at cost to enable poorer nations to respond to the acute phase of the pandemic, while countries like Norway are donating back to COVAX, New Zealand is supporting neighbourhood Pacific Islands, and India is giving away some of what its factories produce. But only an agreed system of fair burden-sharing can ensure sufficient resources to support the global poor in the long term and avoid an increasing rich–poor vaccine divide.

In the absence of this, most support for the wider ACT-A programme has come from only five nations: Germany, the US, the UK, Canada and Norway, as Table 1 shows. In fact, the Bill & Melinda Gates Foundation has so far donated far more than the vast majority of countries have given: around £350 million to the general anti-COVID-19 effort, along with $156 million specifically for vaccines. The table below also illustrates what *should* have happened: what a more equitable distribution of the burden would look like based on a country's capacity to pay, taking into account either their current national income (GNI) or their share of UN payments. Entirely missing from the list of donors are large economies such as China, Brazil and Russia.

Table 1: General COVID Support (ACT-A) and Vaccines (COVAX) Funding Support to Date (March 2021), Major Nation State Donors [*]

	Actual to March 2021 ($m)[†]		% of Total		Alternative Burden Sharing (%)	
	General COVID Support (ACT-A)	Vaccines (COVAX)	General COVID Support (ACT-A)	Vaccines (COVAX)	GNI Share	UN Contribution Share
Germany	2,636	1,954	24%	23%	5%	6%
United States	2,500	2,500	23%	29%	25%	22%
United Kingdom	1,111	1,032	10%	12%	3%	5%
Canada	757	301	7%	4%	2%	3%
Norway	470	390	4%	5%	0%	1%
Saudi Arabia	313	303	3%	4%	1%	1%
Japan	346	337	3%	4%	6%	9%
France	185	122	2%	1%	3%	4%
Spain	147	147	1%	2%	2%	2%
Italy	116	116	1%	1%	2%	3%
Australia	72	67	1%	1%	2%	2%
Republic of Korea	11	10	0.1%	0.1%	2%	2%
New Zealand	23	23	0.2%	0.3%	0.2%	0.3%

Total Pledged (all nations)	11,078	8,559
% of Total	78.4%	85.3%

---

[*] Excludes the $604 million from the European Commission that would place it as the 5th largest donor.
[†] Nation state donations converted to US dollars as of exchange rates 26 March 2021 and subject to variation. General COVID-19 support currently unallocated at time of writing includes CAD 230 million from Canada and EUR 21 million from France (included in general COVID-19 support but not allocated amongst pillars). See https://www.who.int/publications/m/item/access-to-covid-19-tools-tracker

Clearly there is work to be done. In the short term, with no burden-sharing agreement and yet an urgent need to move ahead with vaccinations, the World Bank could extend its grants to low-income countries and both the IMF and World Bank could increase their loans to middle-income countries. But in the long term sustained funding on an annual basis will be needed, and there will have to be better ways of paying for a global vaccination programme than relying on charity.

One option is to lessen the costs of purchase and production. In May 2020 the COVID-19 Technology Access Pool (C-TAP) was created, a global agency created to address issues of technology disparity and promote widespread access for the voluntary sharing of COVID-19 intellectual property and technology. The eventual goal of C-TAP is to provide a globalised vaccine production line with ordinary commercial patents waived to enable generic manufacturing. In October 2020, with the support of 100 developing countries, South Africa and India asked the World Trade Organization Council to waive intellectual property rights for COVID-19 vaccines, tests and treatments until everyone is protected. America and Europe, home to most pharmaceutical companies, resisted, but a temporary waiver should be agreed.

The India–South Africa proposal would, of course, exclude the innovators from profits but it would also leave manufacturers free to dominate the field. Thomas Pogge's proposed Health Impact Fund offers a better and fairer way forward in which a system of payments calculated according to the real-world impact of their innovations would replace the reward that companies automatically receive for monopoly patents. Under this system, the innovators would be paid a fee for each dose of their vaccine administered anywhere in the world; the higher the number of patients immunised with their vaccine, the more the innovators benefit. 'Instead of jealously guarding their know-how,' writes Pogge, 'innovators will be eager to share it so as to give manufacturers confidence that they will be able to manufacture, in large quantities and at low cost, a high-quality product that will pass regulatory scrutiny.'[21] The next step is to boost production through more voluntary licensing agreements and technology transfer into low- and middle-income countries, and to achieve this the WTO's new director general, Ngozi Okonjo-Iweala, has brought major pharmaceutical manufacturers together to explore voluntary licensing arrangements not just for scaling up COVID-19 vaccines but for diagnostics and therapeutics. It is too early to say how ambitious attempts to link Western pharma and developing country producers, like India's Serum Institute, the biotechnology company that will produce the greatest number of 2021 COVAX doses, will ultimately work out.[22]

But even if deals can be done, success depends on some-one meeting the costs. There's no avoiding a basic lesson with COVID-19: finance is not the whole solution, but it is indispensable to a safer world. We cannot continue to rely on charity or voluntary contributions: the virus doesn't care. At the end of this chapter I will suggest a formula for funding global health for the future, but to understand what we have to do to achieve the acceptance of such a system, and to improve the overall coordination of global health, we have to first look back into our history.

We have been here before.

Some lessons from history

Lest we think COVID-19 is a 'black swan' event and that global pandemics are one-offs, it is worth examining the evidence. Throughout history, more people have been killed by pandemics than by wars and lesser conflicts. And indeed it is an equally remarkable contemporary fact that already in this still-young century, we have witnessed five large scale epidemics: SARS (2003); avian flu (2009); Ebola (2014); Zika (2018); and now COVID-19.

Of course, because of our enhanced ability to communicate with each other, we are more knowledgeable than we once were regarding what is happening in other countries. But it is not simply increased awareness; according to the Royal Society, outbreaks have become more common in recent years.[23] Some viruses have evolved with humans over hundreds or thousands of years, and researchers have known about infectious diseases like Ebola since the 1970s and Zika since the 1940s. But while we have become more expert at identifying them and more adept at addressing and coping with them, viruses, bacteria and fungi can now spread around the world with greater speed than ever before by the same means as their hosts: by road, rail and air.

People and goods are travelling at greater volume and rapidity than at any time in history. Trade, travel, tourism and migration have all made it more likely that infections will spread. Budget airlines, huge cruise ships and regular international get-togethers for business and pleasure have extended new opportunities to millions, but they have also created huge risks. It is this depth and breadth of cross-border connections that mean a small single event can have consequences that cascade across the world. In short, greater interdependence means greater vulnerability, putting us more directly at the mercy of unplanned-for events. Once again we are all in the same storm, if not the same boat.

Infectious diseases can also spread more easily within countries today, because more than half of the world's people – nearly 60 per cent – live in closely integrated urban spaces. Soon the cities and towns of Africa – the least-developed continent of the world – will house half their countries' population. Yet, in most developing countries and cities, where people are crowded together and social distancing is difficult to achieve, health systems remain underdeveloped and social protection is often so inadequate that disease spreads quickly. Poverty – and, with it, the inability to isolate oneself by staying off work and facing the resultant hunger – is an aggravating force. So, too, is climate change and the laying waste of agricultural land. In June 2015, *The Lancet* brought together the world's leading experts on environmental health, who argued that a warming climate fuels the risk of disease and 'threatens to undermine the last half-century of gains in development and global health'.[24]

We need to accept that another COVID-19-style event could easily happen again. The question is not whether but when. We must therefore accept the urgency in reforming our global health architecture. We must not make the same mistakes that we have made with COVID-19.

And the WHO's past record might hold the key to the future.

The case of smallpox

There had been many false starts in the eradication of smallpox throughout the middle of the twentieth century: a global campaign agreed in 1959 which failed when only half the fifteen vaccines pledged met the quality standards; a mass vaccination in India planned for 1963 that never generated sufficient donations; and a USSR Cold War effort followed by a US response that also fell short. And so in the mid-1960s there were still 10 million smallpox cases across forty-three nations and between 1.5 and 2 million deaths every year. It was then that the WHO asked members to approve a separate budget for a Smallpox Eradication Unit requiring each member to contribute based on their ability to pay. But the $2m fund was so small, and much of the WHO membership so reluctant to contribute, that the smallpox-infected countries were expected to pay 70 per cent of the costs, and as the team that led the effort later explained:

> [The] lack of resources constituted a serious, continuing problem and, even in the concluding years of the programme, those that were made available barely sufficed to sustain momentum . . . the response was never adequate . . . Success was never a certainty even during the years immediately preceding the last known cases.[25]

But after a whole decade of intensive effort against the odds, by the late 1970s there remained only one country carrying the disease: Somalia. Of course an eradication effort that reduces cases by only 99 per cent fails to achieve its main goal. Nothing short of 100 per cent eradication constituted success. The appeal was still underfunded and it was not until Sweden, which had suffered its own outbreak as recently as 1963, offered a voluntary donation that final contact-tracing in Somalia could proceed. A Somalian man was identified as the last patient on earth with smallpox.[26] In this way a formerly much-feared contagion became the first and only human disease in history to have been totally eradicated.

Not only was this campaign, for all its false starts and underfunding, one of the best examples of international cooperation the world has ever seen: it must also go down as one of the most cost-efficient endeavours in human history. The annual cost of the smallpox campaign between 1967 and 1979 was $23 million set against an estimate that smallpox cost developing countries $1 billion a year and the global economy as a whole $1.35 billion a year. Adding up data for the whole world, the benefit was 159 times the cost – possibly the greatest global public investment in human history, and for a country like India, the benefit was more than twice as great.[27] But it was not just India benefiting. Donors across the globe were repaid many times over. 'The benefits to all countries of eradicating smallpox would appear so great and so clear', one study puts it, 'that it is difficult to understand why there were problems in obtaining the requisite resources and political commitment.'[28] Smallpox eradication was not a prisoner's dilemma. Everyone benefited. It was, as Barrett calls it, 'perhaps the greatest achievement of international cooperation in human history'.[29]

And yet it very nearly did not happen. It was good fortune that Sweden was prepared to pay for the last mile. While many countries had a strong incentive to finance the eradication effort, each would have preferred that another paid.

With eradication efforts persistently hampered by funding problems, and with countries seemingly unable to recognise the huge upsides of action and unwilling to shoulder the financial burden, we should have learned an early lesson with smallpox: that a new system of burden-sharing had to be devised. The eradication of smallpox was not inevitable, and success was such a close-run thing that we should never again have left disease eradication unfunded, trusting instead to chance. But we did.

A one-off?

An unwillingness of countries to contribute, despite the obvious medical and financial benefits of doing so, has thwarted more recent attempts at eradication of other infectious diseases. A campaign started in 1980 set out to eradicate Guinea worm, a water-borne parasitic infection that produces painful and disabling ulceration of the lower limbs. Progress was based on: eliminating the parasite from stagnant water; providing far purer water from boreholes; and reinforcing efforts with extensive health education campaigns. In 1986 cases were estimated at 3.5 million. The disease was endemic in twenty countries in the 1980s but by 2016 that was reduced to three. Only fifty-three cases were reported in 2019. This is huge progress – yet once again it took decades to secure the financing and commitment to get there.

By 2011, we saw the elimination of rinderpest, a rapidly fatal gastro-intestinal infection of cattle that was common for centuries. With a significant impact on food production in the form of milk and meat rinderpest was a real threat to the health of people in Africa and Asia and its eradication is a huge step forward. Yet we could be making so much more progress on other diseases. Take the example of a much more common disease, mainly of children: measles. One study has estimated that if measles were eradicated and vaccination could be discontinued the US could save anything between $500 million and $4.5 billion. Another study estimated that seven industrialised countries (Canada, Denmark, Finland, the Netherlands, Spain, Sweden and the UK) would save sums ranging from $10 million to $623 million if measles were eradicated.[30] Spend a little on eradication, save a lot on healthcare and vaccination. Again, there are huge health and economic benefits that accrue from joint global action.

Despite these large and sometimes successful programmes working to eradicate infectious diseases, our overall efforts still fall short. The hope has been, and remains, that after smallpox, poliomyelitis (commonly referred to as polio) will one day become the second viral disease to be eradicated. The circumstances are the same as they were for smallpox: there is a vaccine and it has no patent. When asked who owns the patent, Jonas Salk, who developed the vaccine, replied: 'Well, the people, I would say. There is no patent. Could you patent the sun?'[31] Yet inadequate funding still prevents the vaccine reaching all the people who need it.

Rotary International, which has contributed $600 million to tackling polio, proposed a fair way of sharing the financial burden across the WHO members, but they found that between 1985 and 2005 only sixteen of the twenty-two richest WHO member states contributed anything, only seven have paid the equivalent of, or more than, their estimated share based on their ability to pay, and six countries were free riders who made no financial contribution whatsoever. Not surprisingly, in 2001 the WHO declared that lack of finance constituted 'the single greatest threat to realising the historical eradication goal' in the case of polio.[32] More recently when, to its great credit, the Gates Foundation moved in to assist, commendable progress toward eradication has been made.

Other infectious diseases are also under attack, with varying levels of generally inadequate support. The search for a vaccination against malaria goes on, despite massive but still-insufficient funding from philanthropic organisations such as the Roll Back Malaria Initiative, as well as various governments. But perhaps because malaria is largely a disease of the developing world and, unlike COVID-19, thus poses little threat to the richer nations, the funding of a vaccine is, for them, a lower priority. And so while modest progress has been achieved, eradication is some way off.

The future of global public health depends on the success of uninterrupted mass vaccination programmes. We are making progress, but we still have a long way to go. In part due to the success of various vaccination programmes, global life expectancy has increased by twenty-five years since 1950, and 6 million fewer children now die before they reach their fifth birthday than in 1990. UNICEF, GAVI and the Global Fund have all contributed to the Expanded Programme on Immunization, which has achieved a steep reduction in river blindness, a 99 per cent reduction in polio infections, the containment of outbreaks of plague, and reduced cholera and yellow fever through effective vaccination programmes.

With a view to eliminating diseases and coordinating the supply of vaccine worldwide, a Decade of Action on Vaccines was launched in 2010 – but again finance was never sufficient. A 2017 study of health spending on 'global functions' found that an additional $9.5 billion was needed each year – more than twice the budget of the WHO – to close the overall financing gap for all global functions, including an additional $3.4 billion needed annually for pandemic preparedness.[33] No doubt we will see this gap close in the near future, but it is a sustained commitment that is required. Funding has always risen and fallen with crises. 'We throw money at an outbreak and, when it's over, we forget about it and do nothing to prevent the next one,' director-general of the WHO Tedros Adhanom Ghebreyesus has said, once again making the case for a new system of funding.[34]

The future of world health

If control of infectious disease was the sole remit of the WHO, it would have its hands full. In recent years, however, it has repeatedly been instructed by its members to do much more. And it has usually been asked to do more with less. For while it has been given directions to extend its reach, it has not been given the powers of execution and implementation, or finance, to do so, amounting to an unfunded mandate.

If its original remit lay in the management of infectious diseases, up to and including HIV/AIDS in the 1980s, it now also covers the world's biggest killers: non-communicable diseases such as cancer, diabetes, heart disease and strokes. Fighting these chronic diseases has meant it has had to shift its focus towards lifestyle, encompassing healthy eating, physical exercise and regular health checks, and including its Framework Convention on Tobacco Control. In its most recent statement of objective, the WHO has committed not only to protecting 1 billion more people from epidemics but also to extending ongoing health coverage to a further 1 billion, and ensuring these people enjoy healthier lives. The WHO of today is clearly a very different organisation from the one that emerged following World War Two. The United Nations calls it 'the directing and coordinating authority on international health', with the task of shaping the health research agenda, setting norms and standards, articulating evidence-based policy options, providing technical support to countries, and monitoring and assessing both progress and impact.

Overextended as it is, the WHO cannot escape the highly charged political environment in which a member-controlled organisation has to operate. Like other UN agencies, the WHO was caught up in Cold War politics, with the USSR leaving in 1949 when a communist delegate to the World Health Assembly declared that the organisation was the battleground of 'two opposing points of view'.[35] Somewhat disingenuously, Russia complained about the lack of priority being given to glaring inequalities in both health provision and outcomes. Under Western leadership the agency focused on practical deliverables, promoting technical assistance to developing countries. In due course the WHO became one of the first UN agencies to offer country-specific capacity-building programmes including for disease control.

The WHO is often accused of mission creep, but in fact global public health in the twenty-first century is still being managed on the basis of a twentieth-century paradigm in which nation states remain the locus of authority and responsibility. In his book *Unprepared*, Andrew Lakoff highlights how too often the agency's role is 'limited to providing technical assistance and issuing recommendations', which may or may not be taken up.[36] The global framework, he says, is little more than what has been 'cobbled together' as 'an assemblage of disparate elements', resulting in an 'unstable consolidation of global health security'.[37] And this limits the WHO's ability to be effective. For while national governments are able to change their domestic laws and build national institutions, there are no provisions in international law that allow an organisation like the WHO to impose obligations on nations. 'Lacking a supranational authority capable of compelling states to behave differently,' writes Professor Barrett, 'the only alternative available is international cooperation – a kind of organised volunteerism',[38] to 'create an aggregate gain, a reason for all countries to come to the bargaining table'.[39]

So today's WHO can only succeed by bringing people together, winning their confidence and urging joint action. It should be empowered by its members and given the authority to organise and direct the pooling and sharing of resources, coordinate donors' activities, and offer economies of scale that overcome market failures in the provision of public goods from data to vaccines.

But we should also see the organisation of international public health as more than one organisation – and instead as a network, single-purpose organisations or funds, many of which are established around the WHO and with the help of the WHO, taking responsibility for implementing, executing and achieving specific tasks like those taken on by the aforementioned vaccination alliances. Assembling scientists, medics and policymakers alongside NGOs and companies and connected together, they would form a network of networks.

Progress in delivering global health will be impossible without an equitable system of burden-sharing to cover those tasks that cannot be discharged other than by international institutions. However, our starting point is, of course, to recognise that under any system national governments cannot evade their responsibility for meeting the majority of health expenditures in their own countries. But according to *The Lancet* Commission on Future Health, by devoting a far bigger share of their rising national incomes to health, over a twenty-year period developing countries could see their mortality rates and life chances converge with those of the richer parts of the world. They could not only meet the 2030 Sustainable Development Goals (SDGs) on health, but, by 2035, prevent 10 million deaths a year.[40]

Later in this book I will discuss how through innovative finance we can frontload expenditure on vaccination and other global goods but it is imperative we now devise a system of national contributions for international health based on each country's relative wealth and their ability to pay. Currently $10 billion of United Nations expenditures and $1 billion of WHO expenditures are covered by compulsory levies which take into account the size of national incomes, debts owed and levels of poverty, with a ceiling on charges paid by the wealthy. Under this formula the US currently contributes 22 per cent of WHO funds, China 12 per cent, the UK, France and Germany between 4 and 6 per cent, and India 0.8 per cent, levies not too dissimilar to what countries pay for UN peacekeeping and the UN's organisational expenses as a whole. But, WHO levies cover only 16 per cent of what it spends, only $1 billion a year – no more than the budget of a small city or a large teaching hospital – and for the remaining 84 per cent, it has to rely on the goodwill of governments and philanthropists and their willingness to volunteer to meet budget shortfalls.

So we will have to raise more, and do so equitably. We could extend the IFFIm vaccination fund so that it can frontload a far higher level of vaccinations, funded by borrowings whose interest and capital repayments are covered by aid agencies. Rich countries could give guarantees upon the strength of which multilateral development banks can leverage up the resources available and maximise their disbursements. The World Bank and regional development banks could be recapitalised to enable them to do more.

As Table 2 shows there is an equitable basis upon which we could fund global health. We should adjust contributions to take into account the differential benefits countries gain from the resumption of trade and from the privileges of world leadership. Permanent membership of the UN Security Council, the G20 and the boards of the IMF, the World Bank and the Financial Stability Board (FSB), positions that give countries greater agency, should trigger greater financial responsibility.

Separately, the floors and ceilings that reduce the financial burden on countries under the current UN formula could be revisited, particularly those that limit contributions from nations with above world average per-capita wealth. This would also see oil-rich states like Kuwait, Qatar, Saudi Arabia and the UAE, who have often given voluntarily, contributing instead to the official fund. Alternative financing options are also available – using the EU's systems for the allocation of resources or the UK government's Barnett formula, where allocations automatically reflect shifts in population.

Table 2: Fair Burden-Sharing Formula
for Global Health[41]

	Share of General COVID Support (ACT-A) – *Donations to Date (April 2021)*	Share of Vaccines Support (COVAX) – *Donations to Date (April 2021)*	UN Funding Formula Share	Adjustment for Above Average GNI Per Capita and Removal of Maximum Contribution Ceiling*	Adjustment for International Status†	Adjustment for Above Average Trade Openness (Trade as % of GDP)‡	**Overall Fair Funding Formula§**
USA	23%	29%	22%	26%	27%	27%	**27%**
China	-	-	12%	12%	13%	13%	**13%**
Japan	3%	4%	9%	9%	9%	9%	**9%**
Germany	24%	23%	6%	7%	7.5%	7.5%%	**7.5%**
UK	10%	12%	5%	5%	6%	6%	**6%**
France	2%	1%	4%	5%	6%	6%	**6%**
Italy	1%	1%	3%	4%	5%	5%	**5%**
Brazil	-	-	3%	3%	3.5%	3.5%	**3%**
Canada	7%	4%	3%	3%	3.5%	3.5%	**3.5%**
Russia	-	-	2%	2%	3%	3%	**3%**
Australia	1%	1%	2%	3%	3.5%	3.5%	**3.5%**
Republic of Korea	-	-	2%	2%	2.5%	2.5%	**2.5%**

* Additional levies added based on scale of above-average GNI per capita; maximum ceiling of 22% on UN style contributions removed (only affects US)

† Based on additional 1% added for China, UK, France and Russia, and USA for Security Council Membership

‡ Trade openness additions calculated on basis of trade as % of GDP, weighting of trade remains lower than GNI per capita; scaled based on higher than world average openness

§ Final adjustments include factoring in a floor on contributions in terms of GNI (only countries with above $200 billion GNI pay), and readjustments for non-G20 countries based on total sum of shares not equaling more than 100%; under this formula, G7 donations cover c.62%, G20 c.93%, EU c.22%.

The sooner we act, the sooner the benefits will accrue, to rich and poor countries alike. For if the cost is in billions, the benefit is in trillions: action is an asset, and inaction is a liability.

The urgency to act

No country will suffer more if we fail to act than Somalia. Somalia was once a defining success of the global health movement, the scene of the final eradication of smallpox. Today, as it buries innumerable COVID-19 victims and faces a second wave of the disease, this country of 16 million people stands out as a desperately poor and embattled nation whose COVID-19 dead and diseased speak to our collective failure.

Somalia's government did attempt some measures to limit the spread of the virus, closing all schools and shutting down all domestic and international flights. Officials tried informing the public via newspapers, posters and warning broadcasts, and a campaign via mobile phones, but they admit that most Somalis are not even aware that the disease exists. Following WHO guidelines and with some financial help, Somalia has appointed a COVID-19 coordinator, and UNICEF and other charities and NGOs have provided hand sanitiser and personal protective equipment. But – in what is now a wearily familiar story – WHO help and international financial support are limited by the budget constraints of all the UN agencies involved. Too little has been done to assist Somalia in building a health system that could have moved quickly to protect the population when COVID-19 struck. With barely any medical support, the most effective protection against deaths from the virus is the relative youth of the population (nearly 80 per cent of Somalis are under thirty). In every other respect Somalia lags behind. It comes 194th out of 195 countries in the global health security index. There is just one doctor for every 100,000 people.[42] When COVID-19 broke out, Somalia had no test kits, no ventilators and little medical oxygen.

Even now, according to the WHO, there is only one hospital that specialises in disease control, and it has only twenty-four intensive care beds. Even when ventilators could be found, often in woefully small numbers (Jack Ma of Alibaba donated 500, but these had to be shared across the whole of Africa), Somalia had only one anaesthetist for every 100,000 people. Now facing a second wave it has run short of supplies of medical oxygen. The government has had little capacity to conduct wide-scale testing and even when health centres received testing kits, days and sometimes weeks passed before results arrived from laboratories.

Ten months into the outbreak, fewer than 27,000 tests for the virus had been conducted in Somalia – one of the lowest rates of testing per population in the world. So it is impossible to know the true rate of infection there. Across the African continent the four countries with the most developed health systems and testing facilities, South Africa, Morocco, Egypt and Nigeria, have reported half of all the continent's cases. Somalia is expecting vaccines to arrive in the first quarter of 2021, but as I write in March, none have arrived, and there is concern that the country has no deep-freeze provision to make use of vaccines such as those from Pfizer and Moderna, which must be kept at a temperature of minus 70 degrees Celsius.

Multiple health failures are compounded by an already inauspicious environment for fighting disease. COVID-19 is hitting a country preparing for its third major drought in a decade and which is already facing the biggest locust invasions and devastation of crops it has suffered for twenty-five years. It has been plagued by civil conflict since 1991, and as rival militias have battled for control, 350,000 Somalis have died as a result of war, starvation and disease and 2.5 million of its people have been displaced. With part of the country still held by the al-Qaeda-linked al-Shabab extremist group, the risk of the virus becoming endemic in some hard-to-reach areas is extremely strong.

Bringing with it interruptions in employment and in the distribution of food, COVID-19 is compounding already grave social problems. A typical income in this war-ravaged country is less than $1 per day – half of what is considered the required minimum to escape absolute poverty. Already more than 2 million of the country's 16 million people do not have enough food and in the absence of humanitarian assistance, nearly a million under-fives face malnutrition. Many live in crowded, unsanitary camps, creating fears that COVID-19 could scythe through an already vulnerable population.[43]

To fight COVID, social distancing is recommended, but in a country where urban areas are overcrowded this advice is ignored in practice, as are curfews and the wearing of masks. With schools closed, pupils congregate in groups, resulting in the easier spread of infection. With 85 per cent of the population lacking access to running water, hand-washing is rare. And even when workers are aware of the risks, they face a terrible choice: to stay at home and go hungry, or go to work and get sick. Worse still, many of the gains in poverty reduction and child health are being reversed. Because of COVID-19, NGOs have left the country, aid has been halted and humanitarian programmes have been cut back. By the summer of 2020, the routine vaccination of 600,000 children for polio and measles – once the pinnacle of global health cooperation – had been curtailed, and deworming of children halted entirely.

And as I complete writing at the end of March 2021, there is nothing more certain than that if current trends continue, Somalia, and countries experiencing similar levels of poverty, will continue to lose out badly. The expectation is that at least 60 per cent of the rich world will be vaccinated by the year's end, or soon after, and it will be grossly unfair and a stain on the conscience of the world if, even under the most ambitious plans, little more than 20 per cent of the developing world's population have had that same opportunity for vaccination. In many countries not even the 3 per cent of the population who comprise the health workforce will get immunised. And, as happened with other infection diseases, as long as countries like Somalia continue to suffer, richer nations like our own will, eventually, be damaged by the consequences. A failure to help Somalia is thus not just a betrayal of the poorest people on the planet, it is putting the global population at risk, too.

In March 2021 twenty world leaders called for a new international treaty to manage infectious diseases and secure universal and equitable access to vaccines and treatments, but they offered no proposal on how this could be financed. What is both frustrating and galling is that even after a year to plan a way forward, the best we can do as an international community to cover the cost of mass vaccination is to run the geopolitical equivalent of a charity fundraiser. Human lives should not hang in the balance, at the mercy of unpredictable and often erratic giving that continues to rely on passing round a begging bowl. What are called 'pledging' conferences can work but only when the demand is for a set amount of money on a one-off basis, whereas to eradicate COVID-19 the world needs to finance a sustained mass immunisation programme over a number of years.

If we are to reach the greatest number of people in the shortest amount of time across the widest geography, it will require new agreements with pharmaceutical companies to deliver lower cost and then generic vaccines, the build-up of manufacturing production capacity in Africa and the developing world, and heightened cooperation between global logistics firms, national armies and local health workers. And so the G7, which represents the richest countries, and the United Nations must urgently agree a formula for equitable burden-sharing between countries and for the expansion of SDRs, multilateral bank resources and innovative finance facilities to frontload the supply of vaccines. The leaders of the G7 should guarantee to cover the majority of vaccination costs until we have eradicated the disease from the face of the earth.

The COVID-19 pandemic will be followed by others. Let us hope our leaders have the boldness and vision to ensure that, when the next virus emerges, the world stands ready. Both our collective conscience and our sense of self-interest dictate that we must think beyond our borders. For our leaders to fail to do so again would be a scandalous dereliction of duty. We must do better. In the words of Dr Larry Brilliant, who worked on the final eradication of smallpox: 'Outbreaks are inevitable, but pandemics are optional.'[44]

3

A NEW KIND OF ECONOMY: A GLOBAL GROWTH PLAN FOR THE 2020S

The post-COVID-19 economy

A year after COVID-19 first struck, many economies and companies are still running at less than 90 per cent capacity – and they may do so for some time. Along with bringing illness – often serious – for tens of millions and death for many hundreds of thousands, COVID-19 initially devastated global production, the global supply chain and global living standards. Nations that, in early 2020, were running at near-to-full employment are now victims of a pandemic-induced recession threatening unprecedented levels of business failure, bankruptcies and debt. The best estimate of the IMF is that even at the end of 2022, cumulative income per head in advanced economies will still be 13 per cent below pre-crisis projections and, with the exception of China, between 18 and 22 per cent lower in low-income countries and emerging and developing countries.[1]

Yes, 2021 has brought new hope, with the emergence of effective vaccines and, in due course, mass vaccination, as well as the economic rebound this will make possible. But we should not confuse this hope with the sustained global recovery the world needs. The fact is that the world economy is heading for another low-growth, high-inequality decade and near-zero interest rates will not restore pre-crisis levels of private investment if high levels of unemployment crush long-term demand. The liquidity crisis of 2020 could easily become the solvency crisis of the 2020s and the scars of long-term unemployment could last a generation.

While all countries will initially benefit from America's $2 trillion fiscal stimulus, I want to demonstrate that there are even greater long-term gains from globally coordinated action. Missing is any concerted plan to rebuild global growth that not only recognises the limits of monetary policy when interest rates are near-zero, but also brings together the world's major economic players – the US, Europe and China – to put under-utilised resources back to work. For, if the major economies used their fiscal headroom to boost infrastructure spending by between 0.3 per cent and 1 per cent of GDP, then the world economy would recover far faster – by an additional $1 trillion, says the IMF, by 2025. And if we are able to achieve a well-coordinated and fully synchronised recovery, as we did in late 2009 in the wake of the 2008–09 financial crisis, the multiplier effect – the spill-over from increased trade and consumption – would be twice as effective in promoting growth, creating $2 trillion of extra economic output. And so great could be the gains in jobs and living standards from intensified international economic cooperation that if we increased investment all round by between 1 per cent and 3 per cent in the coming year, then we could achieve as much as two-thirds of that boost in output – a 1 per cent increase in world economic activity – in one year alone.

We already know that COVID-19 has disrupted traditional manufacturing and service sectors, destroyed hundreds of thousands of jobs for good, radically changed the established work patterns of millions and accelerated big changes like the online revolution. All of these factors combine to force a number of unpalatable choices on policymakers as policy priorities shift from saving jobs and companies to engineering a sustained recovery and, at time of writing, it is not clear what the outcome will be.

The economic response to COVID-19 has been as transformative as the virus itself, not only because it has altered every country's fiscal arithmetic – and will do so for decades ahead – but also because of unprecedented monetary activism, which will eventually have to be unwound. But the rescue operation has papered over major cracks in the financial sector that were left unresolved by the incremental reforms to the financial system after 2009. What is clear is that the huge test the global economy faced in 2020 is not going to be its last momentous test of the decade: it will face multiple challenges over the next few years, for which it does not seem well prepared.

Looking forward, as policymakers also come to terms with the climate change challenge, we can be certain that the future shape of economic policy will be different. Economic growth and social justice will not now be the only objectives a modern economic policy must pursue: environmental sustainability is now a third and equally important goal, which I will discuss in the next chapter, and the need for environmentally sustainable solutions will have to be factored into every aspect of economic policy.

The economy of the future will still be highly interconnected and integrated. Disrupted as global trade and global supply chains have been, and may continue to be because of trade disputes, climate disruption, cyberattacks and of course pandemics – McKinsey predict disruption to firms' production lines for up to two months every four years – talk of 'deglobalisation' is overdone. For while instability in any one country or continent will continue to threaten to spill over to disrupt the stability of every other country and continent, obituaries about the 'end of globalisation' underestimate the opportunities for global growth and development that lie ahead, and the desire on the part of investors, entrepreneurs and companies to seize them.

As I examine where we are, how we got here, where we need to go and how we get there, I want to focus on what I see as the two greatest risks to prosperity: the lurking dangers of global financial instability as unprecedented levels of monetary support are removed; and the weak insipid global growth – what is often called a low-growth equilibrium – that, even without COVID-19, was set to undermine standards of living in the 2020s. I will show that, by working together to devise a global growth plan to which we all contribute and from which we all can benefit, the world economy will grow faster, create more jobs and spread prosperity more equitably to low-income countries and the poorest citizens of the world.

First: the damage done by COVID-19. World economic activity in 2020 was around 6.5 per cent less than it would have been had there been no pandemic. Instead of the global economy growing by 3 per cent, as expected, it shrank by 3.5 per cent in the biggest annual contraction since the Second World War.[2]

By way of contrast, the world economy shrank by just 0.1 per cent in the global financial recession of 2008–09. Of course, the impact worldwide has been uneven: output in many of the advanced economies like Spain, the UK and France has fallen by 9 per cent or more and was thus around 12–13 per cent lower than it might have been. While the US is usually resilient (it fell by 3.4 per cent in 2020 and will grow by far more than 5 per cent this year), all Western economies have been hit so hard that even if they register growth rates averaging around 4 per cent in 2021 it will probably take at least two and, in some cases, five years to recover the output lost. China has recovered quickly, one of the few economies to see its output rising again – a growth of around 2 per cent in 2020. But other emerging market countries from India to Latin America have fared worse and it is now predicted that, by the end of 2021, they will have suffered an output loss of more than 8 per cent on pre-COVID trends.[3] Convergence between countries can no longer be taken for granted, and there is a major risk of a new era of divergence, with developing countries, whose prospects for recovery depend on a revival of trade and what is slow to materialise – access to vaccines, debt relief and financial support from the international institutions – languishing for years to come. Instead of catching up, fifty-eight emerging and developing countries, says the IMF, will fall further behind the West. Already the 2020s are shaping up to be a lost decade for growth.

Even if there were to be a faster bounce-back, unemployment in most countries will remain high. During 2020, millions of workers were placed on half or reduced pay or sent home because they had zero-hours contracts, so were never registered as unemployed. Many of their jobs are now so insecure that they are likely to be terminated in 2021 and 2022. In the biggest economies alone the IMF predicts further job losses of 25 million in 2021 and 20 million in 2022.[4]

While in the first phase of the pandemic growth fell faster than incomes, especially in Europe, employment in the second phase has been falling faster than growth. The estimate made by the UN's International Labour Organization in March 2020 – of a 25 million rise in unemployment, already in excess of the 22 million increase in unemployment during the previous global financial crisis – has had to be continuously revised upwards. In the global tourism sector alone, the IMF estimates, as many as 120 million jobs could be in danger.[5]

The biggest losers from the crisis are the already poor. About 2 billion people around the world work informally, with limited access to social protection or benefits, and the pandemic has pushed around 150 million more people into extreme poverty. The IMF estimates that income inequality rose more sharply in 2020 than it did in previous economic and financial crises not least because those who own shares did well as stock markets, underpinned by government support, boomed. The pandemic has increased both income and wealth inequality between nations, as well as within nations, and a decade of progress in reducing inequality in developing economies has been wiped out. The World Bank reported that remittances to low- and middle-income countries – often the mainstay for poor families – declined by almost 20 per cent. 'The poor are getting poorer,' said Gita Gopinath, economic counsellor and director of the Research Department at the IMF.[6] According to the World Bank, the COVID-19 crisis will throw back poverty reduction worldwide by around four to five years.[7]

But the occupations we are employed in and the ways we work are rapidly changing, too, speeded up by the crisis. At one point during the lockdown, two-thirds of US economic activity was being run from home – perhaps the shape of things to come – and, in the coming years, digital retail trade, which has already risen from 5 to 20 per cent, will rise even more. All this also foreshadows a transformation in the way we produce goods and services that is unparalleled outside wartime. COVID-19 created a tipping point. An October 2020 McKinsey survey of shifts in companies found that many had accelerated the digitalisation of customer and supply-chain interactions and internal operations by three to four years, and the share of digital or digitally enabled products in their portfolios by seven years.[8]

Within the mass manufacturing economies of the twentieth century, a sense of solidarity built up among workers thrown together in factories and workshops. It led to a high density of trade union membership, across Europe in particular, and for a time maximised the wage-bargaining strength of unions. But the workers of the future will not only be far more widely dispersed, but also far more isolated from their fellow workers. This has led respected economists – from Lawrence Summers in the US to Jean-Claude Trichet, former head of the European Central Bank (ECB) – to argue that we should recognise the important role played by trades unions and collective bargaining in raising demand for goods and services in the economy, diffusing prosperity and ending a decade of zero inflation and near-to-zero interest rates.

What we do to sustain and expand growth and distribute economic benefits fairly – and how we deal with deficits and debt – is the subject of the last part of this chapter. But my other question is equally important for prosperity: what happens to the financial system? For the current interventions by central banks may simply be obscuring major fault lines in our global financial system and postponing a day of reckoning.

The context is, of course, the massive global flows of capital and the global sourcing and supply of goods and services, which are the two distinguishing features of today's economic globalisation. We have yet to discover COVID-19's long-term impact on cross border services like air travel, tourism and hospitality. Until the crisis, these were an ever-growing component of the services sector, which, in most advanced economies, makes up around 70 per cent of economic activity.

One quarter of the recent fall in output was caused by the disruption of the very supply chains that characterised the new era of globalisation; the question is whether they have become too stretched and will break down. Of course, the China–US stand-off will affect the level of trade for some years. Already, by 2019, trade protectionism was such that US tariffs on Chinese imports rose from an average of 12 to 21 per cent and Chinese tariffs on US goods increased from 17 to 21 per cent.

The lurch towards protectionism has been accelerated by the closing of borders and the restrictions of medical and other exports during COVID-19, all of which contributed to the large fall in global trade in 2020. A McKinsey survey of 180 products found that 70 per cent of the trade in them was monopolised by a single country, usually China, and as a result companies reported they would like to lessen such dependence within five years by placing a quarter of their contracts elsewhere. But, as I will suggest in Chapter 9, it is in both countries' interests to minimise the disruption and we have to distinguish between temporary and permanent disruption. The history of supply chains, according to a study of sixty-four countries, is that, while they are not robust in the short term in a crisis, they are resilient over the longer term. In other words, they are less good at working through a crisis, but they are far better at bouncing back. As the same McKinsey study found, 93 per cent of firms were not planning on breaking up their supply chains, but rather making them more resilient.[9]

Supply chains – or what are now called value chains, because they include everything from research and development to management and sales – are also changing fast. As the economist Richard Baldwin has argued, the global economy could become more, not less, integrated as teleworking is made possible by the unbundling of legal accountancy and financial services into discrete and semi-skilled tasks that can be accomplished online from low-wage destinations in Africa and Asia.[10]

Of course, as, over time, Asian and African wages rise, and as, also, more and more goods and services become less labour-intensive, some production may move closer to home. Here, however, automation and the use of robots will mean that machines will replace workers and few new jobs will be created. But beyond this reshoring, there is no intrinsic reason why, if trade disputes can be minimised, trade should not recover.

The bigger question is not so much whether the global supply chain will collapse, but whether the financial system that underpins it is resilient enough to ensure that the global economy can work to full capacity.

In the two decades before 2008, what had once been distinctive, largely autonomous national financial regimes gradually morphed into a highly integrated, interconnected and interdependent global financial system. This system now requires such massive flows of capital every minute to sustain the sourcing of goods and services that daily cross-border financial transactions amount to much more than the world's GDP. While foreign claims by the banking system were only 25 per cent of global GDP in 2000, they rose to 60 per cent in 2008. While they then fell heavily during, and in the aftermath of, the global financial crisis, foreign claims stand today at around 40 per cent. This means that any financial crisis is inevitably a global financial crisis.

And that is what we face today.

Learning from crises

While the circumstances are a bit different, we have been here before. The last major crisis was a little over a decade ago and an understanding of its nature, its aftermath and the lessons that were *not* learned is essential for us to consider if we want to ensure a more prosperous decade in the 2020s, one that is not bedevilled by financial crises.

In the first few days of the previous global financial crisis, on Saturday 4 October 2008, President Nicolas Sarkozy of France convened talks at Paris's Elysée Palace. Around the table were: Chancellor Angela Merkel of Germany; president of the ECB, Jean-Claude Trichet; president of the European Commission, José Manuel Barroso; Prime Minister Jean-Claude Juncker of Luxembourg; Prime Minister Silvio Berlusconi of Italy; and myself, the UK prime minister at the time. The purpose of the meeting was to discuss Europe's response to the crisis. We had already agreed on the need to strengthen economic cooperation to deal with the coming European recession and, at my request, Asian, African, Latin American and European leaders had met at a hastily convened informal summit during the UN General Assembly gathering two weeks previously.

By the time we met in Paris, the financial markets had frozen: no one was investing, and few were trading. US Federal Reserve chairman Ben Bernanke later confessed that he had had to act with speed because eighteen of the twenty biggest US financial institutions were in danger of collapse. But, in Paris that day, I did not detect the same sense of urgency among my fellow European leaders. They tended towards the view that it was a US crisis. If the UK was affected, it was because we had fallen too easily and foolishly for an Anglo-Saxon model of capitalism. As a result, they did not foresee the decade-long European crisis that lay ahead.

I argued that European banks looked even more at risk than the US institutions. They were more debt-ridden and more highly leveraged. We had discovered that $500-billion-worth of sub-prime mortgages – the virtually valueless (at the time) assets that were the immediate trigger for the crisis – had been bought by European banks and that these banks, too, were now only a step away from bankruptcy. Simply put, the banks had been running capitalism without capital. I explained that the UK banks were now drawing up plans for recapitalisation – under public owner-ship if necessary – and I advocated an internationally coordinated effort to inject new capital widely across the world's banking system. But there was still no agreement on what Europe should, or could, do.[11]

We considered a number of other options to stabilise the financial system, such as guarantees to bank depositors and the provision of liquidity to the corporate sector. But we were not getting very far. So, after an hour and a half or so of talks around the table, we took a break. At that point, as we relaxed over coffee and tea in one of the Elysée's sumptuously decorated rooms, Silvio Berlusconi, who had yet to express a view on what ought to be done, was overheard saying: 'Amateurs! Amateurs!' Might the only professional businessman in the room have a solution to the crisis that none of the rest of us had considered? 'Amateurs!' He gesticulated emphatic disbelief. 'Amateurs! *Ils sont amateurs*. Don't they realise? We have a photo call in an hour! And none of them have brought a make-up artist!'

Politicians are not intrinsically well suited to dealing with the intricacies of financial stability and economic risk. And, if that meeting was anything to go by, businessmen-turned-politicians might be even less so. This remains the case today. It is doubtful that a group photograph of cosmetically improved politicians would have done much more to reassure the markets – then or now.

While a lack of early political grip was obvious that Saturday afternoon in Paris, the grim truth is that the international community's lack of attention to, and inability to grasp, the escalation of financial risks over the last few decades has cost us dearly and may continue to cost us dearly in the future. Leaders have to be not one, but at least two steps ahead in a crisis. In 2008, we were all behind the curve – and I fear this is happening again.

In particular, at every crisis point in the decade since 2010, politicians, lacking confidence in their own ability to supervise the financial markets, have left the bulk of economic decision-making to the unelected monetary authorities and, during these ten years, central banks have rightly been called 'the only game in town'. And so it was again when the world economy stopped in March 2020 and the authorities stepped in with unparalleled support in the form of loans, guarantees and payments.

To meet and master this new financial crisis, the world's central banks have had to take on even bigger additional roles – far beyond their 2008–09 status as the lenders of last resort to private banks. This time, to prop up capital markets, the Federal Reserve and others have become market-makers of last resort, intervening directly in credit markets – the Fed alone underpinning the financial markets with $23.5 trillion, a sum bigger than the annual output of the US economy and a figure unsurpassed in history.

Financial markets are global, but, in a crisis, support for them has to come from national authorities. As a result, dozens of national central banks around the world, in emerging markets as well as advanced economies, have now, for the first time, offered unconventional monetary support, even buying low grade bonds and guaranteeing to uphold the financial markets in junk bonds and what are often called exotic products. But these welcome temporary interventions to stabilise the economy have – and this is the crux of the first part of this chapter – obscured the vulnerabilities at the heart of the global financial system. And, as the risks taken by the financial sector turn into liabilities on governments' balance sheets, we have, in turn, created a new source of moral hazard. The corporate world has been guaranteed support, whether or not the companies are viable or not. The instruments they have chosen to underpin financial markets – state guarantees – have not only privileged the financial sector, but also allowed stock markets to boom while the real economy is in recession. And, of course, this state underpinning of financial assets inevitably widens inequalities in income and wealth. It has benefited big companies, even near-to-bankrupt ones, at the expense of small businesses, including financially sound ones, and boosted wealthy individuals who own shares over ordinary working households whose wages from work have been interrupted to produce a very skewed economy.

Today, risks have been nationalised even though rewards remain privatised, as was the case after 2009 when economic recovery coexisted with what we called a main street recession. This is now referred to as a K-shaped recovery, so called to describe the two paths of direction that leave the majority under financial pressure amid a boom at the top. But the main form of corporate support is in loans that have to be repaid and, as monetary support is cut back, liquidity problems – a need for cash flow – can easily descend into solvency problems. So, despite the massive injection of resources offered by central banks, the underlying problems of the world's financial system, revealed by the global financial crisis, have not disappeared. They are currently just hidden from view. At some point soon, we will rip off the bandage without ever having sewn up the wound. Our failure to update the global financial system for the era of global capital flows will come to the surface as a major concern once again. As the IMF reported in January 2021, action is needed to address the vulnerabilities exposed by the pandemic. These they summarised as rising corporate debt, fragilities in the shadow banking sector, increasing sovereign debt, restrictions of market access for some developing economies, and declining profitability in some banking systems.

All this raises questions about what the proper role of central banks is: where their responsibilities end and where the direct responsibilities of governments begin. When we talk of the independence of central banks we do not, and should not, imply the freedom of central bankers to do just as they want. It is for the legitimate governments of the day to make sure that, in their deliberations and decisions, employment creation, the fair distribution of rewards and environmental sustainability are not neglected, and there is no doubt that during an era where central banks have dominated economic policymaking these great issues have not enjoyed the attention they deserve.

Recessions

For most of the post-1945 years, recessions and downturns in economic growth, particularly in the UK, have been triggered by inflation. These regular crises started with spiralling prices and wages that led, in turn, to the ratcheting up of interest rates and ended with businesses being unable to cover their loans, laying off people and, in too many cases, going under. Inflation targets were adopted to prevent this – and, while there were many factors at work, like the much lower 'China price', the evidence is that, when central banks were given independent control of monetary policy tools, inflation did drop significantly. But, of course, over these same decades, no one closely involved could overlook the vulnerabilities of a financial system that had been liberalised and gone global.

In the wake of the 1998 Asian financial crisis, I had advocated a Global Financial Stability Forum that would monitor emergent risks in the financial system and provide early warning of crises. At the start of the 2000s, after the US dot-com bubble, the UK proposed that the regular IMF meeting of finance ministers and central bank governors, which I was then chairing, should conduct an annual review of risks to the global economy and – perhaps more importantly – set aside time at each annual meeting to consider these issues, which had previously been ignored or neglected.

Risks in an economy are greatest at the time investors are worrying about them least. By 2006, we were all aware that we were nearing the peak of a long economic cycle. At such a point, with equity prices booming, there is, history tells us, a tendency to believe that 'this time it is different', that house prices, for example, will never fall, and that we can get away with taking more and more risks. We decided to model a possible crash in the financial sector. I ordered scenario planning on how the collapse of a major financial institution might play out. But we soon decided that this should not be restricted to an exclusively UK exercise. After all, the reach of the City's financial institutions did not stop at the UK border. We believed that a transatlantic investigation would yield more insights, so I approached the chairman of the US Federal Reserve, Ben Bernanke, and Hank Paulson, US treasury secretary, as well as the US regulatory authorities, who agreed to be part of a joint simulation of a banking crash.

That simulation took place in April 2007, just a few weeks before I left the UK Treasury to become prime minister. In a transatlantic video conference, we discussed detailed papers already exchanged between UK and US regulators. There were, of course, limits to how effective such an exercise could be. Because awareness of such a simulation might unnerve the markets, we did not include the private sector in our scenario planning. And, while we did consider contagion (how one bank's failure would put others at risk), we assumed that the failing bank was a standalone institution. As a result, we did not go so far as investigating the intricate connections between different financial institutions, nor the more important ties that these individual banks had to the shadow banking sector, which includes hedge funds and huge, ill-defined offshore interests.

Incomplete as our review of risks was, the findings were

something of a revelation and are still relevant to the challenges we face today. We were immediately made aware that, in a crisis, we would be dealing not with a single regulatory chain, but rather with dozens of regulatory authorities across the world, often in competition with each other. And, while we now had the Global Financial Stability Forum to bring regulators together, it took some years to persuade national governments that something more authoritative was needed and we would later create the Financial Stability Board (FSB), to be ably led by Mark Carney.

In the course of our exercise, the then-governor of the Bank of England, Mervyn King, when faced with the collapse of our hypothetical bank, favoured letting the ailing bank collapse. He and others were worried about the 'moral hazard' of any rescue, so-called because, by saving failing institutions, we risked being seen as underwriting the consequences of bad behaviour, thus making such behaviour more likely in the future. This was a serious concern of his and, at the origins of the real financial crisis in August 2008, he would issue a strong warning that failing institutions should be left to collapse.

A week or two later, suddenly and surprisingly, a test case occurred in the UK. On 12 September, Northern Rock, a bank based in Newcastle, approached the Bank of England for liquidity support – and, for the first time in living memory, long queues of people seeking to withdraw their savings from its branches were seen all over the country. Northern Rock's shares dropped by almost a third. A previously respected and successful bank, with a long record of charitable donations from its profits, Northern Rock had taken to acquiring long-term debts in the form of attractively priced mortgages and, when these loans soured, it sought to compensate with expensive short-term loans from the wholesale credit markets. Faced with this crisis, agreeing that the risk of contagion was great and despite the moral hazard involved, the government moved to reassure both investors and account holders. Recognising the gravity of the problem, high-level negotiations followed. Northern Rock became the first UK bank to seek Bank of England funds in the wake of the subprime crisis.

Over the years of these uncertainties, I received regular sub-missions from the Treasury and held monthly meetings with the governor of the Bank of England and we continued to consider possible risks to financial stability. But I cannot recall a memo or any spoken or written warning that a financial crisis was immi-nent or even likely. 'Would there be a world downturn in the next year?' I asked in 2007. 'No,' I was told.

The limitations of our own simulation exercise in the spring of 2007 were reflected elsewhere. I discovered later that the private sector was doing scenario planning of its own, mainly address-ing the risks of a collapse in the emerging market economies. But when, as an off-the-cuff exercise, Lehman Brothers, a vast and long-established New York bank, applied their predictive model to the US economy, they were surprised by the results. Their computer model – named Damocles, somewhat ironically as things turned out – came up with a reading 'above 75', which implied a one-in-three chance of a financial crash within a year. A later reading of 100 suggested the likelihood was 50:50.[12]

But when Lehman's modellers came up with these readings – a result of external debt, a current account deficit and high levels of outstanding credit – they did not take them seriously, despite the US economy's vulnerability being deemed by their survey second only to that of Iceland. Laughing it off as a statistical freak seemed the rational thing to do. Lehman's experts concluded that, as everyone assumed, the US was too strong to fail.

A number of commentators have written about such crises as we witnessed in 2008 as if they were anomalous and rare: 'black swan' events that simply defy anticipation.[13] In fact, crises have long been endemic in our global economy, if less noticed than the inflation-led crises of the latter part of the twentieth century. Hardly a year has gone by without a crisis in at least one continent and there is no decade in recent history in which the world has escaped a major crisis. Of course, the UK itself suffered badly in its deep recessions of the mid-1970s and early 1980s. Another followed in the early 1990s, after the Conservative government's eventually chaotic encounter with the European Exchange Rate Mechanism, but the decade subsequently saw, in quick succession, a series of financial crises across the globe: the Finnish banking crisis of 1991–93; Mexico's 1994 economic crash; and the Swedish house price-related banking collapse of 1990–94.

After I became chancellor in 1997, I observed around the world the Russian financial crisis (1998–99), the Argentinian economic crisis (1999–2002) and the Brazilian crash (1999), but these were minor events compared to the crash that convulsed Asia in 1998–99. I recall how, on Christmas Eve 1998, the governor of the Bank of England came into the Treasury to announce to me that South Korea was bankrupt. During the next few months, I toured Asia and saw at first hand the impact of a crisis that spread to Thailand, Indonesia, Malaysia and Japan.

But the result of the analysis by the IMF into the causes of the Asian financial crisis actually set back what should have been a concerted international effort to create an effective global financial safety net to prevent and resolve future crises. The IMF attributed Asia's instability to alleged fiscal profligacy on the part of Asia's 'spendthrift' governments and recommended punitive spending cuts, which left much of Asia struggling to develop even the most basic of social safety nets.

At the time, I argued for change – in the form of international insurance, perhaps organised through the IMF, that gave emerging economies some protection against the likelihood of future crises – but this attracted only limited support from a global community still unwilling to recognise that there were structural flaws in the global financial system. Asian countries then decided that their only rational course of action was to 'self-insure'. They set about building up their own reserves, even to the point of underinvesting in the infrastructure developments that might have contributed to expanding their potential for growth. Rather than supporting international institutions seeking to organise the global supervision of financial systems, a discouraged Asia had turned away. The world had learned the wrong lessons from the financial instability of the 1990s. And the Asian crisis did not end the run of financial crashes. Even before the global financial crisis of 2008, a still-young century had already seen the US dot-com bubble of 2001, the Turkish economic crisis of the same year and the Uruguay banking crisis of 2002.

The three obvious conclusions from this short overview of several stormy economic decades are that crises are endemic; that our systems for crisis prevention and crisis resolution are wholly inadequate; and that damping down risks in one part of the system does not lessen risks in the system as a whole, with the result that risks move elsewhere. Not only should international regulators have agreed better ways of detecting and preventing future crises, but more time should also have been spent on how best to prepare to solve them if and when they happened. What Eisenhower once said of military crises is as true of economic crises: plans are useless, but planning is indispensable.

It seems equally obvious to me that, given the regularity of crises in the twenty-first century, not least the COVID-19 induced economic crisis that we are currently grappling with, we need to revisit and complete the unfinished business of the G20 of 2009, which had begun well but was not followed through. As *IMF Reform: The Unfinished Agenda* – a pre-COVID-19 report of 2018 by a highly respected group of financial experts warned: 'Sudden stops, like capital flow volatility, remain a fact of international financial life, and the magnitude of the associated capital flow turnaround has, if anything, become even larger.'[14]

Crisis prevention means: first, developing better early warning systems that give us more accurate assessments of emergent risk while accepting that risks mutate; second, improving global financial safety nets to adapt to the allotment of capital between banks and non-banking institutions, ensuring that, whatever befalls us, we protect the most vulnerable; and, third, perhaps most importantly of all, devoting more attention to the underlying problems of the world economy and what can be done to reverse the slowing of the overall growth rate. Together, these are the major challenges to the stability and strength of the future global economy and, throughout this chapter, I shall attempt to explore some ideas on how we might respond to them.

Early warning systems

We've never been very good at this. The 2008–09 global financial crisis exposed what economists had long ignored. Over two decades of enormous expansion, New York's Wall Street and London's City had created ever-more complex and lucrative ways to oil the wheels of the modern global economy. Indeed, the months and years immediately preceding the 2008 global crisis had been marked by unprecedented financial inflows into the US. Over these years, a global financial system had come into being, but governments across the world had done little to monitor, supervise and police it – or even to understand how it worked. Indeed, the US government had actually increased risk by the removal of the 1930s Glass–Steagall Act, which had created Chinese walls between the banks' lending functions and those concerned with active investment or even speculation.

By 2008, in the words of the IMF's chief economist, Olivier Blanchard, this US-led approach could be described as 'all competition and no control'. It was considered sufficient for the authorities to set interest rates, to regulate the size and composition of the central bank balance sheet and to monitor exchange rates. Regulatory controls that could have brought greater stability – limits on loan-to-value ratios, lending and interest rate ceilings, reserve and capital requirements and perhaps, in emergencies, countercyclical margin requirements for the purchase of shares – were out of favour, not least because the very boundaries that the financial system required in the interests of avoiding volatility were what finance itself now opposed. And many banks sought ways to get around those regulations that were in place, in the interest of, as they saw it, maintaining their freedom to innovate or, as I came to see it, paying themselves huge bonuses for taking excessive risks at the public's expense.

For there was an even deeper failure. As trillions flowed around the world in an increasingly interconnected global financial system, there was an implicit assumption that such capital flows were spreading risk across the world – and onto the shoulders of multiple holders – thereby diluting it. This diffusion of risk, it was argued, was bringing about a permanent reduction in the volatility of business cycle fluctuations. Indeed, the idea that risks were widely diffused was central to the standard assertions about the 'rationality' of 'efficient' markets. If the diffusion of risk was made possible by wide and deep markets, then there was no problem: large-scale deregulation could be justified.

The events of 2008 exposed what should have been long been obvious but has been ignored. When talking of the diffusion of risk, we had tallied up, and found comfort in, the range of countries, individuals and financial institutions that were all, in some way, now part of the global system. We should have been looking in more depth at the small number of very large and systemically important global institutions dominating the sector, and their dubious assumptions that their ever-more sophisticated financial engineering made possible perfect risk mitigation. And we should have understood how they had become 'too big to fail' and too dominant for us ever to allow them to go under.

In fact, risk had not been spread evenly across the world; it was concentrated within a few very large institutions that used complex and often obscure instruments, made possible by the development of securitisation, the generalisation of derivative markets and, until the crisis hit, high levels of leveraged finance. Such leverage was boosted by the shadow banking world of hedge funds, private equity firms and other unregulated financial companies that bought collateralised debt obligations (CDOs), mortgage-backed securities, credit default swaps (CDSs) and the like.

It is not necessary to know one's way through any more of the details of the morass of financial acronyms and jargon. All that is necessary is to understand that the very complexity of the system allowed financiers to maintain a certain, intentional obscurity around the asset bubbles they were creating, until, finally, the money ran out, the bubbles popped and the risks they had been taking all along came home to roost. Banks that had held only a fraction of their assets as reserves and had borrowed short-term to make long-term loans or hold long-term securities were exposed as vulnerable when markets for illiquid securities seized up and when depositors rushed to withdraw their funds. The liberalisation of the financial system had become so complex as to make us far less aware of the risks – and thus far more susceptible to them.

The crisis should have been a wake-up call in all areas, but, as Willem Buiter, one of the first external members of the Monetary Policy Committee of the Bank of England, argued a decade later:

> We may know more about the observable drivers of the financial crisis, but not enough to make it likely that we will see the next crisis coming. We still cannot confidently identify asset bubbles, so the bubbles that will precede the next financial crash will not have been identified by those in a position to act.[15]

The post-2009 reforms – entrenched in national and international regulations, such as the Basel framework – required banks to hold adequate capital. They were designed to encourage everyone, including investment banks, to take fewer risks. It worked, up to a point. Banks have not been and will likely not be the main drivers of any financial crisis following COVID-19's disruption of the economy. Because of the post-2009 reforms, US banks almost doubled their core capital to nearly \$2 trillion. And the latest US stress tests – the authorities' measure of the ability of banks to withstand a crisis – found that, even when subjected to the most extreme and rigorous pressure, core capital ratios across the thirty-three biggest banks in the US fell only marginally: from an average of 12 per cent to a still-respectable 9.9 per cent.[16] But European banks, with the exception of the UK's, recapitalised the least and remain under pressure. The 2020 IMF stability report concluded that it is only in America that what they called 'median market-adjusted capitalisation' is higher than it was in 2008.[17]

While the conventional view is that there is no need for more capital, John Vickers, the economist who helped recapitalise the UK banking system, concludes that 'we need to go a lot further in terms of beefing up the equity capital in banks and other financial institutions' and Buiter takes the view that 'systematically important non-bank financial intermediaries remain undercapitalised'.[18]

Trichet's pre-COVID-19 crisis conclusion was radical but realistic: we will have to maintain 'permanently the capacity of public authorities to substitute when needed for the private sector'.[19] Indeed, the lesson of the global financial crisis remains true and as yet unanswered: without better means of crisis prevention, as well as better methods of crisis resolution, crashes will regularly occur. For the risks have not disappeared, but rather moved from banks to non-bank financial institutions – the traditional and reliable as well as the more recent and risky. For example, before the global financial crisis, around 80 per cent of US mortgages originated in banks. A decade on, homebuyers seeking mortgages can now choose the many non-bank lenders that now provide the majority of loans. New or growing companies struggling to access bank loans can turn to a wide range of private-credit funds. At least a fifth of the funds under management at five of the largest private equity firms are currently invested in credit assets.

With the post-2009 reforms focused on banks, it left the rest of the financial system more lightly regulated in comparison, opening the door to 'regulatory arbitrage', which meant, in practice, giving preference to the non-regulated sector. So, while US corporate bank lending has remained low, at 12 per cent of GDP, non-bank loans and securities – which hovered at around the same 12 per cent of US GDP for most of the past century – have risen from an already high 30 per cent in 2010 to 40 per cent of GDP now, with corporate debt reaching an all-time high.

According to the FSB, global non-bank financial assets around the world stood at $100 trillion in 2009, equivalent to 172 per cent of GDP and 46 per cent of total financial assets. Now these assets stand at $183 trillion, constituting 212 per cent of global GDP and around 50 per cent of the world's financial assets.[20]

So as banks have retreated from their traditional intermediation role in response to higher capital requirements, thinly capitalised market makers have stepped in even if they tend to retreat quickly at the first sign of volatility. At the same time, non-banks have acted as the primary transmission mechanism of loose monetary policy to the economy. In turn, credit and liquidity risks have shifted from banks to non-banks' asset managers.

And yet far from learning our lesson about risk from bitter experience, we have watched as the pace of growth of additional leverage at a global level has continued more or less exactly as before the crisis. 'In an interconnected global economy,' Jean-Claude Trichet has written, 'leverage is a vulnerability indicator as to systemic instability. Today this indicator is not reassuring.'

While getting more credit to the real economy is a positive development if happening in isolation without any knock-on effects, the combination of fickle intermediation, the concentration of credit and liquidity risk in less regulated non-banks and rock bottom interest rates is a recipe for future trouble. As seen in

March 2020, such a cocktail of risk can threaten a dash for cash even against the safest asset of all in the financial system, government debt.

So, during these past ten years, the attention of regulators should have been more focused on the financial institutions facilitating the creation of credit and who have been able to access central bank crisis support and yet are subject to little regulatory oversight. And it is a global problem. We have seen the build-up of $3 trillion of more risk-laden — what is rated 'BBB' — debt (which was $600 billion at the time of Lehman's collapse in 2008), $2 trillion-plus of leveraged loans (none of which normally have the kind of protection afforded by the official banking system), and billions of dollars' worth of junk bond debt (standing, as I write, at around levels six times the value of their earnings). Without any official underpinning by central banks, which was absent until a few months ago and may soon be withdrawn again, such low-quality corporate debt, much of it denominated in dollars, can look more like a precarious multi-billion-dollar house of cards than a stable element of a safe financial system.

The FSB, which brings together national regulators, has studied financial firms that are most likely to face sudden liquidity or solvency problems and are big enough to pose a systemic risk to the world economy. In 2010, the magnitude of the risk in 'narrow' shadow investments was $28 trillion or 42 per cent of global GDP. In 2020, risk was identified at $51 trillion or 59 per cent of global GDP, with three-quarters of these assets held in instruments 'with features' that the FSB says 'make them susceptible to runs'.[21] Today, the US alone has investments that add up to a risk of $15.3 trillion — a volume of risk that is itself almost the equivalent of the value of the entire US commercial banking system.

The most at-risk shadow banks, according to the FSB, are companies that make loans and depend on short-term funding. These include some of the world's retail-mortgage or consumer-credit providers; broker-dealers trading securities;

fixed-income and money-market funds; and various entities that provide securitisation-based credit intermediation. And the high-leverage, risk-laden strategies pursued by some non-bank institutions have involved taking high levels of risk in expectation of outsize early returns – be that in long–short Treasury trading strategies, through corporate leverage or by dealing in emerging markets' local currency debt. So while some regulators will favour imposing higher capital requirements on the whole sector, and others on institutions that are big enough to be deemed sys-temically important, which would create other anomalies, a more direct way forward could be to impose requirements depending on the activity. This would mean better supervision of the risk-ier part of lending combined with amendments to redemption terms to better account for the liquidity of the assets in which funds invest.

As we've seen: in 2009, banks tried running capitalism without capital; in 2021, shadow banks are trying to run capitalism, also with the least possible risk-bearing capital – as Martin Wolf, chief economics writer at the *Financial Times*, has helpfully highlighted. 'As before,' he writes, 'reliance on high leverage as a magical route to elevated profits has led to private profits and public bailouts.' It has forced governments and central banks to do for capital markets what they did for the banks in 2009 – underpin them.[22]

At the G20 summit in London in April 2009 and then at Pittsburgh in September 2009, leaders agreed, in principle, on common global standards for bank capital and liquidity, as well as on acceptable ratios for leverage: ratios that would prevent banks' debt far exceeding their equity value, as had happened pre-2008. There has also been an agreement that all major financial cen-tres, bondholders, shareholders and management – rather than taxpayers – should bear the brunt of losses. The objective is to ensure that, when banks fail, they can do so without the massive repercussions on business finances and family lives that we saw in 2008. We must, says John Llewellyn, economist, 'discourage off-balance-sheet activities and put the onus on the proposer to explain why they are in the public interest'. Or as Andy Haldane, the chief economist at the Bank of England, has argued:

> There is likely to be a need for at least as many policy instruments as there are complex sub-components of a system of systems if risk is to be monitored and managed effectively. Put differently, an under-identified complex system of systems is likely to result in a loss of control, both system-wide and for each of the layers.[23]

And, while the FSB has worked to strengthen financial coordination, we cannot say that we have, as yet, proper global oversight and regulation of shadow banking, not even adequate systems for tracking exposures globally. As we know from 2009, when a crisis happens in another country or continent, it's not just their problem, it's ours, too, and so global cooperation to develop better early warning systems and better regulation is therefore the only way of protecting our own interests in our own nations. We require a global repository of financial data modelled on the US financial reporting initiative, the Office of Financial Research, and its European counterpart. And if we are to prevent and minimise future financial crises, our national regulators and international supervisors need to build on the various G20 and IMF/FSB initiatives promoting transparency and better surveillance to create a global financial reporting system that will monitor financial flows, as well as assess systemic risk in the financial system.

Systematic stress-testing should include assessing the coping capacity of not just national authorities but our international systems.[24] Until now, no global agreement has been possible on who, or what, the authority will be, but there can be no doubt that a more integrated worldwide system of risk surveillance is now needed. The three global financial institutions – the IMF, the FSB and the Bank for International Settlements – should work together to construct and continually update what I would call 'a global risk map' – an ongoing survey of financial linkages and vulnerabilities.[25] Surprisingly, the post-2009 response of the IMF to the idea of a surveillance-based IMF – especially the response of the US – was less than enthusiastic. But now, in a world still full of risk, is the time for a new push and what is called the IMF–FSB Early Warning Exercise should be extended as an integral part of the IMF's day-to-day surveillance of the world economy. National as well as international regulators should examine what weapons they may need. Of course, continuous adjustment of asset prices and credit is an essential element of a properly functioning international financial system. Only with continuing innovation is growth in the economy possible. But, on the occasions where our surveillance shows there is too much volatility and violent swings in stock markets, there is a case for action to dampen down these excesses.

Clearly the role of international economic institutions in a globally integrated economy has to be different from the one they played when the world was made up of heavily sheltered national economies. For over seventy-five years, the IMF has concentrated on country-by-country enquiries and assessments, specifically on dealing with the balance-of-payments problems of distressed national economies, and as a result, its energies have been concentrated on the rescue operations that had to be carried out in contexts similar to the closed and sheltered national economies that comprised the world economy after 1945. So country reporting has been the IMF's bread and butter.

But the world has since changed fundamentally since 1945 and a global institution is needed whose primary tasks are providing a comprehensive overview of the global economy, the identification of risks to it and, where possible, the prevention of crises. Of course, nation states are reluctant to accept a loss of control to a more powerful global institution, even if it were to bring more stability, but we should now attempt to build a consensus around reforming the IMF as a global central bank with its primary function to conduct without fear or favour the surveillance of the world economy.

The creation of a global financial safety net

Crisis prevention is one challenge; crisis resolution another. The latter requires one very straightforward change: an adequately resourced global safety net so that, when huge financial institutions fall off the high wire or recessions hit and countries cannot cope, it is not ordinary families with pensions and savings, nor small and medium-sized firms watching from below, who are hardest hit. Our two most recent economic crises have shown us that when crises happen, nations need better and more immediate assistance and that if we act quickly contagion can be limited. And yet, more than a decade on from the big crash and despite the recommendations of a major review ably led by Tharman Shanmugaratnam, senior minister of Singapore, such needs are not yet catered for in the permanent resources available to the IMF or anyone else. Once more, we are unprepared for a crisis.

Improvisation has been the order of the day. In the 2020 crisis, as in the last, the US Federal Reserve has played a huge role internationally, organising currency swap lines modelled on the 2009 intervention that enabled trade and commerce to resume. But it has done so, and continues to do so, selectively to favoured countries with the result that China is now doing the same with its Asian neighbours and beyond. It makes more sense for the IMF to play a far bigger role in intermediating these swap lines as part of a global recovery plan.

The IMF moved quickly in response to the pandemic to create a new facility for providing countries with far easier access to liquidity than in normal times. But countries still fear being stigmatised for accepting IMF support and, worrying that they will suffer reduced access to global financial markets, many have eschewed official help and have been reluctant to ask for debt holidays. But given the scale of the COVID-19 crisis many countries have invested less in vaccination and health than they should have and they are not prepared for the investment in education needed to get children back to school.

So far they have been able to come through without the IMF because, in a welcome shift from ten years ago, developing countries and emerging economies have found it easier to borrow privately in the marketplace. But they have racked up additional debts and will at some point, especially when interest rates start to rise, face a day of reckoning. They complain that down the line, even in the wake of a crisis that was not of their own making and was clearly not caused by the 'original sin' of national profligacy, there will be excessive conditionality in IMF programmes they may have to rely on – something that has been criticised by respected academics, including Harvard's Ricardo Hausmann, as akin to 'a person unwilling to help the victim of a car accident for fear of getting blood on their shirt . . . if these arguments are allowed to win the day, we will ALL have blood on our hands.'[26]

What is needed is a more comprehensive safety net for countries that have, for whatever reason, run short of liquidity. A permanent global liquidity facility should be set up on terms that will offer longer-term loans to in-need countries without the strict conditionality of current financial instruments.

Better and fairer systems for debt relief and debt restructuring are also needed under which private creditors, now a far larger part of low-income countries' loan books than at the time debt relief was agreed nearly two decades ago, cannot avoid their responsibilities. While forty-six debtor countries took up the offer to relieve their debt servicing payments in 2020, an offer that was then extended into 2021 and should be extended further, only a fraction of outstanding debt has been relieved. Once again low-income countries are reluctant to suffer the stigma of being considered unworthy of private credit. Pakistan, the first country to ask for debt relief, stated publicly that if bilateral relief were made conditional on securing commercial relief, it would reconsider its request for help. At the time of writing, just three countries have approached commercial lenders for relief.

In this and in other areas the banks and financial institutions also need to do better. In the global crisis a decade ago, the financial sector relied on national governments to bail it out. But, if the financial sector will not do enough to self-insure against potential crises, governments must protect themselves against the cost to the taxpayer of future financial rescues. So, while I am not convinced that a tax on financial transactions will yield all the results claimed, there is already European support for a globally coordinated banking levy – the equivalent of an insurance premium that would be paid every year by our financial institutions and charged on revenues or profits to cover the potential cost of any future crises.

Getting back to growth

Behind the turmoil of recent years and continuing worries about financial instability is an even bigger underlying problem, endemic to the real economy: an unwillingness of countries to cooperate even when it is obvious that it is in their interests to do so. Asked in 2010 to consider a global growth compact that would speed the recovery from the previous year's crash, the IMF demonstrated that global coordination could achieve 3 per cent higher global growth, create perhaps 50 million additional jobs and take nearly 100 million people out of poverty.

But the global growth compact never got off the ground and because we are seeing a repeat as global initiatives fail to make headway, we have to ask, why? Writing several years ago, the Harvard academics Jeffry Frieden and Dani Rodrik and Yale's Ernesto Zedillo, former president of Mexico, warned that progress on global economic cooperation would always confront at least four major barriers.

The first is, as with other realms of policy examined in this book, the difficulty of convincing nations of the concept of the global public good and the need for some form of cross-border economic governance. In other words, a lack of vision.

The second is the complexity of the internal political and economic domestic challenges faced by the world's major economic entities, which means they have little excess capacity or firepower to take on new longer-term global commitments. In other words, short-termism.

The third is the great and increasing diversity of goals that distinguish each of the major economic powers from each other: for example, the US's worries about holding on to its technological leadership and its privileged position with the dollar as the world's reserve currency; China's priority to become a high-income nation; the problems arising from internal disunity in the EU; and the dependence of emerging markets on foreign investment, which separates them off from advanced economies. In other words, a multiplicity of competing goals.

And, of course, the final problem and cause for scepticism regarding the possibility of new international initiatives: the disappointing record accumulated over the past decade. 'Optimistic anticipation has all too often given way to empty phrase-mongering,' they write.[27] In other words, a failure in implementation because of narrow nationalism.

While realistic about these formidable barriers to cooperation – a narrowness of vision, short-termism, competing goals and failures in implementation – Frieden, Rodrik and Zedillo concluded that macroeconomic cooperation, not least to deal with very large trade imbalances between major economies, will become an unavoidable necessity and could beat the descent into nationalism. And so, against this logic, we need to understand why what started in 2009 as an agreement to coordinate macroeconomic policies for growth ended up a few years later in currency wars, fiscal autarchy and as big a retreat from international economic cooperation as we have seen for fifty years.[28]

In 2009, world leaders agreed to coordinate fiscal, monetary and trade policies in a comprehensive Action Plan. What the IMF called the 'mutual assessment process' – an annual examination of the growth and employment potential of individual economies and the world economy – was to become the basis for coordinated action. But, as I explained in Chapter 1, the early momentum was quickly lost as separate national responses based on austerity came to dominate the economic agenda. As early as 2010, the Seoul G20 summit downgraded the commitment to active coordination to nothing more than vague promises of 'indicative guidelines' that 'would serve as a mechanism to facilitate timely identification of large imbalances that require preventive and corrective actions to be taken'.[29] Instead of the promised global growth compact, collaboration now meant little more than 'identifying' the imbalances between major economies. To its credit, South Korea then floated a halfway house. The idea was that there should be an internationally agreed limit on national trade deficits and surpluses – around 4 per cent for each. This would create a 4 per cent ceiling for China's large surplus and a 4 per cent ceiling for the US's large deficit. For some weeks, this South Korean-led initiative was the subject of three-way private talks. But the US chose to make the proposals public and, when this happened, other countries with large trade surpluses, including Germany and Japan, complained of being kept out of the loop. Very quickly, both the US and China walked away from any possible deal.

The retreat from meaningful action continued. At a meeting of G20 finance ministers in Paris in 2011, the ambitions set for economic coordination narrowed further. Crucial issues of international concern like exchange rates and the coordination of fiscal and monetary policies were now only to be taken into 'due consideration'. The message was clear: national profligacy was the real problem and fiscal retrenchment was the answer. Indeed, as a recent study has shown, ninety countries signed up to 'austerity' policies.[30] The G20 were sending a message that if anything was wrong with the world, it was nothing to do with the international economic system.

And so national protectionism grew. Even when a comprehensive set of IMF reports was prepared highlighting the spill-over effects affecting us all from persistent trade imbalances that restricted global growth, nothing came of it. The IMF continued to show that growth was much lower and job creation much less than it might have been if coordination had succeeded, but now with no international growth agenda worth the name, currency wars became the order of the day, the US accusing China of policies little short of currency manipulation. As Frieden, Rodrik and Zedillo had predicted, when 'left to their own devices', nations end up on 'something of a macroeconomic collision course'.[31]

By November 2014, under the Australian presidency of the G20, a very different kind of a strategy for growth was set in motion. At last the G20 research group had recognised what it characterised as 'a disappointingly weak cyclical recovery from deep recession, weakened productive capacity in key economies and a legacy of vulnerabilities from the financial crisis'.[32] But Australia announced that the focus would be on in-country structural reform rather than cross-border economic coordination. International collaboration would now be little more than the exchange of information and experience. What was called the G20 Brisbane Action Plan set the goal of lifting G20 GDP by more than 2 per cent by 2018. The 'global' element was the creation of a small infrastructure hub based in Australia and tasked to advise countries on how to mobilise private funds for investment in energy, the environment and public amenities generally. But implementation did not follow from the warm words. By the time of the COVID-19 crisis, global infrastructure investment was only a third of the $3 trillion deemed necessary.

So, in what I call a lost decade for many economies, but also for international cooperation, world growth in the years 2010–19 was a disappointing 3.7 per cent. This was only slightly higher than the recession-hit decade of the previous global financial crisis and only a little above the 3.3 per cent annual growth rates recorded in the inflation-prone 1980s and '90s. In the absence of cooperation, the world economy grew far slower than it should have done.

It was the weakness of growth in the advanced economies that marked out the decade. For while the four BRIC countries (Brazil, Russia, India and China) grew by around 5.5 per cent, with China and India growing 7.5 per cent annually, the US averaged only 2.2 per cent, the euro area 1.3 per cent and Japan 1 per cent, with the whole G7 coming in at just 1.7 per cent a year. Once the indisputable engines of the global economy, the G7 countries grew at only half the global rate and at a third of the BRIC rate, and so most of the new growth was generated in Asia.

Even before COVID-19 hit, forecasts for the 2020s were already less optimistic. Now, as China's trend growth rates slip to around 4 per cent annually and India's much-anticipated 'big push forward' remains a promise rather than a consistent reality, the largest emerging markets of the 2020s will be less able to compensate for the low growth that is already factored in for the West and Japan. Indeed, as we have noted, the IMF has calculated that half the emerging markets and developing economies that over the last decade were growing fast and converging towards advanced economies will now diverge, growing very slowly for some years to come.

While the United States is projected to surpass its pre-COVID levels in 2021 the euro area will fail to do so, and even after Japan has tried every expedient to reactivate growth – zero interest rates, aggressive quantitative easing and dramatically expansionary fiscal strategy, budget deficits averaging 6 per cent of GDP, debt in excess of 200 per cent of national income – it can only average around 1 per cent a year for the foreseeable future, with the euro area's potential growth not much larger.

Since 2010, there has been much soul-searching across the advanced economies as to the cause of this anaemic performance, what has been labelled 'secular stagnation' by Lawrence Summers, reintroducing a term coined in the 1930s to refer to both low population growth and a slow pace of technological innovation.[33] Lower growth is attributed by some to trade imbalances – the current trade surpluses in countries like China, Germany and the Netherlands deemed too high and trade deficits in countries like the US, the UK and southern Europe not low enough. But there is a growing consensus that identifies a surplus of savings and a shortage of investment as the source of lower than expected growth. Savings are higher because of greater uncertainty about the future, rising life expectancy (which means that there are more older people saving more), and growing inequality (there are more very rich people with a greater propensity to save). Overall investment is lower perhaps due to a bias against investment in many tax systems, short-termism in financial markets and failings in corporate governance, which again encourages a short-term view. With that excess supply of saving coming up against a declining demand for investment, and causing downward pressure on interest rates, it is difficult for monetary policy to provide the stimulus needed. And with many investors now craving security, being less willing to take risks and invest long term and holding greater financial reserves in case of further shocks, COVID-19 may have accentuated what Keynes called the 'liquidity trap'. This happens when, in expectation of lower growth, people tend to save rather than invest.

Supporters of this theory suggest that these long-term trends will become more pronounced as we exit the pandemic. The global savings glut, they say, will not end. Demographic changes will intensify it and income inequalities will worsen it. Demand for 'safe' fixed-income securities will exceed supply. Left to market forces alone, and despite high levels of pent-up consumer demand, there may be no sustained boom in investment sufficient to generate a return to consistently high levels of growth. There is another dimension to the lacklustre growth rates. Western productivity growth has stalled, not least because, as David Sainsbury's study, *Windows of Opportunity*, shows, the service sectors that are now the biggest job creators are far less productive than the manufacturing sectors where jobs are being lost and more generally because there is too little public and private investment in the real generators of growth – science, innovation and skills.[34]

But some also fear that big firms have become too powerful, labour bargaining power too weak, inequality too entrenched and, because the wealthy exhibit a higher tendency to save, there is now a link between the maldistribution of the spoils of economic activity and structurally weak economic growth.

So the public policy question is: could countries have done – and now do – much more to encourage higher growth and higher employment, not least in the euro area, where a decade of austerity brought growth close to zero (or below) in five of the past ten years?

In 2020, expectations of a quick and sustained recovery rested on the assumption that, as businesses emerged from forced lockdowns, economic life would return to pre-pandemic 'normal', following a V-shaped recovery pattern. Market economies, it was assumed, spontaneously tend towards full employment and thus the only thing the government needed to do was support incomes through the short period of interrupted activity. But the reasoning was faulty. Economies do not bounce back spontaneously – and certainly not after a shock as fundamental as the 2020 pandemic. The scarring effects – lost skills and lost capacity – outlast recessions and linger. Economies have to be helped back to health.

To encourage firms to borrow and invest, quantitative easing aims to drive down interest rates, even to the extent, as happened in Japan and Switzerland, of setting 'negative interest rates' on the reserves commercial and euro-area banks hold at central banks. But it is not, however, the cost of capital – and only the level of interest rates – that determines the amount of investment: it is expectations of profit. Companies will not borrow, even at nugatory interest rates, if their profit expectations are zero. Business investment depends on expectations of profitable sales and thus of rising demand in the economy. Near-zero interest rates are a necessary but not sufficient response: to expect them on their own to restore pre-crisis levels of private investment when unemployment is keeping demand subdued is like pushing on a string.

The 4–6 per cent reductions in interest rates that have been found necessary to counteract past recessions are, of course, not possible in the current low interest rate environment when in some cases, interest rates are already zero or below. This appreciation of the limitations of monetary policy has now led the IMF and others to advocate fiscal expansion, reversing their past championship of 'austerity', and the shift has been called 'the silent revolution in economic policy' as the IMF itself has admitted that the fiscal retrenchment and balanced budget policies of ten years ago may have had a far bigger negative impact than it had predicted.

But monetary policy is a blunt instrument, and while central bankers have looked at the 'transmission mechanisms' by which the extra cash they have created flows into the real economy, they have not been able to channel it to poorer households and instead it has often replenished depleted bank reserves or been deployed to swap financial assets without any direct benefit to economic growth.

By contrast, public spending can be targeted at those who need it in the short term and help lift a country's growth potential for the long term. In a way that current monetary policies fail to do, it can ensure that there is proper protection for the poor, the unemployed and the job insecure and by a fair distribution of the stimulus it can address some of the dissatisfaction that is leading to popular disquiet. As a number of economists have warned us, the danger of not taking fiscal action can be expressed in a simple equation: $QE - F = P$. Quantitative easing minus fiscal action equals populism.

But how fiscal stimulus is managed is important too, especially when we are dealing with a shock to both the demand and supply sides of the economy. Although any direct boost to demand will also indirectly boost supply by increasing national income, the rebuilding of industrial capacity may take time and delays in doing so may risk inflation, and so it is important that governments use their current ability to borrow long-term funds at near-zero rates to invest in rebuilding the economy, not least to green our infra-structure. According to one expert assessment, increasing public investment by 1 per cent of GDP can boost private investment by 10 per cent, growth by nearly 3 per cent, and employment by more than 1 per cent.[35]

Inflation is a risk that, given our historic experience, should never be discounted. Looking at projections for Western inflation over a two-year horizon, price rises in 2021 have to be set against limited wage pressure, a continuously depressed world economy and, outside America, large output gaps and still-limited fiscal stimuli that carry little danger of overheated economies. There are obvious dangers in the longer term, not least because of the changing demographics of China, but as long as inflation and interest rates remain low, governments can service the higher levels of public debt and the economy can grow its way out of debt without always needing to run a budget surplus. And central banks can continue to finance governments, as long as inflation remains low, because it is ultimately the prospect of inflation that forces policymakers to raise rates to levels that make debt costly.

This may look like 'modern monetary theory' (MMT) which calls for the countries that can print their own currency to ignore levels of debt and rely on central banks to provide a backstop. Of course at zero interest rates, as Olivier Blanchard put it, it 'doesn't matter whether you finance by money or finance by debt': there is no practical distinction between issuing debt, which would otherwise incur interest costs, and printing money.[36] But those who advocate modern monetary theory assume deficits can continue to expand almost indefinitely while more mainstream economists want fiscal policy to act as a bridge to recovery and be sufficiently stimulative for monetary policy to regain its traction as interest rates start to rise. This, they argue, needs to happen if we are to manage future downturns with countercyclical monetary policy.

Even before the onset of the virus, the Nobel Prize-winning economist Paul Krugman proposed a permanent US increase in public investment that would add 2 per cent to the budget deficit. He accepted that the debt ratio, which was then below 100 per cent of GDP, would more than double and might eventually reach 200 per cent of GDP. This would, he said, increase interest rates, allowing more scope for monetary easing during future recessions.[37]

But in a crisis, national budgets perform two roles: to steady economic activity through public investment and to pursue countercyclical policy, injecting extra spending into the economy when private spending and investment falters. Both roles are needed today. Fiscal activism can thus take the form of tax cuts or increased public spending. But, since there is no guarantee that the cash released by tax cuts will be spent, public spending is likely to have a greater impact on demand, employment and growth. Keynes argued that if a government sets people to work during an economic slump, even just to dig holes and then fill them in again, the multiplier effect of the workers' earnings and the consumer spending they would then undertake would restore the private sector to higher levels of employment. This logic informed US policy in the pre-monetarist era. The Humphrey–Hawkins Act of 1978 authorised the US government to create 'reservoirs of public employment' to balance fluctuations in private spending.[38] Versions of a job-guarantee programme have also been implemented in countries as varied as Argentina, India and South Africa, though mainly for young people. Such an active employment policy has great merit in dealing with crises, hiring and training a pool of *employed* individuals that expands or contracts with the business cycle.[39] This is in contrast to what Karl Marx called 'a reserve army of the *unemployed*', advocated in some economic theories as the way to stabilise prices and output even at the cost of keeping people out of work.

In the past half-century, we have been thinking about the world economy through the lens of high inflation, which requires us to keep debt low. Now, in a world of low inflation and thus low interest rates, it is possible, it is argued, to afford higher debt. But if deficits and debts – deemed by economists a decade ago to be the most fundamental of economic problems – are feared less, their impact on a nation's economic prospects cannot be ignored. Even before COVID-19 hit, the burden of global debt – public plus private – had reached nearly $200 trillion with the global average debt more than twice the size of the world's GDP. A few years ago, economists had agreed that public debt should never rise above 90 per cent of any country's national income but by 2019 public debt in the advanced economies had risen to 105 per cent of GDP, and it was now 54 per cent of GDP in the emerging markets and 44 per cent in low-income countries. By 2021 advanced economies' post-COVID-19 public debt had risen to 120 per cent, double that of 2007, the year before the global financial crises, but, while debt has more than doubled, interest payments over the last thirty years have halved from 4 per cent of GDP to 2 per cent.

And not all debt is now seen as 'bad', with the IMF distinguishing three types of debt: what is possibly sustainable, probably sustainable and definitely unsustainable. The novel view of what is sustainable does not just depend, as was the conventional wisdom, on current debt and deficit levels, but also on a host of other economic and political factors, not least the reduced cost of managing the debt. The fiscal rules themselves should be rewritten to allow for more active countercyclical policy. Rigid fiscal rules that have, in particular, marked out the euro area for three decades should give way to 'fiscal standards' designed to distinguish in qualitative, rather than just numerical, terms what is 'good' and acceptable behaviour from the 'bad' and unacceptable. While warning of continuing uncertainty over the likely future course of inflation and interest rates, one group of respected experts recruited from both left and right, who include the Nobel Prize winner Joseph Stiglitz and the former US treasury secretary Robert Rubin, have set down conditions and options – extending debt maturities, a greater role for automatic stabilisers such as unemployment benefits, and 'semi-autonomous infrastructure' spending that rises when growth falls[40] – that, if met, would permit the relaxation of previous fiscal rules. Some economists including Larry Summers have proposed a 2 per cent limit to the costs of servicing national debt.

Of course, deficits become unmanageable if inflation runs out of control and if private investment is crowded out. But, with inflation and interest rates still low, the G20 leaders should agree a global programme aimed at significantly raising levels of growth, employment and the demand for traded goods and services – and not just in advanced economies. Of course synchronised action will always be difficult because of the distinctive features of individual national economies – different fiscal rules, inflation targets and levels of dependence on trade – and because of political factors like election cycles, but a global growth compact can bring benefits to every part of the world. By coordinating our support, and with the US fiscal stimulus complemented by stimulus elsewhere, the world will achieve not only faster but more balanced growth.

The IMF has modelled an 'infrastructure push' by countries with the fiscal headroom to do so. As I stated at the outset of the chapter, countries with the fiscal space to do so would raise infrastructure spending by 0.5 per cent of their national incomes in 2021 and 1 per cent a year until 2025. Countries that are unable to meet the fiscal standards set out above would increase spending by 0.15–0.35 per cent of GDP instead.

If countries were to act independently, the boost to global growth would add a not insignificant $1 trillion to the size of the world economy by 2025. But if between now and 2025 countries were to synchronise their policies, we would all benefit from the spill-over effects of the expansion of trade with each other. The world economy would be 2 per cent or $2 trillion bigger. As the IMF puts it, it 'would take about two thirds more spending to get the same output impact in the absence of cross-border spill-overs – that is if countries acted alone'.[41]

I believe we can do even better than that and achieve even higher growth. A bolder fiscal stimulus, raising spending in G20 countries by 1–3 per cent in 2021, could achieve two-thirds of these gains in just one year.

We need a G20 initiative that is not just for the G20 alone. The IMF itself has said that $2.5 trillion will be needed by emerging markets and developing countries to fund their healthcare and social safety nets and to speed their recovery. The United Nations has given a similar figure and the World Bank has estimated that low- and middle-income countries will need between $175 billion and $700 billion a year, that is anything between around $1 trillion and $3 trillion by 2025.

But the limited fiscal firepower of these countries – 2–5 per cent of GDP – is in sharp contrast to fiscal injections that have averaged around 10 per cent in the West. When we take crisis spending on fiscal stimulus and forgone tax revenues together, the contrast between developed economies and developing nations is even starker and indeed shocking especially when we consider we are all dealing with the same virus and the same recession: $1,365 per capita in developed countries against $18 in the least developed countries.[42] But while many developing countries have, until now, been able to borrow in the marketplace, the aid, debt relief and enhanced multilateral bank lending that might have compensated for the collapse in tax revenues and helped to pay for emergency support has been slow to build up, leaving health-care and anti-poverty programmes underfunded and demand suppressed. This has to be rectified.

The first port of call is, as in 2009, special drawing rights (SDRs) – the international money that the IMF can make available to its member states without conditions attached, some of which is already available in unused allocations due to advanced econo-mies and, if the IMF chooses to do so, can be redirected to poorer countries. A decision on a new issue of SDRs would release nearly $650 billion immediately and could advance another $650 billion by 2023, without having to go through the often-interminable process of seeking approval from each national parliament, not least the US congress. The Trump administration objected to the issue of new international money on a couple of grounds: that the money was not needed, and that Iran, Venezuela and China would benefit.

However, the new Biden administration has agreed to one new issue of around $650 billion, just as the Obama administra-tion did in 2010. I favour a second issue within two years. If we allocated new money on the basis of existing shareholdings, then the poorest countries would receive only a fraction of each $650 billion released. Instead, the richest countries should agree to transfer a substantial part of the money to developing countries who need it most.

But we will have to do much more if years are not to go by before crisis-hit countries fully recover. My growth plan would double the resources the IMF and the development banks make available – from $1 trillion to $2 trillion, a move that could, I believe, secure the support of America, China and Europe. When the need is so pressing we should not accept justifications for delay and we should reject those who say we need to conserve resources now because of the long haul ahead or because things may get worse. Action is needed now, not least to vaccinate whole populations, and the international community should not excuse itself from doing more by saying that countries are refusing the help on offer; it may be that the conditions attached to the help on offer should be revised.

The World Bank has promised poorer countries $160 billion by mid-2021. In the Bank's fiscal year 2020, ending on 30 June, the Bank's low-income country facility, the International Development Association (IDA), committed $30 billion, an increase of $8 billion from the 2019 financial year. In the first two quarters of 2021, the IDA's commitments so far amount to $14 billion, and it aims to achieve $35 billion in total annual commitments by the middle of 2021. The middle-income country facility, the International Bank for Reconstruction and Development (IBRD), committed $28 billion in its financial year 2020, an increase of $5 billion from 2019, and then $10 billion in the six months to December 2020, but this is a slower build-up of support than in the global financial crisis, when in just one year this World Bank fund trebled its disbursements from $15 billion to $46 billion.[43]

The Center for Global Development has argued that all development banks could use their existing capital more productively and, according to the Overseas Development Institute (ODI), the multilateral development banks could, while maintaining their high credit rating, release $750 billion more in loans to developing countries that could, for example, cover vaccination, hospital refurbishment costs and the reopening of schools as well as green infrastructure. The current portfolio of the World Bank itself is around $500 billion and this could be raised to $1 trillion. I welcomed the creation of the enhanced IDA facility which, by borrowing on the strength of repayments of loans made thirty years ago, raised annual disbursements to the world's poorest countries by around 50 per cent. But more help could be made available without risking the Bank's high

credit rating. By a less conservative but still prudent interpretation
of the potential leverage that comes from the capital repaid from
historic loans, IDA disbursements could rise beyond $40 billion a
year. IDA itself could use its recently acquired powers to borrow
in the marketplace. There is currently a debate between World
Bank shareholders, pointing to better ways of using the balance
sheet, and the management, calling on shareholders to refinance
the bank, but both sides could agree that the crisis is so severe that
we need both: more capital and more effective leveraging of World
Bank funds. As we discuss in Chapter 6, the Bank will soon need
to be recapitalised for a second time this decade and one radical
proposal – one that would require the support of European countries whose shareholdings would be diluted – would be to merge
the World Bank's low-income and middle-income country funds,
the IDA and IBRD. Such a step, similar to a merger already implemented by the Asian Development Bank, would widen the capital
base and create additional capacity we now need if we are to meet
the world's SDGs.

And we can do more to mobilise private capital for public
purposes, building on the private–public vaccination facility,
IFFIM, as well as creating new guarantee-based facilities like the
International Finance Facility for Education. It can offer guarantees and, when backed up by grants, can lend developing countries
money at very low interest rates.

It is often reported that the IMF has a $1 trillion balance sheet
but perhaps only $700 billion can be deployed, of which currently
$200 billion is committed, nearly $50 billion to one country,
Argentina. If $50 billion is an acceptable risk for bailing out one
country, then issuing $50 billion across developing countries who
have a record of repaying should not be automatically written off
as an unacceptable risk.

The IMF's interest rate-free credit line, the Poverty Reduction
and Growth Trust, is the vehicle through which the new international money SDRs will most likely be passed on as loans to

low-income countries. In the year before the crisis, 2019, it committed $3.4 billion and disbursed $1.6 billion, but in 2020, to the credit of Managing Director Kristalina Georgieva, commitments rose to $9 billion with disbursements even higher. The IMF should maintain that level of disbursement not just in the coming year but until the crisis is over, with the outlays covered over time by the shareholders.

A more comprehensive approach to country-by-country debt restructuring will be needed. But to help pay for its wider interventions in 2009, the IMF agreed to sell gold to the approximate value of $15 billion. A sharp rise in the price of the precious metal means that, since the start of 2020, the IMF's gold reserves have increased in value by $38 billion – undercutting the idea that to sell any gold undermines the balance sheet of the IMF.

All these initiatives require political leadership. The IMF and World Bank are overseen by twice-yearly ministerial committee meetings and by full-time resident executive board members who are in continuous session, but I have found that the big changes we need only happen when we have the direct engagement of presidents, prime ministers and finance ministers. Longer-term reforms – even more ambitious and radical than the emergency global growth plan that I have described – will be essential and I set out some proposals in Chapter 10. No longer can we expect international civil servants however brilliant and well-meaning to manage the world economy without the engagement of national leaders who, in a crisis like this, must accept their responsibility to lead.

Conclusion

The economist Rebecca Henderson argues:

> The institutions that have historically held the market in balance . . . are crumbling or even vilified . . . Free markets only

work their magic when prices reflect all available information, when there is genuine freedom of opportunity and when the rules of the game support genuine competition. In today's world, many prices are widely out of whack, freedom of opportunity is increasingly confined to the well connected, and firms are rewriting the rules of the game in ways that maximise their own profits while simultaneously distorting the market.[44]

And reporting a shift to the left in social democratic parties, Olivier Blanchard has pointedly asked: what comes after capitalism? 'We may be one cyclical downturn away from a need for revolution.'[45] But like Henderson, Blanchard, too, has expressed his fear that, even when 'capitalism is substantially broken', entrenched interests are still so powerful that they will prevent us from doing enough to address insecurity and alleviate inequality. But for me, the issue comes down to an inescapable choice – whether we manage globalisation well through our actions or badly through inaction.

In the 1930s, the task was to prevent depressions and this led to revolutionary changes in macroeconomic thinking much more dramatic than have yet occurred in response to the events of the past decade. In the 1970s and early '80s, the Holy Grail was to end 'stagflation', and this produced neoliberalism and the demand to liberalise, privatise, deregulate and focus on low inflation, even at the expense of high unemployment and widening inequality.

Today's challenge is quite different: it is to elevate the importance in all our economic decision-making of three great concerns: employment, the environment and equality. The IMF now proposes a carbon tax and taxes on excess profits or wealth to address this vicious cycle of mutually reinforcing inequalities. We must create an economic framework that encourages investment, demand and revenues to rise, financial crises to be fought and sustainable and inclusive growth and employment to be delivered across the world. None of this can now be achieved without global cooperation and without nations working together to mitigate risks, regulate fairly, provide support when things go wrong and, most importantly, agree and deliver on a common goal for global growth. This could lift millions out of poverty, bring down unemployment, ensure the world's young people have opportunities and options they do not enjoy today, and make our citizens more secure at home. The very act of cooperation reflects what might be deemed the global paradox: that the ability of nations to best pursue their own self-interest and the prosperity of their own citizens depends upon their willingness to share a part of national sovereignty with others for the global common good. It is to recognise that, in the modern world, the power that may have the greatest potential for good is not the power we exercise OVER others, but the power we exercise WITH others.

Could any or all of this happen? Why not? The second wave of COVID-19 has heightened awareness of the need for a global response to a pandemic, and that response must be carried over into the economic realm. We must all advocate – through our votes and our voices – for equitable global solutions to global problems.

The money in our hands, the spending that pays for healthcare, the savings we hope to pass on to our children all depend on the intricate workings of a global financial system that has let us down not just once, but twice in a single decade. We must now act, as one, to safeguard the incomes of each of us, to fund the social safety nets that we and others rely on, and to deliver on the promise of prosperity for the generation to come.

4

A GLOBAL GREEN NEW DEAL: FIVE ROUTES TO A ZERO-CARBON FUTURE

Summits of world leaders don't just happen. Before anyone sets foot at an international conference in Cancún or New York or Durban or Kyoto or Paris, there will have been complex negotiations, heated arguments and sometimes veiled – and not so veiled – threats. During 2009, I was one of a number of leaders calling on fellow prime ministers and presidents to attend what I hoped would be the most important climate change summit since the Kyoto conference of 1997. It took months of sustained pressure, huge diplomatic efforts and the expenditure of large amounts of political capital to persuade world leaders – from President Obama of the US to Premier Wen of China, as well as every European, Asian, Latin American and African leader – to make the visit to Copenhagen in December 2009.

Following on just nine months from the successful G20 in London, where, on economic matters, an international consensus – and a will to work together – seemed to have been established, we were optimistic of success. But, by the time we met in Copenhagen, we had already had nearly two decades of repeated attempts under the UN to forge collective action on this global problem. I now look back on Copenhagen as a missed opportunity and, in some ways, a tragicomic event with elements of farce. Its failure showed me how difficult it is – and continues to be – to secure global agreement to combat climate change, even when there seems to be the best will in the world.

When, behind the summit's closed doors, the Australian prime minister, rushing to the defence of the US president, engages in a heated war of words with the Chinese ambassador, you have what is called a diplomatic incident. And, when the German chancellor then volunteers that the richest countries will cut carbon emissions by 50 per cent by 2050 and the same Chinese ambassador challenges her right to make such a commitment on behalf of the rich countries, you have the makings of a potential walkout. As I found in my time as prime minister, the future of our environment – a concern about which world leaders might be expected to share common interests and objectives – has the capacity to divide the world, inciting passions in a way few issues can.

I will get back to Copenhagen soon, because it's a vivid illustration of the challenges we still face and the lessons we must learn if we are to meet and master them. As that story and this chapter will show, any attempt to tackle climate change should begin with an understatement: it is a formidable and seriously complex task, one that a series of intergovernmental meetings have not yet succeeded in addressing since the first UN initiative almost three decades ago. While COVID-19 has rightly usurped much public attention and resources, the climate challenge is greater and more urgent now than it ever has been – and it cannot be ignored or kicked down the road. We are already facing our last chance to ameliorate the damage we as humankind have inflicted on our planet. And the response demands a series of scientific and technological breakthroughs, the environmental equivalent of a Manhattan Project or a moon landing. But while COVID-19 can be eradicated by medical advance, climate change can be overcome only if we match the technological solutions on offer with a shared determination across all nations to cooperate together, force companies to disclose and undo their carbon footprints, and tackle entrenched interests who still deny the scale of the challenge. Before I look at potential solutions, I'm going to address the history of the problem in some detail. As you will see, the solutions are interrelated and the pandemic opens a window for change.

There is no doubt we are in trouble. Climate change is with us not in the abstract, and not just as a future risk that is yet to materialise, but is today being played out in real time. Today's manifestations of climate change are insidious and sometimes paradoxical. Recent examples include the rising numbers and intensity of storms, hurricanes, floods and droughts and abnormal weather ranging from subtropical summer temperatures in Siberia to increasing numbers of cities enduring freezing conditions in North American winters – with the latter offering false comfort to climate deniers. A couple of years ago, a US senator brought a snowball into the Senate chamber – as if a rare snowfall in Washington, DC, suggested normalcy and somehow disproved global warming.

Historically, climate change has been measured over centuries and decades – in contrast to the many other global challenges we face, such as wars, terrorism, pandemics and economic crises. Yet climate change has consequences that often include acute events – the increased frequency of tropical storms in the world's oceans, for example, or serious storm-induced flooding in the UK. Such events were formerly considered once-in-a-century, but have recently been recurring within a few decades of each other, and the frequency is increasing.[1]

Worse still, the causes and consequences of climate change are unevenly distributed among nations great and small. In terms of causes, this is because major industrialisation, which is strongly associated with global warming, has been spread across three centuries. Early movers included the UK in the 1700s, followed by Europe and the US in the late nineteenth century, when knowledge of the chemical processes by which the atmosphere traps carbon dioxide and consequently heats up first began to emerge. Nations such as India and China, industrialising much later, perhaps understandably resent pressures from the West. *'Why shouldn't we do now what you did – guilt-free – centuries ago?'* they might fire back.

The consequences of global warming, too, are distributed unevenly around the world, with the worst flooding endured by low-lying coastal nations such as Bangladesh on the Bay of Bengal. Already Bangladesh, with hundreds of miles of coastline, shallow countryside and flood-prone river deltas, is finding that in most years heavy rainfall puts 20 per cent of the country under water at some point. And islands such as the Andamans and the Maldives may be swamped in the near future. 'One day we will disappear,' the leaders of Tuvalu's sinking islands warned us in 2019 – and already Pacific islands are being lost to rising seas and coastal erosion.[2]

Just as dramatic, though with less of an immediate human impact, is the loss of Arctic ice. This has had a triple effect. The smaller the polar icecap, the less effective it is in reflecting solar energy outwards – resulting in raised temperatures and more loss of ice. At the same time, an intrusion of warm Atlantic currents into the East Arctic has exposed long-concealed organic matter, releasing frozen methane deposits – known as the sleeping giants of the carbon cycle – which are as harmful to the atmosphere as CO_2. And the once-unthinkable occurrence of Arctic wild-fires, linked to warmer temperatures and the loss of snow cover, have generated many gigatonnes (billions of tonnes) of CO_2.[3] Atmospheric concentrations of CO_2 have reached the highest level in 800,000 years. All this means that our planet is on course to reach temperatures not seen in millions of years, with hot days, sea levels, and the number and intensity of storms, hurricanes, floods and severe droughts going up.

Since the 1980s, the planet has become warmer than each preceding decade, with the five years from 2015 to 2019 the warmest ever reported. Evidence is mounting that the world is far closer to abrupt and irreversible changes – so-called tipping points – than previously thought. Average global temperatures have increased by 1°C since pre-industrial times,[4] but if we take no further action, they will rise by 1.5–3°C by 2050 and by 4°C or more by the end of the century.[5]

Perhaps the term 'global warming' – with its cosy overtones and accompanying stories of vintners making English and even Scottish sparkling wine – is obsolete. 'Global heating', 'climate change' and even 'climate emergency' are much better descriptors of what is going on. I write this during the UK August bank holiday of 2020, in which overnight temperatures dropped as low as 3°C, making it the coldest August bank holiday in the past fifty years. The year before, the UK baked in a record-breaking heatwave, with temperatures in some places exceeding 30°C.[6] This, surely, should serve as a firm indicator of climate instability, foreshadowing worse, as overall temperatures continue their seemingly inexorable rise.

A recent study published by the US National Academy of Sciences suggests that a billion people will either be displaced or forced to endure insufferable heat for every additional 1°C rise in global temperature. They say that, in a worst-case scenario of accelerating emissions, areas currently home to a third of the world's population will be as hot as the hottest parts of the Sahara within fifty years. Even on the most optimistic outlook, a billion people will fall outside what has been called the comfortable climate niche.[7] As a result of higher sea levels, food insecurity, more frequent natural disasters and significant increases in the number of dangerous heat days, the G30 – an authoritative grouping of economists and recently retired central bankers and finance ministers – has stated that world GDP by 2100 could be up to 25 per cent lower. Already, weather-related insurance losses have increased eight-fold over the past decade to $60 billion. In his book *The Uninhabitable Earth*, David Wallace-Wells vividly portrays the risks: heat, death, drowning, hunger, wildfire, freshwater drain, dying oceans, new plagues and unbreathable air, among other horrors, could all be features of 'normal' life.[8] Bill Gates suggests that, while at its peak, the Spanish flu was responsible for fourteen deaths per 100,000 people, climate change could take seventy-three lives per 100,000.[9]

The 2020s may indeed be our last chance to avoid catastrophic global warming. This makes the transition to a net-zero carbon emissions economy the greatest collective endeavour we face in the decades ahead. Greenhouse gases fell during 2020 due to the huge contraction of economic activity. During the first three months of the pandemic, emissions decreased by 17 per cent, prompting some to say that this offered hope. But while the COVID-19 crisis has reduced emissions, it is already evident that this decline will be only temporary; emissions began to rise again as soon as any sign of economic upturn occurred. For the year as a whole, the decline in emissions is estimated to be 7 per cent, but it took the biggest economic contraction in nearly a century to achieve this reduction – clearly a very high price to pay to address climate change. Not to mention the fact that, to stay within the 1.5°C limit, the world will need to reduce emissions by *more than* 7 per cent every year for the coming decade, while increasing the economic activity needed to create jobs and deliver SDGs. Fortunately, there are better and fairer ways than negative economic growth to tackle climate change.

The CO_2 concentration in the atmosphere will only fall below the critical level if new emissions flow in more slowly than carbon is drawn out. As recently as ten years ago, inflows were almost twice that of outflows, so we will have to do more in future years when a still-rising global population and faster-rising global middle class, whose carbon footprint is twice that of the global poor, are likely to increase the use of energy. In its special report of October 2018 on 'global warming of 1.5°C', the Intergovernmental Panel on Climate Change indicated that, in order to keep warming below 1.5°C, global CO_2 emissions will now have to fall by 45 per cent by 2030 and reach net zero by 2050.[10]

So, for me, climate change is the most difficult global collective action problem the world has ever had to face: we are confronting the biggest market failure in history and no innovator or entrepreneur has yet captured the market for solving climate change. It raises substantive issues of international and intergenerational equity and, of course, free-rider problems on an unprecedented scale, with potentially catastrophic implications. Added to that are the huge remaining uncertainties in the science – how to understand the precise impact of specific concentrations of greenhouse gases in the atmosphere on temperatures, storms and sea-level rise. Sadly, because we are often dealing only in probabilities and not in absolute certainties, sceptics can choose their own data points, hence the aforementioned senator's use of the snowball in Washington. The solution requires uniquely forward-looking political leadership and nothing less than fundamental restructuring of the economy – from energy to agriculture to manufacturing to buildings to consumption.

Learning from failure

Before I suggest some solutions, we need to understand why past efforts to solve this problem have come up short. Nearly thirty years ago, the world's leaders created the UN Framework Convention on Climate Change (UNFCCC) and convened the Rio Earth Summit in 1992 to track a growing recognition of climate change as a global problem. Then, shocked by the damage to the environment but not yet able to quantify the scale of the problem, governments sought to 'stabilise' greenhouse gas concentrations. Already there was worldwide pressure to do so, not least from the world's first youth movement for environmental change, led by an earlier Greta Thunberg – Severn Cullis-Suzuki, a twelve-year-old Canadian schoolgirl – who lambasted world leaders with these memorable words, showing the same passion that has mobilised young people ever since:

> You don't know how to bring the salmon back up a dead stream. You don't know how to bring back an animal now extinct. And you can't bring back the forest that once grew where there is now a desert. If you don't know how to fix it, please stop breaking it . . . What you do makes me cry at night.[11]

There then followed, from 1996, annual meetings of the UNFCCC, called the Conference of the Parties (COP). The 1997 Kyoto conference focused on targets to reduce percentage emissions. Delegates agreed to limit each country's emissions and allowed the buying and selling of emission rights – with the emphasis on more efficient use of energy and the switch to cleaner alternatives. The Kyoto Protocol was heralded as a turning point. It wasn't. History failed to turn.

The US refused to sign up, on the grounds that no obligations were being placed on China, and Canada later departed. While some countries did follow through, the Kyoto targets were soon exposed as not stringent enough. In particular, the Kyoto period – the first decade of this century – coincided with a massive increase in economic growth and emissions from the emerging middle-income countries – it became clear that rich countries simply could not solve the problem on their own. The very foundation on which Kyoto was built was being undermined by the speed at which the emerging markets of the world economy were growing.

The Copenhagen conference in 2009 was supposed to provide a new start. In the run-up to it there was a debate over the most appropriate temperature targets and levels of CO_2

concentrations as we started to understand the scale of the problem. But both the opening of the conference and the way it ended proved to be almost as astonishing as its divisions. As leaders, we planned an agreement on both enforceable emissions targets and financial support for developing countries in their efforts to mitigate and adapt to the impact of climate change. But, with the conference's proceedings developing in an anarchic way, near-insuperable barriers to reaching agreement were placed in our path.

The second week of the conference, when national leaders arrived, began with the Chinese delegate actually questioning the right of the Danish prime minister to chair the conference, which he had agreed to host. It was clear from that moment that, despite the complex negotiations that had been necessary to get us all to Copenhagen, there was no agreement on any agenda, timetable or even process or structure for decision-making, let alone a consensus on what those decisions would be.

One hundred world leaders were scheduled to address the conference, including myself, as UK prime minister. Leaders droned on for hours, making remarks about their nation's importance, good intentions for the future, and on and on. A pre-conference attempt at agreeing the wording of a treaty had failed, bequeathing us a document with so many 'square brackets' around possible clauses (treaty drafting code that the language is contested) that we were virtually starting from zero.

A few of us pressed for a steering group similar to the size and status of the G20. And so a group of around twenty-five people – President Obama, Chancellor Merkel, President Sarkozy and others from emerging markets and developing countries, including the leaders of Indonesia, Mexico, the Maldives and Guyana – met in a small upper room above the conference floor; the world's leading politicians huddled together in the cramped space. Notably absent from the steering group was Premier Wen, who refused point blank to attend this session – the reason being,

I suspect, his fear that he would be pressured into signing up to an agreement that his president had not sanctioned.

For Wen to have joined, I later learned, would have meant going beyond the constraints placed on him by the detailed and tight negotiating remit agreed upon by the Chinese Politburo prior to the conference. This was unknown to us, but it dictated what came next. The Chinese ambassador who was sent into the room in place of Wen felt it necessary to question, stall, obfuscate and generally hold out against any agreement.

It was then that frustrations boiled over, as the Chinese ambassador abandoned all rules of diplomacy, insulted President Obama and then fired back a blank refusal to a German proposal from Chancellor Merkel that rich countries should state in the conclusion to the Copenhagen agreement their commitment to 50 per cent lower emissions by 2050. (It is a measure of how far we have progressed that almost all rich countries have now set targets of net zero by 2050.) Little ground was gained amid this commotion as the Chinese ambassador argued that, because China would itself be a rich country before 2050, it could veto this offer by the contemporary richer countries.

What also distinguished Copenhagen from previous negotiations – and eventually made a deal virtually impossible in 2009 – was the coming together as one faction of the emerging market economies known as the BRICS (Brazil, Russia, India, China and South Africa). They had first met as the BRICS in 2006, but were now, for the first time, operating at a global conference as a single power bloc. Their stated objective was to insist on differential treatment between developed and developing countries; the former had been responsible for most of the environmental damage so far and were deemed rich enough to pay for the mitigation and adaptation required in the latter, whose poverty and underdevelopment entitled them to special concessions.

Copenhagen showed how difficult it was to reconcile the interests and perspectives of developed and developing countries. But, if the answer was to revise the Kyoto model of dividing the world into developed and developing countries, with both having to take on commitments, the main historic emitters had to show that they would lead the way and provide finance for poorer countries.

Of course, we could not object to the emergence of coalitions of countries. The EU had agreed a common position before the event. I had been in direct contact with the US, too. But, while the EU was trying to raise the ambition of the conference, the impact of the BRICS' agreement would lower it. Such was the BRICS' new-found power that they brought any chance of an agreement at the conference, and indeed the conference itself, to an end. President Obama agreed to what he thought was a private meeting with Premier Wen in his hotel, but he arrived to find all the BRICS leaders present. Whether or not his security team had discovered all this in advance, I will never know. But it was there and then, at that hotel meeting, that the president settled for what became, in the view of many, the lowest common dominator deal: there would be transparency in the reporting of national commitments, but no targets binding on any nations in any shape or form. For, when the Chinese ambassador refused Chancellor Merkel's offer that rich countries would do more of their own volition and accept differentiated obligations, a more fundamental problem was exposed: not even the US wanted an agreement that made any national targets binding. The language of what, by 2013, were being called nationally determined contributions (NDCs) – a useful cover for the Copenhagen compromise – has, as we shall see, survived to this day.

It is easy to see now, looking back, why Copenhagen was never going to succeed: the Copenhagen summit occurred at a time when there was still an underestimation of the scale of the problem and an overestimation of the costs that would have to be borne to deliver a solution – in other words, an under-recognition of the urgency we needed to show and an under-appreciation of the benefits that could be gained. At the same time, there was, as

I have shown, massively inadequate political preparation. In retrospect, Copenhagen should be seen not as the culmination of our efforts, but rather as a process that educated us to the difficulties of negotiating international agreements and, as we absorbed the lessons from failure, helped shaped the future direction of climate policymaking around the world. A wholly different approach had to be taken to make the next large summit work. Copenhagen did, at the UK and Europe's prompting, agree to add a global fund that would, as the communiqué stated, amount to $100 billion by 2020 to help developing countries mitigate climate change and adapt to it – an issue that takes on rising significance year on year. The planning of the fund was delegated to a committee, which I jointly chaired during the first half of 2010.

But, despite a series of post-Copenhagen meetings, the $100 billion we aimed for and tried to mobilise for years has yet to be raised. Adaptation alone would cost between $140 billion and $300 billion per year between 2020 and 2030, according to the Global Commission on Adaptation, but the largest emitter, the US, committed just $3 billion, a fraction of what was needed, and only $1 billion had been disbursed by 2020.[12] Yet mitigation and adaptation remain an urgent necessity, more so now in the 2020s. It cannot make sense to say the price of a sustainable economy is to deny electricity to 800 million of the world's poorest people. To deprive them of electricity in the interests of saving the planet would condemn them to continued destitution and means that we are not actually saving the world, but saving only its richest parts. We must find new ways of securing cheaper energy and energy-efficient prosperity for Africa and Asia.

After the 2009 Copenhagen 'turning point that wasn't' and the exposure of deep differences between the major players, the huge challenges that lay ahead formed the subject of a succession of international meetings. A major fall-out from the failed Copenhagen conference was a serious loss of trust among the parties present, with a feeling on the part of developing and vulnerable countries especially that they had been betrayed by the rich countries and the BRICS. This put a major burden on the 2010 COP in Cancún. Felipe Calderón, president of Mexico, and Patricia Espinosa, his foreign minister (now head of the UNFCCC Secretariat), embarked on an all-out diplomatic effort to rebuild trust. The outcome was a formal agreement to establish the Green Climate Fund, which would collect and allocate payments for climate mitigation and adaptation. Important decisions on adaptation and technology were also made – both very important to developing countries. Until Cancún, all UNFCCC decisions needed to be made by consensus. But when the final Cancún Declaration was opposed by one country (Bolivia). President Calderón made the decision that consensus did not mean unanimity and so instructed the COP president, Patricia Espinosa, to lower the gavel. In this way, the Cancún Declaration was approved.

The annual COP conferences of the following years, notably Durban in 2011, focused on mitigation and adaptation and tried to reconcile the different responsibilities of developed and developing countries. But it took six years of multilateral meetings and bilateral negotiations – and many false starts – before a conference equal in status to Copenhagen could be reconvened. A deal was struck, much to the credit of President François Hollande and Foreign Minister Laurent Fabius, at Paris in December 2015. It was, of course, not as good as what we had aspired to in 2009, but it progressed things in a way that Copenhagen had failed to, not least by moving beyond the previous differentiation of developed and developing countries: under the Paris Agreement all countries had a responsibility to act. But the real political breakthrough that had eluded us in 2009 was achieved by the patient negotiating skills of John Kerry, then-US secretary of state, whose outreach over the three years leading up to 2015 persuaded a once-reluctant China to sign up to a carbon accord – though only because we took a different approach.[13]

The achievements and limitations of the Paris agreement

The starting point of an updated stance was to see environmental action not as a cost to be borne, but as an investment that can repay dividends. In 2005, I had commissioned a major report on the economics of climate change, which became known as the Stern Review, after its principal author Sir Nicholas Stern. This was the first official governmental report to show the significant costs faced tomorrow as the price of inaction today. It also itemised the large returns from action, even if these were in the somewhat distant future, and homed in heavily on discount rates: the long-term financial benefits from action, even if the short-term costs were high.[14]

But, after the Stern Review, the argument moved on. The story now is of benefits, not just costs, and of immediate, not just long-term, gains. Smart climate action is today seen as pro-growth, when once it was seen as anti-growth. This new thinking has been encapsulated in the New Climate Economy (NCE) reports by the Global Commission on the Economy and Climate, which show that smart climate policies will spur on growth, not be a barrier to it. They will also drive the introduction of new technology, improve economic efficiency and lower the risk facing investors of being landed with 'stranded assets', leading, in turn, to greater competitiveness, higher investment and more jobs, as well as a better quality of life. The NCE report in 2018 showed that the economic reward for climate action could be conservatively calculated at $26 trillion in the years to 2030.[15]

While much of the detailed work came later, this new thinking formed the background to Paris and the progress that has been made since. Paris brought a better understanding of the scale of the problem, but also a clearer route to delivering action. With the Paris Agreement, which 196 countries signed and which 189 have now ratified, we entrenched a consensus around a new global imperative: to confine global temperature rises to 'well below 2°C above pre-industrial levels'. Of particular importance for countries most at risk from climate change was the adoption late in the proceedings of an additional aspirational target, prompted by the pleas of the smaller island coastal states: to 'limit the temperature increase to 1.5°C', in line with the new evidence on the scale of environmental damage that had since become available.[16]

The agreement required us to abandon the 'road well-trodden'. Even as late as 2013, the European intention was to push for what might be called a 'top-down treaty' of obligations, including penalties and sanctions – the very approach that had failed at Copenhagen. But there was, sadly, no chance of the US congress agreeing to such a treaty and little chance of China and India, which had resisted in Copenhagen, or even Japan signing on either. Instead, the US favoured 'pledge and review' – a bottom-up, rather than a top-down, approach, under which countries could pledge action that would then be monitored and reviewed by peers. And so Paris represented a compromise – a 'ratchet-up' approach to global collective action, under which countries could promise what they were able to, knowing that what they signed would not be legally binding but also that other nations would be monitoring them. The weakness of this approach, of course, is that the commitments to action are not compulsory, thus there are no sanctions if you fail to deliver, and even when taken together they never added up to the global target. In other words, the international architecture we agreed at Paris boasted every important attribute worthy of praise – transparency, periodic reviews, corporate involvement and stakeholders' engagement – except one: a binding obligation on member state countries to honour their promises to cut emissions. Of course, there is a fear that, without compulsion, countries will free-ride, expecting others to take the action they are not prepared to take themselves. But more damaging perhaps is the conclusion countries reach that they need not give priority to anything that would cost them politically with key constituencies – for example, cutting energy subsidies – or would make their domestic industries uncompetitive.

But the new element Paris introduced is the obligation to pledge, monitor, report and review emissions. Every nation is not just required to publish their emissions targets, but also to be subject to an 'international accountability mechanism', which necessitates proper reporting of emissions and a five-yearly updating and strengthening of them. Paris made it possible to think that, with action by both developing and developed countries and, in more favourable circumstances, with cheaper and more cost-effective carbon technologies, progress is possible.

And, since Paris, the world has moved on: more than fifty individual countries have now committed to the ambitious and demanding goal of net-zero carbon emissions by 2050 and over 120 countries, including some as poor as Afghanistan and Tanzania, are actively discussing such a target. A large number of companies and corporations have also pledged to move towards net-zero emissions by the middle of the century. Taken together, this commitment to change is bigger than anything the world has ever previously made.

Of course, those who signed the Paris Agreement already knew that the combination of national commitments announced at and after Paris would not meet the global targets – Paris was only one step towards more ambitious commitments. National commitments made at Paris will take the world down to 56 gigatonnes of CO_2e, but we need to be down to 41 gigatonnes to meet the 2°C target. In order to meet the 1.5°C target by 2100, we need to do half as well again to get down to 25 gigatonnes.[17] And although new commitments have been made since 2019, we know that even if all the current commitments made by countries under the Paris Agreement are honoured, global temperature will certainly exceed the target.

Five years on from Paris, is it working? The Paris deal was

based upon the expectation that the first round of NDCs would be inadequate to solve the problem, but that, over time, the case for climate action would become more compelling, the costs of not acting would become more obvious, clean technology costs would fall, citizens would demand action and the economics, as well as politics, of action would become more widely accepted. Subsequent updates – due every five years after the Paris agreement – were expected to become more ambitious.

To a significant degree, this has been proven to be correct. As of February 2021, fifty-five countries, representing 30 per cent of global emissions, have committed to net zero emissions by mid-century. More than 1,500 major companies and 11,000 cities and towns have done the same. And many more are considering such commitments. This would have been unthinkable at Paris in 2015. These ambitious long-term goals now need to be embedded in the nationally determined commitments for the 2020s. This is beginning: the EU is committed to lower emissions by 55 per cent by 2030 (over 1990 levels) and for the UK the target reduction is 78 per cent by 2035. Many others now need to follow, and then implement these reductions in a disciplined manner. And in 2025 the next round of NDCs will need to be even more ambitious. We are still far from where we need to be, but the momentum is swinging rapidly in the right direction. The question is: 'will it be fast enough?'

For we still are not on track. Overall, there are not yet enough countries or companies willing to take decisions that are sufficiently bold. The reason, however, we can talk meaningfully of a possible 'ratchet' effect – and the difference it can make – is that, every year, not one, but a number of elements of a carbon deal are being 'ratcheted up'. First, the science is becoming clearer and more conclusive. Second, the technology is costing less. Third, our economic understanding of the costs of inaction and the benefits of action is improving. And, fourth, countries, companies, cities and citizens are ramping up their demands for action, putting peer pressure on other countries to follow the 'first-mover' countries that are challenging the laggards to do more – by making their own 2030 targets more ambitious – and shifting the decision-making calculus.

COP26, to be held in Glasgow, is the first of the ratchet points when, five years on from Paris, countries will be required to refresh the NDCs with a strong presumption of increasing their ambition. But the key issue in the run-up to COP26 is operationalising the Paris Agreement with common timeframes in order to give more definition and urgency to the NDCs, variously expressed 'up to 2025', 'up to 2030' and so on. The hope – and indeed expectation – is that the actual commitments will be added to, the ambition stretched further, the determination to act reinforced, and the willingness to work together heightened.

Carbon neutrality by the 2050s is an attainable goal, and it is on a timetable for delivering this target that our attention should now be fixed. For the world to be net zero by 2050, the advanced economies will have to get to that point even quicker. Reaching, for example, the 2030 targets set by the UK (78 per cent reduction by 2035) or the EU (55 per cent by 2030) will require some radical sectoral shifts beyond the decisions to eliminate the sale of gasoline- and diesel-powered automobiles. It is a matter of fact that we could get emissions down faster by 2030 by replacing coal-fired power stations with gas-fired ones, especially if they also attempt carbon capture (trapping CO_2 at the emission source). But a push to net zero by 2050 would require us to cut back on gas-fired stations, so it makes more sense to deliver cheap and reliable zero-carbon electricity as quickly and as widely as possible and seek to eliminate what Bill Gates calls the green premium – the additional financial costs you currently pay for dispensing with carbon pollutants and moving from high-carbon to low-carbon solutions.

COP26 revolves around the credibility of a decade by decade

timetable to reach net-zero carbon. But 'net zero' means not just reducing emissions by making clean and renewable energy cheaper than fossil fuels, but also increasing the sequestration of carbon, reducing the size of the carbon sink. And, because we need to take out of the atmosphere more greenhouse gases than we put in, we must also plant more trees, improve the soil quality, engineer reductions in carbon and use carbon capture, storage and removal.

It is encouraging that over the past decade some action has occurred in most major economies. And countries that have reduced their emissions or emissions trajectories have done so for two reasons: because of their own recognition of the seriousness of the global problem, and because they have perceived the costs of action to be economically acceptable. Of course, countries are not yet doing enough because they perceive the costs of doing *more* to be too high and because the incentives to be a free rider remain too strong. Countries can easily find excuses to weaken their ambition and minimise their contributions in the expectation that other countries will foot the bill. Why would many in the US say their country should undertake the enormous economic cost and risk of cleaning up their economy without guarantees that China, India and others are going to do the same? After all, their logic dictates that, even if an economy the size of the US cleans itself up, we could still face the prospect of warming temperatures if other countries don't follow suit. And why would China and India act as forcefully as they should if the US did not?

The problem is that when a number of countries start to think this way, it's almost impossible to enact change. And, if we don't all commit to action together, any individual country's contribution — even the biggest polluter's, no matter how sizeable — will simply not be enough to put us within reach of our global targets. So, if we have any hope of addressing climate change through international cooperation, the international community will have to show sceptics in Glasgow that 'ratcheting up' can be made to work.

Cooperation can work

We have seen global cooperation being effective. When, four decades ago, scientists revealed that aerosol chemicals had thinned the stratospheric ozone layer over the South Pole that protects us from cancer-inducing levels of ultraviolet radiation from the sun, the world moved quickly to regulate the consumption and production of ozone-depleting compounds. The Montreal Protocol on Substances that Deplete the Ozone Layer, signed in 1987, banned the use of ozone-depleting chemicals worldwide.[18]

And, while man-made ozone-depleting substances continued to increase until 2000, they have been on a downward path ever since. The ozone hole over Antarctica will gradually be reduced as the use of chlorofluorocarbons – banned chlorine-containing synthetic compounds that were once frequently used as coolants – continues to decline and it is now forecast that, in the Antarctic, ozone will be back at its 1980 level by around 2070. In conference after conference, the timetable for phasing out ozone-depleting substances has been accelerated and the numbers of banned chemicals increased. With South Sudan becoming the 197th UN member state to ratify the Montreal Protocol, it has become the one and only UN treaty ratified by every country on the planet. By limiting the use of hydrofluorocarbons under the most recent Kigali amendment of 2015, 105 million tonnes of CO_2e greenhouse gases will be eliminated, making it the single largest contribution the world has made towards keeping the global temperature rise below 2°C.[19]

Why did this work? In part, because the costs of repairing the ozone layer have been far smaller than the costs of addressing climate change. In part, also, because non-ozone-depleting chemicals have been easily produced and, at least in part, because developing countries have been offered sufficient support to implement the global agreements. But one major reason for success is that the Montreal Protocol binds all countries to commitments on a timeline, tailored to their individual circumstances, for phasing out the polluting chemicals, organising national licensing systems and controlling their imports and exports.

While the cost of repairing the ozone layer was proven to be affordable, climate action has, until recently, been seen as too expensive. But with the astonishing reduction recently in the prices of renewable energy, battery storage, electric vehicles, remote-sensing monitoring and smart grids, driven by public support for an energy transition, a new calculus based on low-cost green technology makes action that seemed unaffordable ten years ago now well within our reach.

Any positive emissions would need to be offset by negative emissions, the most straightforward of which would be expanding forest and vegetation carbon storage, in addition to carbon capture and storage and direct air capture technologies. Because climate change is no respecter of national borders and because of the free-rider problem, countries need to have confidence that they will not be acting alone. We need globally coordinated interventions. While the economic costs of mitigation vary across countries, all stand to gain greatly from reduced pollution. The question is: can we reach an agreement on measures that are globally coordinated, nationally implemented and thus binding on all countries?

And, if we are to achieve this, what additional combination of policy tools – from carbon pricing to a renewables push – do we require? What process for international decision-making do we now need that gives everyone the confidence that countries will match generalised targets with the funds to deliver on them?

Of course, it is, indisputably, in a country's national interest, even without global agreements, to deliver on its own climate change mitigation policies and to support innovation, redirect electricity generation towards low-carbon activities and make transformative investments in green infrastructure, environmental efficiency and clean technology. While each country will decide its own energy policies, every single one can – and should – take action to decarbonise their energy sectors and sponsor cleaner, cheaper and healthier forms of private and public transport. We should all be making buildings more energy efficient, creating a circular economy plan (that allows us, for example, to reprocess waste), making their farming more sustainable and doing all they can in pursuit of a biodiversity strategy to protect the fragile natural resources on our planet. This is the wide canvas upon which the EU seeks to reach net zero by 2050.

Cooperative arrangements between cities and companies – one way to move forward when governments fail to agree – can also make a difference. The Global Climate Action Agenda, launched at COP22 in Marrakech in 2016, brings together private actors, local authorities and civil society. It is already boosting cooperative approaches on climate change.

But who will lead? At most points in the past 250 years, we would have targeted the industrialised West as the major polluter and required those countries to deal with the problem they have created. Now, however, China accounts for a higher share of pollution than the EU and the US combined. And, because the advanced economies account for a declining share of global emissions, they cannot successfully mitigate climate change by themselves. It makes sense that China and the West work together to secure carbon reductions, in a deepening spirit of cooperation that I now think is within our grasp.

In the past year or two, however, a new factor has entered the equation: from now on, the majority of global emissions will come from lower- and middle-income countries – like China, India, Bangladesh, Pakistan, Ethiopia, Egypt, Nigeria and Iran – as they industrialise, their middle class grows and their carbon footprint expands. The countries that are part of China's Belt and Road Initiative already account for about 55 per cent of greenhouse gas emissions, but could, by 2030, be responsible for 65 per cent, taking us close to 3°C warming, even accounting for

China's net-zero target for 2060. This has led one well-respected academic writer, Adam Tooze, to propose a new forum for environmental decision-making in which climate change initiatives could be agreed: a G40. This would not only include the world's biggest economies, but also the new lower- and middle-income polluters.[20]

But we must look at the responsibilities countries must assume not just because of their present and future emissions, but also because of their past emissions. The US, China and Europe account for the vast bulk of historic emissions (as my table on emissions at the end of this chapter shows) and they ought to accept the biggest role.[21] The US will also remain the world's top per-capita polluter, among top emitters, consuming twice as much energy per capita as even its European counterparts.[22] Rising carbon emissions in some of the newer polluters arise from the transfer out of China of low-skilled manufacturing work, which is often still under the control of Chinese companies. Europe is indisputably the third partner responsible, not just because of its past and present emissions, but also because of its determination to bring people together. It has led the way in addressing climate change – not least with European climate law requiring carbon neutrality and net zero for all greenhouse gas emissions by 2050 – and, under Frans Timmermans, the dynamic vice president of the European Commission, the continent is already in the process of examining how the energy, manufacturing, transport and food sectors can play their part in a 'just and inclusive transition' to a green economy.[23] Timmermans' ambitious package of policies, announced in December 2019, sets targets to reduce greenhouse gas emissions and enhance forests, farming, green transport, recycling and renewable energy.

With the election of President Biden, the US joins Europe and China in being represented by leaders who agree on the existential threat posed by climate change, the urgent necessity of creating a carbon-neutral world and the importance of international agreements to do so. China's historic announcement of its intentions to reach carbon neutrality by 2060 has been followed by announcements from Japan and South Korea that they will achieve climate neutrality by 2050.[24] With the EU setting its 2050 target in 2019, most major advanced economies are now starting to follow. It is now essential that these long-term goals be made a reality by setting shorter-term decadal targets – the aforementioned NDCs. There is progress here, but also a long way to go. The NDC Partnership is a coalition of 120 governments and twenty international institutions committed to raising ambition in delivering on the Paris Agreement. Coordinated by the World Resources Institute (WRI) and the UNFCCC, the partnership highlights and shares successes and provides technical support for raising ambition.

Setting long-term goals is sometimes easier politically than agreeing on the path to get there. We know that China plans to quadruple the share of nuclear power in its energy mix, to treble the role of renewables and to reforest, but, if carbon neutrality is to happen, there will have to be more ambitious intermediate targets. While China has committed to carbon neutrality by 2060 and has nominated 2030 as a turning point at which emissions will cease to rise and start to fall, it has far less stringent targets than the kind Europe has agreed for 2030 and 2040. Their March 2021 announcement suggests only an 18 per cent reduction in carbon intensity in the next five years, which means that total greenhouse gas emissions will most likely increase.

And, while under President Biden the US is now ready to sign the Paris Agreement, the question is whether the decisive actions that it will need to take – a 45–50 per cent reduction in carbon emissions by 2030 – will be acceptable to the US congress.

A practical first step for President Biden would be to usher in the same kind of climate change diplomacy that Secretary of State Kerry engaged in prior to the Paris Agreement in 2015. Biden should also aim for an EU–China–US partnership to drive to net zero, to enlist India through diplomatic outreach and use the other global forums – including the G20, the UN Security Council and the UN General Assembly itself – to embed a broad-based consensus on change. These initiatives could create the momentum for an agreement at COP26 or a future COP27, which will bring in all 197 parties.

Five priorities

No one can argue that there is a single bullet, a single measure or even a single pressure point for addressing the climate challenge.

The limits to growth are now well known, but a blanket commitment to 'degrowth' at a time of rising population, when so many poor people are seeking to increase their material standards of living, would not work. We aspire to raising poor citizens to the level of median income, and, if everybody in the world had an income level equal to the current median income that we enjoy in rich countries, world GDP would have to increase three times over – not accounting for the rise in the world population. Conversely, if we were to limit any increase in growth while equalising incomes, millions would have to lose about two-thirds of their income.[25] And to take one illustration of the challenge, a stalling of growth in the interest of reduced carbon usage would deprive 800 million Africans of the access to electricity that they currently desperately need. Our aim should be to reduce the price of renewables as quickly and as much as possible – and not to prevent the electrification of Africa.

So, setting aside illusions of 'degrowth' in a very poor and unequal world, we need to think of other strategies: investing in low-carbon technologies; offering incentives and even price guarantees in order to increase demand, investment and supply in renewables; developing negative-emission technologies; and, where possible, spurring innovation with support for ambitious research and development. Where a country's poverty deprives it of the resources to do so, we should, as an international community, step in to help. Every country should also consider creating 'carbon councils' to plan the route to climate neutrality.

There are five areas in which global cooperation is now essential – and indeed a precondition of success – and in which, if we are to meet our targets, binding commitments will have to be agreed:

- First, there is an opportunity thrown up by COVID-19 to use a globally coordinated fiscal stimulus to convert national green recovery plans into a collective endeavour of historic dimensions – and I will suggest how we bring together the advanced world and the developing world in doing so.
- Second, we should seek to agree international rules under which companies everywhere disclose the impact their operations have on the environment and set out their transition plans for sustainability.
- Third, we should begin to create the momentum for a system of carbon pricing that can, in time, lead to a levy on carbon in all parts of the world.
- Fourth, we should invest in the technologies that deliver carbon reduction in a global plan that involves minimising the use of fossil fuels.
- And, fifth, in pursuit of negative emissions, we should invest in afforestation, direct air capture, carbon capture and storage, and other new technologies. All of this is in line with a growing international consensus recently expressed by the IMF, whose policy programme covers these areas. To reduce emissions by 80 per cent by 2050, the programme focuses on green infrastructure investment, carbon taxes (with compensatory transfers to poorer households) and support for renewables.

Let's look at each of the five initiatives in turn.

1. A globally coordinated green stimulus

The recent World Economic Outlook 2020 highlighted that a green recovery is not only environmentally sensible, but can also lay the foundations for longer-term economic success and debt sustainability – in other words, a double dividend. A joint IMF and International Energy Agency (IEA) report found that global spending of $1 trillion per year on clean energy would add 1.1 per cent to global economic growth annually (over three years) and save or create about 9 million jobs a year.[26] Almost every economy in the world needs a post-COVID-19 stimulus and, at a time when the costs of going greener have fallen dramatically, the argument for maximising the impact through an internationally coordinated fiscal injection has been set out in our discussion of the global economy. By the end of 2021, we could, under the auspices of COP26, have brought together all the elements of a global new deal that includes not just cuts in greenhouse gas emissions, but also biodiversity commitments agreed by the Convention on Biological Diversity.

In the previous financial crisis, the green stimulus amounted to $520 billion – one of the most successful being the American Recovery and Reinvestment Act, which supported the equivalent of 900,000 new clean-energy sector jobs. Not all of the total fiscal stimulus promised was spent, and most large companies received bailouts with few strings attached. Indeed, by the time policies of austerity brought it to a sudden end, less than 15 per cent of the stimulus had actually gone to green projects.

As of February 2021, more than $14 trillion has been allocated by the world's governments in response to the pandemic.[27] Global leaders, such as UN Secretary-General Guterres and IMF head Kristalina Georgieva, have been calling for a green, inclusive recovery but, so far, more money is being allocated to 'grey' high-carbon investments than 'green'. As one example, while

$189 billion has been allocated to support clean energy, more than $240 billion has been allocated to fossil fuels.[28]

The initial Trump pandemic recovery package in the US had no focus on sustainability, but instead contained large, targeted relief to oil and gas companies and $60 billion for airlines, offered without conditions. In contrast, the European Commission's €750 billion stimulus has set aside 30 per cent for climate-friendly investments, with a Just Transition Fund in place to help vulnerable regions cut reliance on fossil fuels. The airline bailouts in France have included climate targets although, overall, environmental conditions have been imposed in only two of the country's twenty-six bailouts. Germany has increased support for low-emission technologies. But while China has upgraded its grids and listed new energy technologies and new energy vehicles as 'strategic emerging industries', it has also made new investments in coal.

All countries should examine the new evidence that green projects – clean power, zero-carbon buildings and zero-carbon technologies – can not only help the transition to a low-carbon economy, but also generate higher short-term returns per dollar spent, compared to conventional fiscal stimulus, and can create more employment.[29] Renewables-based electricity generation and energy-efficiency-enhancing investment are more job-intensive than the generation of electricity from fossil fuels. One study reports that $1 million invested in renewables creates seven jobs in the West, while $1 million in fossil fuels creates fewer than three jobs. So jobs from investment in electric cars beat investment in the internal combustion engine. Investment in cycle paths and walking routes now does more to create jobs than building roads. Targeted investments in solar PV, energy efficiency and clean urban transport can generate up to two times as many jobs as the same investments in coal or gas.[30] And, as a report from the NCE shows, shifting to a low-carbon economy could create a $26 trillion growth opportunity and 65 million new jobs by 2030.[31]

C40, a global coalition of large cities committed to climate action, found that, 'across nearly 100 cities . . . and their supply chains, a green and just recovery could create over 50 million good, sustainable jobs by 2025 – over a third more than would be created by investing equivalent funds in a high-carbon recovery'.[32] And the non-profit coalition We Mean Business, using modelling from Cambridge Econometrics, recently found that a green recovery plan would provide an immediate boost to output and employment greater than a 'return-to-normal' stimulus approach that costs the same amount of money.[33]

Most important of all, such a green recovery can go global. There should now be not just a European and a US green new deal, but also an Asian green new deal, a Latin American green new deal, a Middle Eastern green new deal and an African green new deal. In Africa, the best estimate is that a greater number of the millions of jobs required on the continent could come from renewables and energy efficiency than from any current policies. Indeed, this is the time to honour the promises made to the developing world and vulnerable coastal states in 2009 and 2016 that a much greater focus would be given to adaptation as well as mitigation.

The IMF plan, set out in the previous chapter, for a globally coordinated fiscal stimulus – synchronised across advanced and developing economies – would generate twice as much additional growth than if countries acted on their own. The plan allocates 30 per cent of new investment to green projects. I have proposed a five-year $2 trillion stimulus package for the developing world, half of which would be invested in mitigation and adaptation. Its funding would come not just from debt relief, but also from the issuing of new SDRs and enhanced investment by the IMF and the multilateral development banks. This global, job-creating green new deal would invest $1 trillion in a green future for the world's poorest countries and would be the biggest single boost to environmental sustainability ever agreed by the international community. For the first time, rich and poor countries could be marching forward to a better future together.

2. Corporate social responsibility

The focus has, in recent years, been on what governments can do, but it is not just each nation state but each company, especially the major emitters, that needs to understand what contribution is expected of them. According to the World Economic Forum, almost all of the world's top 1,000 multinational companies have supported a green recovery. And more than 1,000 companies have signed on to science-based targets, whereby they commit to decarbonising their supply chains to reach net zero, reporting their goals and achievements each year.[34] Every major bank, insurer, pension fund and asset manager is now calling for the early and full disclosure – by 2021–22 – of climate-related financial risk. The UN Environment Programme Finance Initiative is working with the world's financial institutions, which cumulatively invest over $100 trillion of assets, to ensure global standards that assess environmental costs and count environmental damage when determining future corporate liabilities. Already the guidelines for investing one-third of the world's professionally managed assets – $30 trillion – require the publication not just of financial returns, but also of environmental and social returns. And companies are going beyond simply disclosing their climate footprint. Many are drawing up transition plans, too, moving their focus from their current footprint (what Mark Carney calls the 'static' state) to a 'strategic' state, preparing 'plans to manage down emissions'.[35]

All this represents great progress, but these voluntary approaches need to be supported by government policies. It took 100 years of pressure and the Wall Street Crash of 1929 to make investors realise that they did not understand the true balance sheets of companies and that standard accounting principles and independent auditors had to be required by law. Today, companies have to take the next step towards being responsible stakeholders and accept that they should be required by law to advance agreed environmental goals. After all, the domestic laws that guarantee companies 'limited liability' are not there simply to be generous to company shareholders and directors. They can only be justified if they advance the public good – public good that requires both social and environmental responsibility.

Tougher rules for disclosure that take us beyond the well-known metrics for social responsibility have been developed by the Task Force on Climate-Related Financial Disclosures (TCFD, created by the Global Stability Board and led by Michael Bloomberg) and the Global Pact for the Environment (led by France), with each initiative underpinned by the more general UN Principles for Responsible Investment, the OECD Guidelines for Multinational Enterprises and the UN Global Compact. This is not a requirement that would carry costs for companies but no benefits. The UN Principles for Responsible Investment estimate that those utilities committed to the net-zero economy are likely to see their market values increase by over 40 per cent. But, while reporting and disclosure will speed up the move to 'fifty shades of green' and start changing firms' practices from high-carbon to green to greenest, much more needs to be done. The report of the prestigious G30 states that 'disclosures remain far from the scale the markets need to mainstream green finance and systematically channel investment to sustainable and resilient business models'. The report's conclusion is blunt: the world needs to 'set out a timetable for making TCFD-compliant disclosure mandatory by 2023'.[36] 'Private companies and financial institutions will not fully take the impact of their actions on our climate into account unless public policy forces them to do so.'[37]

With the International Accounting Standards Board ruling that material climate change risks must be included in financial reporting, a first step has been taken towards constructing legally binding obligations. But an important next step would be to require companies to produce impact-weighted accounts that would show their cumulative imprint on the environment. When a Harvard project, sponsored by the leading 'social impact' investor Sir Ronald Cohen, investigated the environmental impact of more than 1,800 companies, it produced telling findings that show the big emitters have a long way to go. It assessed the environmental costs of chemical companies Sasol and Solvay, with $22 billion and $12 billion in sales respectively, to be at $17 billion and $4 billion a year and those of BASF, with its $70 billion in sales, to be at $7 billion. The review also looked at the environmental impacts of oil majors Shell ($13 billion), BP ($8 billion) and Exxon ($39 billion), showing the extent of changes still required by these energy companies in order to meet their own self-proclaimed environmental aims.[38]

There are other ways of accounting for environmental damage. The Accounting for Sustainability project measures six types of capital, including both human and environmental capital, and soon we will have more sophisticated frameworks, standards, certifications, tools and indicators. Of course, it will take time for a new set of accounting standards to be implemented, not least because traditionalists will argue that accounts are about measuring profit and loss. There are, however, US sustainability standards that, after some consultation, are now oven-ready and have been written with a view to being complementary to US accounting standards. The Securities and Exchange Commission could require these to be applied.

In Canada, large businesses that receive loans are now obligated to publish annual reports of their climate-related risks and how their future operations will affect national climate goals. Subscribing to what a group of international lawyers has recently proposed, the Principles on Climate Obligations of Enterprises would advance us to the next stage: concrete requirements for companies not just to disclose and report environmental damage, but also to show the extent to which they are reducing the use of carbon. We need changes in the law that could be agreed globally, but which all countries could enshrine in their national statutes, too.[39]

3. Carbon pricing

The combined impact of an ambitious global green deal and intensive corporate transition plans are not enough. Whether it is a carbon tax or a trade system in which companies buy and sell the right to emit carbon, a form of carbon pricing is going to be needed if we are to put the global economy on a sustainable path. We have to reflect the true costs that carbon imposes on society in the price that consumers pay for products fuelled by or made using carbon. It is, of course, because the price consumers pay for such carbon products is artificially low – we pay only 40 per cent of the true cost of burning coal – that the consumption of everything from cars to pencils is artificially high. Supply is available and cheap because there are abundant resources and they are relatively easy to move. On top of this, the more the middle class grows, especially in urban areas, the bigger the carbon footprint.

Again, we cannot achieve progress at the scale we need without some international agreement that makes polluters pay and incentivises good behaviour. However, the freedom to impose taxes is at the heart of each country's national sovereignty. Indeed, Europe's attempts to harmonise taxes has foundered because of national resistance. Be it beer, wine, cigarettes, champagne, restaurants or petrol, each country has its own culture, its own traditions, its own ideas of what should be given favourable tax treatment or be exempt from high taxes. And, of course, a truly global tax would require support from oil and gas producers like Saudi Arabia, Iran and Russia, as well as the US.

Yet a system of carbon pricing that would incentivise energy efficiency and trigger a reallocation of resources from high- to low-carbon activities is an idea whose time has come. Of course, regulations on emission rates and energy-efficiency standards can make some difference: carbon permits are in use in Europe and California and already forty countries and twenty cities are using the pricing system to impose fees or offer rebates on products and activities with above- or below-average emissions. But few have yet come near to meeting our emissions goals. For, while carbon levies of anything from $40 to $80 per tonne of CO_2e are deemed the minimum necessary to limit warming to less than 2°C, only a limited number of emissions are covered by carbon pricing initiatives, and of these half are still priced below $10 per tonne.[40]

But, if ever there was a time to set globally agreed prices for carbon, that time is now, with fossil fuel prices low and renewable energy becoming more efficient and cost effective. A higher price, triggered by carbon pricing, would mean people drive less and purchase lower-emitting goods, inducing businesses to switch to solar- or wind-generated electricity. A tax of, say, $35 per tonne on CO_2 emissions in 2030 is estimated to increase prices for coal, electricity and gasoline by about 100 per cent, 25 per cent and 10 per cent respectively, thus reducing consumption dramatically.[41]

Attempts are being made in the US to find a way forward on carbon pricing and China is also developing a carbon pricing mechanism. Of course, with the carbon price under the EU Emissions Trading System at around just €25 a tonne, we will have to do far more to achieve the step-change in carbon usage we need.

Could there then be a common global approach? What is called a border carbon adjustment is a way of preventing free riding by imposing taxes on the most carbon-intensive imports from less ambitious countries, although it has to take into account the position of low-income countries. According to *The Economist*, an EU border carbon levy of €30 per tonne would be equivalent to doubling existing tariffs. It would impose an extra 2.8 per cent ($10 billion) on imports from China; 1.2 per cent ($3 billion) on goods from the US; and 5.1 per cent ($2 billion) on imports from India, now a huge importer, like the US and Europe, of carbon-intensive goods from lower-cost countries.[42] China would almost certainly see advantages in agreeing and, if it is prepared to support what Europe already plans and President Biden has already favoured, an international settlement is possible. So, as the IMF suggests, the first step could be a carbon-price floor, agreed between the large emitters.

Perhaps we could then agree on common rules: that the best carbon pricing is at the point fuel enters the market, rather than taxing downstream products, and that pricing be based on the weight of CO_2 produced at an oil refinery or coal mine. And perhaps we could agree on a staged approach, with prices initially ambitious enough to meet 2030 emission targets, but also rising fast enough to meet 2050 targets, without triggering a dash to frontload all non-green construction before it is more highly priced. We could also forge a consensus on what is 'fair', not just *within* countries but *across* countries, otherwise different carbon pricing could lead to 'carbon leakage' and thus the relocation of carbon-intensive industries to countries with lower carbon prices.

Under the 2015 Paris Agreement, most countries have committed to establishing a market mechanism for exchanging carbon credits, but have so far been unable to agree on rules for how to do so. To meet the needs of companies with net-zero emissions plans, a private global market in carbon emissions – with liquid, exchange-traded contracts at its core – is developing, prompted by the Taskforce on Scaling Voluntary Carbon Markets, an initiative backed by more than forty companies. Offsets will compensate for residual emissions that cannot be eliminated. What is today a $300 million market could, according to Mark Carney, turn into one worth $50 billion or even $100 billion.[43] While this offers great opportunities it is very important that polluters not use these markets as a way to avoid their responsibilities to adopt their own science-based targets. The only way in which we will succeed in limiting warming to 1.5 degrees is if all industries – including the so-called 'hard to abate' sectors like steel, cement and ocean shipping – drive down their own emissions.

The Baker–Shultz plan – which resembles the UK climate change levy introduced on companies after 2000 – is revenue neutral, sending the money raised directly back to the taxpayer on a per-capita basis in the form of a carbon dividend.[44] Canada, France and Germany are currently examining how to build support for such a levy and are finding that the most popular way is to return the dividends to the taxpayers directly. Twice, in 2016 and 2018, in the US state of Washington, proposals to tax emissions were defeated in referendums. It is an indication of where overall public opinion is that carbon tax supporters gained only 41 per cent support when they proposed to use the revenues to cut sales taxes and 43 per cent when the revenue was to be directed to green investments. But this policy is not fair to those with the lowest income. Unless we are to tolerate greater inequalities by raising prices for those who can least afford to pay, governments will have to agree to protect those most affected by mitigation by providing targeted cash transfers financed by carbon. Here's the maths: a $35 per ton tax in 2030 would raise 1–2 per cent of GDP. Double that figure, in line with the IMF's recommendations, and assume a $70 per tonne carbon tax for the US (the large coal-using countries like Australia may have to charge more) and a $35 per tonne carbon tax for countries like China, India, South Africa, Indonesia and Iran. Averaging $50 in 2030, carbon pricing could raise significant revenues – typically around 0.5–2 per cent of GDP, which is $500 billion to $2 trillion a year. Then, if, as the IMF proposes, 30 per cent of revenues are used to compensate the bottom 40 per cent of households and the remaining 70 per cent are used for income tax reductions or increases in productive investment, the poorest 40 per cent would be better off overall.[45]

4. Harnessing new technology and phasing out fossil fuels

The challenge is so great that carbon prices alone are not enough. According to the Center on Global Energy Policy, a carbon tax – even one of $50 per ton – would reduce transport emissions very little, perhaps by only 2 per cent.[46] And, as the IEA has reported, investments in fossil fuels – from exploration to power generation – will continue to be massive, totalling $25 trillion between now and 2040, the equivalent of 25 per cent of annual global GDP.[47]

Fossil fuels still provide 80 per cent of our energy needs – almost exactly the same share as thirty years ago – and, under 'business-as-usual' projections, we would be using 50 per cent more fossil fuels in 2030 than what is required to limit the temperature rise to 1.5°C. While the COVID-19 pandemic did cut oil production dramatically, world oil consumption on average is still twice what it was fifty years ago, not least because of inexpensively produced shale oil, and is predicted to rise from 2019's 100 million barrels per day to a peak of 125 million some time before 2050, although some oil companies say the peak has already been reached. While China's oil demand will now top out around 2030 at 14 per cent of the world's supply, emerging market demand will continue to rise as a billion more Asian, African and Latin American citizens join the global middle class, their footprint now twice what it was when they were poorer. Even now, we use 4 billion gallons of oil every day. We used to think that the oil age would end as we ran out of oil. But, just as the Stone Age did not end because we ran out of stone, the oil age will not end because of the depletion of oil reserves. It will end only when we make new decisions, preferably internationally agreed measures, about how we meet future energy needs.[48]

The single largest source of greenhouse gas emissions is coal-fired electricity generation. Two-thirds of the world's coal is used to produce electricity. While, for the first time in 250 years, countries like the UK are now supplying electricity without coal, there are, worldwide, 400 new coal-fired power plants under construction and 700 more on the drawing board. At last count, Chinese investors alone are financing more than sixty coal-fired power plants, part of the Belt and Road Initiative, and US coal firms are currently financing the construction of new plants in

Africa. What's more, 60 per cent of existing coal plants are less than twenty years old and have had \$1 trillion of investment sunk into them that has still to be recouped. Therefore, it is not likely that companies will volunteer to give up coal-fired energy.

Across the board, we are doing far less than is often claimed to make the transition from fossil fuels. While the official figure is that \$400 billion is spent on fossil fuel subsidies that governments still pay out, one recent estimate of the gap between existing and efficient prices – the price that would be warranted if environmental and social costs and lost revenues were taken fully into account – was \$5.2 trillion, 6.5 per cent of global GDP.[49] Fossil fuel subsidy reform has been part of the COVID-19 response in Nigeria, Sudan, Venezuela, Ecuador and India, but, when we contrast this with the much smaller \$25 billion of public money that is spent globally on clean energy research and development, we can see how far we have yet to travel.[50]

Over time, we must bring oil and gas producers, as well as coal producers, on board for a climate change agreement that manages the transition to clean energy. With relatively low extraction costs, Saudi Arabia, Qatar and indeed Russia will outlast the North Sea, African fields in Nigeria, Latin American fields in Venezuela and other well-known, higher-cost producers. But these petrostates can become 'electrostates' – not only manufacturing powerhouses, but also producers of cheap zero-carbon energy for export, either as electricity to neighbouring countries or in the form of fuels like hydrogen and ammonia, which can be used to power factories, buildings and, above all, transport.

Bill Gates has argued that we need to quintuple clean-energy and climate-related research and development if we are to progress clean electricity to what is called the renewable portfolio standard, which would cut the premium paid to deliver non-fossil fuel supplies. This means investing in fission (with the possibility of nuclear fusion some time off), in geothermal energy (recovering energy from hot rocks underground) and in the circumvention of problems caused by the intermittency in output of renewable energy, the seasonal differences in supply and the high storage costs. The IEA says that solar electricity is now being made more cheaply than any other method of production. But, because solar panels currently only convert around a quarter of the sun's energy that falls on them into electricity, new technologies are being developed to increase the efficiency of panels. This demands a commitment to energy and environmental research and development well beyond what is spent as a share of national incomes by the EU and the USA, both of which are far below the 2 per cent of GDP now spent on this by China.

5. Capturing carbon and nature-based solutions

A carbon-neutrality policy requires not only deep cuts in emissions, but also the removal of carbon from the atmosphere. To halve carbon emissions by 2030 and then halve them again in the 2030s and halve them again in the 2040s only removes 87.5 per cent of emissions, so we have to find newer and better ways – such as air capture from afforestation – to generate 'negative emissions'.

Since the Industrial Revolution, humans are said to have emitted more than 2,000 gigatonnes of CO_2 into the atmosphere. The thickening blanket of heat-trapping greenhouse gases causes forest fires, heatwaves and sea-level rises that will only continue to intensify if nothing is done to remove billions of tonnes of CO_2 from the atmosphere. Trees and other forms of vegetation mitigate climate change by sequestering and storing carbon extracted from the atmosphere by photosynthesis. Indeed, nature-based solutions like forestry are so important that they could, over time, account for one-third of what is needed for us to stay below 2°C in 2030. But, while forests still cover about one-third of the planet's land, deforestation, which has been concentrated mostly in South America, Africa and parts of Asia, has speeded up since the 1980s to make way for cash crops, cattle farming and industrial developments, including palm oil. Every minute, according to the UN's Food and Agriculture Organization (FAO), forests the size of thirty football pitches are cut down. The result is that 30 per cent of previous forest cover has now been completely cleared and another 20 per cent degraded.[51]

There is more positive news, though. The WRI has identified more than 2 billion hectares worldwide of degraded land – an area larger than South America – but much of this can be restored, often by combining forests with smallholder agriculture.[52] Right across the board, there is agreement on the need for far bolder intervention to both restore previously forested land and plant billions of new trees. Supported by sixty-one countries, the Bonn Challenge and the New York Declaration on Forests seek to bring 150 million hectares of degraded and deforested landscapes into restoration by 2020 and 350 million hectares by 2030.[53]

From South Korea to Latin America and from Ethiopia to China, reforestation is happening, but more could be done if we cooperated globally. It is thought that 'nearly half of India's . . . 140 million hectares (346 million acres) could benefit from restoration', which could, by 2040, sequester twice India's annual emissions.[54] As the WRI estimated in a study of options for the US, planting trees is the least expensive zero-carbon option and will do more to deliver cleaner water and air.[55] Many such programmes are shovel-ready and can create jobs; what we lack are global financial arrangements that will help those who have the most to do but are least able to pay.

I was involved in the creation of the Congo Basin initiative across six of Africa's poorest countries – initially championed by the Nobel Prize-winner Wangari Maathai and led by Paul Martin, former Canadian prime minister. We had to develop sophisticated methods of surveillance to prevent illegal logging, as well as find funding for the planting of trees. But, through better management of farmland, soil fertilisation and the planting of cover crops when fields were otherwise bare (thus extending photosynthesis throughout the year), we found that we could increase economic activity and improve the environment at the same time. Now, by successfully monitoring what is happening on the ground – as, for example, the WRI is doing worldwide – we can not only account for trees felled and trees planted, but also assess the actual amounts of carbon we are offsetting. This can be extended to all continents – making even more headway, for example, in the forests of Malaysia and Brazil – but only if guarantees of global funding can be agreed by the G20 in advance of COP26.

> Growing rice has a similar climate impact to flying – about 2–3 per cent of global warming. Paddy fields are like giant marshlands emitting huge quantities of methane. Rothamsted Research, in Hertfordshire, has developed 'Direct Seeded Rice' (DSR) which doesn't need to be grown in a puddle so uses less water. The plant has also been bred to grow its first roots and shoots more rapidly which is vital for success in a conventional field system. It's crossed with existing high-yield varieties and initial results are promising. The water in paddy fields does help to suppress weeds and so this system could need more herbicide but the developers believe farm-ready seeds will be ready in a couple of years with most of the world's rice grown this way in a decade.[56]

Reducing the carbon footprint of production processes for the likes of cement, steel and plastics is, of course, far more complicated and, until now, has been far more expensive than planting trees. The technologies include sucking up CO_2 at a coal plant, for example, before it hits the atmosphere – which is known as carbon capture and storage – as well as catching carbon emissions across the entire energy, transport and manufacturing sectors before they are released back into the atmosphere. The CO_2 emissions can then either be stored deep underground or be combined with calcium to produce limestone as a possible replacement for concrete. Ten years ago, the cost of carbon removal was an uneconomic $600 per tonne. Now the cost is more manageable, but government subsidies would be necessary. Here, again, global agreements to pool and share costs would be advantageous and it is positive news that President Biden is being asked to consider global agreements on the future of steel, cement and other carbon-intensive industries.

Carbon capture can also be complemented by other innovative and potentially effective technologies like carbon mineralisation, sea-based carbon removal that will de-acidify the oceans, and direct air capture using scrubbing machines.[57] But this is more difficult because, while there is a concentration of carbon at, say, the coal plant, where we would do what is called point capture when the air at the mine is 10 per cent CO_2, there is a far lower concentration of CO_2 in the air as a whole. There is, of course, no way to capture carbon without using some energy. The question is how much will be used to capture how much carbon? Technology moves forward all the time and, as in the case of solar panels, becomes more energy efficient and cost effective. Again, an internationally coordinated programme of investment in research and early-stage development is a precondition for viability on the scale needed in the coming decades.

Conclusion

If we know 'why' and 'what' we need to do, we should also be clear on the 'how' and then the 'when', so I return to the step-change in international decision-making that is needed to move this global environmental agenda forward. The year 2021 is crucial. The Climate Convention COP26, convened in Glasgow under UK chairmanship at the end of the year, will be a decisive event. In advance of it, the G20, which will meet under Italian chairmanship (preceded by a UK-chaired G7, which – as the table at the end of the chapter shows – contains all the biggest polluters) could take forward all five initiatives I have proposed: a coordinated green recovery plan; new obligations on companies; agreement on fossil fuel subsidies and carbon pricing; the stepping up of investment in new technologies; and the amplification of nature-based solutions. The missing element is finance. Over the course of the next year, we have to agree the funding of a global green deal.

Progress on our environment should not depend, as we have suggested, on a relatively toothless UN Environment Assembly or be wholly at the mercy of a potentially unmanageable COP, which struggles to reach decisions because it has no executive and because its decisions, which require the unanimous agreement of all member states, can easily be blocked or watered down. Nor can progress be guaranteed if we rely on current decision-making forums – the UN Security Council, the G20 and the G7 – all of which are controlled by some of the world's biggest polluters. As we can see in the table below, the five members of the UN Security Council are responsible for 42 per cent of current emissions and 54 per cent of historic emissions.

Over time, we will need a far more effective institutional architecture within which we are capable of agreeing and policing carbon reductions in individual countries and delivering results. But, if we are to make progress at COP26 and future COPs, we will need the conference to be guided by a formal or informal executive that will include the G20 but also go wider to embrace the concerns of the Island and coastal states, the developing world and the emerging markets. And, if this is the case, the agenda will have to include far greater support for adaptation and loss and damage in the poorest countries. Chairing the COP26 in December this year, the UK is in a position to create such a working group that could ensure we build on a new-found enthusiasm to act.

Equally, some of the single-purpose green funds and initiatives that have been agreed in recent years have not been as effective as hoped. The Green Climate Fund – which was established in 2010, is governed by a board of twenty-four country representatives and is shared between developed and developing countries – has raised only $10 billion for a three-year programme – a far cry from what was originally promised. While the main benefits of an adaptation fund will accrue to the country receiving the assistance, mitigation – a public good that benefits all – is best delivered by a *global* mitigation fund that is not tied to one or two powerful states and has a structure that allows it the independence to support the projects that are the most efficient and cost effective for climate change.

Table 3: Shares of global greenhouse gas (GHG) emissions and representation on IMF, World Bank (WB) and UN Security Council (UNSC)

	% of GHG emissions	% of cumulative historic emissions	% of global population	% of IMF vote	% of WB vote	UNSC veto?
China	23.5	8.1	19.1	3.7	4.4	Yes
US	12.8	29.3	4.4	16.7	15.9	Yes
Russia	4.1	7.6	2.0	2.7	2.8	Yes
UK	1.0	6.3	0.9	4.9	3.8	Yes
France	0.7	2.9	0.8	4.9	3.8	Yes

There are grounds for hope: recent bolder climate commitments from the UK, the EU, President Biden and even China; the fact that, for almost a decade, renewable energy investment has exceeded investment in fossil fuels; and the emergence of new ideas that are applying the best of human ingenuity to the problem, which one writer has called the best vaccine against climate change.

I have said that addressing the climate crisis is this generation's moon-shot moment – and there's reason to be hopeful. Time and again, humanity has proven the power of possibility. In the span of one year we have gone from discovering a novel virus to sequencing its genome and developing not one but multiple vaccines with historically high efficacy – that was a moon-shot moment, and humanity delivered.

And just as a scientific remedy was found that started to repair the ozone layer, so, too, a solution can be found for a far greater human-induced problem. There are good examples of innovation being swift and game-changing and manufacturers making a difference. In the Second World War, for example, a wartime substitute for natural rubber had to be found; five years later, the US was producing tens of thousands of tons of synthetic rubber. In the post-war years, clean air legislation reduced pollution in our cities.

In the early 1960s, a manned lunar mission seemed out of reach, but less than a decade of concentrated effort made it happen. Armed only with primitive computing technology and centuries-old mathematics, the world's greatest engineering and astrophysics minds came together and put a man on the moon – an achievement so great the United States and other countries are still seeking to replicate it a half century later.

Now confronted by a different kind of moon-shot moment – a climate crisis – people are beginning to understand that the tools needed to wage this fight are all around us, from hydrogen fuels cells to wind and solar. Indeed in the past ten years, so many countries launched programmes to decrease the cost of solar power that savings of around 75 per cent were achieved by 2020.

But most of all, we will need each other because this is a race only won when we all cross the finish line.

During COVID-19, as we have burned carbon less, millions round the world have seen the benefit: they have looked up at clearer skies and looked down at cleaner rivers, and millions can again envision an environment where if you go for a walk you are helping not hurting your body by inhaling air that is not carcinogenic but clean. And we can do more, even if that is just paying attention to packaging when buying groceries and separating recyclables when we throw out the rubbish. For example, neither Bogotá's surge in cycling and expansion of bike lanes as citizens avoid public transport nor the global COVID-19 work-from-home experiments have required any new technology, but instead relied on new thinking. We can walk or cycle more and, if we do drive, can consider hybrid or electric vehicles.

But we also have to accept that, without a sense of being part of a bigger project, it is difficult to motivate individuals to change their behaviour. And when the world's richest 10 per cent have carbon footprints that are sixty times bigger than the poorest 10 per cent, and when for the last three decades the richest 1 per cent have been responsible for 15 per cent of all carbon emissions, more than the bottom 3 billion taken together, those with the most will have to make a far bigger contribution than now.[58]

But with a more equitable burden-sharing we can build what is needed: a wider global commitment to a shared environmental goal. When, after launching his lunar mission plans, President John Kennedy first went to Cape Canaveral, he asked each member of staff he met there what their role was. The first told Kennedy he was an engineer, the second explained she was a research scientist, the third said he was an astronaut and the fourth said she was a statistician. But, when he came to a woman who happened to be one of the cleaning staff and asked her what she did, she replied in nine telling words: 'I am helping put a man on the moon.' She was proud that she was part of a shared mission. In this way, citizens of the world can be made aware that we are in the battle against climate change together. Most of us have votes and voices that can be directed at our political leaders. People with social media platforms can broadcast the need for change. The climate emergency is indeed an existential threat to the globe. We owe it to ourselves to work together towards progress not as spectators but as agents of change, each of us with the power to reduce all our carbon footprints. Governments can make a difference, but public pressure will be decisive.

UNLOCKING THE WORLD'S POTENTIAL: AN EDUCATION REVOLUTION

I am constantly reminded that, worldwide, education is more important than we may realise.

Sometimes one image can sum up a feeling far more powerfully than any words written or speech uttered. Etched in my mind is a photograph of a three-year-old boy that many will remember and that drives me on in the educational work I do and in the objective I share with millions of teachers and parents to ensure that every child has the chance of an education.

The photograph of a red-T-shirted Kurdish boy, Alan Kurdi, lying face down on a Mediterranean beach, his legs and hands outstretched, travelled the world. But Alan's full story – and its significance – has rarely been told.

Along with his father, mother and brother, Alan had boarded a flimsy boat made of inflatable rubber and was en route from Turkey to Greece. At least twelve passengers were crowded together on a boat that was only five metres long. None had proper life vests for the thirty-minute journey in rough waters to the coast of Greece. Only five minutes after leaving Turkish land, the overloaded vessel capsized. To this day, there is a dispute over who the captain was and whether he had deserted the ship and abandoned its passengers as it flipped over and sank.

Alan had left Turkey for one reason: his mother, who also

died, wanted him to go to school. She wanted him to have the education that had ceased to be available after Syria exploded into civil war: education that Turkey, because of its strained resources, could only offer some of the Syrian refugees. An application promising to sponsor the family had been submitted to the Canadian authorities by an aunt residing in Canada, but, without proper back-up information, it had not been approved and the family had also failed to secure a visa from Turkey. So the Kurdis' journey was a desperate and, as it turned out, deadly last throw of the dice.

The family's search for an education they could not find in Syria or Turkey – and the unacceptable price they had to pay in trying to secure something so basic – made me determined to redouble my efforts. During my nine years to date as a UN special envoy for global education, in a journey that has taken me to schools in every continent, from Timor-Leste off the coast of Australia to many in the towns of Africa, Asia, Latin America and the Middle East, I have heard mothers and fathers express the same determination as Alan Kurdi's parents to do everything in their power to secure the chance of an education for their children.

This experience was both daunting and inspiring, but the clearest message that has emerged from my travels so far is one of a huge injustice. A 21st-century education should be lifelong, recurrent and permanently available – at any age, at any time and for any course of study. Those of us who live in the privileged quarter of advanced societies take for granted what our children enjoy: universal primary education; secondary education that builds on primary teaching to provide a basis for university or higher technical education; access to skilled single-subject teachers; and, increasingly, experience of the recent flourishing of online educational resources and thus a direct line to education whenever and wherever people want it. But around three-quarters of the world's citizens have had either limited access to the most basic of school education or no education at all.[1]

Of course, educational disadvantage does not exist in isolation, and it is widely complicated by the current COVID-19 pandemic and by the fact that millions of people in the world are destitute or on the move, driven by forces such as poverty, climate change, oppressive regimes and lingering genocidal civil wars in Syria, Yemen, Myanmar and elsewhere.

More positively, vastly improved communication and the wide range of innovative educational technologies developed in recent decades give some grounds for optimism that lifelong learning can soon be accessible to all. These vary in scale from iPads and laptops for individual pupils to Massive Open Online Courses (MOOCs) – a concept pioneered in the 1980s by the UK's Open University using the limited resources then available and taking a great leap forward in the US two decades later when, according to the *New York Times*, 2012 became 'the year of the MOOC'. And now, with the assistance of advances in artificial intelligence and a greater understanding of how the brain absorbs and processes knowledge, a more holistic approach to learning makes rapid progress in both educational opportunity and per-formance possible.[2]

But, as I will show in this chapter, the contrast with the expe-rience of children in poorer, less developed societies – societies whose demographics now show rapid growth in the proportion of under-20s, which actually increases the numbers at risk from educational disadvantage – is stark and utterly indefensible.

Education is, of course, a good in itself: few will deny that it unlocks human potential, bridging the gap between what we are and what we have in ourselves to become. Many describe its value – and its impact on us – as dramatic, mind-blowing and even magical, but it is best seen as the gift that keeps on giving. As the brilliant Nobel Prize-winning economist Amartya Sen has shown, education and literacy are the foundation stones of human capabilities, opening up opportunities that give us the freedom to make real choices. And what is true for individuals is also true for countries. No country has made sustained progress economically and socially until it has succeeded in education. Indeed, education is the key that unlocks all our human development goals. Without the information, knowledge and wisdom that education imparts, we could not improve people's employment prospects, guarantee better health, deliver gender equality or enhance quality of life. Education is important to earnings, economic growth and poverty reduction: on average, one year's additional education increases personal incomes by 12 per cent.[3] It is also important to survival: the child of an educated girl is twice as likely to reach the age of five than the child of an illiterate mother, which, of course, creates a virtuous circle as these educated mothers are also more likely to educate their daughters.

Alternatively, if denied education, millions more girls are forced into early marriage or domestic service or find themselves trafficked. One recent study of children living in the slums of Dhaka, Bangladesh, found that, by the age of fourteen, half of them were working and 15 per cent of 6–14-year-olds were out of school and engaged in full-time work, mainly sewing garments, for well beyond the 42-hour limit set by national legislation.[4] Such widespread abuse reminds us that universal education has not been achieved in any country without education first being made compulsory. We can romanticise about the 'pull' of education, but, in the UK, it was the 'push' factor that made education universal. Indeed, the appointment in the mid-nineteenth century of inspectors checking up on school attendance was what forced children out of factories and mines and into schools.

Yet, even in this century when, in almost all countries, school education is required by law, 260 million of the world's school-age children – perhaps 15 per cent of the developing world's children – will not be at school today or any other day, even after COVID-19 is over. Add to that the alarming facts that still only 20 per cent of under-5s are offered any pre-school education and that more than half of our children (800 million) cannot read or write to an acceptable standard at the age of eleven – a figure that could rise to 900 million because of the closure of schools during COVID-19 – and we are describing the theft of the childhoods of millions of boys and girls.[5]

We spend £6,000 a year on the education of a child in countries like the UK and US, but in low-income countries, the cost of educating a child averages just £35, or less than 70p per week. On these figures we value the education of a poor child in a poor country 160 times less. And while educational aid makes a difference, it is not enough. I calculate that even after combining all the education aid money given by all advanced economies and international organisations to African children, the total support is no more than £10 a year per child, barely enough to pay for a second-hand textbook, far less for the teachers' salary or the upkeep of the school building, and it is falling. For while education aid increased rapidly in the first decade of this century and then again in the second half of the second decade, reaching a peak of $16 billion (or £11.5 billion), it has now fallen by $2 billion (£1.3 billion) and may not return to its previous peak before the mid-2020s.[6] With aid less than $10 per child and developing country budgets under pressure, children's chances of securing a good education are slim.

It is commonplace to think that inequalities of opportunity are decreasing. But, with education taking on an even more critical role in what are now knowledge economies, those excluded from education in poorer countries are receiving less help and yet paying an ever-higher price in joblessness, poverty and social rejection. So it is also important to understand several key factors which are intensifying inequalities: the changing nature of work as it affects the developed and still-developing world; the rising demand for higher skills; the considerable challenge in Africa and South East Asia in relation to the funding of education; and as the recent survey 'Inequality in the Developing World' identifies, 'low intergenerational mobility in India', 'declining mobility pointing to rising inequality' in China and 'earnings inequality rising' in South Africa, all due to a growing educational divide. The survey concludes that 'high inequality undermines the maximum use of human potential'.

The right to education

Some of the concepts I have introduced may seem abstract and the challenges involved sometimes difficult to address, but they matter enormously to the young people and teachers I have listened to in Pakistan, India, Bangladesh, Afghanistan, Indonesia, Thailand and South Korea. I have also visited and observed schools in dozens of African countries – indeed, I had the privilege of doing so in Mozambique with the late Nelson Mandela and his wife Graça Machel. In Kenya, I met orphans begging for money for schooling they could not afford themselves. I visited a school for the blind in Ethiopia – with Sir Tim Berners-Lee, inventor of the world wide web – and saw first-hand how just a little new technology exported from the West can assist the world's 35 million visually impaired. In fact, I have seen how computers can be put to use in schools from Uganda to Timor-Leste – though sadly, too often, I have found that no one at the schools has yet mastered the software. I've also visited northern Nigeria several times to learn how their schools – closed down by the threat from extreme Islamic terrorism – could be re-opened and kept safe for girls after a spate of violent abductions by Boko Haram.

And I've travelled widely in the Middle East to see how education can be delivered for displaced children, uprooted and then accommodated in overcrowded huts and tents in insanitary camps. I spent time with young Syrian refugees in Turkey, Lebanon and Jordan, which was a harrowing experience, but did lead to a new proposal from Kevin Watkins of Save the Children for double-shift schools. This shift system allowed for a group of young people to study in their own language from morning to mid-afternoon and for another language group to then study from mid-afternoon to dusk. 'What do you want to be?' I asked a young Syrian refugee holed up in Beirut. 'An engineer,' he said. 'I want to go back and help rebuild my country.'

I've seen the impact of civil wars on schooling not only in the Middle East, but also in the Democratic Republic of Congo and South Sudan. When I visited the latter, a struggling new nation, I had an unforgettable meeting with impoverished young mothers, refugees from Sudan to the north, who were in desperate need of shelter, food, healthcare and protection. However, what they were begging for above all else was their children to have the chance of an education. I remember twenty children being taught in a hut in a village just outside Juba, South Sudan's capital. The hut had no desks, no computers and only a small number of textbooks. What little light there was came only from two small windows. Through one of them, I could see some of the crowd I had walked through to enter the hut – about a hundred children standing in the hot African sun gazing wistfully at education opportunities they could not share. One mother even told me that she had to choose which of her eight-year-old twins would take up the one place available to her family at the 'school'.

But this tiny school was the result of the work of the UN Bangladesh Rural Advancement Committee (BRAC) – a huge development initiative committed to identifying best practice in non-profit organisations. BRAC creates 'opportunities on human rights and social empowerment, education and health' and has recently expanded its commitment in Africa and Asia.

It is difficult to express the conflict of emotions you feel – both the compassion for the children and the anger at the injustice – when you come face to face with barefoot kids; 'AIDS kids'; pupils who, in one school in Kibera, Nairobi's largest slum, were called 'Half-AIDS' kids, meaning that one but not both of their parents had HIV/AIDS; and boys and girls so hungry that they could barely speak. I remember meeting a twelve-year-old girl in Kenya who had HIV/AIDS with tuberculosis as a complication. She was homeless and, as an orphan after both parents had died, got passed around from relative to relative every week because no one would accept her guardianship. Miriam was so desolate that there was no hope in her eyes. I found myself asking what chance she – now perhaps mortally ill – had ever had to make anything of her talents, and, after I returned from Africa, I tried to find out what might be done to help her, but we lost track of her whereabouts and she could not be found.

Again and again, I've seen how children desperate for the chance of an education have lost out because of conflicts and civil wars. In Rwanda's Kigali Genocide Memorial, the museum commemorating the Rwandan genocide of 1994, is a photograph of a boy called David. What he wanted more than anything else was an education so that he could be a doctor. Under the photograph is a plaque that reads:

David, age 11

Ambition: to be a doctor

Favourite sport: football

Favourite hobby: making people laugh

Death: by mutilation

Last words: the UN are coming to save us

But the UN never did. In his idealism and his innocence, David believed we would deliver what had been promised: a UN rescue and then education for him and his friends.

Politicians, some would say, don't show weakness by crying, other than as a media opportunity. But, when I think of David, what he'd hoped for and how we failed him, tears well up.

However, in every place I have visited across the world, I have also been inspired by the enthusiasm of young people – moved by their desire to learn and their willingness to make sacrifices to study. In only a very few places have I encountered pupils who don't want to learn and only rarely have I come across disenchanted teachers who don't want to teach. Almost everywhere, I've been struck by the earnest commitment to education of both children and teachers and the influence this has on children's potential. But one thought always comes back to me: *why do we persist in wasting half our world's future by writing off the potential of half the world's children?* And, from my own schooldays in Kirkcaldy, I sometimes recall Thomas Gray's *Elegy*, a long poem describing wasted potential and lost opportunities in rural eighteenth-century England. Tragedies, too, but on a very small scale compared to what I have seen during my travels: millions and millions of young people denied education because they are in the wrong place at the wrong time in a still-unjust world.

Technology: a game changer with unfulfilled potential

At the height of the pandemic, 1.5 billion children were sent home from school for weeks or months and 1.8 billion for shorter periods of time. This resulted in the upending of our views on where and how education can be delivered. Suddenly, classroom crowding yielded to social distancing; and digital learning – supported from school – could take place at home. The pandemic emergency taught education a sharp lesson. In future, digitalisation, distance learning and a fresh look at the curriculum – together with a wider range of interactions between teachers and students – should form the obvious way ahead.[7]

But the COVID-19 crisis also revealed the worrying inequality in children's access to necessary technology. Already in the developed world, 94 per cent of young people aged 15–24 use the Internet. In developing countries, that figure is 67 per cent, dropping to 30 per cent in the least-developed countries. Most worryingly, young people in Africa, Asia and the Pacific are almost 90 per cent unconnected. And, during the pandemic, more than 460 million children, close to one-third of all school-age children, could not be reached by digital or remote learning programmes due to a lack of either effective policies or access to devices and connectivity. Sub-Saharan Africa is worst affected, with 50 per cent of its students unreachable.[8] And, even in places where access to technology exists, many children still do not benefit. A survey of secondary schools in Bangladesh found that only half of students with access to TV-based learning programmes watched them and only 2 per cent of the 21 per cent that can get online did so.[9] Too often, the provision of laptops was grossly inadequate and overcrowding in housing in the poorest communities proved to be just as great a barrier to learning. Until we connect people everywhere, technology use will accentuate the divide between rich and poor and between the financially secure and insecure. Social inequalities and the digital divide uncovered by the COVID-19 crisis will take vision, persistence and money to overcome.

Almost everywhere in the developing world, I have seen education systems struggling to cope and creaking at the seams, despite the enthusiasm and dedication of teachers, the good intentions of administrators and the ambitions of parents for their children. In recent years, as computing, automation and artificial intelligence have opened up new opportunities for every sector of our fortunate 25 per cent society, we have seen some of our most traditional institutions changed beyond all recognition in appearance and function, too. The design of offices; the layout of homes; bright, clean and orderly factories; spacious, continually restocked shops and supermarkets; even hospitals, which are now recognised – sometimes begrudgingly – by doctors approaching retirement as vast improvements on the hospitals in which they trained forty years previously. In our personal lives, our consumption, our entertainment and our healthcare, there is a relentless force for greater personalisation. Services and products have increasingly adapted to our every need and desire.

Sadly, this transformation has not happened in education. Too many of our schools still reflect the format in place 100 years ago: block after block of stacked identical classrooms, furnished so that pupils sit in serried rows of desks, all facing a special space, sometimes a stage, featuring a teacher and a board. True, flapping black gowns are less common, as is the irritating squeak of chalk on the blackboard, so I guess that is progress of sorts.

Perhaps more surprisingly, the way we teach and are taught – teaching methods – has also changed too little: we still cling to the idea of the teacher as the sage, taking the class lecture by lecture through the same curriculum year after year, sometimes lightened by the occasional joke that usually works annually. Nearly 170 years have passed since Charles Dickens wrote *Hard Times*, but we have not come so far from the 'bare monotonous' classroom Dickens described or from his school board superintendent character Thomas Gradgrind's injunction that, in order to 'teach these boys and girls nothing but facts', 'you have to be in all things regulated and ruled'.

And yet there is now a wealth of research showing that a teacher can often achieve much more as a tutor than as a lecturer, acting as a guide, motivating pupils via one-to-one interactions, supporting them, prompting and monitoring individual endeavours and projects, and encouraging discussion that all can share in, even the shyest in class. This adaptive, inclusive and engaging way of teaching is called 'adaptive and differentiated instruction' – sometimes referred to as 'teaching at the right level' – and is, of course, a far cry from the uniform and standardised delivery of content that was typical of the first industrial age. Not only that, research in cognitive science on the human brain's capacity to incorporate new knowledge has also endorsed this as a more effective way to improve children's learning.

But so embedded were the old ways that it has taken time for technology to improve results, be that in reading, maths or science. A study reviewing the use of technology in 2015 showed that even countries that had invested heavily in information and communication technologies were slow to move to the teaching bubbles and individualised tutorial spaces that place children at the centre of the learning process.[10]

Indeed, artificial intelligence is changing everything else in our world, but, until now, it has had the least influence on education. Even when there are teachers who are far better suited for person-to-person coaching that will encourage, stimulate, advise and reassure students, we still cling to traditional standardised pedagogy. Despite all the evidence that we need both lectures and tutoring to spark the imagination and ambition of children and help them make the most of their potential, too often our education systems have failed to change and, deprived of the resources they need, too often teachers have had no choice but to follow the traditional approach.

However, as technology transforms communication with ever-more sophisticated aids to personalise learning, the world is moving on from 'chalk and talk'. We now know that lectures can be successfully delivered online and transmitted as videos around the world. In this way, the best education is no longer delivered in classes of thirty or forty, but instead transmitted to millions.

Pioneered by Ju-Ho Lee, the former minister of education, science and technology in South Korea, 'High-Touch, High-Tech' learning makes the most of interactive technology, including artificial intelligence, and delivers improved pupil performance in both the classroom and the exam hall by offering individualised learning with an emphasis on tutoring and mentoring. Students 'first remember and understand content through interacting with artificial intelligence and mobile technology (high-tech)', he has explained, 'and then learn to apply, analyse, evaluate what they understand, and finally learn to create, through engaging with teachers (high-touch)'.[11]

The worst aspect of the persistence of outdated methods is that we continue to expect too little of too many of our children. The UN's SDGs in this area are ambitious: every young person will complete not just a high-quality primary education by 2030, but also a high-quality secondary education, with higher education extended to all those with the talent to benefit, funded through a combination of state and private finance, though private investment cannot be viewed as a substitute for public funds. But, when we look at many countries' national plans for education, a different picture emerges. Sadly, they confirm that change will not be transformational in line with the UN's goals. At best, national plans offer only incremental, perhaps fragile, improvements. And, in almost every country in the world, governmental manpower planning projections are predicated not on the fulfilment of the SDGs and thus on universal high-quality schooling, but instead on the continued assumption that the beneficiaries of post-school education will remain a small elite.

The best research suggests that, even by 2040, only 20 per cent of the world's adult population will have post-secondary qualifications and, by 2060, that figure will be a still modest 26 per cent. Such a 75:25 global divide between the education-poor and the education-rich may be the best that can be achieved in the next forty years unless the necessary programme of radical change is implemented. Of course, the wealthier you are, the more likely you are to be in that privileged quarter. But the poorer the country, the less that is devoted to the education of the poorest. While governments in high-income countries spend, on average, about 18.6 per cent of resources on the poorest 20 per cent of children and 21.7 per cent on the richest 20 per cent of children, the governments in low-income countries spend only half as much – 10.3 per cent – on the poorest 20 per cent of children, compared with 37.9 per cent on the richest 20 per cent. Even in a country like the UK, which spends thirty times more per year on a child's education than poorer countries do, five-year-olds from poorer households are still an average of fifteen months behind those from richer households in terms of vocabulary development. So it is hardly surprising that, in East African countries where only $200 a year is spent on the education of those children who are enrolled at school, more than half of these pupils cannot read or write at all by the age of eleven.[12]

Expanding post-school education

University graduate numbers have, of course, risen fast – from 100 million globally in 1970 to 400 million in 2000 and now to 700 million. These numbers look set to rise to 1.1 billion in 2030 and 1.4 billion in 2040 – figures that sound impressive, but apply to a continuously low fraction of the developing world's fast-rising adult population.

By 2040, only 20 per cent of the adult population will have the post-secondary qualifications that most experts think will be essential for the workplace of tomorrow, up from 14 per cent now, but still a small minority. So it follows that, twenty years from now, in 2040, the vast majority of the population – 3 billion adults, including those born this year or currently infants – will not have secondary education completion certificates and will have had either no schooling at all or, at best, an incomplete primary and junior secondary education.

However, when we also look beyond the stock of qualified adults to what should give us a more optimistic picture – the flow of today's children into higher education – we still find a monumental education poor–rich divide. And this is despite the fact that we promised that every child would be receiving high-quality secondary education by 2030 in the SDGs.

Even a decade from now, the majority of schoolchildren will not be enjoying six years of secondary education and, just as today, the opportunity to enjoy a university- or college-level education will still be well beyond the reach of the vast majority of the world's young people. In other words, by the middle of the twenty-first century – by which time, college or university degrees will have become of even greater importance in determining a person's lifetime earnings – only a fraction of young adults will have post-school education qualifications worthy of the name.

What's also frightening to contemplate is that, even in 2040, almost 1 billion of the world's citizens – 12 per cent of adults – will not have had any schooling or will have failed to complete the most basic of primary schooling. This means that they will be functionally illiterate, equipped for only the most basic jobs and condemned never to be able to command decent earnings.

Table 4: Slowing of the global growth of graduates

	Total global graduates (millions)
1970	100
2000	400
2019	700
2030*	1,100
2040	1,400

* Note: while middle-class adults will number 4 billion in 2030, the graduate population will be one-third of that.

**Table 5: Education level attained globally
(total %, excluding under-15s)[13]**

	Post-secondary	Secondary	Primary	Incomplete primary/no education
2015	14	49	17	20
2030	17	53	15	15
2040	20	54	14	12
2060	26	55	12	7

But the grim 2020 COVID-19 pandemic has also shown how quickly educational systems can respond under pressure – and can transform our prior assumptions about their inflexibility. After a salutary and informative crisis, we now have a big opportunity to reorganise. The physical structure of a school can be rethought. Classrooms can be redesigned as learning bubbles to meet new social distancing rules that may be with us for some time; the relationship between teacher and pupil can be reconfigured; and online learning can be made far more accessible to students. There is a chance to do what the UN secretary-general has called for – 'bring education back better' – and this would be nothing less than the revitalisation of what we mean by our commitment to education for all.

Lifelong learning and recurrent, permanent education have featured in UN resolutions for fifty years, but have never been delivered. In a new setting, in which a normal working life involving many changes of job will require lifelong learning, we can resolve to make these resolutions a realistic prospect rather than a distant dream – perhaps by thinking things through from first principles, deciding on the changes we need to make and then pursuing them via an innovative and radical approach.

The education-poor/education-rich gap is, of course, the culmination of long-term trends that previously separated manual and non-manual workers, as well as those with capital from those with no savings or investments whatsoever. A century ago, as stated in Chapter 1, 40 per cent of economic output went to wages and 60 per cent to owners and investors. By the mid-twentieth century, that ratio had shifted: on average, 60 per cent of economic output went to wages and just 40 per cent to capital owners. Now the capital-to-labour ratio has shifted yet again, from 60:40 back to 40:60 – a measure of rising inequality. Those who are simply wage earners with no shares or access to profit-related pay lose out badly. And they lose out doubly because there is both a surplus of unskilled labour and a race to the bottom as nations and companies send their work to the lowest-wage-paying countries.[14]

As a result, the poorest can exert only minimum spending power – to the detriment of national economies. And this lose–lose outcome scenario is not easily reversible without major reforms in the global supply chain. For three decades now, Western workers have been competing against lower-paid Asian workers and have thus been unable to raise their standards of living. This is not good for the consumer economy either because, if the majority of the population has less to spend, growth will then slow, which is one of the reasons a period of secular stagnation is now a real threat to the world economy.

So, while the global middle class has grown to more than 3 billion, its ability to increase earnings will depend less on its hours worked and more on the skills it can bring to the workplace. Indeed, however widespread the gains from cutting consumer prices through technological innovation may be, social tensions will still increase as a result of rising inequality if the capital–labour divide continues to grow and something like a 75:25 education-poor/education-rich ratio becomes entrenched.

Too often, equality of opportunity means the opportunity to be unequal. That is because far too few young people are encouraged through secondary education to go on to be offered places in further or higher education. As two professors, Michael Sandel and Daniel Markovits, have recently demonstrated in separate books, a meritocracy has become entrenched that is in a position to pass on educational advantage to its children. 'Although meritocracy was embraced as the handmaiden of equality and did open up the elite in its early years, it now more nearly stifles rather than fosters social mobility,' Markovits has argued.[15]

Our aim should be to expand equality and opportunity together. Extending compulsory education from primary school to secondary school – i.e., increasing the average number of years spent at school from five years to eight, nine, ten and then eleven years – and dramatically increasing college and university places will, at one and the same time, make skilled labour more plentiful and less expensive, narrowing the gap between the education-poor and the education-rich.

As documented by Harvard economists Claudia Goldin and Lawrence F. Katz, technological advance increases the demand for more skilled and thus more educated workers; and, if workers have flexible skills and the educational infrastructure and provision develops sufficiently, then the supply of skills will meet the increasing demand for them. Of course, qualified secondary school leavers and those able to attend college and university will on average earn more, but, if the supply of qualified secondary school leavers is at – or preferably ahead of – the demand for their skills, these qualified school leavers will no longer be in short supply. This means that they will not be able to command an additional premium based on their scarcity value, so the gap between the wages of skilled and less skilled workers will narrow. It was in this way – by making secondary education a universal right – that, by the mid-twentieth century, the West had won the race between education and technology.[16]

For across the West in the first half of the twentieth century, an acceleration in the number of qualified secondary school leavers reduced what had been the 'high school wage premium'. With a massive growth in secondary school graduates, pay differentials based on superior skills did not rise. The elite of the early twentieth century – secondary school graduates – became the typical school leaver of the mid- and late twentieth century. And, with the resultant decline in income inequality, we ushered in a broad-based prosperity.

Next to soar in the West was college and university attendance. So, while a rapid increase in secondary school graduates caused the secondary school graduate premium to plummet in the first half of the century, the college and university 'wage premium' also began to narrow. Therefore, the gap between high- and low-skilled workers continued to narrow, too, contributing to the overall decrease in income inequality.

For a time, this broadening of educational opportunity worked to create a fairer society. Indeed, the decades before and after the mid-twentieth century comprised the only period in Western history when we managed to sustain both rising incomes and decreasing income inequality. The reduction in inequality was, of course, helped by other forces: the bargaining power of trades unions; social transfers through progressive taxation; the levelling social and economic consequences of mass military and industry; and inflation. However, although all of these eroded the power of inherited wealth, any reduction in inequality would have been minor and even more transient without educational expansion.

And, of course, while pay differentials have narrowed, this was not enough to transform society either. Simply adding more years of education only took us so far. Various injustices persisted. Firstly, six more years at the best state schools offered a higher-quality education than six more years at lower performing schools. And, secondly, in no way did the expansion of further and higher education from a very small elite to a still-small elite have the same impact on equality that the dramatic expansion of secondary education brought when it was made compulsory and universal.

Education and automation

Now we find that the latest wave of rapid technological change requires even higher skills that are far more advanced and diverse than those expected of skilled workers just a generation ago. As machines get better at performing traditional skilled work, education will need to transform itself to deliver skills that cannot be automated away by machines. This includes both higher-order skills linked to using technology in the age of artificial intelligence and socio-emotional and communications skills that artificial intelligence cannot provide. And technology is clearly winning the race between man and machine since, from the 1980s onwards, the increase in the supply of highly skilled graduates has slowed, the demand for high-level skills is outpacing supply, and a global elite of highly educated, highly paid professionals is emerging with an earning power, wealth and style of living that is already distancing them from the rest of society.

So, when Goldin and Katz re-examined the relationship between the supply of and demand for educated workers at the start of the twenty-first century, they found that the US's once-great education system was failing to keep pace with technological change. They also found that: the output of well-qualified graduates had fallen behind the availability of good jobs; graduates' relative scarcity was earning them an education premium and causing a widening of economic disparities; and, as a result, the position of unskilled workers – the supply of whom was far in excess of demand – was deteriorating.

Had the relative supply of college- and university-educated workers increased from 1980 to 2005 at the same rate it did from 1960 to 1980, the college and university wage premium, rather than rising, would have fallen. But, because our long-term supply of skilled graduates has generally lagged behind the demand for their skills, the college and university wage premium today exceeds its high level of 1914, before the twentieth century's education expansion began.

Studies suggest that 35 per cent of all occupations are at risk from automation. And, while more recent studies that analyse jobs rather than occupations produce much lower estimates, this suggests it is too simplistic to say that technology destroys jobs. Change is on the way. Economist Kaushik Basu distinguishes between two kinds of technical change: labour-saving and labour-linking.[17] And economists David Autor and Anna Salomons have found that, over the past forty years, jobs have fallen in every single industry that introduced technologies to enhance productivity. The only reason employment didn't fall across the entire economy is that other industries, with less productivity growth, picked up the slack. 'The challenge is not the quantity of jobs,' they wrote. 'The challenge is the quality of jobs available to low- and medium-skill workers.' But both 'labour-saving' and 'labour-linking' changes can increase inequality in rewards.[18]

The West's recent experience casts a shadow on how the developing world might deal with inequality because the prospects for the poorly educated in developing countries are far worse, with the earnings gap between the educated and the uneducated at 27 per cent.

Far too few college and university places have been created in the developing world, so – with the demand for graduates exceeding the supply – the graduate wage premium is even higher there than in the West. In many countries, there are so few higher education places that there is barely the provision to train the doctors, teachers and lawyers needed and, of course, government grants are so restricted and so small that higher education is a realistic option too often limited to those whose families are rich enough to pay. Technological change is likely to widen the divide within a labour market overpopulated by the unskilled and semi-skilled, which then forces wages down, and the risk to jobs from technological change is said to be 50 per cent higher in India than in the US.[19]

Sadly, developing countries have yet to complete the secondary school revolution. For many of them, despite all the worthy promises made by national governments and the international community, universal secondary education is still a distant dream. So, while the West won the race between education and technology in the twentieth century by making secondary education a universal right, we have yet to make secondary education a right in the world's poorer countries. Put simply, the global supply of secondary education is not keeping pace with the demand for it. And, in the developing world, we are compounding a huge divide between the education-poor – those who are left behind – and the education-rich – those who have educational qualifications and can command a high premium in the labour market. The same revolution that changed the West in the first two-thirds of the previous century is now, in this century, needed across the rest of the world. Universalising educational opportunity in every country at every level – starting in the early years – is perhaps the greatest egalitarian challenge of any generation.

The opportunity now exists to develop the potential of young people previously left behind, but we have to reduce unacceptable inequalities if we are to dramatically increase the numbers of qualified young people. This will expand the numbers entering the middle class, reduce the education premium that separates the qualified from those without degrees, narrow the gap between the education-poor and the education-rich, and halt rising income and wealth inequality. But, if we do nothing to raise the earning power of the 3 billion unskilled and semi-skilled workers who now comprise the bulk of the global labour market, we will be intensifying the race to the bottom as the low-skilled compete with the semi-skilled for far fewer suitable and available jobs.

So the low-skilled are under pressure in both West and East. Lower-skilled workers in rich countries are being squeezed both by technological change that is destroying their jobs and by the competition of lower-paid workers abroad. Some argue that technology was a bigger driver of this than trade between 1980 and 2000, but that trade has taken the lead since 2000. However, while low- and middle-skilled workers in poor countries in Asia have seen their wages rise, further increases are not inevitable, at least not on the same scale. One theory for the rise in inequality suggests:

> In the short run, an additional unit of machine labour that is added to the economy earns its marginal product, but also generates a zero-sum redistribution from labour to traditional capital because it changes the relative supply of the two . . . unemployment would result because workers could not survive working for the market clearing wage without government support.[20]

This is a correction to the standard belief that technological progress lifts all boats. Artificial intelligence – sometimes called 'augmented intelligence' – will only further boost the earning capacity of the few who already have the skills that enable them to derive the greatest benefit from the new technologies.

The wider picture: ways forward

It is clear that, if we are to begin to unlock the potential of young people across the world, we must start with basic education.

Beginning in the 1950s, South Korea revolutionised its schools' education system. Education was made compulsory and about 80 per cent of the educational budget was allocated to primary schooling. When primary enrolment reached 90 per cent, the government then shifted major resources to secondary schooling and only after success there did it focus on university education. Pursuing this principle of progressive universalism in allocating public finances was one of the major recommendations of the global Education Commission. (Although, now that we know that the first forty-eight months of a child's life are more important to his or her development than the next forty-eight years, we should be investing in that period too.) So South Korea has been a pace setter and, based on current trends, 52 per cent of South Koreans will achieve higher education qualifications by 2050, followed by Singapore with 48.4 per cent. Substantially further down these ratings come other advanced economies like the UK (38.7 per cent) and the US (36.4 per cent). Thereafter come lower-tier nations such as Egypt (31.4 per cent), Argentina (24.4 per cent), India (17 per cent) and Brazil (15 per cent). And then, on less than 20 per cent, we find Côte d'Ivoire (11.9 per cent) and the Central African Republic (8.5 per cent).[21]

The UK is an encouraging example, having seen the flow of 20–24s going to university or college rise from 5 per cent fifty years ago to around 50 per cent today. There has also been a big rise in the percentage of university-qualified older adults, too, from 4.4 per cent in 1970 to 5.5 per cent in 1980 to 9 per cent in 1990 to 12.8 per cent in 2000 and to 15.3 per cent in the past decade.

However, while the overall share of graduates in the labour force will increase substantially – to 38 per cent in 2050 – this educated population is unevenly distributed, skewed towards the upper middle class, as it is in the US. There, college students from families in the top 10 per cent earning bracket receive more than 50 per cent of all college degrees, while those in the bottom 50 per cent of the population receive just 10 per cent of degrees. As a result, university- and college-degree holders earn nearly twice as much per hour as high-school graduates.

But we cannot successfully finance the opening up of post-school education worldwide by replicating the model of Western universities in developing countries.

So how can we finance this expansion? In the great majority of developing nations, primary school spending per pupil averages only 15 per cent of the national income per head. When it comes to lower and upper secondary, costs are understandably much higher, at 25 and 34 per cent respectively. And the cost of a college or university education is far greater still when expressed as a proportion of annual income per head – an eye-watering 139 per cent.

Of course, in higher-income Western countries, higher education costs are also very high, making the balance between government, parent and student funding the subject of huge controversy. But, because overall incomes are much higher, the typical cost is not around 140 per cent of GDP per head, but only 40 per cent – much of it shared between the student and his or her family. Here, too, the numbers are not as daunting because the demographic pressures are considerably less.

But there is yet another barrier to overcome. Much of the post-war rise of higher education in the West was made possible with governmental support from grants, loans and scholarships to cover living expenses and, where needed, help with tuition fees. Public expenditures were justified then because the skills being acquired would be of benefit to the whole country. But, now that we have a global labour market alongside greatly increased international mobility, national investment in education is risky. For example, one-third of Indian graduates leave India to work elsewhere, so the case for the Indian government paying for graduates to gain their degrees is diminished. At a minimum, India might have to require students whom the state supported through university to pay back the costs of their education by working in India for a specified number of years, as happens when companies give scholarships. But, if the government cannot subsidise higher education, it becomes a monopoly for the offspring of richer families who can pay their own way. The globalisation of our economy is, therefore, leading to the privatisation of opportunity with the inevitable result that students from lower-income families lose out. I foresee a growing anger with this education divide and the increasing inequality it creates and hence a threat to both economic growth and social stability.

Most of the academic literature on change in tertiary education focuses on issues of knowledge development, skills formation, curriculum reform and transformational interventions to improve quality and relevance within universities. But far less attention has been paid to the evolution and transformation of entire tertiary education systems, including all post-secondary learning options, from universities to vocational training and various forms of micro-learning.

The challenges are: to meet the range of learning needs of an ever-more diverse student population; to respond to the ever-changing demand for skills; and to expand enrolment at prices students can afford. Now, in the twenty-first century, we need a 'new education' that is innovative, diverse and continually relevant to a changing economy. And we must consider the evolution and transformation of the entire tertiary education system as a whole, from the unbundling of traditional universities – distinguishing between leaders in research, certification, and undergraduate and postgraduate education – to various forms of micro-learning, giving prospective students the option of building their qualifications from a portfolio of courses in a range of institutions.[22]

Higher education degrees are thus more likely in future to be more personalised to the individual students' needs. Instead of graduating with a single degree from one university, students may design their own customised degree, micro-learning from a number of online or residential programmes and combining humanities courses with tech courses or communication courses with coding courses – each combination complementing analytical skills with design skills. Data scientists, for example, may need a unique hybrid skillset both in statistics and in the industries they service, which could be as varied as renewable energy or financial services. Indeed, the biggest expansion may be in vocationally oriented tertiary-level institutions, which are able to respond to the labour market demands and may even operate what is often called the revolving-door model, whereby career professionals return to teach relevant post-secondary skills.

And if, in developing countries, we can provide universal access to online education and then combine on-campus university education with online education and post-school technical and vocational training, we would be able to bring the price of post-school education within the reach of millions currently excluded. Of course, the annual costs of new online streams are far lower than traditional on-campus training – one year is estimated to cost the equivalent of 25 per cent of GDP per capita, compared with 100 per cent plus for traditional bricks-and-mortar places. In 2016, the Education Commission that I chaired developed a financing scenario for higher education in low- and middle-income countries. One option was to deliver half of post-secondary education online, 30 per cent as on-campus college and university education, and 20 per cent as on-site vocational education, with person-to-person tutoring and mentoring included. Only by providing education in this way can access to post-secondary education in low-income countries ever reach the levels seen in high-income countries today – 50 per cent by 2030 and almost 75 per cent participation in post-school education by 2040. Per-student costs for post-secondary education have been estimated at around $1,600 by 2030 in low-income countries, $3,600 in lower middle-income countries and $9,800 in upper middle-income countries, which, while more affordable, still requires us to spend four times more on higher education students than secondary school pupils.[23]

So, in theory, this online mobilisation of new technology in the service of education could allow ours to be the first generation in history to make universal, lifelong education a reality. Online education platforms and the burgeoning MOOCs movement have already helped millions of people achieve college readiness and go on to upgrade their skills at prices far below those of more traditional approaches. For example, EdX, a project backed by

Harvard University, MIT and other top institutions, has enrolled 25 million people, from every country in the world, and has so far awarded 1.6 million certificates of completion. They have been joined by private-sector companies like Coursera. UNICAF, an online provider focused on Africa, predicts it alone will have 100,000 learners on the continent by 2023, though this, as a proportion of the African population, is still low. Institutions such as Arizona State University in the US are developing a new model for online courses. Together with EdX, Arizona State University has created the first MOOC programme to offer first-year college-level courses for academic credits. The Global Freshman Academy is geared towards high-school age students who want to prepare for college or reduce the cost of their undergraduate education, while at the same time targeting older adults seeking to return to education. Top-ranked universities such as Georgia Tech, the University of Texas at Austin, Boston University and, in Australia, the University of Queensland offer many of these courses at a cost of just 20–25 per cent of an on-campus course. The University of the People works through thousands of voluntary tutors who prepare students for study at traditional universities.

Another option is to introduce extended online degrees at undergraduate level, with the curriculum sub-divided into stackable, modular programmes offering credentials that enable students to learn on demand in an affordable way throughout their lifetimes. What's more, to stay ahead of the labour-displacing effects of artificial intelligence and automation, catch-up digital-learning opportunities must be further developed. Just one-fifth of respondents to a recent EdX survey believe that the knowledge from their college curriculum is translatable to their current field. The rising popularity of coding bootcamps and part-time, post-college online micro-credential programmes shows that more workers are taking upskilling into their own hands. Job-relevant credentials from online programmes like EdX are on the rise, with more than 3 million people having enrolled in various

MicroMasters programmes since this certification was launched by MIT on EdX in 2015.

Now is also the time to leverage digital technologies to improve college-readiness and expand opportunities for students and workers at all points in their careers, particularly those who can least afford traditional educational channels. So, to serve the growing demands of young people for post-secondary education, we have to be innovative, embrace diversity without lowering standards and offer an online or virtual segment as part of the university and college courses on offer. This should not be done at the expense of personal tutoring, but be complemented by it.

And we must reduce the differential between the education-poor and the education-rich by ensuring that the supply of highly educated people and thus the opportunities for social mobility rise, that more people move from low-paid jobs to higher-paid jobs and that – ideally through their working lives – they will be able to gain additional skills and qualifications through lifelong, recurrent, permanent education.

These policies require far more investment in higher education and schools, but if our societies are to be seen as fair, we must also value those who do personal service jobs and help them secure higher status and better rewards for their work. As one writer puts it: 'Ideally we would like education to keep up with technological change to make sure workers have the skills they need to face this challenge. In practice, there will always be losers and even basic-income schemes can take us only so far.'[24] However, if we can narrow that divide through better rewards for caring jobs in education, health and social services – the importance of which has once again been proven during the COVID-19 crisis – we can show that greater opportunity and greater equality advance together. During the pandemic, we've seen the reterming of many such jobs as 'key workers', but this has not been reflected in increased wages. The importance of these roles to society should be reflected in enhanced recognition and social and economic status, even after the threat of COVID-19 recedes.

While developing countries can and must do far more on their own, achieving universal education without outside support would require them to commit at least 10 per cent of their national income to education, just to cover the costs of primary and secondary schooling; so even if each developing country doubled the share of national income spent on education and increased performance and productivity to the level of the best performing quartile of countries, a large annual shortfall would remain.

Funds like the Global Partnership for Education and Education Cannot Wait, as well as UN organisations like UNESCO and UNICEF, plus a host of great charities, are ready to do more. But there is one way of doubling aid funding: donor governments providing guarantees to the new International Finance Facility for Education, which I have been involved in launching. This facility will not only help protect education funding through the current crisis, but also offer a new stream of affordable financing so that countries do not have to trade off the financing of health and social protection to get children to school. It works through donors providing grants and guarantees that provide multilateral development banks with the capital to borrow. For every $2 billion provided in guarantees by donor governments, the fund can distribute between $8 billion and $10 billion in resources for education. With interest rates low, the additional grant financing needed to cut borrowing costs is so low that, in fact, donor cash contributions of $300 million will deliver that $8 billion–10 billion of education services in countries in need of assistance. Had this fund been available a few years ago, Alan Kurdi could have secured schooling in Turkey, where his family first fled. Indeed, his family would not have felt compelled to cross the Mediterranean if the World Bank or any of the regional development banks had been able to offer Turkey money to build schools for refugees.

In the end, however, it is not the lack of money or teachers or the shortage of school buildings or equipment that forms the biggest barrier to ensuring every child is at school; it is the political will power to promise we will be the first generation in history to ensure every child goes to school – and to mean what we say.

6

THE HUMANITARIAN CHALLENGE: MEETING THE SUSTAINABLE DEVELOPMENT GOALS

I did not think it could happen in the twenty-first century – and certainly not in 21st-century Europe. But, in the summer of 2018 on the Greek island of Moria, three refugee boys, trapped in a run-down refugee camp that would be burned to the ground two years later, came to a devastating conclusion. At the ages of eleven, twelve and thirteen – when, in a better world, they would have been full of optimism at the prospect of a whole life of opportunity in front of them – they concluded that their futures were so devoid of hope, their desolation so overwhelming and their lives so empty that they would attempt suicide.

When a refugee boat capsizes at sea, when a food convoy fails to get through to a besieged town and when a hospital has neither the doctors nor the medical supplies to cope with disease, hope dies. But hope dies, too, when young men and women – with no school or college to go to, no job or career to aim for and no opportunity to fulfil their talents – cannot prepare or plan for a future ahead and cannot begin to dream of a better tomorrow. Easy prey to people traffickers, ruthless criminals and violent abusers, these children face a world in which nightmares happen in broad daylight.

The refugees on Moria were three among millions falling through the humanitarian net, losing out because humanitarian aid is grossly underfunded and because dedicated aid workers have to prioritise short-term emergency rescue, the provision of shelter and urgent action to stave off starvation. Often, the best the UN humanitarian system can do in these circumstances is to prevent suffering, disease and loss of life, but not much more. As Dag Hammarskjöld, the second secretary-general of the UN, reminded us: 'The UN was not created to take mankind to heaven, but to save humanity from hell.'[1]

And the refugees are losing out twice over: once because they are exposed to all the consequences of overstretched and underfunded emergency UN humanitarian provisions; and again because the separate source of funding for their health, housing, employment and education – development aid – is precarious. Development aid budgets, invariably allocated in three- or five-year cycles, cannot easily be relied on to deliver what is needed in the context of a broader emergency.

Every day and every week, this crisis brings home to me the urgency of finding new and better ways to organise and finance humanitarian support. Even before the pandemic hit the world in early 2020 – setting years of progress on poverty reduction into reverse and consigning millions to the prospect of hunger and malnutrition – our humanitarian crisis, aggravated by conflict and climate change, had become so grave that nearly 150 million people were in need of emergency assistance. They comprised children and adults who were caught up in conflict, victims of persecution, casualties of natural disasters like floods, drought, disease, hurricanes or crop failure, or at the sharp end of climate change. The scale of the escalating humanitarian disaster can be measured in many ways, but the official statistics from the UN estimate that a record 235 million people worldwide will need humanitarian assistance and protection in 2021 – an increase of 40 per cent from 2020 – including millions displaced in their own country and millions more forced into exile far from home.[2]

In 2020, the number of people in need exceeded the population of the world's eighth biggest country, Russia, but was still below that of the seventh biggest country, Nigeria. In 2021, the number is already greater than Nigeria's 200 million population and will end the year as large as the world's fifth biggest country, Brazil. These comparisons show the enormous scale of the problem: it is equivalent to a disaster hitting the entire population of one of the largest countries on our planet.

We used to act only when a crisis hit and, even then, we were slow to pass around the begging bowl for help. Now, new and far more progressive ways of coping with humanitarian disasters are being introduced by Mark Lowcock, who is this year completing his term as director of the UN's humanitarian effort, the Office for the Coordination of Humanitarian Affairs (OCHA). Acting early to address humanitarian needs ahead of a crisis is, as he has shown, more effective, as well as more cost-efficient, than waiting until disaster has struck. Pre-emptive action includes building up food stocks, developing insurance as a first line of protection, and long-term investment in supporting farmers and food growers to achieve self-sufficiency. But much more, as he himself says, needs to be done.

Refugees and the displaced

A starting point is to consider how we can do more to help those millions who have been exiled from their country and are now refugees or, because of persecution, asylum seekers, as well as the even greater millions who have been forcibly displaced within their own country.

As I write, there are already 23 million stateless refugees worldwide. This 23 million is the estimated number of those exiled from their country and is equivalent to the entire population of Australia.

But the number of those forcibly displaced from their homes includes not just those who are now outside their home country, but also those forced to live away from their homes in their own country: a total of 70.8 million people, a figure greater than the population of the world's twenty-first most populated country, the UK, and not far below the world's nineteenth, Germany.

So we have to meet the often-different needs of these two groups of displaced people: the larger group of men, women and children who need help within their own countries; and the men, women and children now outside their country, who are part of that larger movement of people – refugees, asylum seekers and economic migrants – around whom there has been so much public dispute in recent years. When we think of a mass of humanity on the move – people smugglers, ramshackle boats and pile-ups of people at border crossings – we often do not distinguish between economic migrants, mainly young people who choose to move country in search of work, and those who have little choice, the men, women and children violently forced out of their homes and countries. Walls have been built, security fences constructed, armies sent to patrol and immigration controls imposed to stop the flow of people from lower- and middle-income countries into advanced economies.[3] A few years ago, those crossing from South America into the US were the biggest of these migrant groups and mainly economic migrants. Now, crossings from Africa into Europe are just as sizeable. Soon, with the population of Africa doubling in the next twenty years, crossings from Africa into Europe will dwarf the numbers appearing on the border between Mexico and the US. News travels fast through mobile telephones – widely used by even the poorest for communication and highly informative about their plight – hence the knowledge of millions of potential migrants, be they refugees, asylum seekers or jobseekers, that they are likely to be better off poor in a rich country than rich in a poor country.

A Nigerian building worker may double his earnings by moving from the Nigerian countryside to Nigeria's cities, but he will multiply his earnings ten-fold if he secures similar construction work in London or New York. Not surprisingly, the absolute number of persons now living permanently outside the country of their birth has increased rapidly from 30 million in 1900 to 230 million today – and this figure will continue to rise as population structures in Africa and East Asia become even more dominated by the under-30s. In one Gallup survey, one in ten of the world's population – more than 750 million people – were reported as saying that they would move to a new country if they had the chance to do so.[4]

But our immediate concern is with those in dire humanitarian need. It is a myth that the majority of refugees gravitate towards 'more comfortable' lives in the richest countries. The fact is that 90 per cent of refugees find themselves seeking refuge in poor countries. They have moved to the country nearest their home in the hope of an early return and, in doing so, increase the problems of poverty and deprivation that already exist in that country. In fact, just ten countries – all of them developing nations, notably Uganda, Bangladesh and Pakistan – host around 60 per cent of the refugee population. And all of these people are refugees for a reason. While floods, droughts, tsunamis and earthquakes can lead to migration, 80 per cent of the movement of refugees from one country to another is driven by civil war and other conflicts, hence the urgent need for humanitarian aid.

In addition, of course, terrorism is playing its part in creating these record numbers of refugees and displaced persons. Militia are bombing schoolchildren in Syria, raping and killing children in Myanmar, and starving people in Yemen by blockading humanitarian help. Poverty is no excuse for terrorism, but, as Jim Wolfensohn, the pioneering former head of the World Bank, warned, it provides a context.

David Beasley, the current head of the UN's World Food Programme (WFP), recounts conversations with mothers he has met.[5] As they explained to him, their husbands joined terrorist organisations to take up a form of remunerated employment and did so simply because their families had no food. So, as Beasley suggests, this makes the WFP the first line of defence – and offence – against groups like Al-Qaeda, Al-Shabab and ISIS. In recent years, thanks to dedicated leaders within the UN system and to the credit of NGOs, whose staff dedicate their lives to helping the dispossessed, the delivery of humanitarian aid has improved.

What needs to be done

Fair treatment of refugees is guaranteed by the 1951 Refugee Convention, but, every day at the peak of the Syrian exodus, around 100 of our fellow human beings were drowning in the Mediterranean Sea, despite often paying $1,000 or more for their voyages to freedom in crowded and unsafe crafts. And, while refugees were assured safe passage by the Geneva Convention, they were denied entry to receiving countries without visa paperwork, refused tickets to travel by airlines that knew they would be held legally responsible for returning them, and turned away by shipping companies whose ships, under European rules, would be seized by the maritime authorities and confiscated if found to be carrying illegals.

And, sadly for refugees, the three assumptions adopted by the 1951 Refugee Convention are all now outdated and incorrect. Back then, it was assumed that: a refugee's exile would be temporary and short-lived; he or she would live in a camp; and a refugee's employment was not a priority because he or she would return home soon. Seventy years on, the average length of exile is over twenty years and the conflicts that force people into exile last twice as long as they did even a few years ago. Today, more than half of the world's refugees are in what are euphemistically labelled 'protracted refugee situations' and, while special provision has been made for Palestinian refugees, the special UN agency that serves them has been operating for years with too little finance. Indeed, in the later President Trump years, it has also been operating with vastly diminished funds from the US, its biggest donor, which affects its ability to provide the comprehensive help – food, shelter, healthcare and education – needed to keep people alive.

Of course, during the Cold War, there was an assumption that refugees from the East would be permanently resettled in the West. After the Cold War, the focus shifted to creating the conditions to enable refugees to go home. Nowadays, the route to the desirable permanent solution – going home – is largely blocked. Fewer than 2 per cent of the world's refugees return to their country of birth. That most refugees live in camps now is a myth. As Paul Collier has shown in his important book *Refuge*, most refugees live in huts, hovels and tents, are largely cut off from one another, and are typically banned from working in the countries in which they reside – a result of concern from locals, particularly in the developing world, who fear that their chances of jobs and decent wages will be undercut by incomers.[6]

But, because the current international system for assisting refugees is based on these three long-outdated assumptions, it still focuses on providing emergency 'first aid' when, in fact, the real challenge is to empower refugee families economically. Given that the average age of exile is nineteen and that the reality is the exiled person will not be going home soon, if at all, simply providing food, shelter and clothing is hardly even a start. The ideal, just goal has to be the restoration of personal independence through creating the means to survive – the acquisition of language skills, training for work and employment. As UN special envoy for global education, I have tried to help governments who are now hosting large populations of refugees – Bangladesh, for example, with Rohingya people displaced from Myanmar, and Uganda, with its Sudanese newcomers – to devise education programmes and long-term thinking about healthcare and employment opportunities needed to give hope to the millions forcibly displaced from their own country and, where possible, help them find a way back home.

Delivering a new deal for the world's displaced millions, whether displaced in their own country or forced far from home, is vital. But they are not the only people in need of emergency humanitarian assistance.

Since the turn of the century, the demand for humanitarian aid has multiplied. In 2005, 40 million people needed this life-saving aid, at a cost of $5 billion. However, UN-coordinated appeals now have to cover 160 million people and, while the total funding received for UN-coordinated appeals was $18.6 billion in 2020 (a record high, up from $17.6 billion in 2019 and $15.2 billion in 2018), this was just over half of its target. the first time since 2016 that the share had dipped below 60 per cent.[7] In 2021, $35 billion is needed, which will reach 100 million people.[8] So to cover all basic needs – food, shelter, healthcare and education – the international community offers, on average, $0.60 worth of help a day to the typical refugee. No one should be asked or expected to survive on such a sum. The 60 million who will not receive any help at all are the other victims of this shortfall.

The last thing they need is abandonment and 'storage' in squalid settings. What we must offer them is hope and opportunity through them gaining personal skills, training and employment. And, to its great credit, the humanitarian programmes of all the agencies of the UN, through mass engagement and cooperation, did manage to reach 100 million recipients across the world in 2020, including 10 million homeless Yemenis, 7.4 million people inside Syria and nearly 6.5 million South Sudanese, covering, in the past ten years, 20 million poor people in those three countries alone. UNICEF provided clean water to more than 30 million, vaccinated nearly a million children against measles and offered psychosocial support to some 3.5 million children. The WFP provided food to more than 90 million people – and did so in desperate conditions, as in Yemen, where they had a budget of only

$0.40 per person per day. And the UN itself has also enhanced its capacity to act immediately when a crisis hits. Its Central Emergency Response Fund has been increasing its resources, but it still cannot keep up with rising needs.[9]

Humanitarian aid relies year to year on the generosity of only a few nations: just eleven countries provide more than 80 per cent of humanitarian assistance and they do so mainly through generous voluntary contributions that are not guaranteed year on year and certainly cannot be guaranteed in perpetuity. For the most part, promises made by political leaders have been long on words but short on delivery.

And, as we found with health in Chapter 2, UN organisations have no guaranteed funding because the UN enjoys no guaranteed funding for most of its work. Every year, as we have discussed when examining the funding of global health, the UN Secretariat receives around $10.5 billion from its members' taxes in assessed contributions. Most of this — $8 billion — is for peacekeeping operations, with only $2.5 billion left over for all non-peacekeeping operations, including staffing, research, advisory work, diplomatic initiatives and humanitarian work. But, because the UN's humanitarian commitments cannot be met within the mere fraction of that $2.5 billion available for aid, the UN has to rely on charity. Putting it crudely, the UN passes the begging bowl around its members. This is a fundamental problem. When the UN was constituted, peacekeeping was seen to be the priority and, for a time, the bills for humanitarian aid were far less than the costs of peacekeeping operations. Now, annual humanitarian needs — $30 billion plus — amount to nearly four times the $8 billion a year needed for peacekeeping.

And humanitarian leaders also have to work to overcome the current fragmentation of provision. In the now-distant 1950s, the UN's pioneering leaders created an agency for refugees, another for food, another for children, another for population, and another for displaced Palestinians — with each agency run separately and having to raise its own funding in separate appeals to governments and private donors.

Of course, the world is doing much better than it once did: in 1971, an Office of the United Nations Disaster Relief (UNDRO) coordinator was established for the first time; then, twenty years later, in 1991, that coordinator became both head of the OCHA and head of the UNDRO. The Department of Humanitarian Affairs was established shortly thereafter and then, in 1998, it was merged into the OCHA, which, from then on, became the UN's main focal point for dealing with major humanitarian disasters. So, today, while no one agency has the overall mandate or the resources, scale, reach, capacity and expertise to guarantee all the necessary support in a crisis, UN humanitarian relief is now coordinated through one body, the OCHA. However, the relief itself is often provided through various UN bodies – the High Commissioner for Refugees, the Relief and Works Agency and UNICEF – and is refined in association with the UN's own development agency, which arose from the merger of a technical initiative set up in 1949 and the Special Fund for Economic Development.

How to finance humanitarian aid

So, while humanitarian agencies valiantly raise funds year after year to cope with crisis after crisis, there is a more basic long-term challenge: can we solve the problem that the UN's founders failed to address and find a way to fund humanitarian aid and the global relief of poverty on a sustained basis? As we have seen, the UN has specific remits to address poverty, but it has limited access to resources and it was not set up as an organisation that issues bonds, levies its members for humanitarian aid or even borrows from banks. However, while the UN has a mandate to tackle poverty but lacks the resources, the World Bank has access to such resources, as well as a widely proclaimed mandate to relieve

poverty. It seems obvious that the two organisations that cooperate on so many issues should work even more closely together to
meet humanitarian needs, but here history matters. The World
Bank has a different view of its remit – not least because, in its
seventy-five years, it has pursued a different path.

The World Bank's International Development Association – its
mission to the poorest countries – emerged only at the end of
the 1950s. Until then, there had been a tug-of-war between the
UN and the World Bank – a battle between the Scandinavian-led
supporters of a UN-based approach and the US-led supporters
of the World Bank. The latter group equated UN control of aid
with third-world domination of its distribution and they wanted
aid for the poorest countries to be channelled through the one
institution they alone controlled: the World Bank.

Behind this lay nearly two decades' worth of too little thought
being given to the potential anti-poverty role of the World Bank.
When delegates were invited to the Bretton Woods Conference of
1944, which would lead to the creation of both the IMF and the
World Bank, their initial agenda mentioned only the 'possibility'
of a bank. But the bank the great powers had in mind was a bank
for the post-war 'reconstruction' of Europe, not for worldwide
development. Only at the last minute was the remit of 'development' added alongside 'reconstruction' and, even then, the
new World Bank focused on the redevelopment of war-ravaged
Western countries rather than the development of the world's
poorest countries. Indeed, the UK's key negotiator John Maynard
Keynes – who, while mortally ill, chaired the committee that
agreed the constitution of the bank – took the view that the UK,
bankrupted by war and in need of funds for reconstruction, would
be a major beneficiary.[10]

As late as the 1960s, little World Bank money was going to the
poorest countries; the world's middle-income countries were
receiving two-thirds of the bank's investments. '"Poverty" was
not part of the bank's charter or working language,' explains the

bank's official historian for that period. 'The subject was never the centrepiece of a statement by the institution during this time and its projects seemed distant from the poor . . . for the most part, the bank appeared to be unmoved by the extent and urgency of world poverty.'[11]

'By 1969,' as the official historian records, 'the "World Bank"', now under the former US defence secretary Robert McNamara, 'had become a bank for poor countries.' On its twentieth anniversary, the bank stated that its principal mission was 'the development of "the economically less developed countries"', the first time that 'it was clearly referring to poor countries, not the undeveloped resources of an Australia or Norway'.[12]

But, even then, as a further review of the bank's role explains, support for some of the world's poorest citizens – the displaced millions in conflict hotspots – was still a minimal part of the bank's programmes. In fact, the author of this review reported that no one then working in the relief and rehabilitation programmes of Liberia, Kurdistan or the former Yugoslavia could be heard to question: 'Where is the bank?'[13] As the premier wholesaler of development assistance, better known for the controversy over structural adjustment, the bank's absence seemed to be taken for granted. Yet, by the time Timor-Leste's struggle for independence burst onto the world scene in the late 1970s, a bank team was in the vanguard of the 'recovery wave'. Indeed, under the presidency of Jim Wolfensohn from 1995 to 2005, the bank came to the aid of the displaced of Bosnia, Palestine and post-war Iraq.[14] Looking back over that decade, a review of bank lending reported that 16 per cent of its funds were now tied up in the post-conflict reconstruction of Afghanistan, Iraq and other countries.

But, given the dramatic escalation of need, it was not enough. Getting the World Bank more involved has been important; ensuring we get the right balance of provision for the future is a whole other challenge. At the World Humanitarian Summit in

2015, a 'grand bargain' was agreed linking all the agencies to a common plan. The idea was that, through more frequent use of cash transfers, a greater focus on displaced families' health and education, and an enhanced emphasis on local management of need and private sector collaboration, all the major development institutions would accord a new priority to humanitarian assistance. And private, voluntary and public agencies have worked more closely in partnership as a result. In the past year, in addition to the billions that multilateral organisations spent on humanitarian assistance, NGOs spent $7.9 billion, the Red Cross $2 billion and other public sector organisations $1.5 billion – all of which sounds like a lot and is indeed progress, but, in truth, is still far too little to respond adequately to emergencies.

And with some countries now cutting assistance even as the humanitarian crisis accelerates, an updated bargain is urgently required. As Mark Lowcock has said, we have to do better than waiting for disaster to strike – be that from wars, earthquakes, floods, storms, famine or disease – before handing around the begging bowl with appeals for funds bringing in the much-needed cash months after emergency support has been called for. Instead, the world needs to plan to anticipate disaster. For example, the Caribbean Catastrophe Risk Insurance Facility offers policies to twenty-one Caribbean states for tropical cyclones, earthquakes and excess rainfall events, and the African Risk Capacity fund, an African Union-led financial entity, shares the risk of severe drought through a continent-wide pooling of risk. While a World Bank pandemic insurance facility has been found wanting in the face of COVID-19 – too slow, too small and too cumbersome – it is possible to envisage insurance providing more effective long-term protection.

As noted earlier, in an ideal world, funding for humanitarian operations should come from a levy of member states. But, to meet today's needs, that would require a four-fold increase in the UN levy to at least $40 billion. The US contributes 22 per cent of UN funds and would be required to pay an extra $6 billion. The UK, Germany, France and China pay around 5 per cent, so would be required to pay an extra $1.5 billion each. And that is before we consider the higher contributions urgently needed to pay for global health – so other options have to be explored. As discussed in Chapter 2, we should consider whether the privilege of permanent Security Council membership, membership of other organisations like the G20 or seats on the boards of the IMF or the World Bank should incur a greater obligation to contribute more to the financing of humanitarian assistance and other global public goods.

Another possibility is for the UN to issue a perpetual bond or, as I explored in Chapters 2 and 5 discussing the funding of health and education, the creation of special purpose vehicles, based on guarantees from donor countries, to address specific emergencies. The mobilisation of private finance was at the heart of the Addis Ababa proposals for the financing of the SDGs. A new approach should focus on a closer partnership between the UN and the one global organisation capable of raising substantial additional resources on a sustained basis: the World Bank. As I explain below, the World Bank should be recapitalised to play a bigger part in financing what is an important part of any remit to end poverty – the proper funding of refugee and humanitarian work.

Sustainable Development Goals

In 2000 and again in 2015 the international community committed itself to anti-poverty goals that were comprehensive, achievable and ambitious – and not for the first time. Since the 1980s the world's governments have been convening summits and embracing targets ranging from the eradication of hunger to universal education and the elimination of killer diseases. Results have invariably fallen short of ambition. During the 1980s, progress in many of the poorest countries stalled because of debt and economic slowdown. The 1990s marked a better decade for human development, especially the reduction of extreme poverty, and progress accelerated after 2000. While the Millennium Development Goals (which set target for 2015 against a 1990 baseline) were not achieved, there was a step-change in the pace of advance, partly driven by debt relief, aid, the creation of global health funds, and a strengthened focus on poverty at the World Bank. Even so, the gap between ambition and achievement was a reminder that the human condition fell far short of the possible. Will it be different under the SDGs – the most comprehensive set of targets ever adopted by the international community?

The SDG targets, agreed in 2015 to be implemented by 2030, include the elimination of extreme poverty, the universal right to education, the ending of avoidable maternal and infant mortality, and attainment of gender equality. Targets were set and deadlines were agreed, but, of course, none of these SDGs can be realised without transforming the prospects of the 70 million refugees and forcibly displaced people. Moreover, this group comprises only a fraction – around 10 per cent – of the world's very poor, so any discussion of poverty cannot ignore an even wider question, one that takes us beyond humanitarian aid: how do we finance adequately and recurringly the SDGs to which the whole international community is committed?

Everywhere I have travelled in Africa and Asia, I have been shocked by the scale of the poverty, deprivation and destitution I have witnessed. Year after year, the international community has passed resolutions, agreed plans, made promises and pledged money to bring an end to these evils. The deadline for the current SDGs is not far off – 2030 – but I am struck not only by the gap between the promises we have made and the reality on the ground, but also by the chasm between what we have achieved and what, through our scientific and technical expertise, we are capable of achieving.

Of course, real progress in extreme poverty reduction has been made. Two billion men, women and children were still in extreme poverty in 1990. By 2018, the number was 650 million. For decades, extreme poverty – measured in 2011 as a purchasing power of $1.90 or less per day, which is clearly not enough to cover the local prices paid for food – was falling at an unprecedented rate. The world saw a decline in extreme poverty from 94 per cent in 1820, to 75 per cent in 1900, to 50 per cent, which was achieved by the 1980s. From then, we witnessed further spectacular falls: to 40 per cent by 1990, 30 per cent by 2000, and 10 per cent by 2010.[15] Much of the progress has been driven by rapid economic growth, especially in East Asia. Sub-Saharan Africa has fared less well on this front, with demography and slow economic growth combining to leave more people in poverty today than in 2000. One of the standout lessons from this period is that inequality and the distribution of wealth matter for poverty reduction. As Martin Ravallion and others have shown, rising inequality in China slowed the rate of poverty reduction after 2000, while falling inequality in Brazil had the opposite effect.[16]

Now, in more than half of the countries of the world, the share of the population in extreme poverty is less than 3 per cent. In countries like Ethiopia, India, Indonesia and Ghana, where more than 50 per cent of the population lived in extreme poverty only a generation ago, poverty has more than halved. One in seven Latin Americans were in extreme poverty before 2000; now that has fallen to one in twenty-five. And both the biggest countries – India and China – have made impressive progress on absolute poverty since 2000, when both had more than 40 per cent of their populations in poverty. In India, the figure is now 12 per cent; in China, just 0.7 per cent (officially zero).

And, at the same time, we have seen around the world the biggest social change in centuries: the rise of a global middle class. Seventy years ago, 90 per cent of the global middle class lived in Europe and North America, nearly half of them in the US alone.

By 1980, 1 billion of the world's population and then 2 billion by 2000 were assessed as being middle class – defined conservatively by the World Bank as those with a daily income above $10. The latest data from 2014 showed 2.5 billion living above $10 per day, including half a billion above $50 per day. Brookings researchers believe that the global middle class could now be 3.8 billion strong, which would mean that, for the first time ever, the global middle class constitutes a majority of the world's population.[17] However, we should not confuse the global middle class with the middle class of advanced economies. People living on less than $10 a day are often one major recession or one health emergency away from falling back into extreme poverty, especially in countries lacking safety nets.

Clearly the greatest advance of the new global middle class is in China, which, since 1978, has lifted 740 million of its rural poor out of extreme poverty. Indeed, 20 per cent of the global middle class now lives in China and one-third of the country's population – around 500 million – has an income at or above $10 a day (2011).[18] Projections indicate that while China will see its population dip, two-thirds – around 1 billion people – will be middle class by 2030. Of course, China still has a high level of in-country inequality – as high as that of the US – but comparative demographics determine that, by then, 25 per cent of the world's middle class will be Chinese. Just one-third of Indians will be middle class, by that date, though that 500 million figure will still be a substantial increase from 120 million today. Africa lags behind. Even in 2030, with 60 per cent of the world's population likely to be defined as middle class, just 10 per cent – fewer than 200 million – will be African and 1.8 billion out of 2 billion Africans will still be living on daily incomes below $10 PPP (2011).

Hans Rosling, whose posthumously published book *Factfulness* is full of masterful insights on development, suggests that we must abandon the traditional assumption of a global rich–poor divide in favour of a four-dimensional split: the 1 billion on less than $2 (the threshold below which, 200 years ago, 85 per cent of the world's population lived); the 3 billion on less than $8; the 1 billion on between $8 and $32; and then the 1 billion above $32.[19]

From figures such as these, writer Steven Pinker draws an optimistic conclusion: 'Numbers show that, over the past seven decades, humans have become (on average) longer-lived, healthier, safer, richer, freer, fairer, happier and smarter, not just in the West but worldwide.'[20] And we can quote Barack Obama when he said that: 'If you had to choose a moment in history to be born . . . you'd choose right now.'[21]

But the real question is, with all our resources and with the benefit of scientific knowledge, technical expertise, technological progress and our amassed experience of what works, are we doing as well as we could? Progress – defined as nothing more or less than 'the accumulated fruits of humans trying to solve problems and succeeding' – is, Pinker says, an indisputable historical fact, not because it was inevitable – it was not – but because of 'the concerted application of reason, science and humanism':

> If poverty, disease and conflict are natural, not unnatural, parts of the human condition . . . the progress we have enjoyed has come from empowering the better angels of our nature . . . These gifts were amplified by ideas and institutions advocated during the Enlightenment and entrenched after the Second World War: reason, science, liberal democracy, declarations of rights, a free press, regulated markets, institutions of international cooperation.[22]

And he sees no reason that such progress should not continue:

> Many of its drivers are not going away. Science and medicine continue to explore their endless frontiers and should keep

delivering increments of understanding that lengthen and enrich our lives. It is true that the ideal of reason is under assault by fundamentalism, fake news, and conspiracy theories, as it always has been. But the reach of reason is also expanding through online resources for education and fact-checking, and in movements for evidence-based medicine, policy and philanthropy.

As illustration of this progress, Pinker singles out growing life expectancy. This averaged only fifty-three years fifty years ago, but now averages seventy-two years. Even in low-income countries, life expectancy is now sixty-two years where, half a century ago, it was little more than half that. Nigerians, for example, now have a life expectancy of fifty-three years, compared with thirty-seven previously.[23]

But is Pinker right to claim that we are continuing to do so well or is he simply complacent? The answer to that question may be 'both'. That the human condition today, as measured by indicators on health, income, poverty and education, is better than at any time in human history is self-evident. But that fact does not merit the development euphoria encouraged by Pinker. Surely the real measure of human progress must be whether or not the human condition, and especially the condition of the most disadvantaged, is commensurate with our wealth, technology, knowledge and – above all – our ethical standards.

Nelson Mandela once remarked that the real measure of any country's moral standing is not its wealth, but the condition of its children. Pinker rightly highlights the worldwide reduction in child mortality since 1950, when nearly 15 per cent of newborns died before their fifth birthday compared to 5 per cent today, as a hallmark of progress. India itself has seen a fall from 25 per cent to 4 per cent. Child mortality in Africa almost halved from 15 per cent as recently as 2000 to 8 per cent now, saving millions of young lives, and in Egypt to less than 3 per cent today. These are gains we should celebrate. But we should also lament the political and moral failures that leave 5 million children dying before their fifth birthday, most of them from infectious diseases that could be prevented or treated with simple interventions taken for granted in the rich world. Progress towards eradicating malnutrition, which is implicated in half of child deaths, has been glacial.

Childhood pneumonia illustrates perhaps more powerfully than any other disease the gap between our achievement and our potential as human community. This year, around 800,000 children will lose their lives to pneumonia, now the biggest infectious killer of children. Almost all of these deaths will happen in the world's poorest countries. Most of them will occur among the most disadvantaged children. That's because pneumonia, which is closely linked to malnutrition, is the ultimate disease of poverty. And here is the real measure of the gap between where we are and where we should be: the vast majority of childhood pneumonia deaths could be prevented through vaccination, or treated with antibiotics costing less than $0.80 and, in more severe cases, medical oxygen. Put differently, almost all of these deaths are preventable. Yet deaths are coming down far too slowly for the world to achieve the SDG ambition of ending preventable childhood deaths by 2030. Look at the world through the eyes of a child threatened with pneumonia rather than through Pinker's metrics and you might have a less Panglossian view of the record on human development.

From a moral perspective, you might also ask questions about inequality. Whatever our views may be on the distribution of income and wealth (more on this below), we should never accept inequalities in for example the chances of child survival. Most people would rightly regard as morally abhorrent the proposition that a child born into the poorest 20 per cent of a population should face a risk of mortality twice as high as a child born into the richest 20 per cent. Yet that is the reality of the world we now live in. Indeed, if child death rates among the poorest 20 per cent were reduced to those of the richest 20 per cent, we would save over 2 million young lives between now and 2030. So while improvements in living standards may make it look as if we have never done better when we look at the changes in living standards, poverty and health over the last 30 years, the gap between where we are and where we should be, given our scientific expertise and knowledge of what can be achieved, has never been wider – and the number of avoidable deaths is the most poignant human measure of underperformance.

Shifting the goalposts

The crisis has set back our ambitions for poverty eradication. When the World Bank and others set out the SDGs in 2015, they predicted that all but 400 million would escape extreme poverty by 2030. By 2020, that had been recalculated upwards to 500 million, but UNICEF and Save the Children believe that the global downturn in economic growth has already left an additional 100 million children destitute, pushing the best estimate for the total number of extreme poor in 2030 to something in the order of 700 million.[24]

But, even before COVID-19, progress on abolishing extreme poverty was too poor to achieve the 2030 target – and was slowing down. In the first decade of the new century, poverty was falling at almost 4 per cent a year – a pace without precedent in human history and twice the rate registered in the 1990s – but the rate of poverty reduction has slowed. At its peak, an average of two persons per second were leaving poverty; just before the pandemic, the average was one person per second; and the prediction for 2021 was one person every two seconds exiting poverty. Now we are moving backwards, more than 200 million off target, and indeed the 'great reversal' may be under way as the numbers of poor grow yet again.[25]

And, when we look at the trends in extreme poverty in more

detail, we find that not every region of the world experienced progress, even in the good years. The immediate cause of our new assessment of 700 million poor in 2030 is the unemployment and deprivation caused by the COVID-19-induced recession, as millions of people have been forced into unemployment and many more have been hit by illness with no social protection. But the longer-term barrier to progress is our inability to reverse slow growth and thus eradicate some of the most extreme inequalities: a failure compounded by the weight of population pressures in Sub-Saharan Africa, where poverty numbers have been rising for some time.

In 1990, more than a billion of the extremely poor lived in China and India. During the past three decades, the concentration of the world's poorest has shifted from East Asia in the 1990s to South Asia in the 2000s and now to Sub-Saharan Africa. According to World Bank forecasts, 87 per cent of the world's poorest are expected to be located in Sub-Saharan Africa by 2030. That means that, even ten years from now, between 500 million and 600 million Africans, half of them children, will still be living below the $1.90 a day threshold.[26] By 2030, on one estimate from the Overseas Development Institute, African children will account for almost half of all extreme poverty, as measured by the $1.90 indicator.[27]

But how adequate is that measure today?

For, while it is true that the world has made tremendous progress towards reducing 'extreme poverty', holding the dividing line between being poor and not being poor at $1.90 a day remains difficult to justify. Lifting yourself above the World Bank's poverty line of $1.90 per day does not banish your poverty and certainly will not, by 2030, remove the risk of destitution if around 30 per cent of the world's population – more than 2 billion of our fellow citizens – still only have between $2 and $10 a day.

Dollar thresholds also systematically underestimate the higher costs of goods and services consumed by the poor. We have to set today's figure of 'around 600 million poor' against the UN Food and Agriculture Organization's calculation – almost certainly also an underestimate – that, in 2019, at least 687 million people did not consume enough calories to sustain even 'minimal' human activity.[28] Other estimates suggest that 2.1 billion suffer from hunger or malnutrition and 1.5 billion do not consume enough calories to sustain 'normal' human activity and are thus, by definition, food-deficient or food-insecure. It would, therefore, be wrong to assert that there are fewer people who are 'poor' than there are people going hungry or malnourished. And, based on current trends, it will clearly take some time for the poorest – almost certainly the world's 200 million subsistence farmers struggling with low-yield crops, half of whom are in parched, drought-prone lands in Sub-Saharan Africa – to escape extreme poverty.

The economist David Woodward put it graphically: the $1.90 measure of extreme poverty implies that a very basic minimum wage – like £10 an hour – is generous enough that it could provide sufficient daily income to a breadwinner to cover all the needs of up to forty people. And that £10 per hour would be the sole income, 'with no benefits of any kind, no gifts, borrowing, scavenging, begging or savings to draw on', since all these potential sources of income are included when calculating the $1.90 a day threshold. Not surprisingly, the World Bank has accepted that the $1.90 figure is too meagre to be used as the reference point. So, if we take thresholds for poverty in lower middle-income countries – at nearly twice the figure, $3.20 a day – and for upper middle-income countries – at three times the figure, $5.50 a day – at least 2.4 billion and up to 3.4 billion people would be assessed as being in poverty today.[29]

An even more robust definition, one that covers what is necessary for achieving basic standards in nutrition, would place the poverty threshold at $6.70 a day, four times the World Bank minimum.[30] Other surveys, which take into account the costs of clothing and shelter, would set the poverty threshold even higher. If, says another expert, we are to cut infant mortality and set a minimum income conducive to normal human life expectancy, the figure should be $7.40, though the New Economics Foundation has called for $8 and Lant Pritchett and Charles Kenny have made a case for setting the global poverty threshold at the level that constitutes the US's poverty line – $15 a day – which would suggest a worldwide total of 5 billion poor people.[31] But, if we were to seek a consensus on the minimum needed to achieve basic nutrition and normal human life expectancy, including the reduction of infant mortality, the figure would probably be $7.40 per person per day. This would mean that about 4 billion people – nearly half the world's population – could be classed as poor, so we would have to conclude that, because of the disproportionate rise in African and Asian populations over recent years, the numbers in poverty have not fallen since the 1980s, but actually risen. As columnist Nicholas Kristof has written: 'Future generations will be baffled at our heartlessness and our indifference to suffering in impoverished countries.'[32] And, obviously, lifting individuals out of poverty cannot be achieved one by one; economies as a whole must make progress and any economy serious about reducing poverty must implement more egalitarian policies.

So an income of $1.90 a day does not even begin to eradicate extreme poverty and the world is certainly not on track to end extreme poverty by 2030. We can only conclude that the continued focus on the $1.90 a day poverty threshold is blinding us to the reality, which is that millions of people no longer classified as poor by the official figures are losing out and will continue to lose out if our complacency is not challenged. So we need greater awareness of poverty as a problem and a rigorous assessment of what we can do about it.

Any analysis of how today's richest countries managed to leave extreme poverty behind would emphasise one central point: we need to acknowledge the importance of social protection policies at the heart of any anti-poverty strategy. Global poverty would be much higher if there were no welfare support, as 36 per cent of people – and, in some countries, more than 40 per cent – escape absolute poverty thanks to benefits they receive through some social safety net provision. But, in low-income countries, according to the World Bank, only a small minority do. Just 18 per cent of the poorest sections have any coverage at all. Even in lower middle-income countries, fewer than 50 per cent of poor people can count on there being any social protection and hardly any of them have social insurance. We can conclude that more than 80 per cent of workers in Sub-Saharan Africa and in less developed countries have no access to any programmes for social protection, as Sub-Saharan African countries only spend an average of $16 per citizen annually on social safety net provision.[33] One of the key SDGs is to achieve, by 2030, substantial social protection for the vulnerable. But, even now, countries in the developing world devote less than 2 per cent of their national incomes to social protection. Long-term measures that establish social protection systems, including pensions and child benefits, and build on the successes of cash transfers – a proven mechanism for alleviating poverty – in sixty countries will help in addressing the underlying drivers of hunger, destitution and child stunting.

So fortunate have Europeans been to enjoy welfare states for almost 100 years that we take for granted how important it is to have a system of provision for the sick, the unemployed, the disabled and the elderly, paid for from social insurance and general taxation, and how urgent it is to extend this to continents where, even in 2021, welfare provision is negligible. An examination of the spread of welfare provision shows how far middle-income countries like India, China and Indonesia, as well as low-income countries, have to travel. India in 2021 is richer than 1880s Germany, but, even now, its 1.4 billion citizens do not have a pension or welfare system that is in any way comparable to Germany's 140 years ago. Indonesia in 2021 now richer than the US of the 1930s, but its 200 million citizens receive nowhere near the levels of social protection that US citizens enjoyed in that bygone decade. China is now richer than the UK of the 1940s, but its 1.5 billion people do not enjoy universal free healthcare on a scale introduced by the UK over seventy years ago. Indeed, China devotes only 6 per cent of its national income on all forms of social protection expenditure, with India even further behind, spending only 3 per cent.[34]

Today, 830 million of the world's people have no clean water. One billion have no proper sanitation. Malnutrition – a close companion of poverty – is rising, too. According to the UN, the number of chronically hungry people increased by an estimated 130 million in 2020 to more than 800 million – about six times the total number of COVID-19 cases to date. And child malnutrition levels are falling far too slowly to prevent deaths from hunger. Moreover, malnutrition carries other non-mortal but nonetheless devastating consequences in the first 1,000 days of a child's life: increasing the risk of low birth weight and health problems; compromising the immune system; and permanently damaging cognitive development.

When he was World Bank president, Jim Kim, who originally qualified in medicine, set himself the objective of ending stunting – the failure to achieve normal child growth and development. Yet the rate of success in doing so is now slowing dramatically. We reduced stunting from an estimated 36 per cent of children in 2000 to 25 per cent today, but – in a decade when, with our increased awareness, knowledge and medical expertise, we should be making the greatest progress – we are likely to be doing only a third as well now. Save the Children estimates that we are likely to see only a 4 per cent reduction by 2030, with one in five of the world's children and one in three in Sub-Saharan Africa showing stunted growth.[35]

Inequality

We cannot ignore inequality. The Pinker thesis becomes more controversial when he says we should not worry about inequality. He underestimates the importance of what should be the third dimension of an anti-poverty strategy: the need to address the inequality of outcomes in one generation that limits equality of opportunity in the next and has, as most economists now agree, become a barrier to economic growth and employment, as well as being socially divisive. The Pinker view is, simply put, that we should not bite the hand that feeds us and that the very same forces delivering immense wealth to the richest, such as entrepreneurship, are also, he argues, eradicating poverty. 'For all the obsession with inequality over the past decade or so, it really is not a fundamental dimension of human well-being,' he argues:

> If Bill Gates has a house that is 30 times the size of mine, it still doesn't affect how I live my life; unless you assume that there is a fixed pot of money and the more some people have, the less others have. What matters morally is not inequality but poverty: how well people are at the bottom. If you can see your child survive, can take vacations or sample the world's culture, and are adequately fit, those are the world's primary goods. But whether you do that to the same [degree] as someone else is really incidental.[36]

This conclusion combined dubious moral principles with questionable arithmetic. There is clearly no simple, universal yardstick for establishing an ethically proper limit to inequality. Some wealth inequality is inevitable – and a desirable spur to innovation. Yet from Plato onwards philosophers have recognised that there is a limit to the level of acceptable inequality. John Rawls invited us to view wealth distribution from behind a 'veil of ignorance' with respect to where we might be placed in that distribution, effectively cautioning against the idea that extreme inequality did not matter. Most religious and moral systems recognise that the distribution of both wealth and opportunity is a matter for ethical concern.

But inequality also matters for the SDGs. Consider two simple illustrations. First, if our aim is to eliminate extreme poverty, then two key variables are paramount: the rate of economic growth and the share of any increment to growth captured by people living below the poverty line. While economic growth may act as a tide that lifts all boats, in societies marked by extreme inequality some boats will rise faster than others – and some boats will be left anchored and sinking. The fastest route to poverty eradication is redistribution with economic growth. An obvious inference is that policymakers need to focus on the levers with the potential to facilitate redistributive growth, including cash transfers, safety nets, social investment in health and education, the removal of discriminatory barriers, and progressive taxation.

Second, reflect on our earlier child mortality example. On a global scale, children in the poorest 20 per cent account for almost 40 per cent of childhood mortality. It follows that interventions successfully targeting this group will, other things being equal, accelerate progress towards the eradication of child mortality more rapidly than equivalent interventions for children born into the wealthiest 20 per cent. Here, too, achieving convergence in opportunities for survival has implications for policy. Far too often, health spending in developing countries is skewed towards hospitals and treatments that are out of reach for the poorest children. Focusing on 'the last mile' for vaccination, investing in primary healthcare and working towards universal health coverage holds the key to equity – and delivering on the SDG ambition.

But billions of people on less than $2, $5 or even $10 a day cannot see their child flourish, enjoy good health, take vacations or sample the world's culture. How, in fact, is anyone supposed to feed, shelter and educate their family, sample the world's culture and take vacations on $1.90 per person per day? And how can we do more for these families if we do not ensure that they have a fair deal when distributing the fruits of economic growth?

Levels of inequality look difficult to justify when 80 per cent of inequality does not arise from the merit or hard work we all admire, but rather is dictated by who you were born to and where you were born – a figure confirmed in the detailed and path-breaking work of Branko Milanović and World Bank researchers.[37] If you were unlucky enough be among the 9 per cent of the world's population born into low-income countries, your typical income per head is less than $3 a day. This is in marked contrast to the good fortune of being born into the one of the world's richest countries, where incomes can average $300 a day and some can range from $1,000 to $10,000 per day.

The evident still-ugly scars of inequality – deep-rooted imbalances not just across countries, but also within countries, linked to wealth, gender and race – are in contrast with the complacency at the heart of Pinker's account. However, even he admits that there is unfairness that needs to be addressed, although he restricts this to 'societies in which the wealthy have too much political power' – which, in many countries, they clearly do.

International development assistance and other transfers from rich to poor countries – remittances, private philanthropy and foreign direct investment – add a fourth dimension to a global anti-poverty strategy. Aid itself has increased from £69 billion in 2000 to £166 billion in 2020. But we must put the figures in perspective. Currently, aid forms: 40 per cent of the income of the climate-hit island states Tuvalu and Kiribati; 30 per cent of the income of the Central African Republic and Yemen; and 20 per cent of Afghanistan's income. However, the aid received by most countries is a fraction of this: 10 per cent for Haiti; 6 per cent for Lesotho; 5 per cent for Nepal; and 3 per cent for Lebanon and Honduras.[38] And, when we look at what that means in practice, aid is worth just $0.20 a day to a Haitian in poverty, $0.40 in Nepal, and less than $1 in Lebanon – to cover not only food, shelter, healthcare and education for individuals, but also the development of these countries' infrastructures.

The shortfall between what rich countries have pledged – 0.7 per cent of their national incomes – and what is actually given – 0.3 per cent – is so big that the very poorest countries alone lose out on more than $50 billion of promised aid each year.[39] Critics will say that aid does not work, that money is wasted and that such transfers create a dependency culture rather than promoting self-sufficiency. They will also say that the continued availability of aid to developing countries discourages a necessary focus on raising domestic taxes and hampers economic growth. Far from helping the poor, aid – so the argument goes – encourages corruption among developing countries' elites and ends up transferring money from the 'the poor in rich countries to the rich in poor countries'.

Of course, aid alone cannot ensure economic progress in poor countries; sensible economic policies are at the heart of what is needed. And not all aid is offered by rich countries to poor countries in pursuit of poverty reduction. Donors often use it to advance their own national security needs, to benefit their own exporting firms or to pursue wrong-headed policies, like the 'privatise, liberalise, deregulate' agenda imposed by the IMF and the World Bank in the 1980s.

And, just as some other forms of intervention – diplomatic, military and economic – do not always work, aid itself will not always yield the results intended. But the evidence I have brought together when in government and subsequently has led me to conclude that aid has made possible huge reductions in infant and maternal mortality, the near-elimination of polio and the suppression of HIV/AIDS through the provision of otherwise unattainable life-saving drugs and treatments. Likewise, aid in support of education and social safety nets has facilitated the entry of a generation of poor children into schooling and has helped with the global reduction of poverty. All these advances would have been unaffordable had they had to be financed from domestic tax revenues; they were affordable only because of aid. And we can show that small amounts of aid have helped deliver some real successes in Africa. The experience of Ghana, Rwanda and Ethiopia is that schooling has been extended into the rural areas, new hospitals have been constructed and vaccination pro-grammes introduced. Moreover, these nations have been building their own national systems of taxation – challenging the allegation that aid will inevitably reduce incentives to raise domestic reve-nues. Aid has clearly contributed to the extraordinary progress in child survival registered by countries like Ethiopia. The real problem with aid today is not that it is ineffective, but rather that it is insufficient.

A major study of forty-seven countries from 1960 to 2000 found that a 1 per cent rise in foreign aid lifted growth in income per person by 0.1 per cent.[40] And another study, led by the World Bank and the University of Maryland, found that every 1 per cent of national income spent on aid resulted in a 0.3 per cent increase in real income per person. Additionally, the detailed evidence painstakingly brought together by eminent researchers shows that, on average, countries experience 1 per cent additional growth – often making the difference between life and death – when 10 per cent of national income is pro-vided from aid.

And, when I look at the needs that remain unmet and recall the overseas visits I have made and the people I have encountered, I can see clearly the difference that the judicious use of aid money can make and what can happen when such aid is not available.

'Why have you abandoned us?' – the five words that a young girl from Syria said to me when she was pleading for help for her country and her family, convincing me that we were doing too little, certainly not too much. This young girl had been forced out of her home in Homs; her family had been forced into exile; her disabled sister had been put out on to the streets. She was now in a shack in Lebanon, her family needed food, shelter and medicine for her sister – and she wanted to go to school.

The double-shift schools system we pioneered with Kevin Watkins of Save the Children – local children learning from early morning in French and English and then refugees learning from late afternoon in Arabic – enabled, at its peak, 300,000 Syrian refugees to go to school. Who could argue that the cost of $10 a week per child was an inefficient use of aid money? But, even when we proved that the scheme worked, we could not raise the extra £100 million needed for Lebanon to have been able to educate all young Syrian refugees. Some 200,000 children missed out – not because there were no schools for them to attend or because there were not enough teachers, but because of a shortage of aid. And those who protest about the cost of aid and allege its ineffectiveness ignore the fact that, when we combine the available resources of all the world's donors and agencies, aid provides developing countries with, as I showed at the start of the education chapter, less than $15 per child per year for their schooling – hardly an overgenerous contribution. Furthermore, all aid taken together offers less than $2 a year per African child for immunisation. Small wonder then that, despite its obvious needs, Sierra Leone has just one health worker for every 5,000 people (we in the UK have one for every seventy-seven). The number of doctors, nurses and midwives covering a population as big as Scotland and bigger than Ireland is no more than 750. When the aid the world offers is so small and the needs of others are so great, can we really say that our aid budgets are overgenerous?

Reversing trends

But aid is there not for its own sake but to advance development – and the ultimate test is not whether we have provided
first aid but whether we have enabled an escape from poverty
and helped deliver a path out to prosperity. We know that aid
that is worth around $150 billion a year can, on its own, cover
only a fraction of what is estimated to be the $2 trillion cost
of achieving our SDGs. So, aid has to be used as an incentive
and, at times, also a lever to encourage in additional forms of
investment. Back in 2014, a joint report from the IMF, World
Bank and the UN envisaged the need for 'a paradigm shift' on
development finance that would 'catalyze and leverage' aid.
The report recognised that philanthropy, worth $500 billion
annually, and remittances, worth $400 billion a year, are,
like $150 billion of aid, a welcome start but, unless they are
deployed alongside other investments, they can only take us so
far. So the report envisaged that some of the world's $85 tril-
lion pool of professionally managed money, including pensions
and insurance funds, could be marshalled through specialised
SDG-linked funds targeted at achieving anti-poverty goals:
green bonds; impact-linked allocations within general funds
and – for maximum anti-poverty results – social impact bonds
where reward is linked to results. The arithmetic is compelling:
if just 20 per cent of the $100 trillion invested in the global stock
market was subject to measurable tests as to whether and by how
much it was advancing the SDGs; and if similarly targeted green
and social bonds accounted for 10 per cent of the $80 trillion
bond market, and such investments formed 10 per cent of private equity's $4 trillion investment pool and 30 per cent of the
$1 billion venture capital and real estate private equity pools,
then the $30 billion we need to invest to deliver SDGs by 2030
would be within sight. Nearly 2,000 asset owners and managers,
who together control around $80 trillion, have signed up to the

Principles for Responsible Investment, which commit them to making socially useful investments, and social impact bonds, the brainchild of Sir Ronald Cohen, will make investment in programmes that help relieve poverty; but the pace of progress is far too slow and once COVID-19 is fully under control it is essential that we refocus the investment community's attention to how we can progress this mobilisation of private finance to meet our 2030 deadline.

A Marshall Plan for Africa

It is Africa that has the greatest needs. As things stand, Africa is the only continent that has not begun to converge in any substantive way with the rest of the world. As the world's poor become ever more concentrated in the continent, it will need more than our immediate rescue plan: it will need a programme for long-term economic development, an African version of the 1940s Marshall Plan that revived Europe. But its starting point will be different. Questioning the impact of aid and investment on Africa, economists often ask why the first Marshall Plan – the US's post-war economic reconstruction plan, which devoted 4 per cent of US national income for four years to stimulating European economic recovery – succeeded, while a very much bigger transfer to Sub-Saharan Africa, over many more years and from many countries, has failed to register similar results in assisting the development of Africa. But to make that comparison is to fail to understand history. Europe was repairing an infrastructure and skills base that had been built up over centuries, drawing on decades of investment and know-how, but most of Africa and Asia had none of these assets to start with. Indeed, history explains why there are so many barriers to success. Africa's imperialist rulers did not build the internal road and rail systems needed to link Africa's forty-four countries and to create a thriving internal marketplace. Instead, they chose to focus on connecting Africa to ports that would export raw materials out of Africa to the rest of the world – a then-customary policy of exploitation. So a new type of Marshall Plan for Africa requires more than investments in battered infrastructure. It requires us to build, often from scratch. Africa's roads, rail, energy and telecommunications alone need between $130 billion and $170 billion of new investment – over twice what is currently being planned.

But, with huge mineral supplies, resources, a youthful population, an Internet revolution under way and plans for integrating the continent's economy, Africa can make progress during the twenty-first century, so I want to close this chapter by outlining what I see as its possibilities that arise from a comprehensive plan drawn up, of course, in Africa but with the support of all advanced economies. Already Africa is developing its own common market: first a free-trade area, then regional – and, perhaps over time, pan-African – customs unions, single markets and even currency unions. And Africans aren't unenterprising. According to the African Development Bank, one in five members of Africa's working-age population starts their own business – the highest start-up rate in the world.[41] But underinvestment in Africa is so acute that the continent – which now has 12 per cent of the world's population and will soon have 20 per cent – sees only 1 per cent of the world's manufacturing, and 1 per cent of foreign direct investment, is home to just 1 per cent of advanced computing services and turns out little over 1 per cent of global graduates. Add to this the fact that its education and social security systems are 100 years behind those of the West and its healthcare systems probably fifty years behind, and it is clear that urgent action is needed.[42]

While aid can never be a substitute for the difficult decisions required to generate domestically generated growth, it can be a spur to the growth that is urgently needed. The Sub-Saharan region will have to create productive jobs at twice today's rate – so at an average of about 20 million each year – to absorb new entrants into the labour force. This is because of population growth. It is a continent whose population will double by 2100, and the region's working-age population will soon exceed that of China – 600 million in 2030 – with a youth share of nearly 40 per cent or 230 million. Africa's fertility rate remains high at 4.4 (only South Africa, at 2.3, is at Western levels). Indeed, unless the economy grows at around 7 per cent annually, it will not be able to absorb the expected additions to the labour force, not least because in recent pre-COVID-19 years, when economic growth averaged 5 per cent, it did not translate into the sustained creation of decent jobs.

Again, the economic and social contexts may dominate the scope for individual opportunity. An estimated 90 per cent of new jobs are still to be found in the low-productivity low-wage informal sector. But, if the gap between the opportunities available and the aspirations of youth is the result of both low growth and a slow demographic transition to lower fertility, there is also a gap between the skills the economy needs and those that school leavers possess.

Across Africa, investment in energy and power is desperately needed and could transform the lives of millions. While the Aswan Dam – which captures the world's longest river, the Nile – produces enough power for about 15 per cent of Africa's needs, the proposed 40-gigawatt Grand Inga Dam on the Congo River in the Democratic Republic of Congo could produce almost three times that amount: 40 per cent of Africa's energy needs. This transformational project is now indefinitely on hold because the investment required has risen from $80 billion to $160 billion.

Africa's tax base is too small to generate the investment it needs and create the social safety net it lacks. Indeed, in 2018, while South Africa's tax-to-GDP ratio stood at 25 per cent, Kenya's ratio was only 16 per cent, Ghana's and Ethiopia's were 11 per cent and oil-rich Nigeria's was only 10 per cent. As a result, the whole of Africa averaged only 17 per cent – with ten countries' tax-to-GDP ratios sitting below 15 per cent and most of the tax revenue coming not from high earners, but from sales taxes paid by all. As the IMF reports, African countries need to raise tax revenues to at least 20–22 per cent of GDP – though this will require a war against tax evasion and corruption, which in turn will require the cooperation of the world's advanced economies. Sadly, Africa scores only 32/100 on the world's Corruption Perceptions Index and, when polled, 59 per cent of all Africans, across more than forty countries, thought their governments benefit only the few.[43]

Until recently, the route to higher prosperity would have been clear: travelling the well-trodden road that started in Europe, then in the US, then in South Korea, Japan and Taiwan, and then in China. It is also the same route now being followed by Vietnam, Pakistan and Bangladesh. Such progress has been based, firstly, on low-cost, low-skilled assembly work – benefiting from both a surplus of labour and its low cost – and subsequently on a shift to higher-skilled, higher value-added manufacturing production. Nowadays, however, technological advance in manufacturing means doubling production for half as many new jobs, thus creating 'premature industrialisation'.

Emerging global trends in manufacturing technology demand new patterns of production. The segmentation of global value chains into a variety of low-cost production locations and the practice of 'component assembly' demonstrate that, in Africa, the future lies in the small number of 'manufacturing enclave' enterprise zones that have sprung up within a few of its forty-four countries – as seen in Ethiopia, Mauritius, Kenya and Rwanda – rather than in highly labour-intensive mass manufacturing.

At its peak, the UK had 40 per cent of its labour force in manufacturing and mining and China had 30 per cent, while Africa has only 6.5 per cent – a figure that is not set to increase substantially, not least because African wages tend to be higher than in low-income Asian countries.

So, starting from a base like that, how can Africa leap forward by creating jobs? Should it focus on agriculture and increasing its productivity? Or on the provision of services – for example, teleservicing and other skills-led facilities – despite the fact skill levels are so poor? Or on tourism? The creative industries? A combination of all of these?

Today, agriculture employs two-thirds of the continent's working population – 200 million – and contributes 20–60 per cent of GDP, depending on the country. And it will, of course, continue to dominate employment in the low- and lower middle-income economies. However, Africa now imports significant portions of its major food staples as current agricultural practices deplete its land and degrade its vital ecosystems. And it is not the exclusivity of land ownership that is the biggest problem. Land in Africa has historically been communally owned, with almost every adult in a village having traditional access rights to some scrap of farmland. The problem is that farming is small-scale and dependent on older workers – the average age being sixty. Eight in ten African farmers are traditional smallholders: in Ghana, 85 per cent have less than 2 hectares; in Uganda, 58 per cent of farms are smaller than 1 hectare; and, in Zambia, half are smaller than 2 hectares. Additionally, technology is minimal, with hoes more likely to be used than tractors, and African countries irrigate just 5 per cent of their cultivated land, compared with the global average of around 20 per cent and the Asian average of almost 40 per cent.

With little mechanisation or deployment of modern farming techniques and minimal use of high-yielding seeds or fertilisers, land yields and output per worker will continue to remain low. But, with a yield-increasing package that includes improved seeds, fertilisers, irrigation, mechanisation and improved farm management techniques, Africa could enjoy a similar agricultural revolution to that of Asia.

Abundant labour and land resources would also encourage market-focused local manufacturing – food-processing, wood-processing, garment-making and leather production – as a prelude to moving into more complex digitised manufacturing. But all this will require prudent macroeconomic policy, access to finance for new businesses and a reduction in the very high costs of transporting goods.

Africa has approximately 30 per cent of the planet's remaining mineral reserves and could better exploit its natural resources, too, including diamonds (it has 55 per cent of the world's output), sugar, salt, gold, iron, cobalt, uranium, copper, bauxite, silver, petroleum, cocoa beans and tropical fruits – the benefits of which have too often been lost to rent-seeking, corruption, higher exchange rates and volatility. Oil may be of declining value, but Africa still has proven oil reserves of 130 billion barrels and produces one-fifth of the global total.

In most African economies, the services industry is the fastest-growing sector for both value-added production and job creation, growing by 4 per cent a year and employing more than 100 million people. And, although the information and communications technology sub-sector is relatively small – accounting for around 1 per cent of the workforce – there are well-known successes within it. World-renowned is the Kenya-based company M-Pesa, which is now the planet's biggest money-transfer system, not least because of investment in the technology by the Central Bank of Kenya. Digital advances such as these allow Africa to bypass the expensive costs of fixed lines and the many other expenditures of the pre-digital era and use mobile telephony to deliver banking, retail, healthcare and education services. However, while 97 per cent of companies in high-income countries use electronic filing or payments, the figure is only 17 per cent in Sub-Saharan Africa. And, though some 150 digital start-ups mobilised a record $1.16 billion in investment across Africa in 2018, that sum represents less than 1 per cent of global incubator funds, which is all the more notable since the vast majority – up to 90 per cent – of Africa's venture capital funding originates from outside the continent. A measure of the catch-up needed is that, in comparison with Africa, India attracted seven times as much capital ($7 billion in 2018) and China seventy times as much (a staggering $70 billion).[44]

Until COVID-19, tourism had also been rapidly expanding in countries like South Africa, Kenya and Senegal, but was still underdeveloped in many countries. Making the continent prosper will require safe access for tourists, but also the same investment in rail, road and air infrastructure that is required for the expansion of other services.

Creative industries, including arts and crafts, sports, leisure parks, gaming software and culinary facilities, amount to a $2 trillion sector – one of the most resilient and fastest growing in Africa – and have great potential for further growth as over the next few years the continent's middle-class consumers expand from 100 million to 200 million. A striking example is Nigeria's booming film industry, which is now the country's second biggest employer after agriculture, employing close to 300,000 people directly and over 1 million indirectly.[45]

As I told African leaders when I was given the privilege of addressing the African Union summit, it is time for Africa to rise. Just as Africa needs the world, the world needs Africa. And, having committed to the anti -poverty goals, the rest of the world has an obligation to work with Africa to achieve them. To not do so – or to make glacial progress – would simply encourage the extremists who say that the West will never keep its word and that our broken promises prove that coexistence between different cultures is impossible.

And any complacency should be resisted. For, as this chapter has suggested, the development issue is not how far we have come, but how far we still need to go; not how much we have achieved, but how much more potential there is yet to be developed to the benefit of us all. Our assessment of how far we fall short in this generation should be all the harsher the greater our capabilities. And, in this respect, the world has become much worse: we know what to do and yet we do not do it. Never before has there been so much avoidable suffering and preventable premature deaths. A friend of mine was at an international conference on Africa and made the point that aid should not flow from pity but from empathy — that we put ourselves in other people's shoes and imagine their pain and plight and we help them because we think about our responsibilities to each other. Her example of this was that she knew of no parent who would not do everything possible for their child out of the love we share for those born to us. However, after my friend's talk, an African delegate quietly took her aside and said one of the most devastating things I think I have ever heard: 'I can't love my children as much as you love yours in the West. I can't allow myself to, because then it would destroy me when I lose them.'

In Africa five children under five die every minute, and most infant deaths — and the deaths she was referring to — are not inevitable deaths but avoidable deaths.

That mother should not have to contemplate a world in which she cannot love her children too much because she is resigned to them suffering early deaths. That mother should not have to live in a world in which families do not, as in some African countries, register the births of their children for months because of the expectation that they are as likely to die in their infancy as survive.

Perhaps, in decades past, we had no choice but to live in a world in which there was little hope or expectation that things could get better quickly. But scientific advance, medical progress, the reach of new drugs and the development of new treatments make it possible to replace fear with hope and resignation with optimism. What is needed is the will to apply what we know. The next few years will test whether the COVID-19 crisis — during which we have all come face to face with suffering — has reinforced or diminished our commitment to help the world's poorest citizens.

And we are at a difficult juncture. For twenty years, the world's development aid budget rose and global poverty fell.

Now, however, for the first time in two decades, global poverty is rising but development aid is about to be cut. If this happens – and advanced economies cut back on aid in the midst of the biggest peacetime humanitarian crisis in a century – we will be depriving the world's most vulnerable families of food, medical treatment and schooling just as surely as if we pulled away the needle from a child waiting for vaccination, whipped away the meal from the mouth of a hungry child or locked shut the school gates on children whose human right to education we promised to uphold. If we allow this to happen, it will take decades to undo the damage. It is right to campaign alongside governments when they are doing good things, but it is also right to campaign to change the minds of governments when they are getting it wrong and to demonstrate that there is an alternative to giving up on the chance of delivering the world's anti-poverty goals.

An African slogan that has been around since the 1980s may be relevant here. The Western slogan TINA – 'There is no alternative' – was often invoked to suggest poor countries had to live with high levels of poverty and inequality and that there was no escape from the harsh medicine of 1980s-style structural reform. But, in Africa, people counterposed with THEMBA – 'There must be an alternative' – and appropriately, in Swahili, a language widely used across Africa, this acronym's first syllable, 'them', means 'hope'. And as we confront an urgent moral issue, this is pre-eminently the time for the whole world to hear and heed the warning first issued by President Kennedy: 'If a free society cannot help the many who are poor, it cannot save the few who are rich.'[46]

ABOLISHING TAX HAVENS:
THE FIRST STEP TO
TACKLING INEQUALITY

If you want to rob a bank, talk to a burglar. If you want to steal a car, ask a car-jacker what to do. And if you want to avoid paying taxes, your best advisers could be some of the world's most prestigious lawyers and accountants. And while finding those counsellors may be easy, the pains and penalties on the rest of society come at great cost. One of the main reasons that developing countries cannot afford healthcare, education and social safety nets for their poor is that they lose so much money through unpaid taxes. And the reason advanced economies struggle with debt and complaints of inequitable public services is that a few companies and individuals avoid trillions in taxes, thereby denying their fellow citizens the revenues needed to pay for essential services and amenities.

To start out to avoid or evade taxes – working with any of a great number of willing agencies – you would normally set up a shell corporation in one of the offshore havens, whose laws still protect your privacy and will prevent the full disclosure of information about ownership to domestic tax authorities. Second, again with suitable help, you would set up a bank account owned by your shell corporation in another equally discreet location – one of the countries, including the US, that has not yet committed to exchange tax information automatically. Then you would arrange to set up a company to buy 'services' from your shell corporation – which could include billing for nebulous things like 'consulting' and subsequently electronically transferring large sums of money for these 'services' to your account. Having been routed through the shell corporation and deposited in an offshore account, that money can now be invested in whatever enterprise takes your fancy.

While, in theory, the profits generated from this investment are supposed to be reported to tax authorities, in practice, that is unlikely – given the complexity and obscurity of these established systems. To find out who truly owns the investments, the authorities would first have to find a way of discovering that you own the shell company too, and then establish links between the shell company and the bank account in question. The more shell companies you add to the chain, the more complete the obfuscation and the more difficult it is for authorities to join the dots.

The complexity of this network of shell companies and offshore trusts, as well as the limited transparency attached to exchanges of information, makes tax evasion not just possible but simple. Not dissimilarly, with the help of that ever-obliging and well-remunerated army of wealth managers and accountants, multinational corporations can shift profits to low-tax havens, through networks of subsidiaries and trust funds. These are currently allowed to transact with each other on the pretence that they do so as though they are separate entities. But this is easily exploited to allow the shifting of profits through methods such as the manipulation of declared transaction prices, the payment of royalties, and the charging of interest on inter-company loans – all of which enable profits to be laundered and emerge largely or entirely tax-free at the end. As described, this could qualify as tax evasion – a crime – but, if there is no outright misrepresentation of the facts, it may also qualify as tax avoidance, which can be lawful or unlawful depending on whether the scheme 'works' for tax purposes or not.

At its heart is the achievement of the same end by similar means: a lower contribution to tax revenues than would be made without manipulation. The game in either case is the cross-border shifting of domestically generated income or profits by transacting with yourself at artificial prices so that the earnings are reported in zero- or low-tax locations instead. And, given the openness of the global economy, this form of corruption has become one of the world's biggest industries.

So, when I was prime minister, I was resolved to take decisive action to end both tax secrecy and tax fraud to take on these glaring and often criminal tax abuses by which vast amounts of money disappeared every year into secretive tax shelters. We knew that it was grand larceny on a global scale and that the revenue lost by tax authorities around the world went beyond billions of dollars. The true figure for the money that escaped tax turned out to be measured in trillions.

But I also knew that we could not succeed as one country alone: we could only do so by concerted global action. For the main reason these individuals and corporations continue to hide so much of their money and shirk their social responsibilities is our persisting failure to bring the tax havens within the ambit of international supervision, as well as our recklessness in failing to require transparency, proper disclosure and an automatic exchange of information between tax authorities.

First efforts to close tax havens

In 2009, the world economy was in free fall. Trade and manufacturing were collapsing faster than at any time since the 1929 Wall Street Crash. Unemployment was rising more rapidly than it had in the previous fifty years. In the face of this crisis, the world might have assumed that its leaders would have their sights fixed firmly and exclusively on planning a global economic recovery.

But, when the G20 met in London in April 2009 to deal with

the global financial crisis, the most divisive and controversial matter on the agenda was not how much of a financial stimulus the international community would inject into the world economy, but rather whether we would summon up the courage to take action against tax havens.

As chair of the meeting, I had identified, along with President Sarkozy, a chance to persuade the new G20 leaders that there was a great wrong that had to be righted, so we wanted to push the G20 to 'name and shame' these tax havens and then throw the full weight of the international community into tracking down and outlawing these shadowy institutions and setting up new global standards. Once agreed and enforced, these standards would ensure that countries the world over would receive the tax revenue they were due and that, in turn, their citizens would enjoy the health services, education, welfare and social safety nets they deserved. Systematic grand larceny that indulged individual and corporate greed was intolerable and had to be tackled. Who could possibly disagree?

But the atmosphere quickly became fractious. So incensed was Sarkozy at the unwillingness of some of our fellow world leaders to act on the issue that he threatened to walk out of the meeting there and then. But so, too, did the president of China, Hu Jintao, who did not want the Chinese tax haven in Macau named.[1] In his view, the G20 had assembled to discuss the way back to global economic growth and not the way forward for global tax policy. President Hu would not sign a declaration that would, in effect, identify his own country as a serial offender, guilty of condoning large-scale tax avoidance.

The main point of controversy was a list newly drawn up by the Organisation of Economic Co-operation and Development (OECD) – a group of thirty-seven, founded in 1961 and head-quartered in Paris, bringing together countries committed to democracy and the market economy in order to stimulate economic progress and world trade. The OECD had investigated the many tax havens around the world that were non-compliant or only partially compliant with international standards of reporting and transparency. Those that had refused to allow exchange of tax information were named as offenders on a colour-coded system and were labelled 'black'. Those part-way to compliance were labelled 'grey' and those in compliance were 'white'. Moving from 'black' to 'white' required a currently non-compliant nation to have signed on to at least twelve exchange-of-information agreements with neighbouring countries. What was so politically contentious was the issue of precisely which countries and regions were to be included on the 'black' and 'grey' lists.

The G20 draft communiqué included wording in support of this OECD initiative.[2] To me, this marked an important moment in international cooperation. While civil servants sitting on expert committees of the OECD had been discussing this issue in depth for some time, this was, in truth, the first time that world leaders had together formally addressed the systemic obscurities and injustices of the global tax regime.

Because the G20 included most of the world's largest economies, our meeting automatically excluded nations and entities relying heavily on their tax-haven statuses, such as Switzerland, Luxembourg, Liechtenstein and the many offshore havens. Had they been present, they too would undoubtedly have tried to block the communiqué.

But, when China stood its ground, we reached an impasse. France dug its heels in for the inclusion of China on the 'black' list, while China wanted to be excluded from that list altogether. An attempt by President Obama – attending his first G20 meeting – to broker a compromise helped ease the tension but did not bring the two sides together in an agreed communiqué.

We had agreed to continue without a breakthrough at lunchtime and, as chair of the meeting, I ploughed on with other less contentious items on the agenda. But as we resumed 'business as usual', I asked my civil servants to arrange a telephone conversation with the OECD secretary-general, Ángel Gurría, in Paris. Taking a few minutes away from the chair, I agreed with him on a compromise in which everyone would save face, but that still represented progress in the global fight against tax havens.

From London, the G20 communiqué would be issued calling for an end to tax secrecy, but it would not mention the tax reform proposals in any specific detail and, in particular, not include reference to the 'black', 'grey' and 'white' labels. But, in Paris, simultaneously with the G20 statement, the OECD, which did not include China in its membership, would name the non-compliant tax havens and indicate the measures intended to end their abuses.

So we would agree with the Chinese that the detail of tax reform was not a matter for this G20 meeting and with Sarkozy that action had to be taken. And the latter would be doubly happy as the agreement would be announced from his own country, France.

So, in April 2009, the G20 leaders declared that 'the era of banking secrecy is over'.[3] Key to this was the OECD's Global Forum on Transparency and Exchange of Information for Tax Purposes (or simply the Global Forum), which would work to deliver this in practice. For the first time and at the highest level, the non-compliance of dozens of tax havens had become a truly global concern, with leaders backing international standards on transparency and exchange of information for tax purposes. On that April day, we had triggered one of the most significant initiatives against offshore tax evasion in history. But, in the meantime, of course, and pending much further work, the offences would continue.

Very little, in my experience, rouses such anger among ordinary people and businesses as the shady world of global tax avoidance and evasion. This is a world that enables the rich and powerful to cheat the system and deprive the nations that provide them with customers, clients and capital of trillions of dollars in tax revenue. And, by taking advantage, this elite minority gains for itself additional luxuries and even more millions or billions of dollars – for reasons of greed, not need – while countries absorb the loss of revenue on the same scale: revenue that would ensure essential public services for middle- and lower-income families. And, year on year, these offences go on and on.

For obvious reasons, these offenders and the practitioners who assist them in offshore tax havens and in allegedly respectable major financial centres, too, prefer to operate in conditions of maximum secrecy and security.

However, in New York in the 1980s, an exception to that rule emerged. This focused on Leona Helmsley, who, with her husband, Harry, ran a real estate empire that was worth billions, which included the Empire State Building and the Park Lane Hotel. They flaunted their wealth, which in part depended on the miserable wages they paid their servants. Leona Helmsley was widely known as the 'Queen of Mean', but the way she treated a housekeeper at her Connecticut summer mansion proved key to her downfall. At Helmsley's 1989 trial for tax evasion, the housekeeper quoted her as saying: 'We don't pay taxes . . . Only the little people pay taxes.'[4] Helmsley was found guilty and went from decades in the lap of luxury to nineteen months in a New York prison cell. Media coverage was huge and her views on taxation undoubtedly raised awareness of great inequality in New York and probably of tax evasion worldwide.

So secretive is the world of tax havens that few members of the public are even aware of just how much they are losing out as a result of these havens' activities. But the anger expressed towards the use of tax havens is justified. They are the ultimate example of one rule for the haves and another for the have-nots.

Only by meticulous research has it been proven just how colossal the scale of this larceny is. The most up-to-date survey, 'The State of Tax Justice 2020', sets out how countries are cheated out of at least $427 billion in revenues every year.[5] Lower-income countries lose the equivalent of 6 per cent of their tax revenue whereas higher-income countries lose 2.5 per cent. Put another way, higher-income countries' tax losses are equal to 8 per cent of their public health budgets, while lower-income countries lose as much as 50 per cent of what they spend on public health. Spread across the world, an extra $60 per person a year that could be spent on health is being lost to cross-border tax abuse. But, because the available public data only allows quantification of the immediate losses due to profit-shifting of the largest multinationals and does not include all financial assets, the total revenue losses to national exchequers from cross-border tax abuse globally is, the Tax Justice Network says, likely to exceed $1 trillion.

According to French economist Gabriel Zucman, at least 8 per cent ($7.6 trillion) of the $100 trillion held in household assets is hidden away in accounts located in tax havens.[6] Other reputable researchers, such as the Boston Consulting Group, put it higher, at around 12–13 per cent of global GDP (closer to $9.9 trillion).[7] But, once non-financial assets like property are included, the figure could, according to the Tax Justice Network, be as high as 30 per cent ($30 trillion) of global GDP.[8] The common ground is that three-quarters of this hidden personal wealth is owned by the world's wealthiest 0.1 per cent, who have teams of consultants, lawyers and wealth managers navigating the waters of these complex international tax schemes. It means that tax avoidance is greatest at the very top of the global 'rich list': the wealthiest 0.01 per cent in the world evade an astonishing one-quarter of all their taxes by sequestering their money in offshore tax havens. Forty per cent of all the wealth of the UK's top 0.01 per cent is held abroad, a pattern likely to be repeated in every major economy.

There is a great number of uses to which these lost taxes could be put and the cost of failing to act on tax avoidance is even higher now than ten years ago, not only because revenue losses have become much larger, but also because the need for tax revenues – given the concurrence of a pandemic and a global recession – is ever greater. The debts of advanced countries, which averaged around 80 per cent of GDP at the end of 2019, are now expected to rise beyond 100 per cent by 2022 and, if these debts are to be reduced, governments need revenues. Developing countries and emerging markets – subject to destabilising flights of capital and facing uncertain economic futures – are struggling to fund not only their sometimes-threadbare social safety nets, but also their health and education systems. However, they have the most to gain from curbing tax avoidance and evasion and from systematic tax collection.

But, if individuals who move their wealth offshore short-change their countries of $182 billion in tax every year, the biggest offenders by far are the multinational corporations that avoid $245 billion in tax annually.[9] Global tax losses are now driven by corporate tax abuse. Lower-income countries lose the equivalent of 5.5 per cent of their tax revenue from corporate abuses, with higher-income countries losing 1.3 per cent.

For it is not just our nations' elites who engage in such accounting chicanery, but also our wealthiest corporations. Global tax losses are now driven by corporate tax abuse. One of the best-known corporate tax practices is an 'inversion', whereby corporations move their formal headquarters – their nominal headquarters on paper only – to a low-tax jurisdiction, even as their production sites, employees and customers remain in their original higher-tax locations. These are known as 'letterbox' companies: companies with few or no genuine ties to the tax jurisdictions they declare themselves headquartered in, other than a simple mailing address.

In this way, corporations can emulate the dubious practices of individuals. The favoured route is to sell themselves goods and services at inflated rates via subsidiaries that are located in tax havens. Of course, there are regulations to stop such practices – including the detailing of market or reference prices for well-understood goods and services, as well as deeming the act of charging yourself well above market rate as fraud — but, as Zucman writes:

> The issue is growing, as a rising number of international transactions within international divisions of a single company — such as the sale of proprietary trademarks, logos, and algorithms — are not replicated between third parties, and hence have no reference price. Firms can sell themselves bananas or shovels at exorbitant prices — it's been done — but the risk is high for companies that engage in such obvious fraud, as they can find themselves caught by the tax authorities, because bananas and shovels are more substantial than the electronic transfers of dubious transactions. There is nothing less risky, by contrast, than manipulating the prices of patents, logos, labels, or algorithms, because the value of these assets is intrinsically difficult to establish. This is why the giants of tax avoidance are companies of the new online economy: such as Google, Apple, and Microsoft. Taxing companies wanes to the same extent as immaterial capital gains in importance.[10]

And, as the IMF recently calculated, $600 billion may be lost to national exchequers in tax revenues through profit-shifting alone, with the OECD countries losing $400 billion and the non-OECD countries $200 billion.[11]

Google — an obvious example — has licensed its highly profitable search and advertising technology to a subsidiary in Bermuda, where the corporate tax rate is zero per cent. Google 'pays' that highly profitable subsidiary billions in royalties each year for the rights to access its own innovations. Similarly, the rights to Nike's Swoosh trademark, Uber's taxi-hailing app, Allergan's Botox patents and Facebook's social media technology have also been registered in shell companies headquartered in tax havens like Bermuda and Grand Cayman. By transferring trademarks, patent rights and other valuable but intangible assets into offshore shell companies, these companies are able to avoid billions of dollars in taxes – and in all these cases there is nothing unlawful to report.

Multinational corporations are responsible for 33 per cent of global economic output, 49 per cent of global exports and 23 per cent of global employment. By registering companies and holding assets in corporate tax havens, corporations can, Zucman and his colleagues estimate, move 40 per cent of their profits to low-tax or no-tax jurisdictions and thus pay little to no tax. Over $600 billion is shifted globally each year to lower-tax jurisdictions such as Ireland, which alone accounts for $100 billion of these profits.[12] On the basis of $1.38 trillion worth of profit shifted into tax havens each year, the Tax Justice Network can reliably estimate that multinational corporations avoid $245 billion in their tax bills.

And this is the tip of the corporate tax avoidance iceberg. According to the IMF, the indirect losses from global corporate tax abuse are at least three times larger than direct losses. So, by multiplying the Tax Justice Network's estimate of direct tax losses – $245 billion – by four, to account for indirect losses, we come close to a figure of $1 trillion in overall losses, both direct and indirect, attributable to corporate tax abuse.[13]

Tax avoidance by multinational companies – as opposed to individuals – is not a marginal activity, but rather central to the way the global economy is run. If tax rates were uniform across the world and not distorted by the zero or low rates charged in tax havens and if, as a result, corporations could not legally shield their earnings from fair taxation, profits that could then be fairly taxed would be 15 per cent higher in EU countries and 10 per cent higher in the US.

So it is now high time to consider how we end these abuses. The first step is to stop accepting the anonymous ownership of companies, trusts, foundations and financial assets, including bank accounts. Current tax havens must either accept international standards of transparency and information exchange or be turned into international pariahs by depriving them of the benefits of membership of the international community and cutting them off from legitimate finance. But, because any solution must also recognise the role of higher-income countries, which, according to the Tax Justice Network, are responsible for facilitating 98 per cent of all global tax losses (OECD countries are themselves responsible for nearly half of all global tax losses), we must, secondly, deal with the continuing impunity of professional enablers of tax abuse, including major international law and accounting firms.

And so, in this chapter, I am also going to set out the case for a wider UN Tax Convention with effective powers of enforcement that will make sure our global tax system not only deals with these abuses, but moves us from a world of tax shelters to one of tax justice. This would guarantee that all but a few – the offending 0.1 per cent and the seriously offending 0.01 per cent – are better off.

If we are to put an end to the mechanisms used to avoid tax, the starting point is to implement the 'ABC' of tax transparency: automatic exchange of information between tax authorities; beneficial ownership registers to ensure transparency as to who owns what; and country-by-country reporting to ensure transparency about multinational companies' profit-shifting, with each country's public registers brought together in what would be a virtual global asset registry.

The main lesson of the past twenty years is that, while effective national tax laws are a precondition of tax justice, international cooperation is essential – indeed, unavoidable – if we are to make sure every country operates and benefits from a fair taxation system. Already unrestricted tax competition between nations has led to a fall in average nominal corporation tax rates – from 35 per cent in 1995 to below 20 per cent today – and, until now, have been falling. Whatever the official rates, effective tax rates are near zero for far too many individuals and companies. We cannot end tax avoidance in one country if we do not end it in all countries. The aim should be to eliminate all hiding places for those who would flout the rules and to prevent anyone, anywhere, devising and using opaque entities or structures to obscure the true ownership of assets – indeed, to make risking such conduct so severe as to be not worth their while.[14]

Case studies: St Kitts and the Caymans

The offshore world is as variegated as it is large. There are havens that specialise in simply hiding true company ownership; others that specialise in laundering money; others whose unique selling point is processing specific kinds of transactions from property to works of art; some that specialise in the peculiar arrangements that focus on avoidance within particular regions; and a few so lax in their rules that, even now, through the use of trusts under undisclosed, often completely made-up names, the true beneficiaries of shell companies still remain unknown and unknowable. There is, indeed, real and lively competition between offshore havens as to which offers the most secrecy and protection. According to the Financial Secrecy Index compiled by the Tax Justice Network, 133 jurisdictions vie with each other in this race to the bottom to secure their share of the offshore market.[15]

Perhaps St Kitts and Nevis – especially Nevis – is nowadays the least open regime in the offshore world, one that specialises in letting its clients create corporations with the utmost anonymity, while hiding who owns what because its authorities simply do not seek to know. In this way, Nevis out-obscures all the established traditional offshore centres: the British Virgin Islands, Switzerland, Guernsey, the Isle of Man, Luxembourg, and even Belize and the Cook Islands. When information from Nevisian companies came to attention in what became the Paradise Papers investigation – resulting from a major leak of financial documents related to offshore centres, which we will return to later in this chapter – the names of 70,000 companies based on that small island became public, but not who actually owned them. Information on ownership is so secret there that even the island's own corporate registry makes a virtue of its ignorance; on both St Kitts and Nevis, even the police and legal authorities cannot prove who owns anything and, as a result, cannot prove whether anything has been criminally acquired. Nor can they begin to show that tax has been avoided on profits – just the kind of confidentiality that criminals and tax evaders are looking for when they send their businesses offshore. The Nevis LLC is a hybrid structure that allows people to avoid identification and taxes at one and the same time. If such loopholes are not closed, it means that the sending of money offshore will continue to deprive national exchequers of the revenues they need, leaving domestic populations defrauded, undersupported and sometimes impoverished.

Not by accident, St Kitts and Nevis is also the leader in what are known as the Citizenship by Investment and Residence by Investment industries, which, as the names suggest, offer citizenship or residence for a price. Much of this can be traced back to a local law passed in 1984, which offered citizenship to foreigners who made a 'substantial' investment on the island. Surely marketed as a way of encouraging investment in local assets, it also offers criminals a convenient way around travel restrictions and an 'escape' option in the event they need to use a second passport. Today, the population of St Kitts and Nevis is about 50,000. But about half as many again – around 25,000 – hold passports but do not reside there.

One recent case of what is now seen to be the biggest international fraud in years – the historic looting of billions from 1MDB, a vast Malaysian state investment fund – sums up all that is wrong. Using Swiss banks and US brokers, lawyers and accountants in the major financial centres, the notorious Malaysian-born financier Jho Low, now wanted for arrest and trial, sent billions out of Malaysia into shell companies across the world in the tax havens of the Seychelles, Curaçao, the British Virgin Islands and other overseas territories. In particular, Low was able to use the criminally negligent tax avoidance systems in St Kitts and Nevis to defraud his fellow countrymen of an estimated \$15 billion, which would have remained hidden for years, perhaps decades, if a whistle-blower and a brave journalist had not exposed the truth.[16]

Beyond St Kitts and Nevis – an exemplar if ever there was one of shady corporate behaviour – the Cayman Islands, which were also used in the Malaysian fraud, are the most intensive offshore financial centre in the world, as measured by the ratio of foreign assets to national income. The territory's foreign assets are valued at an astonishing 1,500 times the size of its domestic economy, with financial services tallying about one-third of GDP.

Briefly blacklisted by the EU for the first time in February 2020, but removed from the list in October that same year after being deemed compliant with international tax rules, the Caymans account for the biggest global tax losses – \$1 in every \$6 – with these islands alone causing other countries to be deprived of over \$70 billion of tax revenues every year.[17]

In as little as two weeks and for as little as \$35,000 in fees, hedge funds can set up shop in the Caymans. This is just a fraction of the time and up to one-tenth the price of incorporating a fund in places like Delaware. Indeed, around 85 per cent of the world's hedge funds are domiciled in the Cayman Islands. No physical presence in the islands – whether office space or staffing – is required, allowing the setting up of a 'nameplate company'. And, in contrast to most other offshore jurisdictions, nothing prevents overseas executives buying or renting real estate in the Cayman Islands – in case you want to check in on proceedings by visiting a luxury beachside property without ever being subject to tax. The Caymans, in this respect, take the prize in any race to the bottom: they have no direct taxes of any kind. There are no corporation, capital gains, income, profits or withholding taxes and no inheritance taxes or death duties either.

This helps explain why today the Caymans are second only to Hong Kong for Chinese nationals seeking to house offshore firms. Using a process called 'round tripping' – when one company sells assets to another party in order to generate sales and then buys back the assets – profits made in China through various means can be routed through the Caymans and subsequently reinvested in China disguised as investment from a foreign country, thus going untaxed.[18]

The Caymans also spearhead what is known as a Special Trusts Alternative Regime (STAR) structure, having created the mechanism in 1997. The defining feature of such a trust is that it can last for ever: the trust need not designate an individual as its beneficiary. It can designate its beneficiary to be anonymous and inanimate by merely setting a purpose such as 'owning shares in a corporation'. These STAR trusts are known as 'dynastic trusts' and can guarantee that a family business is not disbanded by subsequent generations against the stated wishes of the founder. Through such trusts, the Caymans have been accused of resuscitating a form of inheritance that is more akin to medieval practice. Traditional onshore trusts have a built-in life span to ensure that assets held in trusts cannot escape taxation for ever. But, because STAR assets are locked into a trust with no end point and are able to grow tax-free, assets can be passed down within a family in perpetuity without any risk of attenuation. Medieval trusts could only apply to land, but these STAR trusts can hold any type of asset – including stocks, bonds or the assets of a family business. The structure of these trusts affords a client's funds unparalleled protection. In her book *Capital Without Borders*, Brooke Harrington recounts the story of a client of such a trust whose ex-wife had just won a huge marital settlement in the Cayman courts. The client was a beneficiary of a trust and requested an amount so large it would have ended the trust entirely in order to pay the settlement. But the manager of the trust simply refused to fulfil the request and, as the technical owner of the assets under trust law, the courts respected the denial and the funds remained untouched by the marital dispute.[19]

While the Caymans are currently trying to revamp their image as a fully compliant and legal financial centre (and it is important to state that their model is technically legal by the letter, if not the spirit, of the law), we cannot forget the territory's involvement in prior crises and scandals and must ask why, in the ten years since the last crash, we have not done more to root out the dubious practices that not only siphon off much-needed public revenues, but also cause financial instability. The origins of the global financial crisis and the activities in the Cayman Islands eventually turned out to be related. The Lehman Brothers bank – the most dramatic bankruptcy in the autumn of 2008 – was found to have parked tens of billions of toxic assets in off-balance sheets in Cayman special purpose vehicles, subsidiaries created by a parent company to isolate and diminish financial risk. When Bear Stearns, another high-profile casualty, collapsed, it transpired that two of the largest hedge funds the bank had bailed out in 2007 were incorporated in the Caymans, which, of course, had enabled Bear Stearns to hide the truth about its true position. And, when Citigroup suddenly reported massive losses from subprime activities, it turned out that the corporation had set up special investment vehicles – a type of special purpose vehicle that earns a profit by capitalising on the difference in interest between long-term securities and short-term debts – based in the Caymans in order to move the positions off its balance sheet and away from the oversight of US regulatory authorities. These special investment vehicles were responsible for two separate taxpayer bailouts. And the first round of the UK banking crisis was triggered by the collapse of Northern Rock, which had been using Cayman facilities in ways that obscured its by-then disastrous position.[20]

But we should actually have learned and acted a decade before the financial crash. Earlier, in 2001, it was discovered that the

US energy company Enron had used hundreds of unregulated Cayman subsidiaries to keep billions off its balance sheet, causing severe market disruption when the company collapsed. If these balances had not been hidden away, regulators might have been able to intervene earlier – and perhaps the worst of the crisis could have been avoided, forestalled or mitigated.

But the Caymans still resist transparency. The UK passed the Sanctions and Anti-Money Laundering Act in 2018, requiring all overseas territories – including the Caymans – to disclose all company owners through a public register. Of course, each of the UK's overseas territories seeks to operate as an almost entirely self-governing jurisdiction and, in fact, the UK only rarely exercises its powers to intervene, using what are known as 'orders in council'. In 1991, it did so to outlaw the death penalty and, in 2000, it acted again, decriminalising homosexual acts. But Alden McLaughlin, premier of the Cayman Islands, called the act 'colonial despotism' and argued that 'the attempt by [the UK] parliament to legislate for this territory . . . is unlawful and we do not accept it'.[21] Only persistent pressure led him to yield and concede that his country would create a public register of beneficial owners – the beneficial owner being the person who ultimately owns, controls or receives profits from a company or legal vehicle, even when the company legally belongs, on paper, to another person or entity, like an accountant or a shell company – by 2023.

But, if some of the worst crime-concealing functions of these tax havens' offerings are being slowly addressed, what is now called the shadow banking system has been left largely intact. This is because, in this area, there has been much less international pressure to bring about change. As happened in the run-up to 2008, the risks associated with the off-balance-sheet behaviours of US banks are again building up, as we discussed in Chapter 3. In 2015, Reuters assessed that just six US banks were holding a total of $3.3 trillion of securitised loans in off-balance-sheet entities in the Cayman Islands alone.[22]

Lifting the lid

We are now in a much better position to ensure the transparency, disclosure and automatic exchange of the information we need. That is largely thanks to action following the disclosure of a huge volume of secret documents to the German newspaper *Süddeutsche Zeitung* in 2016 – the Panama Papers. Included in the original release were 12.7 million files and more than forty years of data from a tiny law firm, Mossack Fonseca, based in Panama. Despite its small size, it was nonetheless one of the world's leading creators of shell companies – advising the world's elites on how to sequester their money offshore. Enclosed in the files were exposés on world political leaders – including the prime minister of Iceland, the president of Ukraine and the king of Saudi Arabia – as well as drug traffickers, celebrities, billionaires and more. More than 200 countries around the world were found to be connected to this one small firm in Panama.[23]

And the subsequent release of the Paradise Papers – 13.4 million files held by Appleby, a leading offshore law firm with offices in Bermuda – implicated some of the world's most prestigious royal families, as well as major donors to, and members of, President Trump's administration. For example, Wilbur Ross, Trump's commerce secretary, was shown via the Appleby documents to have used a web of Cayman dealings to retain a financial stake in Navigator Holdings, a shipping company that includes, among its top clients, Sibur, a Kremlin-linked energy firm, which, in 2016, had paid Navigator more than $23 million. Kirill Shamalov (ex-son-in-law of the president of Russia, Vladimir Putin) and Gennady Timchenko (a billionaire sanctioned by the US government in 2014 because of his links to Putin) both have large shares in the company. Another major Navigator client is PDVSA, a state-owned oil company controlled by the authoritarian Nicolás Maduro, president of Venezuela – a nation sanctioned by the Trump administration.[24]

No US ethics report had uncovered any of this; it took the Paradise Papers to expose enormous potential conflicts of interest concealed within Cayman holdings. And it was thanks to the Panama and Paradise Papers that we learned the full extent of the taxes that go unpaid by major multinationals. We should not have to rely on leaks for information on decades of malpractice as our main weapon in the battle against global tax injustice. What is needed is broadly based, effective, international action that will uncover and deal with persistent offending.

Exchange of information

There is an obvious reason for the continuing growth of tax evasion and avoidance today. Since the 1980s and especially in the past twenty years, global flows of capital have far exceeded local and national flows. While governments once prevented even small sums of money going overseas, the abolition of capital controls created the free-for-all that has made the global tax evasion industry possible. Warning us that this new era of 'banking without borders' has facilitated the avoidance of tax liability and showing how the decision of one jurisdiction to restrict access to information adversely impacts on all of us, the OECD's 2000 report proposed: 'Ideally, all Member countries should permit tax authorities to have access to banking information, directly or indirectly, for all tax purposes so that tax authorities can fully discharge their revenue-raising responsibilities and engage in effective exchange of information.'[25] But – over twenty years later – achieving international consensus on the nature and the implementation of measures against tax avoidance and evasion is a battle still being fought, and will be throughout the third decade of this century.

The first step forward came in 2002 with an international agreement to support model tax information exchange agreements.[26] These were special-purpose agreements between two countries – taking, until 2009, a bilateral rather than multilateral approach – for exchanging tax information, with countries signing 'double taxation treaties', invariably incorporating an article that legislated for cross-border administrative cooperation. Yet this was not enough. Many countries did agree to exchange information, but only with a very limited and specially selected number of partners. Seven years on from the 2002 agreement, there were around fifty jurisdictions still refusing to exchange tax information – including information related to secret bank accounts – not least because, as long-term beneficiaries of avoidance schemes, they had a lot to hide. By 2009, when the UK welcomed the G20 to London to discuss our response to the financial crash, the majority of jurisdictions covered by the OECD's work – seventy out of 125 – still permitted bank secrecy and had yet to agree to lift restrictions that prevented the exchange of tax information.

I had long felt that the best way to deal with the secrecy around tax havens was to press for the automatic exchange of tax information. Countries that hosted foreign citizens and international businesses would ideally transfer all financial information relevant to the tax affairs of the individual or the company back to their home nations. Then it would not matter where the money was held: the home nation would now be able to assess what was owed to it under its own tax laws.

The urgency of agreeing such a policy had been firmly impressed on me during the EU's own internal efforts to battle tax avoidance and evasion. Worried about tax avoidance by the many German savers who were setting up bank accounts in low-tax Luxembourg, the Germans wanted a harmonised savings tax to apply to every country in Europe. Thousands of ordinary German citizens were travelling to Luxembourg to place their savings in its banks, then recrossing the border once a year to collect their dividends. All attempts to persuade these individuals to declare such savings income to the German tax authorities had proved fruitless. Luxembourg's bank secrecy laws made sure of that.

Exasperated by the loss of revenues incurred through this tax avoidance, Germany and the overwhelming majority of European leaders had, by the turn of the century, agreed a new policy to solve the problem. They favoured a single, uniform, Europe-wide, one-size-fits-all tax rate on savings. No matter where your money was, it would be taxed at the same rate. If Germans held their money in Luxembourg, the Luxembourg authorities would transfer the tax revenues back into Germany.

The answer the European Commission devised – a centralised uniform tax across Europe – accorded with the commission's broader ambitions, which viewed the harmonisation of taxes, and hence a single Europe-wide tax, as the obvious next stage of the establishment of the currency union and the euro. In practice, this policy made Europe more federal than the US. Even the US, a federal nation, does not require uniform tax rates across all fifty states.

Britain now stood alone in championing the automatic exchange of information on taxation as the most appropriate and effective way of preventing tax avoidance. We did so because we knew that the European policy raised more questions than it answered. We all agreed that savings should not escape tax by being transferred from one country to another. But I saw quickly that there was one fatal flaw in the proposal to harmonise taxes within Europe: if we legislated to impose a European savings tax, thousands of European savers would simply move their savings outside the EU – to Switzerland, Liechtenstein, Hong Kong and tax havens elsewhere in the world – and do so with the expert assistance of local tax lawyers and accountants. A Europe-only tax harmonisation was progress, but it would prove powerless to prevent taxpayers using countries outside of the EU to save and grow a great deal of money without paying a cent in tax.

I had to persuade other European leaders that there were better routes than a blanket, harmonised one-size-fits-all approach, which, if implemented, would result only in Europeans sending their savings out of Europe to low-tax or no-tax jurisdictions. My proposal involved rejecting the harmonisation of tax rates in favour of an exchange of tax information between national tax authorities and the insistence that the new policy apply to the whole world, including financial centres like Geneva, New York and Hong Kong.

We had to accept that we were living in an integrated global economy whose reach went far beyond the confines of Europe's borders. The only effective way forward was via broader international cooperation – agreements not just within Europe, but with all the main financial centres, too. And, if this could be achieved, an even bigger prize was within our grasp: a binding European agreement that would include the exchange of information with both European and non-European financial centres, which would make it possible for us to move forward towards a new global agreement – one that would require the automatic exchange of information everywhere, together with the blacklisting of those uncooperative tax havens who refused to play ball. Automatic exchange of information on that scale would unlock billions escaping tax in offshore centres. And so I raised the obvious question: if we could persuade Europe, could we persuade the rest of the world?

Action now

Now we return to where I started this chapter – the 2009 G20 summit. The impetus generated by the G20 and OECD in 2009 meant that, to escape being named and shamed, every country had to sign at least twelve bilateral agreements to exchange tax information. That led to 300 such agreements being signed between the April summit and the end of December 2009 and, in due course, led to signatory countries disappearing from the list of non-cooperative jurisdictions.

However, from 2009 to 2017, the exchange of information was

more limited than most of us had envisaged – mainly agreements to exchange information 'on request' and usually only in cases where the requesting authority had a suspicion of tax evasion or avoidance. Only a minority of member countries required automatic reporting by banks and, as a general rule, such information was limited to interest paid and the amount of tax withheld on these interest payments.

The Convention on Mutual Administrative Assistance in Tax Matters now fought for the rapid expansion of the network of exchange-of-information agreements, offering a more straightforward alternative to a lengthy process of negotiating bilateral arrangements. Today, it monitors the equivalent of nearly 8,000 bilateral agreements. Tax information relevant for taxation purposes can now be obtained from about 130 other jurisdictions, including all G20 and OECD countries, practically all international financial centres, and an increasing number of developing countries.

In 2013, in a follow-up set of decisions taken after I had left the UK government – and, in this instance, agreed by the G20 as well as the OECD – leaders also officially endorsed the automatic exchange of financial information as the new global standard.[27] Now tax authorities were able to obtain information previously beyond their reach. This meant that, when tax evaders tried to hide money offshore, the chance of detection would be enormously increased. A taxpayer weighing the costs and benefits of hiding money abroad could no longer ignore the costs associated with tax evasion on the assumption of a low-to-zero probability of detection. With the implementation of the automatic exchange of information, participating jurisdictions could now access information on the foreign financial accounts of their residents. From 2017, many members commenced the automatic exchange of tax information.

But the wider plan for transparency, disclosure and the automatic exchange of information has still not been fully implemented – and the main obstacle has been the stance taken by the US. The US's own Foreign Account Tax Compliance Act requires other countries to send tax information relating to US citizens to its Inland Revenue Service (IRS), but it does not require the IRS to hand over information to other countries in return. But, beyond that major gap in international collaboration, other developments that followed the G20 in 2009 sparked an international network of exchange agreements: a sharp rise in the volume of information exchanged automatically as well as on request; and a lifting of much of the veil of secrecy allowing tax evaders to hide their assets offshore. By 2018, at least 100 jurisdictions had committed to automatic exchange of information under the OECD Common Reporting Standard.

Now almost all of the trillions of dollars in private wealth held offshore are retained in jurisdictions that have agreed to exchange financial account information automatically. When tax authorities first started receiving large volumes of new data, information on more than 11 million financial accounts was exchanged. This figure grew to 47 million financial accounts in 2018 – the total value of which was more than $5 trillion – and, in 2019, to 84 million financial accounts holding €10 trillion.[28] The number of bilateral agreements to exchange information increased from around 4,500 in 2018 to around 6,100 in 2019. All this amounted to the largest exchange of tax information in history and the culmination of more than two decades of international efforts to counter tax abuse, but there is still much more work to be done. We have to circumvent attempts to create 'non-reportable' financial assets, designed to mimic the benefits of financial account holdings without having to disclose ownership, thus obscuring the true tax residence of accountholders and defeating the requirement to exchange information. If the rules for transparency and disclosure can be easily sidestepped by accountancy firms and legal advisers, automatic exchange of information is a hollow promise. For, while we can name and shame countries or regions identified as tax havens, offshore financial markets, flags of convenience and economic free zones, these shelters sadly exist not just because they are based in far-flung overseas territories or in rogue, 'bandit' states, but also because they are organised in and from some of the most advanced economies in the world. In fact, as economist Branko Milanović argues, so-called 'rule of law' areas, including London and New York, are now acting as enablers of worldwide avoidance.[29] Without new laws that require banks and legal and accountancy firms to fully report dubious activities and improper implementation of the rules, huge sums of money will still remain outside the scope of tax authorities.

Obviously, through the automatic exchange of financial account information, a new channel is created via which tax authorities can be alerted about potential abuses. But we have yet to plug the gaps in transparency and in disclosure that arise from well-known avoidance mechanisms, like the use of beneficial ownership to obfuscate the true holders of sometimes huge assets. In 2015, the Global Forum and then the G20 agreed to include a new requirement: full information about ownership has to be available and accessible for all legal persons, legal arrangements and bank accounts. Practice would be monitored internationally – sixty-one countries have now been subject to reviews – in order to further limit the risk of 'letterbox' companies being misused to conceal financial flows. But, as we have already found, it is not enough to agree a legal framework for compliance; the laws must be effectively implemented and rigorously enforced in practice. While the Financial Action Task Force and the Global Forum continue to allow countries to implement three different approaches, many gaps remain in place: the narrow scope of legal vehicles subject to registration; the high thresholds in the definition of beneficial ownership; and the lack of effective sanctions. These gaps cannot be closed until all countries establish and properly supervise a centralised and public register of beneficial ownership for all legal vehicles. Bearer shares – where the owners of shares are not, and need not be, identified – are one means of sustaining tax avoidance. Since 2009, over thirty jurisdictions that allowed bearer shares have abolished them. But there is as yet no agreement, as one day there has to be, on the outright prohibition of bearer shares.

And so, extensive as the membership of the Global Forum has become, there are still too many countries and too many dubious practices that escape scrutiny – and a tax system can only be as strong as its weakest link. Many countries exchange information with only a limited number of other countries and thus cover only a fraction of relevant transactions. And there are still twenty-eight members of the Global Forum that, even now, have failed to sign the multilateral convention. Twenty-six of them are developing countries, sixteen of which are in Africa, five in Asia and a further three in Latin America and the Caribbean.

So, while the major restructuring of global tax policy that started just over a decade ago did turn a new page in the battle against tax injustice, much more still needs to be done to ensure that there is no going back and no repetition of, or return to, the innumerable and often outrageous tax scandals of the past.

In the next stage the United Nations now has a big role to play and under its auspices a global convention on transparency in the reporting and exchange of information should be assembled. 'There is no international tax convention to compare with the United Nations Convention against Corruption and United Nations Convention against Transnational Organized Crime, which have nearly universal coverage,' stated the interim report of the High-Level Panel on International Financial Accountability, Transparency and Integrity for Achieving the 2030 Agenda.[30] And accordingly, the panel's final report, published in February 2021, recommended such a tax convention as one of three elements of a sweeping reform. The convention would be negotiated on a globally inclusive basis, which, the panel write, 'will provide the basis for legitimate action against any jurisdiction that is undermining global norms and damaging the legitimate tax base of any country. It would also create a universal and more effective mechanism for international tax cooperation.'[31] In other words, a UN-led convention that could require proper disclosure and reporting of incomes would cover not just the nations currently in compliance, and able to access information, but all countries. The convention would also create the legal foundation for the second element of the reform, an intergovernmental body to be established under UN auspices, to oversee the setting and implementation of international tax rules. This would be supported, thirdly, by a Centre for Monitoring Tax Rights, to collate, analyse and publish data on the extent of international tax abuse.

One further reform that would enhance transparency and commands increasing support is the creation of a worldwide financial register to document the true ownership of stocks and bonds – including the beneficial ownership of companies, trusts and foundations. This would draw on national registers and on other sources of reporting, such as the listing requirements of major stock exchanges – for example, those imposed by the SEC in the US; and on the country-by-country reporting of multinational companies, as this data is increasingly made public.

Some companies – Vodafone, Philips and Shell, for example – have already agreed voluntarily to publish, for each relevant country, their profits and the tax paid, and the names of all their subsidiary entities, using the most robust standard, which is that published by the Global Reporting Initiative.[32] All individual companies are not yet required to publish their data, however, even though the OECD standard created in 2015 mandates that all large multinationals must report the information privately to their home tax authority. While the detail has to be worked through, the member states of the European Union agreed in March 2020 to require multinationals to publish their country-by-country reporting.[33]

When multinationals are required to report and the ultimate

beneficial ownership of legal vehicles and of the holders of financial accounts disclosed, we will be able to deliver on the aspirations set out by the G20 in 2009 and reinforced in 2013. A worldwide register managed by either the OECD or better still the IMF or UN, based on the UK pilot project carried out by the Independent Commission for the Reform of International Corporate Taxation, would bring together all existing registers and widen the scope of the disclosures required.

Devising policies to counteract avoidance and evasion is difficult enough, but even more difficult is securing an actual agreement among countries with diverse needs and considerations. In 2013, the G20 countries also established a consensus – since joined by many more countries – that the single goal of corporate tax reforms should be to ensure that multinationals from Google and Apple to Amazon and Facebook are taxed where their economic activity takes place and where their profits are generated. There is now a highly developed European plan for a common consolidated corporate tax base (CCCTB) to allocate profits of multinationals not on the basis of dubious legal devices, but on the basis of objective metrics that will include company turnover, numbers of employees, the location of physical capital like factories, and sales – precisely the data that should be published under country-by-country reporting. Because tax would have to be paid where economic activity takes place, rather than where profit has been declared, profit-shifting into tax havens would be barred. Taxation is not an EU competence, of course, but a national matter and, although there is now a proposal on the table to decide tax policy by majority voting, unanimity is currently required if the EU is to move forward together. And, as I found many times over the years, tax decisions can easily be blocked by those countries with links to tax havens that benefit most from the status quo. Not surprisingly, Germany and France remain exasperated by countries – such as Luxembourg, Ireland and even the Netherlands – that have failed to clamp down on abuses.[34] Some say that any consensus may be possible only if, instead of seeking 'harmonised' tax rates, the EU settles for tax bands, allowing a range of, for example, between 15 per cent in the least progressive country to 25 per cent in the most, as happens with the current sales tax regime.[35] But, under the new European proposals, which could increase corporate tax returns by 20 per cent, companies could not siphon off expenses to subsidiaries to hide where profit is being made. Profits of subsidiaries would be relabelled and consolidated in the profits of the larger corporation.

The advantage of the new European approach is 'formulary apportionment', which is something already practised in the US. This means that the profits of multi-state firms are calculated nationally and then distributed in proportion to the activity in individual states, which then tax them. So, building on action in the US, where Lawrence Summers and others have recently set out detailed anti-avoidance proposals, there is a real chance Europe and the US can work together to secure a global agreement.[36] The OECD has now also recognised the need to go beyond the discredited 'arm's length' approach and introduce at least some elements of apportionment, which would make profit-shifting more difficult. There is also agreement on the need for a global minimum corporate tax, which would make profit-shifting less attractive. And, with over 135 countries and jurisdictions now involved, the decision-making process has been opened up well beyond the OECD's own more restrictive membership.

That OECD reform process has been revitalised by the new US administration's stronger preference for multilateral engagement. Some elements of formulary apportionment may be included in the deal now pencilled in for July 2021, although it will likely stop well short of the proposed common consolidated tax base or of the system already in operation among US states. The stronger consensus appears to be around the plans for a global corporate minimum tax rate. An ambitious proposal could unify many countries and eliminate much of the incentive for profit shifting.[37]

But much more needs to be done. While a minimum tax rate may now be acceptable, agreement has still to be reached that would secure an outright ban on profit-shifting, and the OECD's current reform proposals would only reduce the global losses from profit-shifting by 2–5 per cent of the OECD's estimate of total losses. And too many exemptions are slipping through the net because the 'black/grey/white' system of labelling is not working. And so, with the pandemic driving pressure on health and other budgets and making finance ministries more aware of their lost revenues, more and more are increasingly restive at the lack of progress. As I write, France and an increasing number of other countries, exasperated by the delays, have decided to go ahead unilaterally with digital taxes, to be imposed on selected gross revenue streams of large digital companies. Of course, these taxes alone will not come close to recovering the revenues lost, and broader multilateral measures will eventually be required.

The answer is to subject the countries that refuse to cooperate in the banning of dubious practices to sanctions and levies proportional to the costs that these tax havens impose on others. Because even the bad performers are undercut by the worst, there is growing awareness on the part of countries like Switzerland that they are losing out to the Caymans of the world. 'The important point is that tax evasion earns Switzerland much less than what it costs the countries that are victims of it,' argues one exponent of major reform.[38]

There is some hope – not just because there is greater awareness of the cost of tax avoidance paid in poorer health, education and social safety nets in every country, but also because of three other changes in official sentiment. First is the growing interest taken by international organisations, including the UN and the IMF, in tackling tax abuses. Second is the shift in China against a free-for-all in places like Macau. And the third sign of progress is the promise made by the new US administration, with President Biden stating that he 'will lead efforts internationally to bring transparency to the global financial system, go after illicit tax havens, seize stolen assets, and make it more difficult for leaders who steal from their people to hide behind anonymous front companies'.[39]

By this time next year, I would like to see the UN Convention I outlined agreed and a UN monitoring centre with a mandate to collate, analyse and publish annual assessments of data on profit-shifting and offshore tax evasion. This would raise public awareness and provide policymakers with a crucial resource to target the causes of revenue losses. The next stage would be, as recommended by the UN panel, the creation of a genuinely globally inclusive, intergovernmental body to oversee future tax rules. The convention would also provide for comprehensive, global delivery of the ABC of tax transparency: automatic exchange of financial account information; public registers of the beneficial owners of companies, trusts and foundations; and public country-by-country reporting from multinational companies – and thus end the scourge of tax abuse now and into the future. But the aim must be to ensure there is no escape route for tax havens – and the ultimate sanction is to exclude them from the benefits of membership of the international community. This can be done by economic sanctions, placing substantial tariffs on their trade or simply refusing to trade with them, and by refusing to recognise them in colloquiums, summits and assemblies of nations. But where they are prepared to change there should be international support for them to identify and pursue alternative paths of economic development.

Of course, tax avoiders and evaders will always seek to exploit any new loophole or weakness in the legal and regulatory frameworks across the world. Now, however, in the wake of the sacrifices ordinary people have made during the concurrence of a pandemic and a global recession, the exposure of tax abuses and the growing desire to remove them present a real opportunity to change the system. It should be possible at this point to build the necessary consensus for progress immediately now that, in April 2021, the US has for the first time announced its support for a global minimum corporate tax. The proposal for a 21 per cent minimum tax rate goes beyond the more modest OECD plan for a 12.5 per cent rate and we would raise $540 billion worldwide. If, however, we agreed the 25 per cent minimum rate proposed by the Independent Commission for the Reform of International Corporate Taxation and insisted on apportioning the tax burden to the countries where economic activity actually occurs, we would raise $780 billion, with the additional revenues gained by low-income countries large enough to pay for nearly half their health spending.[40] This would begin to ensure that tax avoiders who have a duty to pay their fair share of taxes – and can afford to do so – actually make their contribution to the financing of public services that are more in demand than ever. Public support for action is growing. Until now, the subject has been so technical and complex that tax abuses were known only to lawyers and accountants, but tax avoidance has become so rampant and glaring that recent polling conducted in June 2020 in seven countries – the US, France, Germany, Italy, Poland, the Netherlands and the UK – has shown 90 per cent support for two reforms: ending the use of tax havens and tying any public support that companies receive to their history of paying tax.[41] So together, if we act as a global community, the sordid, secret world of tax abuse can be beaten for good – and our world will be better and fairer as a result.

8

ELIMINATING NUCLEAR WEAPONS: TOWARDS A DECADE OF DISARMAMENT

On a weekend in early September 2007, I flew from my home in Scotland to an urgent meeting with the foreign secretary and senior Foreign Office officials at London's Heathrow Airport. It had only been a few weeks since the Queen had asked me to form a government and I was already dealing with a long list of problems: an outbreak of foot-and-mouth disease; another of avian flu; and a terrorist incident. Next on the agenda would be a run on the Northern Rock bank – the first casualty of the impending financial crisis. I now had another crisis to add to that list.

At Al-Kabir, a remote site in Syria in the middle of the desert, far from any major city, the Israeli intelligence agency Mossad had obtained photographic evidence that the Syrian regime was developing a nuclear reactor similar to that in Yongbyon, North Korea, and that the Syrian leader, Bashar al-Assad, was well on his way to making Syria a new nuclear power in the Middle East.

Unless it were destroyed within six to nine months, the reactor could become operational. The US, Israel and the UK had already agreed that action was necessary. Israel favoured a US strike, but President George W. Bush and I were against that. In the aftermath of the Iraq War, a Western air strike would be even more controversial than one by the Israeli Defence Forces and would cause far wider repercussions. On 6 September, in an operation named Outside the Box, the Royal Air Force verified Israeli claims by photoreconnaissance and Israeli strike aircraft destroyed the facility. History in the Middle East was repeating itself: twenty-six years earlier, in 1981, the Israelis had bombed the Osirak nuclear reactor in Iraq, preventing that troubled country from developing a nuclear weapons facility for – as it turned out – quite a long time.

Controversial as the 2007 Operation Outside the Box might have been, it remained secret until very recently, when its existence was confirmed by Israel. Inside and outside Syria, there were walls of silence. Not even the Syrian army's chief of staff or the defence minister were aware what was going on at Al-Kabir; only a small circle around the president was in the know. And, since Syria was a signatory to the Nuclear Non-Proliferation Treaty (NPT), it could not complain that its attempt to acquire nuclear weapons had been thwarted. No one outside Syria wanted the world to know. If Israel had declared its involvement in the strike, a humiliated Syrian president might have thought it necessary to retaliate.

But that pre-emptive attack prevented Syria becoming the world's tenth nuclear-armed state. This was important in itself for preventing escalation in the Middle East. In a few years' time, with a desperate Syrian government proving itself willing to use nerve gas – another banned weapon of mass destruction – against its own people as it fought for its very survival, we found out just how fragile a state it was. And, however horrific the Syrian Civil War has been, a collapsing nuclear-armed state that hosted resilient and determined non-state actors like ISIS would have been far more of a danger for the country, the region and the world.[1]

The destruction of the Al-Kabir site also served to prevent a possible new wave of proliferation. If the facility had become operational, other states in the region might have found themselves with a nuclear-armed neighbour and some would then consider whether a nuclear programme of their own was necessary to safeguard their security.

International rivalry in nuclear weaponry goes back a long way. Germany dropped out early, largely because many of its best physicists were Jewish and had relocated to the UK and the US. Stalin was kept well informed about the Manhattan Project thanks to effective espionage, which meant that, by the time of the successful US test at Alamogordo, New Mexico, in July 1945, his own programme was not too far behind. In 1945, the US became the first – and, to date, only – nation to use nuclear weapons in war when it attacked Hiroshima on 6 August and Nagasaki three days later.

The instant devastation and mass casualties inflicted on Hiroshima and Nagasaki, together with the lingering horror of radiation-induced illnesses, was salutary. The world had learned that the realities of nuclear war were truly horrific. The Soviet Union tested its first nuclear weapon in 1949, the UK followed in 1952, France in 1960 and China in 1964. That, and an understandable wariness of the consequences of nuclear conflict, led to a period of relative stability, which endured until the early 1960s, when the Soviet Union covertly installed nuclear-tipped medium-range missiles in Cuba. A sequence of photographic reconnaissance, sabre-rattling and much anxious brinkmanship began on 14 October 1962 and took the world the nearest it has come so far to an all-out nuclear war. A young and untested President Kennedy wisely kept the US's over-eager and competing military forces on a short leash, setting aside his joint chiefs of staff's plan for air strikes and a ground invasion. Instead, on 22 October, he declared a naval blockade that would prevent the maintenance and expansion of the Soviet Union's Cuban arsenal. Those of us who were alive then found ourselves contemplating the possibility that quite soon we might not be.

As President Kennedy sought to enforce the blockade of Cuba, he did not know that the Soviet B-59 submarine, which the US navy was trying to force to the surface, was in distress. With falling oxygen levels and without communications, the submarine was unaware of the blockade or the escalating crisis. What President Kennedy also did not know was that the submarine was armed with nuclear weapons. Unsure of whether a war had already broken out, the submarine's captain wanted to launch a nuclear torpedo. The boat's political officer agreed. But, under the rules of engagement, the ship's three leading officers needed to agree before nuclear munitions could be used and, were it not for the good sense and restraint of Vasily Arkhipov, the submarine's second-in-command, nuclear weapons might have been fired and the US would have almost certainly felt obliged to respond. When details of this event became public in the early 2000s, Arthur M. Schlesinger Jr, an adviser to President Kennedy, described the incident as the 'most dangerous moment in human history'. Until then, we also had not known that, in the event of a conventional US attack, the Soviet commander had authority to use tactical nuclear weapons.[2]

Fortunately, Soviet ships paused then turned back. Nikita Khrushchev, a realist and a mature survivor of two world wars, deserves as much credit as Kennedy and was happy to accept, in return, the removal of batteries of short-range nuclear-tipped Thor missiles based in Turkey, near his own border. He was also content that this concession remained, for the time being, secret: a precedent somewhat prefiguring aspects of Operation Outside the Box more than forty years later.

In 1963, President Kennedy predicted that there could be as many as 'fifteen or twenty or twenty-five nations' becoming nuclear states by 2000, a year he did not live to see. And, after the Cuba crisis, he observed that 'living under a nuclear sword of Damocles, hanging by the slenderest of threads, capable of being cut at any moment by accident or miscalculation or by madness' was a grim prospect for humanity, but one more likely as a result of the uncontrolled spread of nuclear weapons.[3] So a consensus soon emerged in favour of an international agreement to limit the spread of nuclear weapons. In 1968, the UN General Assembly endorsed the NPT, which entered into force in 1970. The NPT remains the most widely subscribed arms limitation or disarmament treaty in history.

In the five decades since the crisis, the vast majority of states have agreed not to pursue nuclear weapons. There are four exceptions – Israel, India, Pakistan and North Korea – all of which were notable NPT absentees and have since acquired nuclear weapon capabilities. Several other countries – including Libya, Iran, South Africa, Syria and Iraq – have also, at some point, been on a path to do the same.

No account of illicit nuclear proliferation in the 1970s would be complete without an understanding of the role of the maverick Pakistani nuclear scientist Professor A. Q. Khan, who, with others and undetected for years, offered expertise on a commercial basis in uranium enrichment centrifuges, triggering devices, missile technologies and even nuclear material. At the height of his influence, he was a public icon in Pakistan and the government's science adviser. His clients are believed to have included North Korea, Israel, Libya, China and many others. After a trial in absentia for espionage in the Netherlands resulted in a four-year prison sentence, which was overturned on a technicality, he fell from grace. Now in his mid-eighties, he is still Pakistan-based and allowed to travel abroad only when accompanied by secret agents of the Pakistani military establishment, which may or may not be reassuring.[4]

His legacy lives on, but now, in 2021, we also find that the nuclear-armed states within and beyond the NPT are rearming – buying and building ever-more sophisticated weaponry. Some are even reviving the concept of so-called low-yield or tactical nuclear weapons, which could be put to use in a 'limited' nuclear war, though few experts believe that any nuclear war, once started, could be limited.

So now, one by one and driven by rising regional and local tensions, Middle Eastern and North African states are considering acquiring nuclear weapons. It is conceivable that the nuclear club could expand from today's nine to as many as sixteen in the near future: Saudi Arabia mirroring Iran in acquiring nuclear weapons; the UAE and Qatar following suit; Turkey next; then possibly Egypt; and perhaps even a second attempt by Syria. A new nuclear arms race could be under way in the world's most volatile region already.

What's more, the security guarantees that the US has given its allies in Europe and Asia over the past seventy years are beginning to look threadbare. In return for guarantees – including one of territorial integrity – from Russia and Western powers, Ukraine gave up the nuclear weapons it had inherited from the Soviet Union in 2014, formalised in the Budapest Memorandum on Security Assurances. Yet, despite these commitments the US and the UK – the two Western signatories to the agreement – stood by when Ukraine's territorial integrity was abruptly violated by Russia. The response of the West was underwhelming, nothing more than the imposition of economic sanctions.

The Joint Comprehensive Plan of Action, better known as the Iran nuclear deal, is an agreement reached in 2015 between Iran and a group of world powers – the US, the UK, Russia, France, China and the EU – and, like any treaty, it has its limitations. Many of its most significant constraints would last only between ten and fifteen years and it did not limit Iran's ballistic-missile development, but it did place a short-term ceiling on Iranian nuclear activity and made provision of international inspections to verify Iran's compliance.

When Donald Trump assumed the US presidency in January 2017, one of his first actions was to denounce the treaty as 'the worst deal ever', seemingly because it was one of the achievements of his predecessor, whose legacy he has successively sought to destroy ever since. In 2018, the US formally abandoned the treaty. Iran's response was predictable – a bill to withdraw from the NPT has been introduced in its parliament – and, also predictably, an Israeli politician and former defence minister, Moshe Ya'alon, announced: 'We see signs that countries in the Arab world are preparing to acquire nuclear weapons . . . Israelis are not willing to sit quietly with Iran on the brink of a nuclear or atomic bomb.'[5]

And it was almost inevitable that, in 2018, Saudi Arabia's young and rising Crown Prince Mohammed bin Salman, more widely known as MBS, announced in a US TV interview that, if Saudi Arabia thought Iran had nuclear weapons, he would immediately pursue nuclear weapons, too. 'If Iran developed a nuclear bomb,' he said 'we will follow suit as soon as possible.'[6] Statements that have led to commentators calling Saudi Arabia the number one proliferation concern in the world. In a private briefing to Goldman Sachs, which was later leaked, Hillary Clinton predicted that, in the wake of Iran, 'the Saudis are not going to stand by. They're already trying to figure out how they will get their own nuclear weapons.' 'But,' she added, 'then the Emiratis are not going to let the Saudis have their own nuclear weapons . . . and then the race is off.' And this, it seems, is the case.[7] Dr Paul Dorfman, the chairman of the Nuclear Consulting Group, a consortium of academics and other leading experts on nuclear affairs, is now warning of UAE intentions to produce a nuclear weapon. And, with perhaps other potential nuclear weapons partners in the Middle East in mind, UAE officials have already said that they are willing to share their nuclear expertise with other newcomers to the nuclear club.[8]

Indeed, there is now some evidence that, during President Trump's time in office, Saudi Arabia has benefited from US help in the secret development of a civil nuclear capability. A bill in the US Senate has sought to bar the US Export–Import Bank from financing the transfer of nuclear technology and equipment to Saudi Arabia in the absence of any agreements on nuclear cooperation. But, in yet another break from past presidential practice, President Trump's administration refused to support it. And so, as a result of the Trump presidency, the inclination to go nuclear may have increased not just because they felt there were many in America who would allow them to do so, but also because there was no certainty that the US would not one day leave them to their own devices in the region.

And indeed there was talk of Saudi Arabia, jointly with the UAE, buying Westinghouse, the US-based nuclear power company. And there was further speculation that the US was transferring nuclear technology to the UAE and Jordan. Even if this were blocked, Middle Eastern powers can now acquire nuclear technology with relative ease. Saudi Arabia has already helped fund Pakistan's nuclear development and there is some reporting that suggests oil-rich Saudi Arabia is considering an arrangement with cash-strapped Pakistan, whereby the latter could deploy some of its nuclear arsenal on Saudi soil. Additionally, Saudi Arabia has not committed to the most advanced type of International Atomic Energy Agency (IAEA) observation or the IAEA's Additional Protocol, which allows widespread inspection of nuclear and non-nuclear facilities and has extensive reporting requirements.

The UAE, which opened its first nuclear reactor in 2020, has insisted that it intends to use its nuclear programme for civil energy only. But, as Dorfman has argued, 'the nature of Emirate interest in nuclear may lie hidden in plain sight – nuclear weapon proliferation'. While the UAE points to its collaborations with the IAEA, which bars it from uranium enrichment and other possible bomb-development activities, its rival Qatar has lodged a complaint to the IAEA, calling the UAE nuclear programme 'a serious threat to the stability of the region and its environment'.[9]

Egypt plans to build a power plant with four nuclear reactors, which will make it easier for it to acquire nuclear weapons. Turkey is a member of NATO, but now increasingly estranged from its allies. Its president, Recep Tayyip Erdoğan, has suggested that he may choose to develop nuclear weapons regardless of what Iran does. In 2012, a Carnegie Endowment report stated that Ankara 'has left its nuclear options open' and the German Ministry of Defence declared in 2015 that 'the Western intelligence community now largely agrees that Turkey is working both on nuclear weapon systems and on their means of delivery'.[10] So it was no surprise when, in September 2019, Erdoğan complained that it was 'unacceptable' that Turkey could not have nuclear weapons. Later that month, at the UN General Assembly, he claimed that the NPT regime of five recognised nuclear-armed states was illegitimate. 'Some countries have missiles with nuclear warheads. But the West insists we can't have them. This, I cannot accept.'[11] And the danger is that we now see the growth of what has been called 'an autocratic nuclear marketplace', where strongmen leaders buy and sell nuclear weapons.

And on to North Korea, more of a present danger. Its hereditary dictator clearly refuses to give up the weapons he already has – only a few dozen missiles and nuclear warheads, but a modest investment that he has played quite well. An impoverished prison-like state with a starving population, North Korea claims it has also tested missiles that can reach the US and indeed may be preparing to test a new long-range submarine-launched missile. Kim Jong-Un – aware of what happened to Ukraine, where US security guarantees mattered little, and also aware of what happened to Iran after it agreed not to pursue nuclear weapons – shrewdly manipulated President Trump away from his early ravings about who had the bigger nuclear button.

May 2020 marked the fiftieth anniversary of the NPT, a landmark agreement that became the bedrock for global efforts at nuclear arms control. July and August 2020 marked the seventy-fifth anniversary of the testing and subsequent use of nuclear weapons in Hiroshima and Nagasaki – the first and only time such weapons have been used as an instrument of war. Efforts to curb their use have been ongoing ever since. The central bargain of the NPT is that, in exchange for not pursuing nuclear weapons, non-nuclear states are able to access the other technological benefits of nuclear energy, while nuclear weapon states make sustained and meaningful efforts to bring about full nuclear disarmament. In part because of the NPT, in part because of a taboo against their use, three-quarters of a century has passed without nuclear weapons being used again in conflict.

Nuclear proliferation: learning from success and failure

But can we learn from the successes in preventing proliferation to countries that have considered being nuclear weapon states such as Sweden, South Africa, Libya and various countries in Europe?

As the Cold War began, an elite group of Swedish politicians and military commanders, faced with the threat of the Soviet Union, decided in secret that they needed nuclear weapons. It took until 1958 for the Swedish government to reveal this and it admitted that, a few years earlier, it had reached a level of technical sophistication that would allow it to produce a nuclear bomb. While the government asked parliament to decide between what it called 'protection research' on nuclear weapons – which parliament voted for – and 'construction research', ministers continued to follow the latter course. It was not until 1968, after twenty years of nuclear planning, that an explicit decision was made to abandon a bomb in favour of a new fighter aircraft programme. Later, by 1972, Sweden had scrapped its work on uranium enrichment and had signed the NPT. Cost was an issue, as admitted in 1968, but, more importantly, Swedish lawmakers came to the view that Sweden's historic neutrality and its international reputation as a peacemaker were best guaranteed by the renunciation of nuclear weapons.[12]

South Africa's experience confirms that a country's international status and its global reputation matter: not just because a non-nuclear state is rewarded by the international community, but also because it is saved from the humiliation of isolation.

From a decision by incumbent prime minister Pik Botha in 1974 right through to 1989, South Africa pursued a nuclear weapons programme, enjoying international help to build up its civil reactor while, at the same time, secretly developing a 'limited nuclear deterrent capability'. The official motivation for a nuclear weapon, as Frederik de Klerk – South Africa's last white president – explained, was to counter the Soviet Union's expansionist policies in Southern Africa. It was to be a deterrent, but, because of the country's apartheid policies, South Africa was becoming more and more isolated in the eyes of the rest of the world and, for that reason, assistance from the international community in the event of Soviet aggression or invasion would not be forthcoming.[13]

By 1989, South Africa possessed six Hiroshima-type nuclear weapons, with a seventh on the way. However, by then, the weakness of the Soviet Union had been revealed, its expansionism in Africa had been stalled, and the justification for nuclear weapons had evaporated. De Klerk explained that, if you were a supporter of having nuclear weapons, the rationale for this fell away as the nature of the threats changed fundamentally. Instead, nuclear weapons were becoming, as he put it, 'a rope around my neck . . . you have something which you never intend to use, really, which is unspeakable to use, which would be morally indefensible to use'. Even though, as he said, 'inner conviction weighs heavier on the scale than international pressure', he added:

I wanted to end the isolation even before we finalised agreements through the constitutional negotiations. And one of the important things to achieve re-acceptance into the international community would have been to take an initiative, without any pressure from outside, to bring this programme to an end, to sign the NPT, to dismantle our nuclear weapons and to prove to the world that we weren't playing games, but that we were very serious about fundamental reform in South Africa.

Some argue that de Klerk gave up South Africa's nuclear weapons because he did not want them to fall into the hands of the new African National Congress government under Nelson Mandela. De Klerk vigorously denies this claim: if South Africa had remained a nuclear-armed country, it might have been ostracised. Even Israel, it must be noted, has never publicly admitted to its nuclear weapon status, presumably for that reason. By the same logic, losing the benefits of acceptance in the international community may not worry the leadership of Iran today, but it may do so in future, and the threat of pariah status may be a reason other Middle Eastern countries could be persuaded to desist from becoming nuclear weapon states.

Some would argue that the case of Libya is so unusual that it carries no wider lessons. Even when the dictator Colonel Gaddafi renounced nuclear weapons, he continued to be distrusted by the international community; though others argue conversely that, had he kept his nuclear programme, his regime might have survived. But, again, we should note the considerable international pressure on Libya, and the isolation Gaddafi faced and was seeking to end. In 1968, Libya became a signatory of the NPT, ratified the treaty in 1975 and even enhanced its non-nuclear status with a safeguard agreement. But all that time Gaddafi was drawing on Soviet nuclear expertise and then on the Pakistani Khan network to 'speed things up', as Ma'atouq, the head of the Libyan nuclear programme, explained. 'We wanted to make the supplier a one-stop shop. We used no other suppliers. Our original goal was to do so between 2006 and 2008, and, if the programme was accelerated, by 2007, with a year to spare.'[14]

President George W. Bush, who had long threatened to destroy the Libyan nuclear facility in the same way Israel would later destroy the Syrian facility, claimed that, once Iraq fell, the Libyan regime would be forced to come to its senses and renounce nuclear weapons. Indeed, Silvio Berlusconi also reported a call with a fearful Gaddafi, who was anxious that Libya would be the

US's next target after Iraq. And there is some audio evidence of a panicked Gaddafi, in conversation with Prime Minister Mubarak of Egypt, saying he was convinced that the US would attack Libya once the Taliban had been crushed in Afghanistan.

'The administration overstates Iraq, but its critics go too far in saying that force played no role,' concluded Bruce Jentleson, the foreign-policy adviser to Vice President Al Gore. 'It was force *and* diplomacy, not force *or* diplomacy, that turned Gaddafi around,' wrote Jentleson – 'a combination of steel and a willingness to deal'.[15] (Indeed, before 2000, Gaddafi had made an offer to President Clinton to renounce nuclear weapons, but he was not taken seriously until reparations for the Lockerbie attack had been agreed and Gaddafi had publicly dissociated himself from terrorism in the region.)

But, when Libya agreed to join Middle East multilateral arms control talks in 1999, the atmosphere had changed and, subsequently, the events of 9/11 probably did more to modify Gaddafi's view than Iraq's situation. 'We found ourselves in a different world, so Libya had to redesign its policies to cope with these new realities . . . We needed something bold, something big enough to have impact,' he said. 'Shock therapy! We knew the Americans would not find yellowcake in Iraq – as we warned them – but that there was yellowcake in Libya and that this card was worth something . . . I saw WMD as a card in our hands.' The invasion of Iraq was 'the best time to play that card'.[16]

But, of course, they too recognised, as did de Klerk, that the 'card' – a nuclear weapon – was not one they could use. As Ma'atouq recounted:

> I'm an engineer, a practical man. And I said: 'Let's assume we have these weapons. What would we do with them? Who is the target? Who would we use them against? The US?' We had no delivery system. Yes, nuclear weapons are a deterrent, but it's better to have nothing at all than a deterrent without a means of delivery.[17]

Proof that the US now had the details of the Libyan nuclear weapons programme brought things to a head. Evidence included intercepts of a conversation about the nuclear programme between Libya's nuclear chief and Professor Khan and the discovery in October 2003, on a Libyan-bound cargo ship seized by NATO allies, of nuclear materials and centrifuge parts sent by Khan. By then, Gaddafi had secretly spent $300 million – $100 million on nuclear equipment and material alone.

In December 2003, Gaddafi dramatically declared Libya's abandonment of its nuclear weapon ambitions, but Libya gained little from its gesture. The country remained on Washington's list of states that sponsored terrorism; full diplomatic relations were not restored until 2006. Indeed, Khan stated that Libya lost more than it gained: 'Don't overlook the fact that no nuclear-capable country has been subjected to aggression or occupied, or had its borders redrawn. Had Iraq and Libya been nuclear powers, they wouldn't have been destroyed in the way we have seen recently.' And he insinuates that, as a nuclear weapon state, North Korea – which, in 1994, agreed nuclear restraint, yet secretly expanded its enrichment programme, before leaving the NPT in 2003 and carrying out nuclear tests in 2005 – has stronger bargaining power than Libya. Khan may be wrong: the more important reason North Korea can withstand pressure is that it is protected by a major power, China, in a way that Libya has not been.[18]

Eastern European countries –most of all, Ukraine – found themselves in possession of nuclear weapons after the breakup of the Soviet Union, but they did not have the economic strength to maintain the weapons, so negotiated them away – 2,000 warheads in total – in return for financial support. And, when we look at what is common to those who renounced nuclear weapons, we can see that economic weakness is indeed an important consideration, but, of course, as we shall find with India, Pakistan and North Korea, not decisive. What may matter more is the vulnerability of countries to their neighbours, which has to be balanced against the threat of 'pariah' status and isolation and whether or not the country has any protection under a nuclear 'umbrella'.

Could we deter nuclear proliferation by extending guarantees of protection with a larger nuclear shield? As early as 1967, the US congress took the view that 'reliance on nuclear guarantees constitutes one of the most important elements in many national strategies for coping with the superior military capability of adversaries. In this situation, operating under the umbrella of a superpower's nuclear armaments constitutes a logical and strategically sound approach.'[19] But congress knew that this depended on the strength of the US guarantee. The congress paper stated that some proliferation analysts were concerned that the erosion of a 'credible' US nuclear guarantee – due to perceived shifts in the political will to employ a military response in situations in which the US is not directly threatened – had decreased the strength of this disincentive.

This statement was relevant to India, which, from the mid-1940s, had ambitions – and plans – to become a nuclear weapon power. When Prime Minister Nehru acquired reactors from the US and Canada, he insisted India would use them only for peaceful purposes. What changed was the humiliation India suffered from its defeat in its 1962 war with China and the further humiliation of having to beg a reluctant US for help with supplies and fighter planes. Nehru and his successors determined on a bomb. While the US, which had been, under President Eisenhower, closer to Pakistan, now helped build a new Indian army, with six US-armed mountain divisions, to face China, India felt that the US was doing more to arm Pakistan. Even when selling F-104s to Pakistan, the US would not sell India any high-performance jet aircraft. And so pressure for a nuclear weapon grew in India, not least from India's main opposition party.

Reviewing the US's possible options in the event of another Chinese attack on India, Secretary of Defence Robert McNamara told President Kennedy in 1963: 'Before any substantial commitment to defend India against China is given, we should recognize that, in order to carry out that commitment against any substantial Chinese attack, we would have to use nuclear weapons.' The Kennedy response was unequivocal: 'We should defend India and therefore we will defend India if she were attacked.'[20] But, if Kennedy was prepared to offer a non-nuclear India a security guarantee that would remove the need for India to acquire nuclear weapons, his successor, President Lyndon B. Johnson (LBJ), was far more equivocal. 'You Kennedy people got a lot of good ideas, but you also do a lot of things that seem to me to be pretty silly,' LBJ complained to one of Kennedy's tougher advisers, Robert Komer (known as 'Blowtorch Bob'). 'Now I want you to explain to me this India–Pakistan business.' Indeed, LBJ had to be persuaded that, if the US's most important strategic goal in Asia lay in preventing communism, US influence in India was more important than in Pakistan. 'You don't make foreign policy on the basis of who you like and who you don't like,' Komer told LBJ. 'Pakistan has 100 million people. India has over 500 million people and, if we're going to try to do something with South Asia as a counterweight to China, we better look at India as first priority and not at Pakistan, which is one-fifth the size.' To which LBJ fired back: 'I'm not sure I agree with you and I still think that we've maybe gone overboard and that we're not giving our Ayub [the then-leader of Pakistan] a fair deal. But I want to tell you that that's a pretty doggone convincing explanation that you gave me.'[21]

The US did consider helping India acquire nuclear weapons as a counterweight to China. In one paper, it was argued that a successful Indian nuclear weapons programme might relieve the US of future military burdens that it might be called upon to bear if India refrained from 'going nuclear'. But the US stopped short of supporting what would have been nuclear proliferation and accepted that, 'nevertheless, we believe adverse effects . . . outweigh this consideration':

From the standpoint of our non-proliferation objectives, the most direct impact of an Indian pro-nuclear decision would fall on Pakistan (where technical capabilities are limited) and Japan (where technical capabilities are large). However, an Indian pro-nuclear decision would also, to some extent, lower inhibitions against proliferation everywhere (possibly even in Western Europe), and, if both India and Japan should 'go nuclear', the effect would be substantial although not necessarily decisive in and of itself.

But the US security guarantees – a promise to defend India if attacked by a nuclear weapon state – were never forthcoming. And, though India did abandon the chemicals weapons it first tested in 1964, it has carried out another five nuclear weapon tests since, including its first nuclear fusion test in 1998.

Could history then have been different if the US had provided the security guarantee? What is certainly true is that, once the 1960s saw India actively begin its mission to acquire nuclear weapons, the decade would culminate with Pakistan acquiring its weaponry – making a conscious decision to do so as a result of its defeat in its 1971 war with India. Then Pakistan suffered the partition of the country, the surrender of 90,000 soldiers at Dhaka, the loss of Bangladesh, the loss of half its population and the destruction of the long-held dream of a single Muslim state. It was a deep national humiliation. So, in January 1972, the new president, Zulfikar Ali Bhutto, secretly convened the country's top fifty scientists. Bhutto said that Pakistanis would sacrifice everything and 'eat grass' to get a nuclear deterrent and he was offered help by Professor Khan, who, with the assistance of the Pakistani Inter-Services Intelligence agency, stole sensitive centrifuge technology from his new employers at a nuclear facility in the Netherlands.

With additional help from China, Pakistan built its bomb in the 1970s, even as the US was trying to prevent this. To no avail, the

US imposed sanctions on Pakistan in 1990 for building the bomb and cut off the supply of F-16 jets that Pakistan had already paid for. When Pakistan, like the rest of the world, discovered India was testing its nuclear arsenal in May 1998, it resisted pleas from President Clinton not to test its own devices, including an offer of billions more in aid, and Prime Minister Sharif's 'new clear vision' for Pakistan was proudly proclaimed on posters around the country. Unlike the post-Soviet states of Eastern Europe that exchanged their nuclear stockpiles for dollars, Pakistan would not be bought off. As a result, a new cycle of nuclear proliferation was set in motion, with Pakistan's scientists about to be enlisted to help both Iran and the Saudis in their desire to develop nuclear weapons technology.[22] So America's policy to 'cap, roll back and eliminate' the nascent Indian and Pakistani nuclear build-ups through incentives, threats of sanctions and censures failed, and we risk a global marketplace in nuclear weaponry developing.

Could all this, too, have been avoided? De-escalation became very difficult after India acquired a bomb. But there was another reason civilian leaders wanted nuclear weapons: to offset the power of a Pakistani army that had ruled the country since 1958. Moreover, Bhutto not only saw nuclear weapons as a symbol of national virility, which evoked popular support, but may also have believed that nuclear weapons could provide a shield behind which to conduct low-intensity conventional war against India, believing that India would not escalate or retaliate for fear of triggering nuclear war.

Twice in conflicts between Pakistan and India, nuclear weapons looked to be on the point of use: first in 1999, when India activated all of its three types of nuclear delivery vehicles and kept them at Readiness State 3; and again, two years later in December 2001, when India held Pakistan responsible for an attack on the Indian parliament in New Delhi. It took President George W. Bush and Secretary of State Colin Powell almost a year to talk the two countries down and to remove the threat of escalation.

The classical model of nuclear deterrence assumed that neither the US nor the Soviet Union would be careless enough to allow proxies to commit terrorist or conventional attacks on the other's homeland. However, Pakistan does not enjoy a monopoly on the legitimate use of force in its name and India may not always hold back when attacks can be traced back to somewhere in Pakistan. Meeting immediate security concerns – and reducing the possibility of nuclear weapons being used – will require greater transparency, enhanced dialogue and confidence-building measures all round but, more importantly, it will depend on restraint from leaders. When India suffered an attack on its homeland in 2008, Prime Minister Manmohan Singh resisted the pressures to strike back in order to avoid an escalatory cycle of retaliation. He forgave Pakistan, whose leaders signalled regret for the terrorist attacks while denying direct responsibility for them. And after a period of escalating conflict over Kashmir, the source of three wars since 1947, their leaders have concluded, as evidenced by the words of Prime Minister Imran Khan, that a permanent military stand-off is harming their economy and environment and their long-term national interests. 'National security', he said 'is also about non-traditional issues like climate change and food security which threaten Pakistan and its overall security.'

Over the past seventy years, the major powers have offered non-nuclear countries differing levels of assurance that have prevented proliferation, at the apex of which is the agreement within NATO to come to each others' defence. Assurances to non-nuclear states have included the more basic guarantee to deliver conventional weapons for self-defence; promises of direct military help; and even the provision of missile defence systems (as the US have done in South Korea). So important have such assurances been that when they seemed less than certain under President Trump, countries traditionally resistant to going nuclear were tempted, it appears, to reassess their options; South Korea by considering developing enrichment and reprocessing capabilities, and Taiwan, some allege, by putting itself in a position where it could produce a nuclear weapon in just a few years.

We can reflect on what kind of assurances could have prevented India or Pakistan acquiring nuclear weapons, but it is more important to ask what kind of assurances might be needed to prevent future proliferation. This applies not just in Asia but in the Middle East and Africa, where assurances regarding what the US or its allies could do to positively assist a country need to be accompanied by concrete proof that they will honour the Non-Proliferation Treaty's third pillar to seriously negotiate multilateral nuclear disarmament. We are right to complain about Russia's increased dependence upon nuclear weapons, but we should also find ways to move beyond the message sent out by Britain's March 2021 decision to increase its nuclear warheads from the current 220 to 260. Instead, in the spirit of the NPT and President Biden's first official statement on his new American strategy, we should show that we have a plan to downgrade the role of nuclear weapons in all our defence strategies. It is to that I now turn.

Risks beyond proliferation

Our efforts to reduce nuclear risk cannot stop at counter-proliferation. As long as the governments in charge of the world's nine nuclear arsenals continue to possess such awesome power it is incumbent on all of them – and us – to reduce, and hopefully eliminate, the risk of their use.

During the Cold War and in the period following it, there were important moments in which nuclear risk-reduction was taken seriously – and major progress was made. Often these steps forward came after leaders had walked to the nuclear brink and back. And, right from the invention of the nuclear bomb, there have been attempts at an even bolder course: not just to restrict the growth of nuclear weapons, but also to secure international control of nuclear weapons. Understanding that a nuclear weapon was not just 'another weapon' and believing it to be too dangerous a weaponry to be left in national hands, the then-US secretary of state pressed President Franklin Roosevelt for a world peace organisation that would ensure international control of the bomb. By late 1945, Roosevelt's successor, President Truman, who had resisted any idea of further nuclear bombings after Nagasaki, was contemplating some form of international control of atomic energy, 'seeking through the UN to put the control of the dangerous aspects of atomic energy beyond the reach of an individual nation'.[23] A combination of US nationalism and Soviet intransigence prevented any progress. At various points, world leaders have pleaded – as UK Prime Minister Attlee did when the use of nuclear weapons in Korea seemed possible – for international management of the new weapons.

But sufficient political will to create international norms and treaties did not come until after the Cuban Missile Crisis of 1962. By 1963, the US, the UK, the Soviet Union and over 100 others agreed the Partial Test Ban Treaty (PTBT), banning atmospheric nuclear testing – the prelude to the NPT of 1968. By 1972, the US and the Soviet Union were able to agree the Anti-Ballistic Missile (ABM) Treaty, which limited systems designed to intercept nuclear missiles, thus potentially reducing an opponent's ability to launch or respond to a first strike.

As in the 1960s, the nuclear brinkmanship of the 1980s gave way to diplomacy and arms control. President Reagan used a March 1983 speech to condemn the Soviet Union as an 'evil empire'.[24] That same month, Washington announced it was developing missile defence systems, known colloquially as Star Wars, and that it would build up its armed strength in Europe – compounding already deep-seated fears in the Soviet Union that the US was trying to undermine its ability to retaliate against a first strike. In November 1983, NATO began a military exercise. The exercise, named Able Archer, simulated the transition from conventional warfare to nuclear warfare. Soviet KGB officers from around NATO reported an increase in military activity and Moscow began to fear Able Archer was being used as cover for a Western nuclear first strike. The Soviet Union ordered its nuclear forces to be placed on high alert, with planes in East Germany and Poland loaded with bombs and submarines deployed. Able Archer eventually ended without Soviet fears being realised, but it was not until the defection of the KGB resident in London in 1985 that Western leaders discovered how Moscow had viewed the threat and how Soviet misinterpretation could have led to war.

Profoundly affected by the Able Archer saga when the world had again come so close to nuclear war, President Reagan began to push for arms control. The then-senator Joe Biden – a trusted operator across the aisle, who had already visited Moscow on arms control business for previous Democrat administrations – was sent by Reagan in 1983 on a clandestine mission with Republican senator and later defence secretary William Cohen, carrying a private message from the president regarding 'a new approach to arms control'. A 1986 meeting of the US and Soviet leaders in Reykjavík established trust and led to the Intermediate-Range Nuclear Forces (INF) Treaty. This prohibited both sides from possessing or developing missiles with a range of between 500 and 5,500 kilometres – weapons of ranges designed for use in battle rather than to deter. The INF Treaty was the first treaty to ban an entire class of nuclear weapons and it signalled to the world that both sides were actively committed to reducing the risk of nuclear use.

Following the collapse of the Soviet Union and the relatively peaceful end of the Cold War, Russia and the US again pushed for a reduction in the risk of nuclear war. Presidents Gorbachev and Bush Sr agreed to the Presidential Nuclear Initiatives to reduce their stockpiles of so-called 'tactical weapons' – weapons that were built not for deterrence but for use in war. From 1991 to 2010, Washington and Moscow signed a series of treaties that limited their nuclear arsenals.

New tensions

Warmer relations between Russia and the West had made weapons reduction possible. But, distracted by the challenge of terrorism and tensions in the Middle East, leaders failed to seize the opportunity for further and more lasting disarmament. Arguing that the US needed to build up its defences against so-called rogue nations like Iran, Washington withdrew in 2002 from the 1972 ABM Treaty and tore up what had been an important source of stability between Russia and the West. Moscow now cites the US move as a justification for Russia's growing nuclear capabilities.

Russia's aggression towards Ukraine since 2014 and its illegal annexation of Crimea showed once and for all that the post-Cold War calm was over. Now successive US and European administrations list great power competition – rather than terrorism – as the biggest strategic challenge facing their nation. Moscow has grown and modernised its nuclear arsenal and openly threatened nuclear use against NATO nations. China is developing its nuclear capabilities. The US is investing even more money in its nuclear budget. Nuclear tensions are back and one of the most concerning features of the post-Crimea era has been the gradual erosion of the hard-won system of international treaties and agreements governing nuclear weapons. The US withdrew from the Iran nuclear deal it had negotiated and again threatened military action against Tehran. Russia's violation of the INF Treaty, through the development and deployment of missiles that threaten Europe, became clear, destroying that landmark agreement, too.

Rising tensions and collapsing multilateralism would be concerning enough if it were once again two great powers standing off against one another. It is all the more worrying because the twenty-first century won't repeat the same bipolar order of the Cold War or the unipolar order of the past thirty years. Instead, in a multipolar order, several nuclear-armed states will face off against each other. The two-power race is becoming, for the first time, a three-power race with the Trump administration alleging that Beijing will double its nuclear stockpile by 2030. The principal source of nuclear risk for the first seventy-five years of the atomic age was fraught relations between Washington and Moscow. Nuclear risk in the next seventy-five years will come from Beijing and Washington, New

Delhi and Islamabad, Pyongyang and Tehran, as well as NATO and Russia. It needs only one of these relationships to fail for humanity to come closer to an existential threat.

Mankind's second nuclear arms race is under way, offering what Pope Francis has referred to as 'a false sense of security'.[25] All major weapon holders are engaged in what they call modernisation, but for some it is, in fact, an expansion of their arsenals. Russia is expanding the variety and capabilities of its nuclear delivery systems, with its newly deployed INF Treaty-breaking SSC-8 missile, which could conceivably hit NATO's European allies with little warning. And the most concerning aspect is the development of lower-yield nuclear weapons, which could be used in battle, rather than as a last resort, thus lowering the threshold of nuclear risk.

Technological change

New technologies, such as Russian underwater drones or American hypersonic weapons, which create new military capabilities and possibilities are also creating new mortal threats. This recent arms race is exacerbated by destabilising technological change through artificial intelligence (AI), quantum, offensive cyber, counter-space and hypersonic weapons. And new nuclear weapon capabilities are convincing – or, perhaps more accurately, deluding – nuclear strategists into the belief that an arms race can be won.

And so, in 2021, we have to ask: could a new Cold War ever stay 'cold'? Of course, technological change has always thrown up new possibilities – from the development of intercontinental ballistic missiles (ICBMs) to the building of anti-ballistic missile defence systems, new modalities (as outlined above) and the militarisation of outer space. But what is different today is the sheer scale and pace of change, as well as the qualitative transformation in the lethality of weapons and the way in which new nuclear and non-nuclear capabilities are entwined. The risks are obvious. As with the advent of offensive cyber capabilities, the race is on to hack into nuclear systems in order to subvert and disable them.

Governments will tell us that their systems are 'air gapped' – in other words, that they are not connected to the same Internet that the rest of us use. The UK government reports its submarine-based weapons are both 'air gapped' and 'sea gapped', adding to their security. In reality, no nation can guarantee the complete security of its most up-to-date, state-of-the-art technologies. In 2010, Iran discovered that its supposedly highly secure air-gapped nuclear programme had been infected by Stuxnet, a computer virus that caused many of the centrifuges used to enrich uranium to fail. Similar possible cyberattacks on command-and-control systems add another layer of uncertainty.

States develop nuclear weapons when they feel insecure and contemplate using them when they feel severely threatened. As nations scramble for dwindling natural resources – one of the forces that lies behind the world's largest migration of people in history – tensions, conflict and war become more likely. So it is not just a polluted and unsustainable global environment that is a deadly risk; it is, sadly, the potential for conflicts over the consequences of climate change to morph into deadly nuclear conflict, making it imperative to work to build a security architecture for a multipolar world.

Over recent years, individual arms control agreements have not only been torn up, but the nuclear arms control architecture itself has also withered on the vine: a nuclear test ban treaty has not been implemented; the Conference on Disarmament has failed for twenty years; the most detailed and stringent regime in the history of nuclear arms control, contained in the INF Treaty, has collapsed; and the next NPT review is at risk of stalling.

So, while the threat caused by nuclear weapons may have been overshadowed by pandemics, financial crises and trade conflicts, it has quietly grown to the point at which, some argue, the very idea of 'arms control' and 'risk reduction' is dead. And it is the frustration that other non-nuclear weapon countries feel at the lack of progress, together with the failure of the nuclear weapon states to implement the disarmament provisions of the NPT, that led to the Treaty on the Prohibition of Nuclear Weapons that came into force in January 2021 – a global agreement now ratified by more than fifty countries aiming to ban nuclear weapons in their entirety. Of course, the next nuclear near-miss might reinvigorate efforts towards a return to multilateralism and risk reduction – but there is no guarantee that it will be just a near-miss. Our task now is to build a security architecture that can both prevent and resolve crises.

Steps to greater security

The first step is the simplest: to salvage and protect what we have – in particular, the NPT and its three principles. (One: that states agree not to develop nuclear weapons. Two: that states gain access to the enormous benefits of nuclear technology. Three: critically, that the states that possess nuclear weapons agree to pursue serious negotiations on multilateral nuclear disarmament.) To defend this vital treaty, its signatories must demonstrate progress across all three of its pillars and not just rely on success in the first two. Buttressed by efforts to prevent the export of sensitive technologies, arms control, the IAEA monitoring system and the threat of sanctions for violating non-proliferation obligations, the treaty has stood most of the tests of time. The Cooperative Threat Reduction programme, the Global Threat Reduction Initiative, the Proliferation Security Initiative and the Additional Protocols have all provided powerful new tools for detecting activities that violate the NPT and endanger world security. The confidence provided by the IAEA verification system – that nuclear equipment and materials are not to be diverted to the production of nuclear weapons – has made the widespread use of nuclear energy for peaceful purposes possible.

A clear signal that states remain committed to the NPT and its principles would be a revised Iran nuclear deal (and alongside it some commitment by Iran to stop the sponsorship of terrorism in its region). And given the recent weakening of North Korea by famine and COVID-19, China may have some scope for leverage in using its considerable influence over Pyongyang more effectively, possibly bringing hope that North Korea might halt and eventually reverse its nuclear ambitions.

Perhaps the most important historic lesson that today's leaders need to relearn comes from Presidents Reagan and Gorbachev. The two leaders were able to agree in the 1980s that 'a nuclear war cannot be won and must never be fought'.[26] What came to be known as the Reagan–Gorbachev doctrine, jointly articulated at their 1985 summit in Reykjavík, opened the door to the greatest period for reduction of nuclear risk in the history of nuclear weapons. In the two decades that followed, treaties were agreed, stockpiles reduced and the Cold War was brought to an end in a way that few once imagined it would be: peacefully. But the statement offers us more: converting their eleven words from mere rhetorical flourish into purposeful action again would not only represent an acceptance of the rising dangers of nuclear conflict, but also be the basis for a strengthening of the global non-proliferation regime and for an eventual halt to the second nuclear arms race.

Reagan and Gorbachev cannot be dismissed as starry-eyed idealists who did not understand the realpolitik of the world they lived in. No one could say that a Republican president and a Communist Party general secretary were anything other than realists. But, while his nuclear policy remained based on the idea that the US 'must prevail', Reagan wrote in his memoir that he thought that those who claimed a nuclear war was 'winnable' were 'crazy'. He called for the abolition of 'all nuclear weapons', which he considered to be 'totally irrational, totally inhumane, good for nothing but killing, possibly destructive of life on earth and civilization'.[27] This vision, an unequivocal expression against the notion of any nuclear use, challenges the established doctrines of nuclear deterrence and is widely cited – for example, by Sweden – as the inspiration and starting point for very recent attempts to break the current nuclear deadlock.

The nearest a sitting president has come to delivering a reduction in the status of nuclear weapons since the early post-Cold War days is President Obama's initial effort after 2009. 'I state clearly and with conviction America's commitment to seek the peace and security of a world without nuclear weapons,' he declared, adding that it was in the US's interest, and that of all other nations, that the nearly 65-year record of nuclear non-use be extended for ever.[28] In Prague in April that year, he called for an end to Cold War thinking and for the US to reduce the role of nuclear weapons in its national security strategy. He also argued in his Nuclear Posture Review, released in 2010, that 'the massive nuclear arsenal inherited from the Cold War era of bipolar military confrontation is poorly suited to address the challenges posed by suicidal terrorists and unfriendly regimes seeking nuclear weapons'.[29] As a result, he substantially narrowed the conditions under which the US would use nuclear weapons: only in defence of the vital interests of the country and its allies in extreme circumstances. One of Obama's initial acts as president was to call the first of a number of nuclear security conferences and, in the twilight of his presidency, he went to the Peace Memorial at Hiroshima and called for 'a moral revolution in response to the growing dangers of nuclear war'.[30]

But, sadly, apart from the signing of New START in 2010, which capped Russian and American nuclear forces, the Obama years ended up with less to show for his efforts than he had promised or hoped for, and in truth, while arsenals did shrink at the end of the Cold War, there has been too little progress since. And to pass New START through a stubbornly uncooperative congress, Obama had conceded a massive modernisation of the US nuclear arsenal: a major upgrade of the country's ageing nuclear complex, including production facilities and laboratories, with a controversial price tag nearing $100 billion. This was the first stage of a programme that has since multiplied to include command-and-control systems, all the delivery vehicles of the nuclear triad (bombers, ICBMs and submarines), refurbishment of existing warheads and the development of a range of new warheads and weapons.

A lasting contribution to rethinking nuclear strategy came from the 'gang of four' or – better still – the 'four horsemen of the apocalypse': Henry Kissinger and George Shultz, former secretaries of state; William Perry, former secretary of defence; and Sam Nunn, former senator. Their joint articles from 2007 onwards proposed what they called global zero: a pathway to the elimination of nuclear weapons. Nuclear deterrence, they argued, came with risks and costs that were now unacceptably high, so they endorsed setting the goal of a world free of nuclear weapons. This was to be achieved by seeking a solid consensus for reversing reliance on nuclear weapons globally as a vital contribution to preventing their proliferation into potentially dangerous hands, with an ultimate goal of removing them completely.[31]

They agreed that, while nuclear weapons were essential to the Cold War, the end of the Cold War made the doctrine of mutual Soviet–US deterrence obsolete. And, even where there were threats from other states (and deterrence remained relevant) or from terrorists (for whom deterrence does not work), reliance on nuclear weapons was becoming increasingly hazardous and decreasingly effective. What's more, 'a new nuclear era . . . will be more precarious, psychologically disorienting, and economically even more costly than was Cold War deterrence'.[32]

Not only will old forms of deterrence not work, they suggested, but it is far from certain that we can successfully replicate the old 'mutually assured destruction' framework with a growing number of potential nuclear enemies worldwide without dramatically increasing the risk that nuclear weapons will be used. New nuclear states do not have the benefit of years of step-by-step safeguards put into effect during the Cold War to prevent nuclear accidents, misjudgements or unauthorised launches.

To hold to outdated ideas was as if we believed in nuclear deterrence only in the same sense that Pascal famously suggested one should believe in God: because the cost of doing so in error is lower than not doing so in error. Perry has followed this up most recently in his book *The Button*.[33] And so, if the leaders of the world's nuclear-armed states – in particular, those of the US and Russia – were able once again to declare that a nuclear war cannot be won and therefore must not be fought, it would send a powerful signal of intent to the world.

Fortunately, there is no need to reinvent the wheel when looking for early courses of action. Anyone who subscribed to Reagan–Gorbachev doctrine would have no need to build up their nuclear arsenals and no need at all to test them. Nuclear weapons have been employed only twice in war, but there have been an estimated 200 nuclear tests around the world since Trinity – the first successful nuclear test – in July 1945. Efforts to stop testing are by no means new. Test bans were central to President Eisenhower's early arms control efforts in the 1950s, but only after the Cuban Missile Crisis did we see a ban on atmospheric tests. In 1963, 126 states (notably not France, China or North Korea) ratified the PTBT, which prohibited atmospheric nuclear tests. Thirty years later, as the Cold War ended, the Comprehensive Nuclear Test Ban Treaty (CTBT) banned all nuclear explosions anywhere on the planet.

But, while the CTBT was agreed in 1996, it will not enter into force until current nuclear states such as the US, China, Iran, North Korea, India, Pakistan and Israel ratify it. While the US has been observing a moratorium on nuclear testing, there have recently been calls by some Republicans for testing to start again. They accuse China of secretly testing a 'low-yield 'nuclear weapon, which China denies. In the past, Joe Biden lobbied hard for the US to ratify the CTBT and is of the view that the US has no need to test. He said in 2017: 'We know more about our arsenal today – and its reliability – through stockpile stewardship than they did when testing was commonplace.'[34]

Asked in the course of his presidential campaign, 'Do you agree that a verifiable, global ban on explosive nuclear testing is in the national security interest of the United States?', his answer was:

> Yes. Bringing the Comprehensive Nuclear Test Ban Treaty into force is in America's security interest. The United States conducted more tests than any other country and has adequate data from decades of tests. A binding and verified agreement would constrain advances in nuclear weapons by other nuclear powers or countries that would seek to obtain a nuclear weapon reducing our reliance and excessive expenditure on nuclear weapons.[35]

Indeed, when he was vice president, Biden said that the secretaries of defence and energy certified each year that the country's nuclear stockpile continued to be 'safe and reliable' without need for nuclear testing and, 'by all accounts, that remains true today'. In a more recent statement to the *Nevada Independent* in 2020, he said that the new testing in Nevada, where the first tests were done, is as reckless as it is dangerous and any resumption of them is delusional. He asked:

> How can the United States persuade North Korea not to test and to give up its nuclear weapons, and how can we persuade Iran not to pursue nuclear weapons, if we set the destructive example of testing nuclear weapons for coercive purposes? It is not the time to discard our mantle of non-proliferation leadership, when there is no justifiable purpose for conducting a nuclear test.[36]

This is an indication that, as president, he will seek to put pressure not to test on countries like Pakistan and India, as well as North Korea. The US should immediately pursue ratification of the CTBT through the US senate. Washington and the other signatories to the treaty should publicly call on all the other hold-outs to do the same, especially China. Beijing can demonstrate its claim to global leadership by signing this treaty.

A commitment to ban the production of highly enriched uranium and plutonium for nuclear weapons, and thus implement a Fissile Material Cut-off Treaty, would signal a desire to reduce the role of nuclear weapons in the future. Commitments to do so have been made repeatedly by the UK including when I was prime minister. A large number of complex components are required to build and deliver a nuclear warhead: from the technology to spark a nuclear fission or fusion reaction to the delivery systems necessary to break through enemy air defences. But at the core of every weapon, whatever its design, is fissile material. A proposal to ban the further high enrichment of uranium and plutonium first emerged in the 1960s, but in 1993, after President Clinton called for a multilateral convention to ban 'for ever' the production of fissile materials, the UN General Assembly agreed by consensus on the 'banning of the production of fissile material for nuclear weapons or other nuclear explosive devices'. The treaty envisaged would, as its name suggests, cut off the existing stockpiles of fissile material.[37]

Efforts to negotiate a treaty have been blocked in the Geneva-based Conference on Disarmament, which requires unanimity among its sixty-five members. Four of the nine nuclear-armed states – France, Russia, the UK and the US – have all publicly declared that they have stopped production of highly enriched uranium and plutonium. A fifth state, China, is thought to have stopped production, making an eventual treaty seemingly more likely. Of course, the other four – Pakistan, India, Israel and North Korea – who do not have the same reservoir of supplies, are among forty-four countries that have yet to sign up to and ratify the treaty. Pakistan fears being locked into a treaty at a point when its uranium and plutonium stockpiles are inferior to those of India.

One option to make progress towards a critical treaty banning the production of fissile material would be to take the treaty out of the hands of the Conference on Disarmament, which has been unable to reach a consensus on its work programme, and hand it over to the United Nations General Assembly, where unanimity is not required. Sovereign states would, of course, have the right to vote against a treaty, but a negotiated treaty helping to further entrench an important norm would make the world safer. If a country objected, be that Pakistan, China or any other country, it would be making it clear to the world that it wants to significantly grow its nuclear arsenal. The international community would then be able to judge this as it wishes.

Sole purpose

Beyond multilateral efforts to prevent proliferation, nuclear-armed states have another powerful lever to pull. They can amend their military doctrines and narrow the scope for any nuclear threats or weapons use. Nuclear-armed states are often clearer about the circumstances in which they would *not* use nuclear weapons. Indeed, all five major nuclear weapon states have issued declarations – admittedly non-binding – that they will not use or threaten to use nuclear weapons against states in compliance with their obligations under the NPT. But, if they were consistent with the Reagan–Gorbachev doctrine that a nuclear war cannot be won and must not be fought, they should also commit never to use the threat of nuclear weapons to further any ambitions that have been pursued by non-nuclear means.

Today, some states prefer ambiguity, leaving their potential foes uncertain as to how they would respond to a conventional attack. But, even if the use of nuclear weapons in response to conventional weapons or weapons of mass destruction makes little strategic sense, the US nuclear review of 2019 referred to the 'extreme circumstances' in which the US would consider the use of nuclear weapons as 'significant non-nuclear strategic attacks' against 'US allied or partner civilian population or infrastructure, and attacks on US or allied nuclear forces, their command and control, or warning and attack assessment capabilities'.[38]

Notwithstanding the UK's redefinition in March 2021 of what would prompt their use of nuclear weapons: if nuclear-armed states, in particular the P5 group of leading nuclear weapon states, could agree that they will only consider nuclear use to deter or respond to a nuclear attack or an attack on nuclear command, control and communications infrastructure, this would help to reduce the chance of miscalculation in the case of rising tensions. A willingness to contemplate 'sole purpose' would reassure non-nuclear states that their nuclear-armed neighbours take seriously their responsibility to reduce the risk of nuclear use. In March 2021, the new Biden White House released its interim guidance on national security to act as a framework for its numerous foreign, defence and security policy reviews. In its guidance, the administration said it 'will take steps to reduce the role of nuclear weapons in our national security strategy'.[39] Advancing a 'sole purpose' doctrine would be one important way to achieve this goal.

First use

Following a sole-purpose agreement, nuclear-armed states should enter into negotiations on a 'no first use' commitment. 'No first use' means not initiating a nuclear war; not being the first to pull the trigger. It would not, of course, preclude the use of nuclear weapons as retaliation in response to a hostile strike, but it would exclude pre-emptive action. The argument for a declaration of 'no first use' is that, without it, a nuclear weapon state not only increases its chances of nuclear conflict, but also assumes, in contradiction of the Reagan–Gorbachev doctrine, that a nuclear war can be won.

Long-standing US policy has been to reserve the option of striking first, arguing that this makes war less likely. But it is often forgotten that, as early as the late 1940s, George Kennan, who wrote the famous letter warning of the inevitability of a Cold War, favoured a declaration of 'no first use' and of 'single use', abandoning any threat to counter conventional war with nuclear attacks. He thought it 'improbable' that the Soviets would use nuclear weapons and proposed that the deterrent consist of a minimal number of bombs. Over thirty years later, in 1982, Kennan joined the Kennedy administration's defence specialists, Robert McNamara and others, in calls for a 'no first use' policy. They argued that even a limited use of nuclear weapons would be catastrophic and a prelude to all-out nuclear war. The West should not rely on nuclear weapons to deter a conventional invasion of Western Europe or to deal with an accidental outbreak of conventional war anywhere. Increased conventional arms spending would be the best alternative to a 'first use' policy. In his memoirs, Kennan said that his advocacy of 'the adroit and vigilant application of counterforce', which had justified an aggressive nuclear stance, had always been misunderstood.[40]

'No first use' is the declared policy of India and China, but, of course, with varying degrees of reliability. China will 'unconditionally not use or threaten to use nuclear weapons against non-nuclear weapon states or in nuclear weapon-free zones and will never enter into a nuclear arms race with any other country'.[41] Indeed, China has called for an 'international legal instrument' to prohibit the 'first use' of nuclear weapons. But many in the US believe that China might be increasingly willing to use nuclear weapons first and early, even in a conventional war.

While India has a declared policy of 'no first use', Pakistan has issued no more than 'negative security assurances' to non-nuclear-armed states. Israel has not acknowledged its possession of nuclear weapons and thus has never made any nuclear doctrine public.

Of course, the most obvious practical challenge to any 'no first use' policy is the danger from North Korea, which has publicly declared a policy of 'no first use', but says that this is only valid 'as long as the hostile forces for aggression do not encroach upon its sovereignty'. The country regularly threatens to use its nuclear weapons against neighbours and the US.

In other countries, ambiguity remains the order of the day. The UK's 2015 National Security Strategy and Strategic Defence and Security Review promised to 'use our nuclear weapons only in extreme circumstances of self-defence, including the defence of our NATO allies. While our resolve and capability to do so if necessary is beyond doubt, we will remain deliberately ambiguous about precisely when, how and at what scale we would contemplate their use, in order not to simplify the calculations of any potential aggressor.'[42]

And, while the UK is willing to commit that it 'will not use, or threaten to use, nuclear weapons against any non-nuclear weapon states party to the [NPT]', provided that the state is not 'in material breach of those non-proliferation obligations', it now reserves the right to 'review this assurance' if a state were to develop not only chemical or biological weapons but also, in a toughening up of conditions that was announced in March 2021, other emerging non-nuclear technologies that could have the effect of weapons of mass destruction. 'We have never said that there will be no first use,' a government minister explained to the Lords Committee in 2018, 'and nor should we.'[43] The 2017 Defence and National Security Strategic Review reaffirmed France's equally ambiguous position that 'the use of nuclear weapons would be conceivable only in extreme circumstances of legitimate self-defence'.[44]

In its 2014 Military Doctrine, Russia reserved the option to use nuclear weapons in response to an attack using any type of weapon of mass destruction and in response to a conventional attack that placed the 'very existence of the state . . . under threat'. Indeed, some defence analysts now allege that 'Russia's military and civilian leaders' appear 'to believe that they could use low-yield nuclear weapons in small numbers to cement victory in a landgrab against NATO'. Clause 19 of the 'Conditions under which the Russian Federation Transitions to the Use of Nuclear Weapons' includes the possession of reliable information about the launch of ballistic missiles to attack Russian-controlled territory.[45] This opens the possibility for Moscow to launch Russian nuclear weapons not on confirmation of a nuclear attack, but simply on warning. In fact, Russia is developing and deploying capabilities, such as its SSC-8, aimed at restricting NATO's ability to reinforce itself across the Atlantic and coercing allies, in breach of the spirit of the INF Treaty.[46]

Ambiguity may destabilise the mind of an opponent, but it also increases the likelihood of misunderstandings. If it is unlikely that a state would respond to a non-nuclear attack with a nuclear weapon, should they not say so? The US 'has a de facto "no first use" policy', according to William Perry, who argued that, to demonstrate that the primary US goal is not domination but deterrence, such a policy should be formally declared. In the early years of the Obama administration, there were serious discussions about the US adopting a 'no first use' policy. The biggest obstacle turned out to be concerns among some Asian allies, and even among NATO allies, who argued that the credible threat of a US first strike was one of the most powerful deterrents against an increasingly assertive China and an aggressive Russia. And, of course, the US's most recent post-Obama Nuclear Posture Review in 2018 justified rejecting a 'no first use' policy on the grounds that the US needs to remain flexible to deter both nuclear and non-nuclear attacks.

But this was not the position of President Biden when he

responded to the Council for a Livable World's question – 'Should the United States review its current policy that reserves the right to use nuclear weapons first?' – with a blunt 'yes'.[47] Indeed, on his campaign website he said: 'The sole purpose of the US nuclear arsenal should be deterring – and, if necessary, retaliating against – a nuclear attack.' As president, he will work to put that belief into practice, in consultation with allies and the military.[48] He is already on record in 2017 stating:

> We made a commitment to create the conditions by which the sole purpose of nuclear weapons would be to deter others from launching a nuclear attack . . . Given our non-nuclear capabilities and the nature of today's threats – it is hard to envision a plausible scenario in which the first use of nuclear weapons by the United States would be necessary. Or make sense.

He went on to say that he was 'confident we can deter – and defend ourselves and our allies against – non-nuclear threats through other means'.[49]

Major force reductions

After a period of consultation about what measures could be taken to address any allied security concerns, I would favour the US seeking international agreement on 'sole purpose' and then 'no first use', and would make it conditional in only one sense: that this is a promise made to all countries, both nuclear and non-nuclear, who fulfil the obligations of the NPT. This could also be extended to include other important non-proliferation treaties, including those on testing and on the production of fissile materials, once they are negotiated and come into force. There is no better way to indicate the importance of these treaties than to put them at the heart of efforts to reduce risk. And there is no better way to prove that the purpose of weapons is to deter than to eliminate those not needed to respond to an adversary's first strike.

If a state declares that it will use nuclear weapons only if it or its allies are attacked with nuclear weapons, then the only weapons it needs are those designed to survive a first strike. Defence experts generally conclude that submarine-based weapons, given these boats' ability to hide in expansive oceans, are the most survivable. Land-based missiles, such as the US's ICBMs, are the most vulnerable, because they can be easily located and targeted using satellites. They are therefore also the most destabilising. This is because in a crisis, states might fear that an adversary will try to take out their ICBMs, so they may feel pressure to use them before they lose them, which is why they are considered to be on 'hair trigger' alert. Imagine a scenario in which, for example, a nuclear power received a false alarm that another power had launched a first strike, and therefore felt the need to launch its weapons before they were taken out: a so-called 'launch on warning' posture.

Land-based nuclear weapons are thus the least appropriate for a country that doesn't plan to attack an adversary first. The countries possessing land-based nuclear weapons, including the US, China and Russia, should seek agreements to reduce and eventually eliminate these arsenals. Of course, the US holds an advantage in its conventional long-range precision strike capabilities, and other countries would want to replace their land-based nuclear capabilities with enhanced conventional capability, but a major reduction in nuclear risk would have been achieved while sustaining deterrence with both conventional weapons and a less risky nuclear arsenal.

Nuclear weapons do not exist in a vacuum. Nuclear weapons are, of course, used to project power in the world, but they are there because states perceive themselves to be insecure. The last UK Labour government established the P5 dialogue between the five nuclear weapon states recognised by the NPTs; it also reduced our dependence on nuclear weapons and pioneered new work on nuclear disarmament verification. And of course, we cut our nuclear weaponry and are, I believe, the only country that can genuinely say it has the minimum credible deterrent. But had we felt that the threat from nuclear-armed adversaries had diminished, we would have been inspired to do more to pursue even greater reductions; I would have declared a policy of 'sole purpose' and 'no first use', which I now propose the UK government moves towards with its allies.

If NATO's Eastern European allies and the US's Asian allies felt more secure in the face of a renewed Russian threat against them, then they may be more willing to support efforts by the US to reduce the role of nuclear weapons in its strategies. If Russia did not feel insecure because its role as a leading military power was under challenge, it may well not be announcing, as now, an enhanced role for nuclear weapons. And, if Iran did not feel that its existing capabilities were insufficient to deter its neighbours and the West, then there would be little prospect of it again choosing to expensively pursue nuclear weapons.

We can argue about the credibility and the legitimacy of the stances countries are taking to justify the build-up of their nuclear weaponry, but no progress will be possible on arms control if we disregard their security concerns. If states are to reduce the role nuclear weapons play in their defence, they will inevitably rely more on – and seek to increase – their conventional military capabilities. If, say, NATO and its thirty members were to feel able to reduce their reliance on nuclear deterrence, they would have to either be confident that the threat from Russia has receded or assess that their conventional capabilities in Europe are now sufficient to defeat Russia in the event of a Russian attack. It may seem counterintuitive to some, but, if European countries who have not yet done so honoured their commitments to invest 2 per cent of their national incomes on defence, they would be strengthening conventional deterrence, itself a positive step towards nuclear risk reduction.

In Asia-Pacific theatres, US guarantees fall short of a NATO-like alliance, but Washington's commitments are also an important stop on potential proliferation risks. Take the needs of a country like Australia. Australia has recently affirmed that 'only the nuclear and conventional capabilities of the United States can offer effective deterrence against the possibility of nuclear threats against Australia', but – given the recent unpredictability of the US – it is 'essential that the ADF [Australian Defence Force] grow its self-reliant ability to deliver deterrent effects'.[50] In the absence of a strong US military role in the region, countries that are worried about China's increasing military power – such as Australia, South Korea and Japan – will call for independent nuclear deterrents of their own. Herein lies the greatest challenge. How can the US and the wider West provide the necessary military support to protect these non-nuclear-armed states and discourage proliferation – but, crucially, do so without exacerbating the threats from China and Russia?

This is where the US could lead by example. Even if other states in possession of land-based nuclear weapons are unwilling to abandon their capabilities, the US, which has, of course, its own submarine-based missiles and long-range bombers, could put its ICBMs on the table in a future arms control negotiation. To do so would send a strong signal to the countries that feel threatened by the US's strategic nuclear arsenal that Washington has no desire to strike their homelands.

How other nuclear-armed states responded to this gesture would also signal to the rest of the world where the greatest current source of nuclear risk comes from – be it from the US and its allies or from others. Hypothetically, a China that continued to grow its nuclear arsenal and refused to sign up to a test ban or to discontinue further uranium enrichment, would reveal itself to be one of the most significant sources of nuclear risk – and its partners around the world could act accordingly.

With declarations not to use nuclear weapons first, and never to use them at all other than if attacked by nuclear weapons, the international community will then be in a stronger position to pressure, sanction and isolate countries that fail to comply with the NPT.

Conclusion

The changing of the guard in Washington, effected over a violent and dramatic two weeks in January 2021, together with the highly probable exclusion of the 45th President from any future in politics, may at best transform the nature of geopolitics and achieve the rescue of numerous sabotaged international agencies that were de-funded and despoiled over the years 2016 to 2020. And it is perhaps not naïve to assume that the prospects for nuclear disarmament will benefit accordingly.

Most of this chapter has been about nuclear risk reduction: how we can effectively prevent the possession or use of nuclear weapons by any one state. But there are more basic questions at issue. In 1932, already worried about the growth of fascism in Europe and anxious to find a way to prevent what he sensed was the descent into another world war, Albert Einstein, the world's most renowned physicist, began a correspondence with Sigmund Freud, the world's best-known psychoanalyst. 'What would curb the aggressive instinct in man?' he asked, aware that such behaviour invariably drowned out any feelings of altruism and empathy and any desire for solidarity and cooperation. Laws, said Freud, were important but were not enough. Education was the key to cultivating the better angels of our nature. Raising Einstein's alternative way forward is important because ever since the hideously explosive and life-destroying power of nuclear weapons was revealed, the scientists who built on Einstein's work, such as J. Robert Oppenheimer and his colleagues in Los Alamos (who began work in 1942 and almost unbelievably delivered usable weapons by 1945), recognised immediately that what they had created had huge lethal potential. As a result they almost immediately campaigned to create a taboo around the weapons' possession and use. As we have seen, the fifty-year-old NPT has had some success in curbing the spread of nuclear weapons, but it has failed to establish a universal taboo.

At one point in the early 1950s, when fighting the Korean War, President Eisenhower told his defence chiefs that, in order 'to keep the attack [on Korea] from becoming overly costly, it was clear we would have to use atomic weapons'.[51] This appeared to contradict his famous 1953 'Atoms for Peace' speech to the UN, when he had expressed America's 'determination to help solve the fearful atomic dilemma — to devote its entire heart and mind to find the way by which the miraculous inventiveness of man shall not be dedicated to his death but consecrated to his life'.[52]

But, two years later, in 1955, he suggested that, 'in any combat where these things [i.e. nuclear weapons] can be used on strictly military targets and for strictly military purposes, I see no reason why they shouldn't be used just exactly as you would use a bullet or anything else'. To which Secretary of State Allen Dulles said that, if this was to be their policy, they had to solve a moral problem: the 'inhibitions on the use of nuclear weapons that made them unacceptable'. He told Eisenhower that 'somehow or other we must manage to remove the taboo from the use of these weapons'.[53] But he could never remove the taboo in its entirety. A recent poll showed that fewer than 20 per cent of US citizens support possible US 'first use' of nuclear weapons. By contrast, disapproval stands at 63 per cent and is the majority view held by US citizens regardless of gender, age, race, education, income, region of residence or, importantly, political party.[54]

If revulsion against nuclear weapons was enough to change policy, we would have achieved more in the past seventy-five years, but people also need to believe, as Reagan and Gorbachev agreed, that such weapons must never and will never be used. They have to be sure there will be no hiding place, no safe haven, for those who threaten our long-established nuclear peace, especially since after seventy years of a two-power nuclear stand-off in which nuclear weapons were never used, the world has become more dangerous: a world still nuclear armed, but far more unstable.

This generation lives with the grim threat from multiple nuclear powers, some principally regional – as in South Asia – and some global, namely the US, Russia and China. The US and Russia, with by far the world's largest arsenals, have the greatest responsibility to reduce this threat. Russia, in particular, must roll back its increasing reliance on nuclear weapons, its dangerous developments of new and destabilising delivery systems and its inflammatory rhetoric. China also has a critical role, with its growing arsenal and its important role in global politics, including holding the key that can unlock nuclear de-escalation in North Korea, Pakistan and, indirectly, India.

We should test the willingness to consider 'sole purpose' and 'no first use', and to agree bans on both testing and producing highly enriched uranium and plutonium for nuclear weapons. All this would require backing up with a change in military positioning and defence postures and – almost certainly – with fresh economic incentives for wayward states to do the right thing. For example, North Korea is unlikely ever to give up its nuclear weapons without strong pressure from China, though Kim Jong-Un's current serious problems with COVID-19, mass starvation and a failing five-year plan give him a strong economic incentive to comply – especially if he concluded that non-compliance was more of a threat to his regime than disarmament.

The renewal for five years of New START by Russia and the US in January 2021 and intense discussions on a new Iranian treaty, which may or may not be conditional upon Iran's discontinuation of the sponsorship of regional terrorism, brought about through the appointment of a US secretary of state who was one of the brokers of the original treaty, may go some way to renewing compliance on the part of Iran. Meanwhile, the US appears to be seriously engaging in non-proliferation diplomacy; hopefully President Biden can propose a ban on testing and on the expansion of fissile materials, and outline a more advanced position on 'sole purpose' and 'no first use'.[55] This could lead other nations to respond in kind, and thus we have a chance in this generation to reverse the world's reliance on nuclear weapons, prevent their proliferation into dangerous hands, and chart a clear pathway to ultimately eliminating them as a mortal threat to our world. For sixty years on, Kennedy's words still ring true. We are still 'hanging by the slenderest of threads, capable of being cut at any moment by accident or miscalculation or by madness'. I conclude now, as he did then, that 'the weapons of war must be abolished before they abolish us'.

PART THREE

Shaping Our Future

9

'ONE WORLD, TWO SYSTEMS': AVOIDING A CHINA–US COLD WAR

'China first', 'America first'

In the currently COVID-19-dominated world, it is ironic that the two countries that will decide whether there are global solutions to global problems are China, where the virus seems to have originated, and the US, which has been arguably among the hardest hit.

And – because one is the established power and the other is the rising power, now threatening to match and even overtake the former – we moved during 2020, in the words of Henry Kissinger, from the 'foothills' to the 'mountain passes' of a potential Cold War, with major implications for the entire world.[1] 'If we walk down the path of confrontation – be it a cold war, a hot war, a trade war or a tech war', President Xi of China told the World Economic Forum in January 2021, 'all countries are going to suffer.'[2]

Of course, the competition and conflict between the US and China goes back to well before COVID-19 sickened and killed millions. Over the past three decades, I've had some experience – and, for a period of time, a front seat – dealing with and trying to understand both sides, and I believe that such experience can shed light on what the future is likely to bring.

In 2008, I responded to a request from Tibetan leader the Dalai Lama to meet him during his pilgrimage to the UK. It was a sensitive request and a sensitive visit. The Chinese government did not want any UK prime minister to give him the time of day.

The Dalai Lama was and is widely recognised as one of the world's most respected moral and religious leaders. He also claimed the political right to rule Tibet. The UK had rushed to his aid in 1959 when he had been forced to flee from his country. One of our newspapers made world headlines when it published what it said was the journalistic scoop of the decade: an exclusive interview with the Dalai Lama as he flew out of Tibet into exile. In fact, the Dalai Lama had left Tibet on foot and travelled out over the mountains. Continuing global interest in this leader is such that his writings and thoughts have always attracted large and admiring audiences in the UK and beyond. Everywhere he travels, to the annoyance of Chinese authorities, he makes news.

I felt an instinctive sympathy for someone fighting for his religious freedom and human rights and I was convinced it was right to meet him. I was careful to distinguish between his religious and his political status, so I decided to meet him not in Downing Street – the centre of government – nor at the House of Commons – the home of parliament – but, with the Church's permission, at Lambeth Palace, the home of the spiritual head of the Church of England, the archbishop of Canterbury. In this way, I would recognise his importance as a religious leader without inflaming the controversy over his political ambitions.

To no avail: China interpreted my meeting in May 2008 as UK support for the Dalai Lama's political designs and cut off high-level contacts with the UK for six months. Only when President Hu and I met a number of months later with other world leaders to discuss a global response to the financial crisis did he signal that the freezing of relations was over: 'Things are now better than they were.' Ice broken – just!

The UK policy on Tibet that I had inherited was a relic from imperial days and irrelevant to the changing situation. The UK had once supported total independence for Tibet. Yet not even the Dalai Lama was proposing independence. He wanted to be the leader of a devolved Tibet that had a high degree of autonomy within a federal China. On my instructions, we amended the long-standing but wrong-headed UK policy and brought it in line with current realities and the stance of most other nations.

But, a few months later, when the UK's new Conservative– Liberal Democrat coalition had been agreed, its two leaders, who had castigated me for meeting the Dalai Lama in church premises and not on state grounds, issued an open invitation asking him to meet them in Downing Street. Not surprisingly, relations with China soured even more. China froze high-level contacts again; strategic discussions were postponed; and a proposed prime ministerial visit to China was cancelled on the orders of the Chinese authorities. Attempts to break the new ice were to no avail. In desperation, the UK offered a series of cultural visits, including asking the entire cast of *Downton Abbey* – then one of China's most popular TV series – to tour China. Dame Maggie Smith notwithstanding, China would resume full diplomatic relations only in its own time and on its own terms.

Ten years ago, I was already seeing at first hand the way the wind was blowing. The sheer rigidity of the Chinese stance may have surprised those who had heard Chinese leaders talk of the 'peaceful rise of China' and might have concluded that, even if only on tactical grounds, China would, in the words of a former leader, 'hide its brightness and bide its time'. But I could see that China now had a very clear view of its status in the world and what it could demand of other nations. You were either for China or you were against it – and giving any time to the Dalai Lama, even on church premises as a religious leader, fell into the latter category. Even before 2010, such attitudes were rigidly held: those who had imagined that China would give ground to Western ideas about human rights and religious freedoms were already, it seemed, being proved wrong.

Within a few years, China appeared to be further hardening its

line and justifying its inflexibility on issues of human rights and religious freedom by repeatedly citing the UN Charter in its defence. It
specifically cited Article I's support for 'the principle of equal rights
and the self-determination of peoples'. Nothing Chinese leaders
said ever mentioned that the very same article referred to 'respect
for human rights and for fundamental freedoms for all without
distinction as to race, sex, language or religion'.[3]

Instead, China focused on the section of Article II that required
that countries 'refrain . . . from the threat or use of force against
the territorial integrity or political independence of any state'. So,
seventy years on from its adoption, the Chinese government had
selectively weaponised the UN Charter to justify what most of
the world views as illiberal and authoritarian behaviour.

And, of course, as the US under President Trump walked out
of UN organisations, including the Human Rights Council, China
gained in power, even to the point of winning a seat in 2020 on
the five-member panel selecting the rapporteurs who carry out
UN investigations into human rights abuses. When, a few months
later, the UN debated China's curtailment of political freedoms
in Hong Kong, China's supporters – led by Cuba – mustered the
votes of fifty-three countries, whereas a UK-led expression of
concern could secure only twenty-seven.[4]

Throughout its 75-year history, the UN has been repeatedly
criticised for pulling its punches and for its inability to reconcile
its charter's defence of human rights everywhere with its charter's
doctrine of non-interference anywhere. As a result, it has veered
from an emphasis on civil and political rights in one decade to
giving priority to economic and social rights in another. Indeed,
in 1969, when the UN's commemoration of twenty years of the
Universal Declaration of Human Rights justified a special conference, convened in Iran, in what seems now to be a travesty
of any concern for human rights, the Shah of Iran was lauded
by delegates from all over the world for presiding over such a
celebration, even though, at the same time, he was ordering his

infamous SAVAK secret police to hound, torture, imprison and murder human rights activists.

But now with China justifying its human rights record by claiming that its interpretation of the UN Charter permits it to do whatever it wants behind its own borders with impunity, onlookers could be forgiven for thinking that, while we may have one world, we have two value systems.

And not only has China sought to demand unconditional acceptance of its fixed positions. All too often the US has, too. I admit to being shocked when I discovered how many American officials viewed the transatlantic relationship in which the UK takes such pride as more subservient than 'special'. This came home to me in an interesting, but so far unreported, series of exchanges between our two countries at the time of the Iraq War.

After the carnage of 9/11, when my predecessor Tony Blair rightly stood 'shoulder to shoulder' with the US, the bonds between our two countries became stronger than ever. President George W. Bush and Prime Minister Blair launched their nations into the Iraq War together. They worked as an indivisible team, with day-to-day contact over phone and video, jointly timed statements and press conferences, and carefully choreographed public interventions to display an unbreakable Western alliance.

But, as I examined events more closely from my position as Chancellor of the Exchequer, the special relationship was beginning to have a few of the features of a master–servant relationship and looking less like a partnership of equals. In a minute I saw of a crucial meeting between the president and the prime minister, Tony was reported as saying that the US and the UK had different roles to play: Washington would lead on the policy; London would lead in its presentation. 'You mean that you could even make Dick Cheney look good?' George Bush joked in response, referring to his powerful and widely vilified vice president.

Before we look forward, it is instructive to look back. Of course, with its unsurpassed military and economic power, the

US was the dominant power from as far back as 1940. Back then, Winston Churchill, the incoming UK prime minister, headed for Washington and spent weeks in residence at the White House, effectively begging President Roosevelt to abandon the US's neutrality and come to the UK's aid. He admitted openly that the UK and its allies would not be able to win the Second World War without help: only if the US entered could the free world be saved from the brutal Nazi domination already inflicted on most of Europe.

Churchill, as we now know, regularly lost his arguments with Roosevelt over Allied military strategy – not least the UK's opposition to the D-Day landings in 1944 and its desire to win the war from the Mediterranean and through Italy. At the root of the disagreements was the US's perception that the UK's agenda was to use the war to preserve an unreformed British Empire. Meanwhile, the UK harboured its suspicions about Roosevelt's Atlantic Charter, which, with its bold enunciation of the Four Freedoms for people everywhere in the world, signalled that the imperial age was doomed.[5]

Roosevelt was careful never to allow the world to think the UK–US relationship was anything other than special. In public, the two leaders presented a united front, leaving no space for the public to see anything other than an unbreakable bond. Roosevelt was always careful to accord Churchill an equivalent status at the top table.

In the early 1960s, President Kennedy never complained when his much older UK counterpart, Prime Minister Harold Macmillan, spoke of the UK as Greeks to the US's Romans; of the UK as the mature, thoughtful counterweight to the impulsive, less mature US. Instead, Kennedy allowed Macmillan to be seen in the eyes of the world as the trusted and valued adviser of a much younger president.

Macmillan played the role with some success. He managed to negotiate UK access to the nuclear weapons system based on

Polaris submarines. But, while the UK claimed to have a wholly independent nuclear deterrent, Polaris was a US system, built by US scientists and engineers, to an extent that is only likely to be fully acknowledged in history books a century from now. Even the UK's 'independent' defence policy looked like it was dependent on the US.

In the 1980s, the Margaret Thatcher–Ronald Reagan relationship had flourished, with the two sharing an interest both in neoliberal economics and in ending the Cold War. But it was not all plain sailing. As Thatcher let slip to me in a private conservation, the basis of their relationship was that 'he was more afraid of me than I was of him'. However, when it came to managing the global issues of the day, she complained of not being listened to. When she sought to be the bridge between Russia and the US – 'I like Mr Gorbachev; we can do business together' – she was generally ignored, although, in due course, Reagan's relationship with Mikhail Gorbachev later thrived, as I shall go on to describe.

When it came to the UK's response following the Argentinian invasion of the Falkland Islands, the US quietly provided critical intelligence support and weaponry – in particular, vital Sidewinder air-to-air missiles – but generally refrained from explicit expressions of support, for reasons perhaps rooted in the Monroe Doctrine, formalised in 1850, which rejected transatlantic interference in the Americas. Perhaps an especially intriguing example of a special relationship?

In the early 2000s, Prime Minister Blair and President Bush discussed in private how the UK–US relationship might evolve. But what came forward from the Americans was something no British leader could be comfortable with: the possibility of the UK joining the US security apparatus as some kind of associate member, with the UK sitting alongside the president and vice president, the National Security Council, the FBI, the CIA and the Joint Chiefs of Staff. If this initiative had become known, there would have been a public outcry amid allegations that the UK was being treated not just as the fifty-first state but as a sixth agency. None of this transpired and the tried and effective system of high-level intelligence-sharing continues in its traditional form: for example, within the Five Eyes collaboration that includes Canada, Australia, New Zealand, the US and the UK.

In the old unipolar age from 1991, after the collapse of the Soviet Union, the US had regularly and happily chosen to act multilaterally within the UN and in support of the WHO and other international agencies. But, following the collapse of the Soviet bloc, a neoconservative right-wing Project for the New American Century emerged in 1997 'to promote American global leadership' – a grandiose initiative that left the US's allies unimpressed.[6] It lapsed in 2006, but worse was soon to come. In a multipolar age, US policy was becoming more demanding of its neighbours and its allies. In 2016, Trump went much further, declaring 'America First' and proceeding with a simplistic, xeno-phobic, anti-Europe, anti-NATO agenda – to the puzzlement and concern of the world's liberal democracies.

Much of this involved substituting tariff wars for diplomacy, with China and its vast and rapidly growing economy as the pri-mary target. With President Xi recently entrenched for the long haul and unchallenged, the stage was set for a Trump–Xi standoff, though Xi had the advantage of job security. As Xi intransigently pursued growth and strong expansionism in his efforts to engage and invest around the world, a future of 'one world, two systems' became a real possibility. But few would have predicted just how fast the China–US relationship would deteriorate. At the turn of the century, after all, the US invited China into the World Trade Organization, later defining the country as a potential 'responsi-ble stakeholder'.[7]

But nothing illustrates better the downward spiral in the China–US relationship and its descent from multilateral coop-eration to two competing power blocs than the response to COVID-19. China and the US, confronting a common virus and a common world economic recession, with the knowledge that the virus could not be fully eradicated in one country until it was eradicated in every country, found themselves unable to cooperate and were reduced to a war of words as to who was to blame for what went wrong. Trump's twittering non-diplomacy, using terms like the 'China virus' and 'kung flu', did little to improve things. Rather than using the seventy-fifth anniversary celebrations of the UN in September 2020 to reaffirm common values, the world was forced to watch a slanging match and witness a blame game between the two countries.

'We have waged a fierce battle against the invisible enemy, the "China virus", which has claimed countless lives in 188 countries,' Trump proclaimed. 'We must hold accountable the nation that unleashed this plague onto the world: China.' And, just in case the world's leaders had not got the message, he concluded: 'The United Nations must hold China accountable for their actions.'[8]

This prompted Xi to fire back that 'any attempt of politicising the issue [of the virus] or stigmatisation must be rejected'. Indeed, their speeches to the UN showed that the two leaders might as well have been on different planets. Xi donned the garments previously worn by the US and presented himself as the foremost champion and defender of the multilateral system the US once built, which Trump had just denounced. 'COVID-19 reminds us', he said, 'that we are living in an interconnected global village with a common stake.'[9]

Declaring China to be a benevolent power that wished no ill on anyone, Xi omitted to acknowledge his country's growing unilateralism: its aggressive strategy of militarising the South China Sea; its repressive laws in Hong Kong; its dark threats to the independence of Taiwan, the self-governing island that China regards as Chinese territory; the persecution of religious minorities; and, of course, its policy of binding Asian and African countries into a new Chinese sphere of influence through lending money to them on terms that make them highly dependent on China.

Despite all their differences, Stalin's Soviet Union supported the creation of the UN and signed important treaties with Roosevelt and Truman. Kennedy and Khrushchev were able to find sufficient common ground to avoid a nuclear confrontation. Gorbachev and Reagan ended the Cold War. And yet, by contrast, the only message of significance to emerge from the seventy-fifth anniversary of the world's biggest diplomatic forum was that of a widening schism between today's two great powers.

It was left to the secretary-general of the UN, António Guterres, to describe what was happening in front of his eyes as the planet started to move 'in a very dangerous direction': 'Our world cannot afford a future where the two largest economies split the globe in a Great Fracture – each with its own trade and financial rules and Internet and artificial intelligence capacities.' Such a divide, he concluded, 'risks inevitably turning into a geo-strategic and military divide':

> We must avoid this at all costs . . . We face a foundational moment. Those who built the United Nations seventy-five years ago had lived through a pandemic, a global depression, genocide and world war. They knew the cost of discord and the value of unity . . . we face our own 1945 moment.

We must, he was saying, 'rebuild and reset', just as leaders had done in the aftermath of the Second World War, otherwise we will return to the chaos and anarchy of the pre-war and war-time years.[10]

The opportunity now comes with the new Biden administration. But the China–US standoff is happening at a time when the balance of power in the world is itself changing at speed. Flashback three years to two international meetings kicking off on the same day in 2018: the G7 in Canada and the Shanghai Cooperation Organisation (SCO) summit. There could be no more visible sign of a new world disorder and of a changing of the guard – as well as the problems that brings – than the contrasting pictures that emerged from the two summits happening thousands of miles apart on the same weekend.

The G7 summit in La Malbaie, Quebec, which comprised the US, Canada, Europe's four biggest economies and Japan, broke up in disarray and discord when Trump not only refused to sign any communiqués – the first time this had happened since the formation of this organisation in the mid-1970s – but also bitterly denounced the Canadian chairman of the summit, Prime Minister Justin Trudeau, for 'false statements' that were 'very dishonest and weak'. It also produced the iconic picture of the world's leaders standing and glaring at Trump, who was seated, his arms crossed in defiance.

With only one unsurprising exception – the US's opposition to the Paris Agreement – the summit's members had initially appeared to agree on: a communiqué that referred to the need for 'free, fair, and mutually beneficial trade'; the importance of fighting protectionism; a joint demand that Moscow 'cease with its destabilising behaviour'; and a pledge to 'permanently' ensure Tehran's nuclear programme remained peaceful. But this consensus was thrown to the winds by Trump insisting on the US getting its way on everything and agreeing to nothing if that wasn't the case. Indeed, Trump went on to multiply the divisions within the G7 by calling for Russia, then subject to Western sanctions because of its invasion of Ukraine, to be readmitted to the organisation. Here, unmistakably, was 'America First', dismissive and unashamed.

But, while the West was exposing its disarray, Eastern unity was on show in the coastal Chinese city of Qingdao under the leadership of China. The country's state-run newspapers proudly contrasted the two events, boasting of the SCO summit as harmonious and anti-protectionist, in counterpoint to the G7. As one Chinese state newspaper concluded: 'The G7 summit has served as another reminder that it is the Trump administration that is challenging the international rules-based order.'[11]

Present at the SCO conference, which had been staged regularly since 2011, were not only the leaders of Russia, Kazakhstan, Kyrgyzstan, Tajikistan and Uzbekistan, but also, for the first time, the prime ministers of both India and Pakistan. Iran, which had announced it was seeking full membership of the SCO, had observer status, alongside countries seen by the West as part of its sphere of influence – Afghanistan and Belarus – whose communiqué pointedly stated that they wanted to 'focus on seeking common ground while setting aside differences and pursuing mutually beneficial cooperation'. And, while primarily an organisation dedicated to economic cooperation, the China-led summit endorsed a plan of action to implement what it called the Treaty on Long-Term Neighbourliness, Friendship and Cooperation between their Member States and talked of building 'a community with shared future for mankind'.[12]

Of course, India, for one, is not signed up to Chinese hegemony and has withdrawn from the new Regional Comprehensive Economic Partnership, the deal that brings most of Asia together by cutting tariff and non-tariff barriers to trade. The quadrilateral security pact India joined with Japan, Australia and the US in 2007 as a counter to China is currently being strengthened. Equally Russia would continue to claim it enjoys military superiority over China. And, furthermore, there is far more in common between Europe and the US than the G7 summit's disputed communiqué implied. But the one conclusion to be drawn from these events and the experience of recent years is that, more than ever, there are not just two competing powers, but potentially two competing power blocs and two competing systems: 'America First' and 'China First'. We have entered the Biden–Xi years with each nation perhaps now less willing to compromise or seek out common ground and each nation now ever-more insistent that its own definition of what is in the interests of the global community should take precedence. And so we have to ask: will we eventually see a Sinosphere in which global networks of trade and innovation once based in the industrialised West are replaced by those based in a dominant China?

China's rise to power

We cannot ignore the context: the changing balance of economic power. Before examining whether there are ways to resolve the differences between the two countries, we have to distinguish between the permanent, structural characteristics of the China– US relationship, which are being written in stone, and what are simply the day-to-day disagreements that can arise because of personalities and events, but are often transient concerns.

A future of 'one world, two systems' has always been a possibility because of the rise of China and Asia. China's rising economic power is well documented: from 4 per cent of the world economy as recently as 2000 to 16 per cent now. It is the biggest manufacturing power, the biggest trading power, the biggest iron and steel producer, and now a world leader in some of the most significant new industries like solar power, electric cars and battery technology – all accompanied by an additional ambition to lead the world in artificial intelligence by 2025. Indeed, economist Branko Milanović writes:

> If China's growth continues to exceed Western countries' growth by two to three percentage points annually, within the next decade, many middle-class Chinese will become wealthier than their middle-class counterparts in the West. For the first time in two centuries, Westerners with middling incomes within their own nations will no longer be part of the global elite – that is, in the top quintile (20 per cent) of global incomes. This will be a truly remarkable development. From the 1820s onward – when national economic data of this kind were first collected – the West has consistently been wealthier than any other part of the world. By the middle of

the nineteenth century, even members of the working class in the West were well-off in global terms. That period is now coming to an end.[13]

Table 6: GDP % shares of global total (current prices)

	2000	2010	2020	2030	2040	2050
Europe	27.9	27.3	21.7	18.3	16.0	13.7
US	30.6	22.7	23.9	21.8	20.0	18.1
Asia*	24.4	26.7	32.4	33.9	36.4	39.4

*Of which:

	2000	2010	2020	2030	2040	2050
Japan	14.6	8.6	5.4	4.0	3.5	3.0
China	3.6	9.2	15.8	16.9	17.6	18.6
India	1.4	2.5	3.4	4.4	5.7	7.2

China's progress is indeed remarkable. GDP per capita in 1978, at the time of the initiation of rural reforms, was only around $1,500 – so low that it was still half that of the UK at the time of the Industrial Revolution. By 2015, it was more than $12,000; China had achieved more economic progress in forty years than the UK had in a century and a half (1770–1914). But, even so, it will take time for China to achieve its ambition to match high-income countries. China's income per head is still only about 25 per cent of that of the US.

As Milanović writes:

In 2013, the gap between the median income of an American and a Chinese person was 4.7 to 1 (and 3.4 to 1 when set against the median income of an urban Chinese resident) . . . it will take some time to narrow. If China continues to outperform the United States by about two to three percentage points of per-capita income growth every year, the average income gap between the two countries will still take about two generations to close.[14]

Whether China will spring the 'middle-income trap' – a term used to describe a country's inability to graduate to high-income status – is, as yet, unclear. When I last met President Xi, his first words were that the middle-income trap was his country's biggest economic worry. And escaping it is becoming more complicated, as China's rise has also been accompanied by a widening of inequality. According to Milanović, the share of income held by China's 10 per cent increased from 21 per cent to 31 per cent between 1988 and 2013. Inequality calculated across all adults, measured by the Gini coefficient, rose from 0.27 to 0.45 over the same period. For better or worse, these are approaching Western numbers.[15]

But, while it accounts for half of Asia's economic activity, China benefits from the progress of Asia as a whole: its alliances put it at the centre of an Asia that now accounts for two-thirds of global growth and 40 per cent of global GDP and is home to half of the world's twenty fastest-growing economies.[16]

China and the US: the ten issues of contention

Tension between China and the US is far more difficult to moderate and wind down because there is not just one concern at issue between the two major powers, but rather at least ten major disputes, ranging across economic, military and political spheres and including disagreements over global governance.

The five key economic issues are: trade; currency; intellectual property; industrial policy; and technological leadership, which encompasses serious allegations against China of forced technology transfer.

And the five key non-economic issues are: human rights, from the persecution of religious minorities to the status of Hong Kong; the long-standing open dispute over Taiwan; nuclear weapons proliferation; climate change; and a range of military and security challenges, including cybersecurity, the Chinese build-up in the South China Sea, China's growing influence across Asia and Africa, and the matter of who will enjoy military supremacy in the Asia-Pacific region.

Since 1945, the US has seen itself as the guarantor of Asian security, careful – in most decades – about cultivating its alliances with China's neighbours, proud of its more recent pivot to Asia and unwilling to accept China as the region's hegemonic power. When the well-respected Brookings Institution recently organised an all-party China event, more than half the audience agreed that US and Chinese interests were 'fundamentally incompatible' and that their relationship now amounted to a zero-sum game, under which any gain for China meant a weakening of the relative position of the US and vice versa. A global survey in October 2020 by the Pew Research Center found that negative perceptions of China had reached record highs in the US, as well as in other major economies.[17]

Once we understand the fundamental and profound nature of these divisions, we can understand just how much we are at risk of an era of conflict. Take disputes over China's management of its renminbi currency: they are not limited to US complaints about competitive devaluations; the accusation is much graver, one of currency manipulation. Even more worrying, US criticism of China's persecution of religious minorities has often broadened into the very serious charge of genocide, with an equally inflexible response from a China now issuing dark threats of retaliation if the rest of the world dares to take it on.[18] Equally fundamental are the disputes over the future of the Internet, with dark warnings of a 'splinternet' whereby two wholly separate global systems will permanently reset the way global technology is managed.

Already the US complains of the 'great firewall of China', the cyber-screening system that Beijing uses to keep out unwanted foreign Internet communications.[19] This standoff goes to the heart of economic rivalries. While, twenty years ago, Europe and the US dominated the products, solutions and development standards, there are now, as a result of China's technological leap forward, two competing paradigms: the Western vision of a free, open and market-led technological future, the downside of which is the quasi-monopoly powers of private companies, as governments pursue a hands-off strategy; and the Chinese vision of an Internet controlled and regulated by the state and subject to widespread surveillance.

Of course, the US and its allies are now more aware of the need for supervision of the existing infrastructure that underpins global networks. But China claims that, to regulate self-driving cars, 'holo-sense teleportation' and the Internet of Things, a 'New IP' is needed both to track individual users, authenticating and authorising addresses, and to sanction 'shut-up commands', which ban unacceptable users. Anticipating what might happen in the next decade, former Google CEO Eric Schmidt thinks that 'the most likely scenario is not a splintering but a bifurcation into a Chinese-led Internet and a non-Chinese Internet led by America' – a 21st-century version of the iron curtain, though this time a cyber curtain splitting the world in two.[20]

The China–US standoff exposes an ungoverned realm: even as space and cyberspace have become new domains of potential conflict, there are no China–US weapons reduction treaties, no communication channels, no agreed code-of-conduct 'hotlines' (as there were between the Soviet Union and the US during the Cold War) that could minimise the chances of nuclear weapons being used. There are not even hotlines via which one country could quickly clarify the other's intentions and de-escalate tensions at the height of any military or security incident or misunderstanding.

This is particularly important because, in the future, de-escalation and deterrence will have to be managed without the obvious unchallenged hegemony the US enjoyed in the unipolar age from 1991 to 2020. Given China's harassment of US aircraft and naval vessels, minor incidents risk escalating into major military confrontations. Admiral Wu Shengli, the former naval commander of the People's Liberation Army Navy, has warned that any such incident 'could spark war'.[21]

In fact, Asia contains four hotspots where China and the US are at odds: the South China Sea, the East China Sea, the Korean Peninsula and the Taiwan Strait. But the great imponderable is certainly a Chinese move against Taiwan. While, for years, China and the US have managed their disagreement over Taiwan, it is also the most dangerous potential flashpoint. To prevent the deployment of US forces to the region in the event of a Taiwan takeover, China, it is thought, would be prepared to mount a 'digital Pearl Harbor': early cyberattacks against the electric power grids around key military bases in the US.

Michèle Flournoy, a defence expert who has advised successive US administrations, has written of the difficulties that arise from this very distinctive Chinese military approach. China has built up 'anti-access area denial' capabilities to prevent the US from projecting military power into East Asia. 'System destruction warfare' is shorthand for precision strikes on US logistics, forces and bases, as well as electronic, kinetic and cyber attacks on digital connections and systems inside US battle-management networks, hitting command, control, communications, computers, intelligence, surveillance and reconnaissance. For all this, she says, the US has, until now, left itself ill-prepared: any asset the US has within the first and second island chains encircling China would be at risk, along with a whole lot nearer home. To counter these threats, the US will almost certainly now deploy more expeditionary air units, more highly mobile marine and army units, more long-range unmanned carrier-based drones, unmanned underwater vehicles and guided missile submarines – all with high-speed strike weapons.[22]

Military and industrial strategy come together because of China's idea of 'military–civil fusion' – that technologies, from nuclear systems to autonomous vehicles and renewable energy batteries, are for dual use. In other words, they are assets and processes to support both civil and military projects. At the root of this build-up, which many argue is the real underlying driver of the China–US conflict, is a long-term national effort to dominate the foundational technologies critical to future innovation, including: semi-conductors (in which Taiwan has the capacity that China wants); supercomputers; quantum computing; bio-technology genetics; autonomous vehicles; artificial intelligence; robotics; 5G; and next-generation communications.

Hence the accusations China faces over the unfair use of industrial policy to undermine fair competition, as well as US sensitivities over any Chinese lead in artificial intelligence, robotics, quantum computing and autonomous vehicles under the contention that this is a threat to US military superiority. It is for these reasons that both Republicans and Democrats have stepped up US 'economic nationalism', with both parties suggesting it is increasingly difficult for the two countries to participate in one another's economies or in cross-border supply chains. And this, as former US Treasury secretary Hank Paulson writes, will not only leave 'American and Chinese technology systems and standards . . . separated', but will also ensure the global system and its standards are 'Balkanized'.[23]

But it is not just US national security concerns that threaten to usher in two systems of product regulation, industry standards and Internet rules. It is also what is seen as a new-found Chinese desire for self-sufficiency. China's recently announced economic model – based on 'dual circulation' theory – is seen by many as the trigger for decoupling the two economies across all four areas of economic activity: the flows of goods, capital, people and technology. And, of course, as Paulson has recently argued, decoupling – if embarked upon – would become a self-fulfilling prophecy as, the less global trade there is in one decade, the less inclined countries will be to work together in the next.

Climate change is another policy challenge, one we discussed in greater depth in Chapter 4. Here, with its ambitious and highly significant promise to be carbon-neutral by 2060, China seeks to work with the world. But, as we explained, it has yet to set out the stages by which it will reach this goal and, even now, Chinese companies continue to invest heavily in coal. The US has oscillated between President Obama's support for the Paris Agreement and Trump's renunciation of it and now Biden's support for it again, but the test will be – as we set down in our discussion of climate change – whether either of the two nations is prepared to agree to be bound by a timeline of specific commitments starting from now.

When we combine these ten areas of potential disputes, it is clear that we are a long way from Kissinger's assessment of ten years ago that China and the US need each other because 'both are too large to be dominated, too special to be transformed, and too necessary to each other to be able to afford isolation'.[24] They are still the large, dominant and connected powers they have been and, before the rise of the new nationalism, a way was found to tolerate differences. However, as of now, there are growing suspicions of each country's long-term intentions that will take China and the US closer to confrontation.

Two power blocs and two systems

The tension is not just about the fate of two nations, but about the fate of two power blocs. Just as the US is demanding more of its Western allies, the latest example being pressure on NATO's European members to pay their share of the costs of defending the West, China, too, is dictating the terms on which it will cooperate with its neighbours. Through the Belt and Road Initiative within Asia, Africa and the Middle East, as well as its '17+1' strategy for building links with seventeen countries in Eastern and Central Europe, the conditions China sets for borrowing and debt repayment make such intrinsically weaker economies far more dependent on China. And this is reshaping the geopolitics of the world.

At the risk of getting lost in the alphabet soup of new organisations' acronyms, let us look at what is actually happening. The question now is: how quickly and how far will this process take us towards two entirely different structures for international decision-making – two parallel but rival systems, one dominated by the US, the other by China? Already, even with its narrower focus on infrastructure investment, the Asia Infrastructure Investment Bank (AIIB) mirrors much of the work of the World Bank. In addition, together with the BRICS, China has created the New Development Bank (NDB) and a BRICS Contingent Reserve Arrangement, the latter a safety net intended to address shortages of liquidity.

China also runs the Silk Road Fund, which was designed to give financial support to the Belt and Road Initiative linking China to Europe via a land route through Central Asia and a sea route through the Indian Ocean. In total, China has invested about $1 trillion over the past fifteen years in infrastructure in Belt and Road countries. The rise of these China-led institutions can be attributed, at least in part, to China's fear of being marginalised within, or even excluded from, the current global institutions. The US's demand, in the recent recapitalisation of the World Bank, that loans and grants to China be curtailed is one example of this. It is not difficult to imagine the recently formed AIIB and the NDB becoming alternative development banks to the World Bank.

Nor does it require a huge leap of imagination to envision an Asian Monetary Fund (AMF) as an alternative to the IMF. China's willingness to offer currency swaps and fiscal assistance to weaker Asian economies creates an alternative to existing IMF and US Federal Reserve support – and usually on less draconian terms.

Japan floated the idea of an AMF in 1997 after it became convinced, in the light of the Asian financial crisis, that it needed a regional safety net that could be deployed quickly, without the extensive conditionality then demanded by the IMF. But this was opposed not only by the US, but also China. Instead, the Asian countries built a surveillance organisation, the ASEAN+3 (Japan, China and South Korea) Macroeconomic Research Office (AMRO) and agreed to create a network of currency swaps, later known as the Chiang Mai Initiative Multilateralisation (CMIM), with a link to the IMF. In time, the CMIM has become more like a regional fund, as envisaged in the original AMF proposal, and it is not only becoming more independent of the IMF, but the total size of the swap network is also increasing. As a result, the CMIM now duplicates the structure of the IMF, with its own contributors, its own system of voting shares, its own formula for allocations and its own maximum swap amounts.

Because these two support networks each has its own distinctive surveillance operation, tension between the two is possible. And, just as the European Stability Mechanism transitions into a European Monetary Fund that is able to support ailing euro-area economies, so, too, could the current arrangements morph into a fully fledged Asian Monetary Fund.

Already the seeds have been sown for two competing trade systems, not least because, in 2017, the US walked out of the Trans-Pacific Partnership (TPP) it had previously negotiated with eleven Asian and US allies. The TPP was specifically designed to keep China out, so the US was unprepared when its eleven partners realigned in 2018 as the Comprehensive Progressive Agreement for Trans-Pacific Partnership (CPTPP), raising the grim possibility that an organisation originally formed to keep China out could result in China being in and the US out.

Side by side with the CPTPP, which China has not yet joined, is the larger Regional Comprehensive Economic Partnership (RCEP), which covers one-third of the world and one-third of the world economy. The RCEP brings China, Australia, New Zealand, South Korea, Japan – the five Asia-Pacific states with which ASEAN has existing free-trade agreements – and other smaller Asian states together in the most ambitious, most geographically dispersed free-trade deal ever negotiated by developing countries.

Of course, the divergences in income between the RCEP sixteen are far greater than those in Europe or in the US, with Australia's GDP per capita of more than $55,000 swamping that of Laos, Vietnam and Cambodia, each with incomes below $2,500 per capita. But, because the RCEP is now the world's biggest trading area, covering around 2 billion people and accounting for one-third of global income, and is also the first-ever trade agreement linking China, Japan and South Korea, global trade is expected to increase by almost 2 per cent. Moreover, the very existence of the CPTPP and the RCEP side by side might rekindle interest in an even broader regional integration, with the Asia-Pacific Economic Cooperation forum being the pathway to a free-trade area of Asia-Pacific. Whatever happens, China's increasingly dominant position in Asia could leave the US looking weaker, more isolated and more excluded – which might prove to be the trigger for further conflict.

But at least the dollar reigns supreme for now, having successfully fought off the euro and the renminbi, and the US continues to control the main channel for international payment and clearing, which it is able to monitor through SWIFT, a Belgium-based organisation that collects information on all financial transactions and then allows that data to be overseen in the US. What kind of challenge, if any, will be mounted to what has been called the extraordinary privilege that the dollar still enjoys as the world's main currency?

In 2009, Governor Zhou of the Chinese Central Bank argued for IMF SDRs – the international money agreed in 1945 – to replace this dollar-centric global monetary order and for IMF-issued currency to become the international medium of exchange for the official sector, for intervention in foreign exchange markets, for central bank swaps and for bond issuance by national governments and international organisations. 'A super-sovereign reserve currency not only eliminates the inherent risks of credit-based sovereign currency,' he wrote, 'but also makes it possible to manage global liquidity.'[25]

He argued for the inclusion of the renminbi in the international currency basket and went on to describe the benefits of using SDRs for invoicing, for settlement and as a store of value in private as well as official transactions. If this was not acceptable, he favoured the internationalisation of the renminbi, which would, over time, require other countries to peg their currencies to the renminbi or be pegged to a basket that attributes a large weight to the renminbi. He wanted the Chinese currency to be used as a currency of denomination of bonds issued by international financial institutions such as the World Bank and the Asian Development Bank.

This is China's current agenda: it wants future contracts priced in yuan – the basic unit of the renminbi – and it also wants yuan-denominated oil futures, which would allow exporters like Russia and Iran to avoid US economic sanctions and circumvent the US dollar, thus increasing the use of the yuan and accelerating a progressive de-dollarisation, with predictable consequences for the US's prestige and significance.

Indeed, in its economic response to COVID-19, China has shown the importance it attaches to creating the right conditions for internationalising the renminbi. Instead of slashing rates to combat the economic impact of the pandemic, China has kept its main interest rate relatively high, making these assets attractive when interest rates in other major economies are at zero or below. Chinese authorities understand that you cannot internationalise your currency without large and liquid bond markets.

China's plans to create the world's first central bank digital currency are, it appears, the most advanced of any country's and it is teaming up with private payment providers that have a global reach, such as Alipay and WeChat Pay. Already today, in most major Chinese cities, there is little or no cash in use. At restaurants, shops and cinemas, customers point their phones at QR codes to pay instantly. There is even a possibility, albeit a remote one, that bank customers outside China might begin to prefer the Chinese central bank digital currency to cash or their own domestic digital payments. The European Central Bank is sufficiently worried to lay out its own contingency plans for a central bank digital currency ready to defend the euro from encroachment by others.

For all these reasons – the ten disputes – there has been a fracturing of the existing architecture for international cooperation. When Trump decided a G20 that included China was of no benefit to him and effectively closed down the summit when its health committee sought a cooperative approach to COVID-19, he also mooted the idea of a G11 meeting in Washington. His G11 would have included India, Australia, South Korea and Russia – a blatant attempt to build a global organisation that excluded China. The Biden proposal differs from Trump's, but could have a similar impact on future relations with China. His principal foreign policy officials, secretary of state Tony Blinken and national security adviser Jake Sullivan, have both written persuasively of the need for a league of democracies, and Biden himself has proposed a 'summit of democracies' – in effect, a G10 of the West plus Asian opponents of China, namely Japan, India, Australia and South Korea, as well as some other smaller countries, but excluding those seen as undemocratic and authoritarian nations like Russia and China.[26]

'One world, two systems'

Harvard University's Graham Allison has consistently warned us
of the Thucydides Trap: a rising power not only threatening the
established power but also ending up in conflict with it.[27] Faced,
until recently, with the options of containment, cooperation
and confrontation, the typical pre-Trump response, according
to commentator Fareed Zakaria, has been a combination of
engagement and deterrence. The rising tension under the Trump
presidency, says Zakaria, signalled 'a treacherous conflict of
unknown scale and scope that will inevitably cause decades of
instability and insecurity . . . A cold war with China is likely to be
much longer and more costly than the one with the Soviet Union,
with an uncertain outcome.'[28] But, if Zakaria were to suggest that
the replacement of Trump by Biden might change things, Henry
Kissinger appears to disagree: he even fears an accident scenario
similar to that of the autumn of 1914 when, through misunderstandings, the great powers stumbled into war.

'The *positive*-sum metaphors of healthy *economic* competition
are giving way to the *zero*-sum metaphors of *military* competition,'
writes Paulson, who has talked of an economic cold war and even
of an 'economic iron curtain'.[29] And Kevin Rudd, the Mandarin-
speaking former Australian prime minister, who has acquired
an expert knowledge of China and the thinking of President Xi,
also fears a 'great unravelling of the global rules-based order' into
mutually exclusive and separate systems. He talks of a standoff so
divisive that it makes great power hostility once again the organising principle of international relations.[30] Author James Crabtree
goes much further:

> Xi [has] quietly unveiled an economic strategy fit for a new
> Cold War . . . This gradual decoupling between China and
> the West will be far more significant than the divisions of the
> Cold War . . . China's intention is the gradual creation of a new

economic 'Sinosphere', in which global networks of trade and innovation that once focused on the industrialised West flow back and forth to China instead.[31]

No rerun of the Cold War

But, at least for now, the China–US standoff is no straight rerun of the US–USSR Cold War. The image of 'the iron curtain' was sketched by Churchill in his Missouri speech of 1946 to explain how an ideological barrier between East and West was now morphing into a physical one – spanning thousands of kilometres of barbed wire, fortified ditches and concrete walls, controlled by mines, watchtowers, tripwires, alarms and soldiers – that prevented any cross-border contact.[32] Later, in August 1961, the Berlin Wall was to become the iron curtain's most visible symbol.

But there is, as yet, no such physical separation between China and the West and there is still considerable contact, mobility and intermingling. In the Cold War years, we saw little interaction between Soviet youth and Western youth, whereas – at least before COVID-19 – many thousands of Chinese students were welcomed to universities and colleges in the US and Europe (and hopefully will return). There are regular academic exchanges between both countries, with Western universities now siting campuses in China itself, and there is no ban on students or on a cross-cultural dialogue, although, at one point, there were proposals discussed by the Trump administration to ban Chinese students from US university campuses.

In the Cold War years, trade and commerce between the Soviet Union and the US was minimal. Today, the economic and business interlinkages between China and the US are so deep and so integrated that most economists accept it will take a generation to break them. Unlike the economically isolated Soviet bloc, modern-day China is integrated within the entire global economy.

The distinctive features of the Cold War were: the underlying threat of mutually assured destruction; zero economic engage-ment; ideological competition for global hegemony; and proxy wars waged across Latin America, Africa and Asia. The Cold War became, essentially, a military standoff. But, while China is building its security and military strength – it already has the biggest navy in the world – and is not passive – it has fought border skirmishes with India – it has not, unlike the US, formally entered a war for forty years (since the Korean War), with the exception of a limited three-month interven-tion in Vietnam. The strength of its defence forces matters to China because, bordering fourteen countries, including India, it has reason to feel insecure. But it continues to think of the battle for economic leadership as the main area of geopolitical competition.

Rudd has called it 'Cold War 1.5': not a hot war or a cold war in the manner of the Soviet Union–US standoff. And, if we were to convince ourselves that a fundamental fight to the finish is now under way for the ideological as well as economic leadership of the world, then we may be surprised to find that China has been far less successful than the mid-twentieth-century Soviet Union in disseminating and winning support for its basic values across the world. Lee Kuan Yew, former prime minister of Singapore, was consistent in his argument that 'China will never become a democracy or an honorary member of the West'.[33] But what he believed was that China's millennia-long history has bequeathed it a set of civilisational values about order and the dominant role of the unitary state holding power over both individuals and civil society. It denotes a world view that he considered to be at odds with the basic values of the West, but is conveniently consistent with the thinking of Xi.

That such a world view resonates very little with Western cultures makes it difficult for China to exercise soft power. Of course, if this were indeed a battle for ideological domination, then the conflict between the two leading powers would be bound to intensify. But the ideological disagreements between the two sides seem more muted than those we experienced in the Cold War, with, perhaps surprisingly, their disputes on fundamental economic issues like the role of markets subdued. In short, Chinese people seem more attracted to Western ideas of consumerism than the Soviet people, and Chinese leaders have watchfully approved the rise of markets and corporations that the Soviet leaders would never have countenanced.

Some even talk of convergence. Branko Milanović believes that the economic systems of China and the US share three defining characteristics: most of the work is done as paid wage labour; the majority of the means of production are, in fact, privately owned; and much of the economy is run on the basis of markets that are decentralised.[34] This suggests that the real dispute is not, as in the Cold War years, about the existence of markets, but rather about their role and whether they are to be seen as synonymous with the public interest or subservient to it. Guided by self-interest and the desire to expand its material wealth, China has, unlike the old Soviet Union, embraced market principles in important areas. And, while US economists will argue that the untrammelled operation of free markets is a non-negotiable principle of a liberal democracy and thus to be automatically equated with the public interest, Chinese economists will argue that markets are in the public interest, but only when certain conditions are met.

The unique characteristic of the socialist market economy, they claim, is that companies are obliged to work to publicly set objectives, albeit those defined by the Communist Party and the Chinese state on behalf of the public. In this way, China's 'socialist market economy' is heavily dependent on state subsidies and thus, as the US sees it, unfair competition. China would, of course, argue that the difference in attitudes to markets between the two countries is a matter of degree.[35] Until the 1980s, most countries had highly interventionist industrial policies, and the US, it is claimed, still has an industrial policy, particularly in support of defence manufacturing, as evidenced by the 'Buy American' policy of Trump and the talk of 'economic nationalism' under Biden. In other words, the US is as keen to protect its industrial base as China.

In both countries, Milanović sees the concentration of economic and political power in the hands of an elite: on the one hand, economic power being converted into political power in the US, where the very wealthy have increasing control over the political system; and, on the other hand, political power being converted into economic power in China, where the Communist Party has increasing control over the economy.

But there is, of course, a fundamental difference between the rule of law as practised in the US and rule of law as exerted by the Chinese government. Because the rule of law would limit the power and discretion of the party and the state, China offers no legal security to individuals or companies, and this makes China's restriction of human rights an issue on which little agreement is possible.

Xi's recent embrace of 'dual circulation' theory has been interpreted by some as a prelude to the complete decoupling of China from the West; but, in purely economic terms, it is possible to exaggerate the break with the past. The expression 'dual circulation' denotes an administration determined to have its cake and eat it. Xi is on record stating: 'The new development pattern is not a closed domestic circulation, but an open domestic and international dual circulation.'[36] He is not discarding a previous commitment to 'international circulation' – which favoured the promotion of exports – in favour of 'domestic circulation' – an economy geared only to serving the domestic consumer market.

At least for now, 'dual circulation' seems to be more about the diversification of the economy than its decoupling, with China rebalancing the economy in a more protectionist era, away from what it considers to be a dangerous overdependence on exports, towards a more consumer-driven economy. 'We should increase the dependence of international supply chains on China,' Xi recently said, 'and establish powerful retaliatory and menacing capabilities against foreign powers that would try to cut supplies.'[37] Measures to cope with Western sanctions may be on the drawing board, with self-sufficiency the long-term objective, but they will have to wait until China is actually rich enough to be self-sufficient. For the moment, China does not wish to lose its export markets.

And there is another important difference with the Cold War. From the late 1940s, the old Soviet Union explicitly rejected the international rules-based order, but China has not done so. Instead, it seeks to present itself to the world as a champion of it. I was in Davos in the front row for Xi's now-famous 2017 address. His words were tailored to a Western audience, full of references to Western history and literature, from Charles Dickens' tales of Victorian England to Abraham Lincoln's inspirational speeches.[38] Just as in his address to the UN in 2020, he sought to persuade his listeners that China did not want to pull down the post-war order, only reform it for changing times. And so, if we in the West are not to lose the benefits of this post-1945 inheritance, we would do well to think, even in the face of a more aggressive nationalism, what common ground we can establish around a policy of responsible international cooperation – an issue I return to in the conclusion of the book.

Ten problems, ten possible ways forward?

As we've seen, there are ten areas of contention between the US and China. We have rejected a future of 'one world, two systems' and any idea of a condominium. There are so many areas of dispute that a 'grand bargain' is impossible. Indeed, the language of a 'grand bargain' is inconsistent with the views of both those who believe containment is the only way forward and those who talk of a future of 'strategic competition'. And there is no possibility of a reset, as if we can go back to where we were before. Too much has changed; but there is scope for a recalibration at some time in the future as long as we do not forget that our aim is to convince China's ruling elites that it is in their country's best interests not to build a rival world order but to continue operating within the current international order, albeit a reformed one.

One route to achieving this has been sketched out by the anonymous author of a 'long telegram' on the China–US conflict published by the Atlantic Council late in 2020. His – or her – missive is modelled on the famous George Kennan letter of 1946 that pinpointed the inherent and ultimately fatal weaknesses of the Soviet regime. The security official agrees that the overriding objective should be that China reject a 'two systems' future, but central to the plan for achieving this is an American destabilisation strategy to 'exploit' what the author calls 'the divisions within China'. The argument is that 'the central focus of an effective US and allied China strategy must be directed at the internal fault lines of domestic Chinese politics in general and concerning Xi's leadership in particular' and with a view to 'changing their objectives and behavior and thus their strategic course'.[39]

I fear that the anonymous author overplays the extent of internal division within the Communist Party. President Xi rose to power as pro-Western reformers lost ground in the wake of the global financial crash and, while he is unlike any other ruler in China over the last forty years, there is no real expectation that China will collapse soon or that it will capitulate.

For that reason I think that the approach that Rudd and Paulson take presents a more realistic way forward that I favour: issue-by-issue cooperation that will demonstrate the benefits of working within the rules-based international order. Paulson calls it 'targeted reciprocity': joint working; an 'I'll help you if you help me' approach in areas of policy where cooperation can be seen to yield mutual advantage. Rudd writes of 're-stabilising' the China–US agreement with what he calls a rules-based, 'deeply realist' policy of 'managed strategic competition'. In other words the two powers could agree to sidestep matters where no consensus is possible – on which they would agree to disagree – and instead focus on two types of relationship: managed competition in areas like trade; and collaboration in areas such as climate change.

This was, we were told, Biden's strategy when, as vice president, he dealt with Xi. In 2013, amid concern about Chinese attempts to create a sovereign air zone in the South China Sea, Biden told Xi:

> We don't accept this action on your part and won't abide it. We will fly our B-52s right through the zone. At the same time, if we can join together on climate and move that agenda down the road for the whole world, we are ready and willing to work together.

Translated to today's context, that means, as National Security Adviser Sullivan, who attended the meeting, says: 'Biden will push back hard where necessary on Hong Kong and the other issues and push ahead where interests converge on climate and pandemics.'[40] This 'push back, push ahead' view suggests that Biden will not seek to reset the relationship to where it was before, but to recalibrate it for the times we live in now.

Blinken talks of the replacement of 'cooperation where possible and competition where necessary' with a strategy that combines collaboration, confrontation and containment. Indeed Sullivan suggests a sequenced approach. While, historically, the US has sought to 'cooperate first and compete second', Sullivan argues that the best approach will be to lead with competition, follow with offers of cooperation, and to refuse to negotiate any linkages between Chinese assistance on global challenges and concessions that could encroach on US interests. 'Cooperating with China should not be seen as them somehow doing us a favour,' Sullivan has said. 'The fact that we should cooperate on things that are in both of our interests does not, and will not, mean giving them concessions.'[41] And President Biden's first speech addressed to an international audience as president – at the Munich Security Conference in February 2021– reflected this thinking. Not only did he define the future as one of 'long term strategic competition' with China and call it a battle between democracy and autocracy, but the new president, who had once called President Xi 'a thug', indicated that his starting point was to 'push back' against Chinese 'economic abuses and coercion that undercut the foundations of the international economic system'.[42]

But such tough talk – and predictably tense first meetings between the Biden team and China – does not change the impression that on many, though certainly not all, of the issues where disagreement currently exists, a way forward can be found. For, as daunting as the issues of contention seem, there are potential solutions within reach for the majority of the problems, making a form of managed coexistence possible. We could call it planetary realism, a new partnership of rivals, or reciprocity on matters where common interests can be found. And we should remind ourselves that, in many of the disputed areas, we have been here before. As Mike Froman, US trade representative during the Obama administration, writes:

> A bilateral accord that imposes binding and enforceable requirements on China to dramatically increase its intellectual property rights enforcement, prohibit forced technology transfer, adopt meaningful disciplines on state-owned enterprises and open vast portions of the Chinese economy to market competition, including from US firms, was more than 90 per cent complete [under the Obama administration, before Trump took office in 2016].[43]

And, while we now have added complications, including Huawei, fears about the military as well as civilian uses of new technology and heightened trade disputes, there are persuasive reasons why it is still to the benefit of both countries to work closely together on a programme of reform.

While 40 per cent of US companies in China say they are already planning to shift at least part of their production, the reality is somewhat different and not all signs are so negative. While China's exports to the US fell, exports from Vietnam – a key destination for China's relocation of industrial plants – jumped 21 per cent. The West is still trading with China, even though increasing amounts of Asian exports are coming through Vietnam.

When trade is a higher share of China's national income (60 per cent compared to the US's 30 per cent), it is not in China's interest to give up on exporting to the US or in the US's interest to give up on exporting to China. Indeed, even during 2020, when geopolitical relations were frozen, some economic opening up was taking place and positive reforms long sought by the West were being introduced.

It will take time for China's Asian trade treaties to build a strong internal market within Asia. Indeed, with its $50 billion trade deficit with China, India is reluctant to open up its water, energy, transport, telecom and health sectors to China. Of course, the US's high and currently rising balance-of-trade deficit with China will always be an issue of contention for the US, and China will have to do more to keep its promise to boost its purchases of US farm goods. However, while major multinational companies like Apple have already transferred some production into Vietnam and the rest of Asia, they do not see this as a hard-and-fast alternative to staying in China and selling goods to the rapidly expanding Chinese middle class. They want to do both. Trade will not die. It will continue.

The China Securities Regulatory Commission has confirmed that foreign firms will, this year (2021), be permitted to take 100 per cent ownership of onshore ventures, thus removing a number of the obstacles obstructing foreign companies. Although restrictions on Chinese firms operating in US stock exchanges have created a new complicating factor, US and European banks and financial services companies are now able to move into China; Western investors are interested in investing in the new digital currency China is backing; and Chinese stocks are increasingly appearing in Western stock indices, and just as Chinese investors now have a share in America, investors from all over the world are beginning to own a share of China, even if they do not realise it.[44]

For the moment, China's higher interest rates are making Chinese assets more attractive to foreign investors. And, while foreign firms have less than 2 per cent of Chinese banking assets and less than 6 per cent of China's insurance market, a number of breakthroughs have occurred recently: American Express became the first foreign credit card company with onshore operations in China; PayPal became the first foreign company to provide online payment services in China; and S&P Global became the first licensed company to conduct credit rating services in China's domestic debt market. At the same time, there has been a steady increase in foreign ownership – now more than $600 billion – of Chinese stocks and bonds.

Better trading relations are in the interests of the West, too, where middle-class standards of living still depend on the 'China price' – consumer goods imports from China at lower prices than Western manufacturers can offer. In 2018, the most recent year for which full figures are available, 82 per cent of mobile phones and 94 per cent of laptop computers imported to the US were from China. The US still buys around one-fifth of all Chinese exports. Sales to China matter, too; even Hollywood now enjoys more revenue from China than any other country in the world. Branko Milanović argues that there would be zero net real income gain from a collapse in trade.

China–US trade will, therefore, remain important to both countries for years to come, with the two sides aware that de-globalisation threatens mutual slower income growth. Economic professor and commentator Michael Pettis is right to argue that domestic disputes over who gets what encourage trade wars, but this very same domestic problem – people's desire for continuously rising incomes – also limits the extent to which, if standards of living are not to fall, trade disputes can be pursued to the bitter end.[45]

Both the US and China seek technological supremacy. The US is close to another 'Sputnik moment' – a term coined in the Cold War years when the US realised it had fallen behind its competitors – and, while in most sectors it still enjoys leadership over China, it knows it must invest heavily to keep pace. After state funding and hold-ups in licensing foreign companies, issues related to intellectual property are high on the list of not just the US's worries but Europe's, too, and, indeed, the European Commission has proposed a 'Transatlantic Trade and Technology Council' to set joint EU–US standards on new technologies in a bid to prevent Chinese dominance.

But, as China moves from being a low value-added economy to a high valued-added one, its government will start to share the US's interest in protecting intellectual property.

Indeed, China has now set up a special international court to deal with intellectual property cases. 'Strengthening IPR [intellectual property rights] protection is . . . the biggest incentive to boost China's economic competitiveness,' Chinese officials recently wrote in a document released by the Central Committee of the Communist Party. The guidelines advise 'speeding up the introduction of a punitive compensation system for infringements of patents and copyrights, and strengthening the protection of trade secrets, confidential business information and their source codes'.[46]

Intellectual property disputes are thus not insoluble. When intellectual property theft and forced technology transfer became the issue in the trade negotiations in 2018, China agreed to instruct companies to refrain from such practices. The initial agreement fell apart because of a disagreement over how it was to be implemented. While the US insisted on new laws, China proposed a state council directive, though this is an issue that seasoned negotiators should be able to find a way to resolve.

Industrial policy is on the agenda in the US as well as China. The US National Security Strategy also now argues that US companies in key industry sectors must be supported as strategic assets. The US House of Representatives has launched a new task force to examine how to maintain the Pentagon's technological edge over Russia and China, but perhaps we can exaggerate the extent to which technology is a security issue and security is technological.

What China has to do is show that it has ended its policy of forced technology transfer and then radically reduce state subsidies and restrictions on foreign investment. It has a long way to go. While China is attracting more foreign investment, not least because current returns are attractive, Chinese markets still lack some of the features of a modern financial regime, but I believe that, over time and out of self-interest, if only to cut the exceedingly high cost and inefficient use of state subsidies, Chinese markets will follow the advice of Vice Premier Liu He to phase these subsidies out, while, at the same time, following his advice to remove the regulations that continue to obstruct foreign companies and China–US joint ventures.

It is in the interest of both China and the West to find a third way for the management of the Internet. A start to resolving the Internet battles has been made with joint statements from the G7 and the G20, which have committed their members to good behaviour online, but, of course, malicious conduct continues. Shared ground may be found on a code of ethics and perhaps even on framing basic research, with respect to biotech and artificial intelligence. But whether a third way for managing the Internet can be found within the existing International Telecommunication Union without creating a new institution is open to question. It would force the West to reduce the power of big tech and the East to reduce the intrusiveness of state surveillance, and it would require us to empower the user – and thus increase transparency online – while accepting the continuing need on security grounds to monitor suspicious activity. While international diplomacy has solved equally difficult problems before, this looks to be a difficult if not impossible negotiation.

The US's long-held fear of competitive Chinese currency devaluations is, at least for now, proving to be unfounded. The Chinese yuan has appreciated dramatically against the dollar, but, rather than allowing the currency to drift down, the Chinese Economic Work Conference of December 2020 pledged to 'maintain the basic stability of the renminbi exchange rate at an appropriate equilibrium level' in relation to a basket of international currencies, only one of which is the dollar.

While the People's Bank of China has extended renminbi swap lines to thirty countries and is seeking to tie Chinese bilateral development aid to the use of the renminbi, little progress has been made in securing the currency's international adoption. This is not least because, in 2015, in response to an increase in financial volatility and the flight of capital overseas, China chose to tighten its capital controls and thus to maintain greater domestic freedom of action at the expense of greater internationalisation of the currency. So, today, more than 85 per cent of global forex trading involves the dollar and nearly 40 per cent of the world's debt is issued in dollars. In 2008, non-US banks had \$27 trillion in international liabilities denominated in foreign currencies, two-thirds of that in dollars. The latest data from the IMF show that nearly 62 per cent of global foreign exchange reserves are held in dollars and that the problems that beset China in 2015 when it toughened its capital controls and downgraded internationalisation of its currency have yet to be resolved.

Some economists have argued that it is impossible for China to combine the domestic autonomy it wants and the fixing of exchange rates with free capital flows and that these objectives cannot be met simultaneously. If China is to boost the use and acceptability of the renminbi in international transactions, it will have to ensure the free flow of capital and market-led adjustments of its exchange rate as well as enhance financial market liquidity, financial transparency and the reliability of contract enforcement. If China were to do this – and it will take time – the rest of the world should welcome it. As its economic power increases, China will undoubtedly press for countries to diversify their reserves and for the issue of public bonds in their currency and in the international currency, SDRs. A natural evolution is for the IMF to offer loans in renminbi. This should be no great problem for the US or the West, but for China the rise of the renminbi as a reserve currency is a marathon rather than a sprint.

The most fundamental ideological differences arise over human rights, not least because of very different attitudes to the rule of law. On the defensive – after recent clampdowns in Hong Kong, arrests for critical comments on the response to COVID-19, and the silencing of its most famous entrepreneur, Jack Ma, but most of all because of religious suppression – China has vowed to take no lectures from the West and is widely attempting to shut down international criticism. It is no accident that, in March 2020, China fought hard to win a seat on a five-member panel that selects UN rapporteurs on human rights abuses. The very officials who have targeted Beijing for imprisoning more than a million Uighurs in 're-education camps' in Xinjiang now report to a panel that includes China.

The Labour government of 1997–2010 proposed, and then engaged in, a human rights dialogue with China. Of course, China was an unenthusiastic partner, defending, as always, its right under the UN Charter to do whatever it wants within its own territory. But the dialogue was never abandoned and the UK continued to raise concerns about the treatment of religious minorities and individual human rights activists.

During this period, I was invited by Premier Wen to join him in answering questions from Beijing citizens at what he told me was the first town hall meeting his administration had convened. The questions that came to us were about what the Chinese government would do to improve schools, housing and healthcare and to cut pollution. Because there were no questions about the suppression of human rights, the foreign press accused Wen of a stitch-up, which, they said, was characteristic of a regime that did not allow people the freedom to express their true opinions. That may be, but my sense was that the citizens who spoke were indeed concerned about poor standards of public services and the polluted state of their environment.

When I asked Wen what he made of it, he referred me to the millions of texts, emails and communications over the Internet that, even then, his government was receiving every day from citizens, which, he said, he and the Communist Party dared not ignore. 'The Internet will bring democracy to China,' he proclaimed. I am not so naïve as to believe things will change overnight or that a communist party that is now tightening its grip will voluntarily surrender or even temper its power. The persecution of religious minorities and the use of forced labour camps offends our beliefs in the importance of religious freedom and of freedom of association, and the UK government has joined others in condemning these abuses.

But maintaining the human rights dialogue – and being unafraid to raise abuses – is still a better way forward than giving up. And there will be, over time, a rising demand, particularly on the part of China's new middle classes, for citizens' voices to be heard. Championing a human rights dialogue may well reap rewards over the next decade.

That other great issue of controversy, Taiwan, is never far from the surface either. Perhaps all that we can hope for is a continuation of the tacit commitment from China not to unilaterally alter the status quo that has endured for several decades. But whatever its own ambitions, China will have to accept that the US is a Pacific power with a network of alliances and partnerships in the Asia-Pacific region, naval operations in its major waterways and armed forces with an ability to strike in crises. There can be no better illustration of this battle for regional hegemony – and the priority the US accords to its effort to contain China in the Indo-Pacific – than that Biden's first presidential summit with world leaders, held online in March 2021, was the Quadrilateral Security Dialogue with his principal Eastern allies Japan, India and Australia.

The path ahead

The Chinese government's own stated objectives, I believe, hold the key to the future. Of course, its international agenda includes bold plans for modernising and expanding its military firepower, developing a security zone that ties neighbouring countries to it, and including the Middle East and Africa, as well as Asia, in its sphere of influence. At the heart of China's security strategy is, as we have seen, self-defence: pushing the US back behind the 'second island chain', undermining and, if possible, unravelling the country's Asian alliances within Asia. But China's leadership still thinks that it is in its interests to build a better relationship with the rest of the world because its main domestic objective is to keep the Communist Party in power, which, in turn, requires the maintenance of the unity of the country and the minimisation of any possibility of, or justifications for, popular unrest.

And that, China has concluded, requires the country to give priority to delivering on its well-advertised ambitions for higher levels of prosperity from now to 2050, including doubling the size of its economy by 2035 and reaching Western standards of living fifteen years later. In other words, China's leaders know that the survival of their regime depends on achieving a level of prosperity that cannot be guaranteed, at least for many years to come, without maintaining its trade with the rest of the world.

Of course, there will always be a partnership of rivals and a 'protracted duality' in relations, in which conflict containment and cooperation will coexist. But I have suggested that – by looking at problems not in terms of a grand bargain, but on an issue-by-issue basis – ways forward can be found – ones that will minimise the areas of disputes, while recognising no possibility of agreement on key issues, and, perhaps also, improve the longer-term stability of the global economy and civilisation.

As I have suggested, we should build on China's explicit endorsement of the international institutions. The rhetoric is of a 'convergence of interests' that will create a 'global community of interests', in terms similar to most (but not all) Western leaders. What that means, they state, is that, when there is an accumulation of converging interests, there will be a solid foundation of common interest upon which to build.

The West should reflect. While we are still in a position of relative strength, our global influence today is less than it was even ten years ago, and this decade is perhaps the last one in which we can mobilise sufficient power on our own to reshape those 1945 institutions for a new age. While the US remains *primus inter pares* and while China focuses its energies on becoming the high-income nation it wants and needs to be, a window of opportunity is open in which the US's new leadership can reshape and reform the global system and find a better modus operandi with China. And it's in all our interests to encourage and support this effort.

But a long career in politics has left me far from starry-eyed. Problems cannot simply be wished away. Those who talk of 'one world, two systems' are right to fear not just two clashing value systems, but also two separate yet parallel sets of international institutions. It seems likely that it will be messy for some time. I do not underestimate the difficulties of avoiding a 'two systems' future that divides, rather than unites, the world. I also do not shrink from standing up to China – or any country, for that matter – when we disagree fundamentally. In China's case, the biggest disagreements with the US are largely concerning human rights. In the case of the US with China, they are mostly about who is to run the world.

All of us can agree that competition is as unavoidable as cooperation is imperative. But, on the issues for which solutions are conceivable if given sufficient political will and effort, we should work for a strategy for cooperation rather than conflict and for stability rather than a permanent standoff. Just think of the opportunities in agriculture, telecommunications, renewable energy production, pharmaceuticals, and healthcare if the scientists, medics, entrepreneurs and social reformers of both countries could find better ways of working together – and then consider the benefits that would flow not only to each country but to the poorest parts of Africa and Asia. In the next chapter, I will set out how I believe we can improve collective decision-making at an international level. But the China–US standoff is not the only barrier as we seek to solve the complex problems the world faces: nationalism – especially, as we have just seen, populist nationalism – is an even greater obstacle.

TACKLING POPULIST NATIONALISM HEAD ON: FROM NATIONALISM TO PATRIOTISM

The contemporary rise of nationalism, of course, long predates COVID-19, but, as the pandemic stopped the global economy dead in its tracks, exacerbated cross-border tensions, particularly trade disputes, and highlighted income inequality in richer countries, it poured fuel on nationalist fires. This new protectionism contributed to racism, especially against Asians in the West, which somehow turned into general anti-immigrant feeling in many countries. The fact that the virus affected the poor, elderly and minorities disproportionally didn't seem to dissuade the xenophobes. But the roots of this problem run deep and were sown over many years. The solutions – again to be rooted in a multi-global, not just bipolar, world – will also take a while to bear fruit.

I feel it is right to end this book examining nationalism in more detail because, as has been clear throughout, be it in our attempt to limit the damage caused by climate change, end nuclear proliferation or rebuild our shattered economies following the pandemic, the block in all areas lies in a seductive and corrosive force – nationalism. Even if we found a way to end the current stand-off between China and the US and prevent a 'two systems' world, still the power that nationalist movements wield will leave us struggling to build a community of nations willing to work together to address global poverty, pollution and pandemics.

The unabashed isolationism of President Trump's 'America First' was by no means peculiar to one country. In recent years, populist nationalism has gone global: now, with the rise of 'Russia First', Hungary First', 'China First', 'India First' and 'Turkey First', 'my tribe first' movements are multiplying around the world.

It is an uncomfortable fact that, even as migration and inter-marriage change homogeneous societies into heterogeneous societies, governments everywhere have been retreating into their national silos – raising tariffs, closing borders, building walls and restricting immigration – and it is this regressive step backwards, with nations turning to the false comfort of populist nationalist solutions, that has characterised much of the decade just passed.

Indeed, the politics of this new nationalism are quite differ-ent from the old, familiar battles between East and West, the long-drawn-out struggle between capital and labour, or the century-long confrontation between socialist and capitalist ide-ologies. For our failure to work together, we can blame a new generation of strongmen leaders, who have fuelled sectarian pas-sions. But, in many countries, a dangerous nationalism has taken hold among large sections of the population and it is important to understand why.

If, since 1945, we have thought of our planet as divided between the free world and the unfree, open economies and closed econo-mies, socialist and capitalist states, then the return of 'tribalism' suggests that the biggest dividing line in the world today is between those who stand for an inclusive and cooperative world, with nation states working together to address shared problems, and those who – even in our interconnected, integrated and inter-dependent world – glory in isolationism and an often grandiose, delusional sense of superiority.

Thirty years ago, the fall of the Berlin Wall appeared to signal a new chapter in world history, one characterised by openness and mobility. Old barriers appeared to be coming down. Such were the hopes placed in this new world order that prominent commentators wrote of history moving in only one direction. They hailed it 'the end of history' and remarked upon the triumph of a dominant ideology that favoured the market economy and capitalist democracy, as well as a new form of enlightenment that would, over time, transcend national cultural differences and traditions.

Yet, today, there are twice as many walls dividing countries than there were thirty years ago. Trump's border wall separating the US from Mexico is only one of many new walls now being built. Currently, a total of sixty-five walls are either in operation or in the process of being built, with forty-five countries now separated from their nearest neighbours by barbed wire, electronic fencing or other physical barriers to entry. Such separators are being planned, for example, between Malaysia and Thailand, Costa Rica and Nicaragua, Estonia and Russia and most recently the Dominican Republic and Haiti.[1]

We all lose out through our collective failure to work together, so, in any study of the world as it is, it is important that we examine what can be done to counter the claims of populist nationalists and protectionists. There are not only global problems in need of global solutions, but also, as suggested in my Foreword, ungoverned spaces and no-go areas – including polluted oceans, warlord-controlled states and tax havens – so the chaos that arises from our collective failure to act is a threat to the stability and sustainability of our whole planet. Current 'no man's lands' cannot be brought under control by nation state-only policies; the approach requires sustained international cooperation. And the issue certainly cannot be addressed by the new tribalism we are witnessing in so many parts of the world.

In this chapter, I will seek to define 'nationalism' and chart its rise over the past few years. I will also close on a note of optimism, because I am certain that the forces of political nationalism, which have done so much damage to the global common good over this past tumultuous decade, can be overcome – so long as we understand why nationalism has become so potent and we commit to the radical and courageous steps necessary to defeat it. My views on this have been formed both by personal experience and by talking to and reading a wide range of authors who have studied nationalism in depth, especially before, during and after the Second World War and throughout the later Balkans conflicts. I will trace my journey in some detail in the hope of making my case for solutions all the more convincing because of its grounding.

What is nationalism?

When we talk of nationalism, what do we mean? I believe it was the author George Orwell who came closest to understanding the nationalist phenomenon. Schooled at an English preparatory school and then the elitist Eton College, he did not proceed to university, but instead joined the colonial police in Burma, from which he resigned quite early and in disgust. He subsequently led a precarious life – as a tramp, as a sometime rural shopkeeper in England and as a dishwasher in Parisian restaurants – while slowly mastering the arts of journalism and novel-writing during the Great Depression. In the 1930s, when a democratically elected government in Spain was overthrown by the fascist General Francisco Franco, Orwell joined the country's legitimist Republicans. During the civil war, he was wounded and even narrowly escaped being killed by a hard-line, Russian-backed communist movement that was striving to dominate the anti-fascist forces.

Back in London, he worked for the BBC (later unkindly caricatured as the Ministry of Truth in Orwell's novel *Nineteen Eighty-Four*). By 1945, he was recognised as a successful author and an established political authority. Even when he was dying from the pulmonary tuberculosis that would end his life at the age of forty-six, he continued to think and write with a legendary clarity. *Animal Farm* – a coruscating demolition of post-war communism in the guise of a children's book – has been read by many, many millions. For these reasons – and, most of all, because of the first-hand experience he gained in Spain, Europe and across the British Empire – his views on nationalism and patriotism command respect to this day and will for years to come.

In his 1945 essay *Notes on Nationalism*, Orwell makes an important distinction between being a nationalist and being a patriot. Patriotism was, for him, very simple and straightforward: the love of your country. Of course, this is what modern nationalists claim, too: they insist their focus is on the innocuous task of nation-building and the preservation of a culture and traditions that (they claim) do not exclude or marginalise anyone. Nationalists equate their ideology with the need to belong and they stress the importance of community – of an 'us'. Indeed, they will almost certainly argue that their nationalism is about loyalty to the nation – with no requirement to choose between this or other loyalties – and it is definitely not about any resentment of, or grievance against, those who are not part of your group.

But Orwell would have none of this. For him, nationalism represented a moral descent from a peaceful recognition and legitimate celebration of the virtues of the land you call home to a dangerous outlook that views life as an endless struggle between 'us', the insiders, and 'them', the outsiders.

'By "patriotism",' he wrote, 'I mean devotion to a particular place and a particular way of life, which one believes to be the best in the world but has no wish to force on other people.' But nationalism is, first of all:

[T]he habit of assuming that human beings can be classified like insects and that whole blocks of millions or tens of millions of people can be confidently labelled 'good' or 'bad', but

secondly – and this is much more important – I mean the habit
of identifying oneself with a single nation or other unit, placing
it beyond good and evil and recognising no other duty than that
of advancing its interests.[2]

Nationalism, Orwell suggests, entrenches an 'us versus them'
mentality that defines our identity – the way we see ourselves;
our view of the world – the way we see others; and the ultimate
goals we feel summoned to pursue.

A patriot, as Orwell states, can happily accommodate people's
multiple identities – Scottish, British and European, for example –
and many loyalties, not least to our family and to our religion. A
patriot can feel part of what the philosopher Adam Smith called
'circles of sympathy', whereby our sense of identity is built from
a strong commitment and connection to our immediate family
and then spreads outwards to our neighbourhood, our town, our
country and our continent – including all and excluding none.
Even where the boundaries of a nation are not the same as the
boundaries of a state, as in multinational states like the United
Kingdom, patriots need see no contradiction in feeling affinity to
both, even if to different degrees. Seen in this light, patriotism is
a sentiment that is inclusive and healthy. But nationalism, Orwell
says, cannot easily accommodate multiple identities. Instead, it
seeks absolute loyalty to the nation, and it forces people to make
a choice between affinity to the nation and other affiliations. For,
while patriots are comfortable with multiple identities, identification with the nation – for nationalists – has to be prized above all
else. As Orwell puts it, loyalty to the nation goes 'beyond good
and evil': it is 'my country, right or wrong'.

Even those who want to define their nationalism as 'civic', not
'ethnic', find it, he suggests, difficult to resist the descent into
ethnic nationalism. The political scientist Karl Deutsch, who
distinguishes residence from ethnicity, spells out the dangers.
Patriotism, he ventures, is a term applied to all, irrespective of

ethnicity, while nationalism tends to be an appeal to an ethnic group. 'Patriotism', he states, 'is an effort or readiness to promote the interests of all persons born and living within the same patrie', while nationalism is 'promoting the interests of all of those of the same nation'.[3] And so, while civic nationalists will claim, he suggests, that their community includes all who are residents, regardless of birth or background, they will, too often, do little to challenge or dispel the sense that their main appeal is to a nationalism of 'blood and soil'.

There is another dimension to this. What matters to a patriot, argues Maurizio Viroli, a well-known professor of politics, is an 'attachment to a way of life'. To a nationalist, however, what matters is a connection to the spiritual and cultural unity of the people. Nationalism is an 'attachment to the ethnic, cultural and spiritual homogeneity of a nation', he writes, while 'patriotism refers to the love of the republic and the political institutions that sustain it'.[4] For a patriotism rooted in the concrete culture and history of a particular place and people can avoid the dangers of intolerance by appealing to something that is not exclusive, like a general love of liberty.

Nationalism defines not only our own identity, but also, says Orwell, our attitude to others. Patriots generally bear other nationalities or countries no ill will and are often curious about, not hostile towards, the culture of others. But nationalists, he argues, capitalise on the fear of 'the other', even to the extent of inventing enemies where none exists.

The nationalist, who will usually talk of his nation as 'eternal' and 'everlasting', will tend to draw on an often-ahistorical view of the past – claims of oppression and discrimination – to detail a series of grievances and resentments, usually more imagined than real. 'The smallest slur upon his own unit, or any implied praise of a rival organisation,' Orwell states, 'fills him with uneasiness, which he can relieve only by making some sharp retort.' Indeed, populist nationalists will often target people for blame – often demonising immigrants or foreigners or ethnic minorities – for anything and everything that has gone wrong, as was vividly demonstrated over the course of US politics from 2016 to 2021.

Orwell is, of course, taking an extreme view of nationalist ideology at its worst, but he also finds that nationalists and patriots are set apart by their differing aims. In the spirit of Orwell, the Dutch historian Johan Huizinga writes that patriotism is 'the will to maintain and defend what is one's own and cherished', thus the exact antithesis of nationalism, which is 'the powerful drive to dominate; to have one's own nation, one's own state, assert itself above, over and at the cost of others'.[5] And, indeed, if we are to believe Orwell, nationalism is usually driven by what are, in the end, unrealistic assertions of an absolute, all-or-nothing form of sovereignty, more relevant to medieval times than to today's interdependent world where sovereignty is usually shared. In some countries, this absolutism is expressed in demands for a repatriation of all decisions to domestic control; in others, it is in the calls to stop all immigration or to redraw borders to reflect ethnic identities. The unlimited, undivided and unaccountable sovereignty that nationalists seek is, of course, impossible to deliver in our economically integrated and technologically interconnected world. For there can be no doubt that every country's independence, even that of the richest and most powerful country in the world, is constrained by its *inter*dependence, whether that is through membership of international organisations like NATO or through trade treaties and cross-border arrangements. But Orwell argues that the aim of the nationalist, ignoring these economic and political realities, is 'to secure more power and more prestige' – what he calls 'power-hunger tempered by self-deception'.[6]

Other writers – and, most eloquently, Isaiah Berlin, one of our best-known twentieth-century philosophers – have drawn a distinction between positive nationalism and negative nationalism. Berlin counterposed concepts like benevolent nationalism and aggressive nationalism, liberal nationalism and illiberal nationalism, pluralistic nationalism and monolithic nationalism – and so on. Jewish and sympathetic to the Zionist movement, Berlin was drawn into such linguistic gymnastics not least because of his enthusiastic support for the creation of Israel. He felt he had to defend and support the nationalist sentiments that gave rise to the country's birth and seemed essential to its survival. But it is Orwell's distinction that has, for me, more resonance, for he is making a contrast between an ethos and an ideology: between the ethos of a patriot, a natural and strongly felt emotional sentiment towards one's country, and the 'us versus them' ideology of a nationalist, which is, for Orwell, 'ethnic tribalism' and can only be challenged by 'a moral effort'.

Nationalism can take a number of forms. As populism it can both target foreigners and be anti-establishment, defining the world in terms of a struggle not just between 'us' and 'them' but between an elite and the rest. It can attack a business elite for holding too much influence at the centre or accuse a political elite of betraying the people they govern. What both approaches have in common is their desire to impose a nationalist narrative that reinterprets their country's history as the 'real people' having been betrayed. Indeed, behind slogans like 'Make America Great Again' and 'take back control' are attempts to blame elites for threatening the very existence of the country's institutions, values and traditions.

Nationalist movements can, of course, lead not only to a breakdown of international cooperation, but also to the rise of secessionist movements. While the world today consists of 195 states, there are 700 ethnic communities and 7,000 linguistic communities. Nationalists seek to realign political boundaries along ethnic and linguistic lines.

Every day, there are stories of ethnic groups demanding status and recognition. In the past few years, referendums have voted to create breakaway states on ethnic lines, most recently South Sudan out of Sudan and Bougainville out of Papua New Guinea, but the most dramatic recent redrawing of borders, which we discuss below, has been in post-Cold War Central and Eastern Europe. Today, most contemporary states contain several culturally distinct groups whose language, religion, tradition and historical experience make them see themselves as distinctive and special. As a result, the multi-ethnic, multinational state is the most common form of government and, in part because of this, a far greater share of the world's population lives in federations than in unitary states. Nationalists, however, tend to reject the idea of sharing sovereignty across multinational boundaries and will fetishise sovereignty above all else.

There are now only a few countries – such as Japan, South Korea and Hungary – that are 95 per cent ethnically homogenous. Given the greater mobility of people and the fact that migration has become so common – 260 million people are living in countries in which they were not born – we might be tempted to conclude that the appeal of ethnic nationalism could wither over time. Not just intermingling but also intermarriage make it possible for us to speculate that ethnic divisions should start to dissolve. But, of course, the opposite seems to be true.

Instead, nationalists have capitalised on the fears of the 'other'. And, rather than bringing ethnic groups closer together, the greater mobility of people – and the presence of many ethnic groups in individual countries – has intensified an old debate, from the US to China, as to how states can foster unity among people with diverse cultures. As the sociologist Andreas Wimmer and colleagues have argued, based on a study of minorities in Switzerland, Belgium, Singapore, Nigeria and other African states, there can be no national integration without political inclusion.[7] However, in environments in which a number of ethnic groups inhabit distinctive territories within a state or form distinctive communities within provinces or regions, the challenge all face is to devise and evolve policies that make for inclusive societies.

The evolution of nationalism in our century

But what lies at the root of these protectionist and nationalist uprisings? To respond to people's concerns, we need first to understand them. One explanation for the rise of nationalism in the West is the decline of other significant sources of loyalty – class, religion, locality – once salient forces determining people's identities. This has created a vacuum that nationalism has filled. Of course, deindustrialisation has weakened the power of trades unions and labour movements. These were at their strongest when there were large, crowded factories and workplaces in which the mass mobilisation of huge cohorts of like-minded, waged employees could join and wield real power. At the same time, traditional community organisations – like cooperatives and social and sporting clubs – have declined in number and strength as families have been forced to leave these communities to find work and as young people have become more mobile, both geographically and socially, and thus less rooted in the towns and villages of the Industrial Revolution. In addition, the more traditional churches and faith groups have lost millions of adherents, finding it difficult to adapt to a new individualism that has downgraded the importance of religion in many people's lives. Put simply: if you are no longer defined by your occupation or your class, your religion or your social club, there is a vacuum left for national identity to fill. Together with the rise of the Internet, the politics of personal liberation has also challenged the old, relatively stable, hierarchical and often deferential societies that formerly constrained people's expression of individuality. Indeed, another reason identity politics has become more important than ever is that it places an individual's inner feelings, the desire to express those feelings and the search for status and recognition at the very top of the agenda. Each nationalist party will, of course, claim that the conditions it faces are unique and particular to its own country. But nineteenth- and twentieth-century political

nationalism was fuelled by common experiences of cultural discrimination, economic exploitation and political exclusion – all of
which were highly significant in the anti-imperialist movements
of recent decades.

Twenty-first-century nationalism is, I believe, being driven
forward by forces that are as strongly felt and as immediate: economic insecurity ('I feel my generation is doing worse than the
last'); perceptions of diminished social standing ('No one listens
to us'); a sense of cultural loss ('My country's not what it used to
be'); and a loss of trust in conventional politicians ('They're all
out for themselves').

And this has intensified in recent years. When I left office
as prime minister in 2010, just a year after the successful G20
summit in London discussed earlier in this book, hopes were
still high that the kind of global cooperation that had marked the
summit would prevail. But leaders like myself, who clung to this
belief, had – it is now clear – already been given plenty of warning
to the contrary.

Earlier in the decade, when I was chairing an IMF summit
of finance ministers at the organisation's imposing Washington
headquarters, an angry group of demonstrators attempted to
invade the building. Anti-globalists were blaming the IMF for
the economic problems then facing the world. As I looked out
on the crowd, I alighted on one prominent banner proclaiming:
'Worldwide Campaign Against Globalisation'. The idea of a global
coalition of anti-globalists may seem, at first sight, so full of con-
tradictions that it should be ignored, rather like an 'Anarchists'
Steering Committee'. But the creation of an international alliance
of anti-internationalists was exactly the project that a number of
populist nationalist leaders had begun to embark upon and, as the
new decade progressed, it would sweep aside our naïve hopes for
international collaboration and cooperation.

This reaction was – again, in retrospect – entirely predictable. The global financial crisis had upended the entire premise

upon which globalisation was based: that, by liberalising markets and opening up trade, all nations and all people would benefit. Instead, those already in possession of secured property, high-skilled jobs and reliable assets found themselves protected, while those without discovered that a rising tide did not, in fact, lift all boats. Little wonder that, as the promise of Western liberal democracy failed to be realised, nationalists moved in to question the rules of the game and to exploit people's justified sense of resentment and fear. For too many people, globalisation appeared akin to a high-speed train careering away, not just out of control, but seemingly uncontrollable, too.

Trump's former strategist-in-chief Steve Bannon and a group of right-wing nationalist leaders were among the first to take back the initiative from the 'globalists', seeking to appeal instead to the growing numbers of dispossessed and disillusioned people in Western societies. And what I saw through the window of the IMF's office in Washington some years before turned out to be a portent of things to come: a global movement of nationalist factions, often financed through foreign funding, using common messaging to whip up popular and even xenophobic fury against what they considered to be out-of-touch elites.

It is these anxieties that are being weaponised by national-ists. Trump, for example, regularly claimed that the US was being 'exploited' and 'taken for a ride' by both its competitors and its allies, and of course one of the claims to power made by Presidents Putin, Xi and Erdoğan is that they will reverse national humiliations visited upon their countries in the past. Viktor Orbán, the prime minister of Hungary, has convinced many of his countrymen that they are being overrun by an invisible army of immigrants.

What follows are promises 'to take back control' in order to 'make my country great again'. For there is, undeniably, a wide-spread feeling now that whether at a national or international level, an insensitive establishment and faceless bureaucrats who live far from where we live and work, who we do not know and who will never listen to or interact with us, are making decisions that dictate the outcomes of our lives, giving us less and less say over what affects our jobs, livelihoods and community life. Nationalists calling for a repatriation of control offer an alternative view. As prominent right-wing strategist Lynton Crosby wrote, explaining his recent success:

> People see the international money markets decide the value of their currency. They see global technology companies move their profits around the world to minimise tax. They see all these things over which they have no control. And so, when they see someone they feel can give them hope that they can reassert control over their lives and over their country, a lot of people will opt for it.[8]

Indeed, nationalist movements feed off and very much target the real sense of cultural insecurity felt by many communities across the West, seizing upon the mass movement of refugees, who have been forced to flee from war or famine in Africa and the Middle East. These refugees are then scapegoated to represent the embodiment of the dangers of a globalised world.

To take one example of this at work, many UK voters will recall the pro-Brexit, anti-European, anti-immigration poster headlined 'Breaking Point', which became a notorious feature of the UK 2016 referendum on membership of the EU. It pictured a queue of dark-skinned, bearded men. All women and all white faces were blanked out to give the impression of a threatening phalanx of Muslim men invading our homelands. The poster built upon an earlier Brexiteer's claim that 90 million Turks would soon have the right to enter and work in the UK, free of any visa controls. The allegation was that Turkey would soon be joining the EU, so unlimited Turkish migration to the UK would thus be permitted under European rules guaranteeing EU citizens freedom of movement across the entire union. (At the time of writing, Turkey has yet to join the EU and is unlikely to do so in the foreseeable future and of course most Turkish citizens want to stay home in Turkey.)

The original photograph used, however, was not actually of a line of people marching into the UK or congregating anywhere near it. The photo was of a group of refugees who were pictured walking in line on a mountainous road from Croatia to Slovenia. Some pro-Brexit campaigners apologised for the racist slurs contained in this propaganda, but, in a clear demonstration of the simultaneous anti-immigrant populist nationalism being fuelled in other parts of Europe, Orbán's Fidesz party adopted the same image of immigrants, publishing the very same poster, though this time under an even more arresting slogan: 'STOP!' Orbán did this despite the telling fact that Hungary's immigration rate is, and continues to be, among the lowest in the world. Indeed, such was the xenophobia he was able to incite that a running joke emerged suggesting there are now more anti-immigrant parties in Hungary than there are immigrants.

That same photograph appeared again a few months later in the hands of the Spanish Vox party, as they, too, sought to make anti-immigrant sentiment the defining feature of their populist, nationalist platform in an election campaign against Pedro Sánchez, the well-liked socialist prime minister.

Nationalists, it seems, favour global campaigns! Or maybe they just can't afford fresh photographs. What they have in common is that they capitalise on fear.

Nationalism in Europe today

A Europe that prides itself on its democracy and its social market economy – both of which were forged over fifty years ago in the wake of two world wars that were, in their origins and essence, profoundly European – might now be accused of forgetting why in the post-1945 decades unification was such an obvious and necessary development. Twenty years ago, Europe was planning full economic integration and contemplating a federal state. Today, against a backdrop of Eastern Europe's fragmentation into ethnic enclaves and the UK's recent withdrawal from the EU, we are now seeing outbreaks of disfiguring populist nationalism, even in mainland Europe's more economically advanced and once-securely liberal democratic nations.

For years Belgium has hovered on the edge of dissolution. Spain has been destabilised by the strength of both a pro-Catalan nationalism and an anti-Catalan, neo-fascist nationalism. Marine Le Pen's *Front National* – now renamed National Rally – remains a threat to stability in France and as I write trails French president Macron only narrowly in the opinion polls. And, although Italy now has a technocratic government ably led by Mario Draghi, former head of the European Central Bank, the country's politics have been driven in the past decade by two populist nationalist parties – the *Lega Nord* (Northern League) and the *Movimento 5 Stelle* (Five Stars Movement) – both of which, having pushed the established parties aside, are now themselves vulnerable to other nationalist factions, such as the more extreme *Fratelli d'Italia* (Brothers of Italy).

Even social democracy's long-time cheerleader Sweden – as well as its Nordic siblings Norway, Finland and Denmark – is, alongside the Netherlands, home to powerful, far-right, xenophobic movements. In early 2020, we witnessed the fracturing of the Norwegian coalition just because the prime minister promised life-saving medical treatment – on compassionate grounds – to the infant son of a Muslim mother whose husband was linked to jihadism.

With the United Kingdom's departure from the European Union, the centuries-long internecine struggle between Irish nationalism and Ulster unionism has been reignited in a fundamental and an almost insoluble dispute over where the border line with the European Union now lies: dividing the island of Ireland, and in doing so challenging the desire of Irish nationalists to feel Irish, or dividing Britain from Ireland in the Irish Sea, and in doing so challenging the desire of Ulster unionists to feel British. Northern Ireland – recently blessed by peace and prosperity, in part because of its inclusion in the European Union – now lives uneasily in both the UK and the EU.

And – while Germany's nationalist right may have suffered electoral setbacks, with the Free Democrats making headway in its place – the chancellor-designate and CDU leader Annegret Kramp-Karrenbauer (AKK) had to resign her chancellorial ambitions over her party's accommodation of neo-right nationalist factions. Her political downfall was triggered by her party's decision to join with the far-right AfD (whose leader, Björn Höcke, as a German court agreed last year, could be termed a 'fascist') to elect a state mayor. There is now a vocal Values Union within the governing CDU calling for a more nationalistic, even xenophobic stance. One power broker who is highly influential in the race for CDU leadership is the young health minister Jens Spahn, whose politics resemble the populist nationalism of Sebastian Kurz, the Austrian chancellor. Spahn is a centre-right politician who might be leaning slightly more to the right in order to take votes from the AfD, but he is on record complaining that German's very identity is at risk and that the German language is under threat not only from too much English being spoken in cafés, but also from Arabic-speaking Muslim 'machos'.[9]

Nationalism has made it difficult for Europe to cooperate even on issues of peace and war, as was recently demonstrated when it was unable to agree on Chancellor Merkel's plan to enforce an arms embargo against Libya through a European naval mission in the central Mediterranean. On paper, all relevant players in the region – Turkey, Qatar, Egypt, the UAE – and even Russia and the US supported the UN arms embargo and the demand for a ceasefire. But, when the Austrian chancellor argued that naval assets in the Mediterranean were serving to encourage migrants to risk the perilous crossing and that EU vessels would be 'a ticket to Europe for thousands of illegal migrants', Europe found itself committed to a naval mission for which few countries were willing to offer naval vessels. And, with Italy and France often on opposite sides, there has been no meaningful EU strategy for de-escalating conflicts, not just in Libya, but in Syria, too.

Today, the EU is also divided on how outward-looking and how global Europe should be, as well as on how close its relationships with Russia, the US and China should be. But both concepts of the EU as a *Weltpolitikfähig* – a Europe relevant on the world stage – or a 'geopolitical' Europe – the brainchild of Ursula von der Leyen, the president of the commission – have floundered, even though Europeans need a renewed sense of cohesion and strategic purpose if the continent is not to look like an appendage of the US or part of a Eurasia dominated by China and Russia. 'We cannot claim to be a "geopolitical power" or a "geopolitical commission" if we cannot solve problems in our immediate neighbourhood,' warned Josep Borrell, the EU's foreign policy chief, in December 2019, highlighting the power of nationalism to prevent progress.[10]

In the east of Europe, warring nationalist factions also continue to threaten the peace. Turkey, Greece and Cyprus are embroiled in escalating disputes including over maritime boundaries and gas exploration rights in the eastern Mediterranean.

Across the Balkans and beyond, ethnic politics is also highly potent. When asked, in a very revealing survey, if there are parts of neighbouring countries that really belong to them, 67 per cent of Hungarians and 60 per cent of Greeks confirmed their ambitions to add to their existing territory, as did 58 per cent of Turkish citizens. Around half the population of Poland (48 per cent), Slovakia (46 per cent) and Bulgaria (58 per cent) also supported their country's right to territorial expansion. And even Germany – the twentieth-century history of which was dominated by annexations – found that 30 per cent of its citizens believe there to be neighbouring territories that actually belong to Germany, reminding us that the very conflicts that scarred an entire century have not, as yet, been buried for good.[11]

Fortunately, few of the more recent European nationalist parties have been sufficiently successful to gain power outright, but they have shaped the politics of the times. I have highlighted Europe because, after its experience of war in the twentieth century, it did far more than any other continent to attempt to heal divisions and counter political nationalism – and yet it is back. However, an equally depressing story can be told of mutual suspicions breeding division and disunity across both Africa and Asia, not least in bitter disputes over territory between India and China or India and Pakistan. Neither of these continents has ever approached the levels of economic or political integration now achieved in Europe. There is no common currency, no common banking union, no common monetary, fiscal or social policies, and no institution with the overarching powers of the EU. The African Union has tried hard to unite Africa but been unable to prevent border conflicts and civil wars across the continent, while Asia's major forums like ASEAN survive only because they limit the scope of their decision-making to those areas in which they can operate on the basis of consensus.

Over time, as we have suggested in the previous chapter, China may seek a form of hegemony across Asia, but Asian unity will always be difficult to achieve under any umbrella when such strong nationalist sentiments exist. One recent example of how deeply such nationalist passions can be felt was the 2020 Kyoto mayoral election in Japan. In that contest, the dominant issue was not immigration – of course, it was hardly likely to be in a country that has fewer immigrants than any other – but rather an equally isolationist desire to ban or reduce foreign tourism, which many locals were holding responsible for the desecration of some of Japan's historic sites and cultural icons.[12]

Why nationalism is a danger to us all

All this has a contemporary manifestation: vaccine nationalism and medical protectionism have led countries to close their borders, thus preventing the transfer of medical goods, even when in surplus. A failure by the European Commission to successfully coordinate the supply of vaccines encouraged member states to 'go it alone'.

But the recent nationalist uprisings I examined have also led me to reconsider a long-held view that, if only national leaders would show themselves willing to embrace a more internationalist world view, we could make rapid progress in solving global problems in need of globally coordinated solutions. Now I have a better understanding that, while leaders can and *do* shape public opinion, often for the worse, the bigger impediment to globally coordinated action is not a weakness in the global consciousness of leaders, but rather – whether engineered by populist leaders or not – the sheer strength of a nationalist consciousness among people worldwide.

I have identified four concerns that have given rise to nationalism in our century: economic insecurity; diminished social status; cultural loss; and political exclusion that stems from the sense that politics is being run by a far-removed professional elite. What these four points add up to is a strong feeling among millions of struggling families that they are being treated as second-class citizens, hence the appeal of a populist nationalism that gives them status and recognition and even suggests that the insecurity from which they suffer constitutes a form of cultural discrimination, economic exploitation and political exclusion.

But you should not have to form a separate state, demonise your neighbours as enemies or view the world as a struggle between 'us' and 'them' in order to establish your right to be treated as a first-class citizen. Indeed, no one should be made to feel that their individuality is unappreciated, their dignity is disrespected or their right to equality of opportunity is denied. Economic, cultural and political justice are essential elements for a society to free itself of the divisive features of nationalism. So, today, the challenge to our global leaders is to respond in kind – to understand and empathise with citizens in nations large and small, navigating an uncertain and insecure world, and to provide an alternative to political nationalism that speaks to everyone's need to be heard and ensures all communities are respected and protected.

In this chapter, I've attempted to define, chart and explain the rise of nationalism over the past decade. I've also set out my views on the dangers of following nationalism's path and how it could stunt our efforts for global cooperation by default. But the question is: what can we do to prevent populist nationalists dictating the next stage of world history? In my view, there are at least four ways. The answer will lie in new measures that bring about redistribution, recognition, representation and reform – not least a reform of our international institutions in order to make them adequate vehicles for cross-border cooperation for the delivery of a more just world. While social justice was once thought of as a matter to be pursued by individual states, it must now underpin our international order too.

First response: addressing economic and social insecurity

So, firstly, we have to address a concern that appears to be present in all nationalist uprisings and often lies at their root: economic insecurity. If we take the experience of the world's wealthiest country as an example of how perceptions have changed, we find that, while 90 per cent of US citizens born in the 1940s said they expected a better standard of living than their parents, only 50 per cent of the post-1980 generation now say this. Other advanced economies record a similar response.

In the decades after 1945, Western economies grew and

incomes grew, too. Inter-class mobility was higher than today and inequality much lower. Indeed, the Western industrial work-force was considerably wealthier than the other three-quarters of humankind. Back then, incomes and job security did not depend on competition with the developing world and, of course, capital was less mobile and migration was much more limited.

But the opening up of the world economy ushered in a new era of capital flight and global wage competition, as a result of the shift of manufacturing to the East, pressure on Western workers from Asian competitors, and the impact of job-saving technologies like computerisation and digitalisation.

Until recently, in what was a golden age for Western manu-facturing, Western workers using advanced Western technology were able to outcompete Asian workers using less advanced Asian technology. But, today, Western workers using Western technol-ogy are being outcompeted and even displaced by Asian workers, who are now using the very same Western technology, but being paid far less to do so. Across all the richest economies, this shift has resulted in lives being uprooted by closures, redundancies and the collapse of whole industries, such as mining, textiles and steel. In turn, this has forced those who once had high-status, secure and relatively well-paid manufacturing and mining jobs into low-skilled service employment.

There is, of course, an ongoing and important academic debate as to whether trade or technology has been the more important cause of job losses and depressed living standards.[13] But, irrespective of your view on the relative merits of trade or technology as the driver of change, there are few who do not agree that technology will continue to transform our society and that this automation of skills will intensify as industrial robots replace manufacturing workers, computers outnumber human brains, sensors do the work of human eyes and artificial intelli-gence renders even some of the most advanced professional skills redundant.

Populist nationalists depict 'foreign' workforces as the culprits, the main barrier to good jobs and rising living standards in the West, hence Trump's proposal to bring back this lost manufacturing work to the US. But, even if there were more work in the West, it would not mean more workers: automobile, shipbuilding and computer assembly workers would simply be displaced by robots that use even more advanced Western technology and do so more cheaply.

The worsening economic position of displaced manufacturing workers who now find themselves in relatively low-paid service jobs also reflects a growing divide between rich and poor, which some argue is a recurring historical phenomenon in the history of protests. It worsens when 'elites' start reserving larger portions of economic gains for themselves, tighten pathways to mobility to favour their families and resist taxation of their wealth and profits, thus starving the already decaying public services of the resources they depend on.

Nothing will eradicate the very strong feeling in certain families that, having once being part of labouring aristocracy, they have now been relegated to lower-status jobs and are being treated badly. In the past, there was another route out of poverty through education. But many poor families will now remain poor because they are also education-poor. As we spelled out in Chapter 5, the way forward lies in a radical extension of educational opportunity to those whose lack of skills currently denies them access to well-paying jobs.

Protectionist attitudes do, however, impact economic growth as they force governments to restrict trade and restrict immigration. They also add to the pressure for more public spending and higher domestic wages, which could actually reignite inflation. So the answer to economic insecurity is not a new form of protectionism. And it is certainly not the closing of our borders, the banning of imports, the discouragement of incoming migration or the sheltering of domestic industries. The better way forward is, in fact, to invest in upgrading people's skills so that economies can create the well-paid and highly valued employment opportunities we need for the future.

However, we have to deal not only with the economic insecurity people experience, but also the pain and anger often felt by people whose lives have been turned upside down by occupational and industrial changes. Rather than being simply 'left behind' or 'left out' – wording that suggests failure or blame – many families in declining towns and inner cities feel like they have been 'pushed out', even 'shut out', from the benefits of globalisation. And this is what they are reacting to. They feel ignored, neglected, overlooked. It is not just economic insecurity, but a deeper sense of cultural loss and injured pride. And, indeed, it this belief that no one else speaks for them that provides the fuel for populist nationalist movements.

This was brought home to me when listening to what people were saying about the UK's relationship with Europe at the height of the Brexit referendum discussions. Ever since the Industrial Revolution, working people in the North and the Midlands were at the centre of English and British life. They were proud to be the coal miners who kept the lights on for all of us and they were proud of their manufacturing enterprises, which produced everything that the world demanded – from ships and razors to lathes and locomotives. Indeed, these workers' skills were widely admired. But, today, these same communities live in towns defined by economic decline – with high unemployment, deserted high streets, abandoned factories, boarded-up churches and community centres, and occasional lingering slagheaps – as well as a sense that they are little valued.

Dr Lisa McKenzie is a sociologist who worked on the Great British Class Survey at the London School of Economics (LSE). She surveyed the East Midlands and found that all too many of the hard-working families, who had once taken such pride in their skills and in the contribution they made to their country, now felt – in their own words – 'at the bottom' and 'like a different species'. Reduced to packing boxes or stocking shelves in warehouses, they were losing a sense of their own self-worth and the pride in their once-vibrant, now depressed community.[14]

She even quoted one woman who, referring to those much wealthier than her, asked: 'We don't exist to them, do we?' Indeed, McKenzie found feelings of anger and pain that left people devoid of hope. Contrary to popular depictions, these people's motivations, particularly in voting as Brexit nationalists to leave the EU, were not rooted in any form of racism against immigrants (despite this being, as we have seen, a major part of the pro-Brexit campaign). Instead, the underlying feeling was resentment towards the 'out-of-touch' political elite, living in a different world, who did not understand these communities' needs or aspirations. A common reaction was: 'Who in London thought of this?'

'They knew they were at the bottom,' McKenzie concluded, so their anti-establishment, pro-Brexit vote was registered in order for them to be 'heard' and 'visible'. They needed to be listened to and respected and they needed someone or something to stand up for them.

Indeed, many of these people feel not only pushed to the fringes of their national community, but also deprived of the roles and respect normally accorded to full members of it. And their diminished status – an inequality based on differences in esteem, not just material arrangements – has sharpened the existing resentments over declining employment and economic prospects. In the past, communities could feel pride in being part of a strong labour movement that championed a more human social order. Now they feel that no one speaks on their behalf, and as Arlie Hochschild has described in her examination of Rust Belt communities, feelings of hurt and 'wounded pride' can help populist movements recruit people to their cause.[15]

But it would be wrong to conclude that nationalism arises

when communities have burned all their social capital. According to new research into America's changing political landscape by a group of economic geographers at the LSE, the biggest reaction to 'being ignored, neglected and suffering long-term decline' occurs among 'strong, but declining communities', which means that 'these places still have greater levels of social capital than more dynamic and unequal areas of the US'. The US election of 2020 – in which President Biden did best in the suburbs, but less well among the white working class of the Rust Belt – was, as one of the researchers tweeted, a confirmation of the LSE paper's argument. 'Donald Trump was voted for not in places with high individual income inequality, but mainly in places that have been in long-term economic decline.'[16] As the paper itself says:

> [It] is precisely the long-term economic and demographic decline of the places that still rely on a relatively strong social capital, the decline of many areas of the American Rustbelt and the Great Plains, that helped forge the economic success of the US for the best part of a century, that is behind the rise of populism in the US.

The rise in the populist vote, the authors continue, 'represents a reaction of strong communities in which individual losses are strongly identified with collective losses'. Indeed, it is because these communities have been so strong and cohesive that they react so badly:

> This social capital has played a role in the swing of votes within communities driven by a growing feeling of frustration, increasingly known as the rising geography of discontent or the politics of resentment. These so-called 'places that don't matter' have had enough of seeing their people leave and their jobs go and have used the ballot box to exact revenge on a

system they consider offers little to them . . . when these communities suffer long-term population and economic decline,
the very social capital behind the cohesiveness and former
dynamism of these areas can also channel the growing anger
and resentment felt by those being left behind.

Better jobs, better-paid jobs, better opportunities for young
people and a ladder of opportunity out of what are often 'dead-
end' starter jobs is one way of addressing economic insecurity, yet
another is to invest heavily in education to equalise opportunities.
But there is a political dimension to this, too – an increasing
dissatisfaction with the monopolisation of politics by the professional classes and the feeling that these leaders are so out of touch
that they cannot solve the problems they have been responsible
for creating. In a recent survey 42 per cent of Germans, 52 per
cent of British and 65 per cent of French think that their elected
politicians and leaders are 'mostly corrupt'; only 39 per cent of
Germans and 32 per cent of British trust their political parties and
the figure falls to 16 per cent in France and 17 per cent in Italy.[17]
People need to believe that their leaders will listen to them and
speak for them and so, as I suggest in the conclusion, political
parties will have to change.

Second response: developing a patriotism without nationalism

Our second step is to recognise the importance of belonging
and find ways to encourage a positive patriotism, free of the
divisive features of nationalist ideology – a patriotism without
nationalism.

By espousing patriotism without nationalism, we reject the 'us
versus them' or 'insiders versus outsiders' view of the world and
we end the blame game. This is a form of patriotism that does
not define our future in terms of an ahistorical view of the past
and does not condone the indefensible claim that, in our modern

interdependent world, national sovereignty can be unlimited and absolute.

But, first, we have to remove all justified and previously unaddressed grievances that fuel nationalist resentments in the first place; we have to eliminate all forms of cultural discrimination, economic exploitation and political exclusion; we have to show that equality of citizenship – irrespective of race, gender, sexuality or religious beliefs – exists not just in theory, but in practice, too.

In *The Lies That Bind*, cultural theorist Kwame Anthony Appiah asks not only 'what gives us identity?', but also, in particular, 'what makes "us" a "we"?' What makes someone 'one of us'? Or, to phrase this in an alternative way, what gives us identity as individuals, but also identities as a collective? And how are these two concepts related to one another? Appiah writes:

> Every identity comes with labels and ideas about why and to whom they should be applied . . . Each person's sense of self is bound to be shaped by his or her own background, beginning with family but spreading out in many directions to nationality, which binds us to places, to gender, and such categories as class, sexuality, race, and religion which all transcend our local affiliations.[18]

This is important, he notes, because 'your identity shapes your thoughts about how you should behave, and it affects the way other people treat you . . . and how you fit into the social world'. For Appiah, identity is absolutely central to your character: it not only gives you a strong sense of who you are, but also a reason for doing things, for living life as you live it. And who can deny Appiah's point that, the more change hits us, the more we need to be anchored and feel part of something bigger than ourselves?

But, as Appiah also notes, identity does not develop in isolation – the desire to be part of a community and to have a sense of belonging is fundamental to our human nature — and, of course, there is a downside to this. The 'clannishness' activated by identity is, Appiah believes, a basic feature of human psychology, but, if it gets out of hand, it can also provoke an 'us versus them' form of nationalism.

And the ties that matter to people are not just national, but local and multidimensional, too: the loyalties we feel towards our family, our neighbourhood, our town, village or city, our religious, social and class ties — all of which bring us together as members of larger groups. So we cannot allow nationalist ideologues to ignore the importance of the many aspects of our culture. Indeed, in the conduct of our everyday lives, these familial and community ties are of far more immediate importance to us than our national identity, but it is typical of populist nationalist ideology to subsume local loyalties and imply that there can be only one source of loyalty — loyalty to the nation.

It makes sense to recognise the importance that a loyalty to 'place' has in people's lives. We can do this by devolving power to local communities to empower elected local representatives — for example, elected mayors — who, in contrast to those appointed by and defending what can often seem to be a distant state, are more aware of local needs and can bring decision-making closer to people in public services as appropriate. In other words, we counterpose localism to nationalism. Embracing the idea that 'sense of place' matters in our everyday lives, progressive politics should be rooted in local communities, with a focus on local improvement, while also being able to transcend them for the common good. And so we should value and empower local councillors, mayors or, in Scotland's case, provosts in villages, towns and cities across our countries as a vital force in our democracies.

I am sure I am not the only one who feels rooted in my local community, where I have lived for most of my life, but I see no contradiction between that bond and the simultaneous feeling that I am a global citizen. Saying that does not make me some rootless 'nowhere man' – I am simply someone who draws his identity from a chain of connections, beginning in my county and region, then in Scotland, then in the UK, then in Europe and ultimately in the wider world.

And, while I am proud to be a patriot, my patriotism is not warped by the intermediate distorting mirror of nationalism. My loyalty to Scotland is, for me, part of a concentric circle of loyalties that starts with that true sense of place – what is local – but also encompasses a sense of shared purpose as an internationalist.

As an ideology focused on the nation above all else, nationalism will always undervalue the pride that people have in their neighbourhoods, their communities and their regions. In contrast, we should recognise and champion the importance of local democracy, community action and regional identities alongside national identity, and this is what a patriotism free of nationalism can do.

Berlin shared the same insights as Appiah about the importance of belonging. He was even close to Orwell's view of patriotism when he wrote that the 'desire to belong to a community or to some kind of unit . . . is a basic human need'. Berlin's thesis was that we all need an identity, an 'I', but we also need to belong to a community, an 'us', which will differ from others in language, customs and culture. Over the past 400 years, this 'us' has usually been a 'national' community. As he put it:

> If the streams dried up . . . where men and women are not products of a culture, where they don't have kith and kin and feel closer to some people than to others, where there is no native language, that would lead to a tremendous desiccation of everything that is human.[19]

So to sum up what we mean by 'patriotism without nationalism': we mean a respect for identity and a recognition of the importance of belonging. Being a patriot means being inclusive and being sufficiently comfortable with one's own identity to never feel needlessly resentful of others or harbour imagined grievances against them. Being a patriot means accepting that there are multiple sources of identity and loyalty and this includes valuing, and celebrating, your neighbourhood, village, town or city, and your region as well as your nation. Being a patriot means being curious about, not hostile towards, the culture of others – what I would term interculturalism – and this is rooted in the equal consideration of and respect for everyone else's traditions. Moreover, because patriotism is akin to an ethos rather than a doctrine, it does not seek to impose itself on others or force people to make unpalatable choices. Love of one's country, for a patriot, leaves one free to visit, enjoy and love other countries, too.

So is it right to warn of the divisive consequences of both nationalism and patriotism and the nurturing of a more exclusive 'clannishness'? Or can we encourage 'us' patriotism that avoids the 'us versus them' rhetoric of nationalism? One writer whose early writings favoured the former approach, but whose later work proclaims the benefits of the latter approach, is Martha Nussbaum, the US philosopher and legal scholar. For years, her writings rejected nationality as 'a morally irrelevant characteristic' and deemed national boundaries to be 'morally arbitrary' (although she stopped short of championing what she termed 'a strong cosmopolitan argument').[20] Now, however, she argues that a sense of a national identity is something to be valued.

'All decent societies need to guard against division and hierarchy by cultivating appropriate sentiments of sympathy and love,' she writes, and it is the 'nation state' that forms the legitimate focus of these sentiments, rather than the worldwide community of human beings.[21] Indeed, patriotism is capable of purifying nationalism's distasteful characteristics, while preserving its positives: the celebration of distinct national cultures and the empowerment of people to identify proudly with the traditions of their homeland. Nussbaum adds:

A nation that pursues goals that require sacrifice of self-interest needs to be able to appeal to patriotism in ways that draw on symbol and rhetoric, emotional memory and history . . . Emotions directed at the nation and its goals are frequently of great help in getting people to think larger thoughts and recommit themselves to a larger common good.

People, she suggests, are more likely to be influenced and inspired by powerful symbols and rhetoric, especially in the pursuit of abstract principles like justice, 'and it is this that leads to the formation of political emotions'.

So, for Nussbaum, 'love of country' is not seen to be 'morally dangerous'. Instead, provided it is 'globally sensitive', patriotism should be welcomed as an emancipatory force. But it should be a civic, 'purified' patriotism – a patriotism based not on ethnolinguistic or religious homogeneity, but solely on compassion for the predicaments of others.

This is not the same as the constitutional patriotism favoured by German philosopher Jürgen Habermas, who makes the case for taking emotion out of patriotism in order to find 'a functional equivalent for the fusion of the nation of citizens with the ethnic nation'.[22] Habermas wants to escape from what he feels is the nativism that surrounds kinship and ethnicity and instead build loyalties around political values we can share. He believes that Europe ought to collectively relinquish the political culture of ethnicity and national identity and replace it with a culture based on the common values of liberty, social responsibility and fairness. Unfortunately, as prime minister, when I tried to rebuild a sense of 'Britishness' around shared values (via a series of speeches), I found that I had little success. What I thought were commonly held British values, the public saw as vague generalities. To talk of a country built on freedom, fairness and social responsibility was seen as too abstract. It did not evoke or instil the same sense of loyalty as pride in the history and tradition of your country does.[23] Nussbaum probably got closest to explaining this when she referred to 'the human mind' as 'quirky and particularistic' – 'more easily able to conceive a strong attachment if high principles are connected to a particular set of memories, symbols, narrative and poetry'.

So we should champion a patriotism without nationalism. We should acknowledge the importance people attach to their history, traditions, institutions and way of life, while also rejecting anti-immigrant and xenophobic rhetoric and an adversarial view of the world. We should reaffirm the principle that public policy decisions that affect our lives be made, where possible, closest to where people are and do what we can to empower local representatives as well as national politicians, so that people can acknowledge and celebrate all aspects of their identity including their pride in their local communities. We should celebrate the wider cultural diversity that now exists and recognise that the challenge everywhere is to promote cross-cultural dialogue and understanding. Most of all, the patriotism we espouse should not only reject all forms of discrimination and exclusion but encourage all citizens to be active participants directly involved in shaping their country's story.

Third response: building a society of states

Next on the list, we have to persuade people of the case for a society of states built out of a modern and realistic view of what sovereignty means.

For most of us, sovereignty means territorially bound, relatively autonomous states with the power to direct their own national economies. But some – like John Bolton, former US national security adviser – take an absolutist view. For Bolton, any international agreements are 'unquestionably a formula for reducing US autonomy and reducing our control over government'.[24] His is a view of national sovereignty that is unlimited, indivisible and accountable to no one – more akin to the ancient and all-but-forgotten divine right of kings. Nowadays, the sovereignty of any ruler is, in practical terms, limited by the constitutions we live under, the laws we inherit and enact, the treaties we sign, and the obligations we accept in return for agreed benefits.

Sovereignty is, of course, divided within states when there are federal arrangements in place that restrict the power of those at the centre. But it is also divided between the nations that choose to undertake responsibilities as members of international organisations in return for rights. Indeed, this sharing of sovereignty is not only a feature of the EU, in which each country has to meet agreed obligations, it also lies at the heart of all international organisations, including NATO, the WTO and the UN. Just as an individual state within the US would damage its ability to shape events by refusing to send its quota of representatives to the federal congress, so, too, would a country compromise its wider influence by walking away from international institutions and denying itself a place at the decision-making tables of the world. By refusing to participate in joint endeavours that cross borders, we narrow our options and weaken our ability to control the decisions that affect our lives. My argument is that responsible international cooperation does not undermine the role of nation states, nor need it weaken the patriotic pride most citizens rightly feel for their country.

To repeat what I said in Chapter 1, I am not endorsing 'some abstract concept of global government', nor am I interested in returning to 'old arguments between globalists and nationalists'. I am simply making the case for international cooperation.

Fourth response: making our international institutions fit for purpose

Unfortunately, as long as states continue to claim – even in our interconnected and interdependent world – that their sovereignty is unlimited and indivisible and that they are accountable to no one but themselves, our 'global order' will be unstable, easily portrayed as anarchic, and little more than a bundling together of poorly resourced international institutions, too weak and ineffective to ever unite the world or bring people together.

The final counterweight to nationalism is good international institutions that people can feel proud of and so we must rebuild our current institutions as representative, effective and capable of gaining public endorsement by balancing our desire for national autonomy with our need for international cooperation. In Chapter 9 I discussed how a future of 'one world, two systems' will not serve the interests of even the two dominant powers, far less meet the urgent needs of the poorer citizens of the world. Like nationalism, it offers us a zero-sum world in which one side must lose so that the other can win. Similarly, it would be nothing less than a tragedy if we were to fail to find better ways to cooperate and simply allowed ourselves to descend into a world made uninhabitable by climate change, and the collapse of our global ecosystem, and rendered ungovernable with millions of forcibly displaced, homeless people feeling they had nothing left to lose.

But the root problem we must overcome is not a pandemic or pollution or poverty – for all of these are avoidable and soluble – but rather our failure to work together as nations, transcend our differences and seek to govern as guardians of the same planet. In other words, we have to stop assuming that we can meet global challenges with nation state-only solutions.

Of course, joint working across borders has to be seen to yield benefits in living standards and quality of life. To deliver such results we must not only cultivate a habit of 'acting together' – sponsoring new friendships and partnering with neighbours – but also reshape our international organisations to make them fit for purpose. As academic scientist and global campaigner Jamie Metzl put it, the world needs an updated operating system based on recalibrating the relationship between the power of nation states and that of international institutions.[25] A lethal pandemic that is still a long way from being eradicated and the associated economic recession that is affecting millions globally both remain, to this day, test cases for whether and how we can, in the words of António Guterres, cooperate to succeed and 'build back better'.

And there are grounds for hope. In recent years, in response to the rising tide of nationalism, the world has retreated from the broad visions of global cooperation, but it is encouraging that very few countries have walked away entirely from cross-border alliances and collaboration. Indeed, no country – not even the nations in which 'my tribe first' is the dominant ideology – has removed itself from the UN or resigned from the most important global institutions like the IMF, the World Bank or the WTO. Even countries outside the West – many of which played little part in the creation of these organisations, but are keen to reform them – have not threatened to leave.

In fact, there are many 'minilateralist' or 'plurilateralist' initiatives now in effect or being planned, which suggests a willingness to engage with cross-border cooperation. These include: variable-geometry organisations like the Paris Peace Forum, which seeks to unite the West; the Alliance for Multilateralism between France and Germany; Biden's proposed 'summit of democracies'; and many 'coalitions of the responsible', such as the recent Canadian initiative to bring countries together under the banner of the UN to discuss enhanced economic collaboration. There is even talk of a 'middle-power moment' – smaller countries that sit outside the great power elite coming together – and of 'Gulliverisation' – a large alliance made up of small or unaligned countries – but these cannot, on their own, reach what economists term 'escape velocity', i.e. achieving the minimum level of support that would make them game changers.

The proliferation of so many informal groupings is itself testimony to the gaps and deficiencies in the post-1945 global architecture. It is clear that, if international cooperation is to flourish again, the global order will have to be reformed. The BRICS and most developing countries want to move beyond an international system designed almost exclusively by those who held power at the end of the Second World War. Indeed, as we have seen in previous chapters, these nations favour reforms that would improve financial stability, environmental sustainability, common security and access to global public goods, since re-ordering our international institutions is not an end in itself. We should all champion reform because we believe that prosperity, in order to be sustained, must be shared and because, if it is achieved under the right circumstances and with the right intentions, everyone can benefit. At all times, we have to show that growth, employment, opportunity and quality of life are improved when we work together.

But how might a policy of responsible cooperation work? In a recent publication for the Carnegie Endowment for International Peace, a group of writers – comprising, in the main, pro-Biden Democrats, who also reject the Washington Consensus, 'America First' and a future of 'one world, two systems' – asks us to choose between two approaches to managing the global order. The first is what the writers call a 'socially liberal approach, focused on economic justice, climate change, and non-military means of foreign policy advocated by progressives'. This they reject in favour of a second approach, an international policy that would:

> Address the downside risks of today's more interconnected security, economic, and social environments much more directly and pay more attention to ensuring that the benefits are more widely shared . . . [and then] advance a shared prosperity and global security through international leadership, engagement, and positive-sum thinking; as well as maintain a robust defense posture to undergird US diplomacy, foster global stability, and ensure continued access and integration with the global markets on which the US economy depends.[26]

In other words, they make a distinction between what they would define as idealistic and realistic approaches to global cooperation. While I see differences of emphasis, I see little of substance that divides these two approaches. Both favour increased cooperation. Both want to reconcile the national sovereignty they are used to with the international cooperation they know we need. Both focus on our damaged environment as an existential threat and see climate change as the great foreign and domestic policy challenge of the twenty-first century – a test of whether we can find ways to work together. Both set out proposals to strengthen our international rules-based order and both know that we cannot do so without winning support for reform. And both would, I believe, favour the case-by-case cooperation that I am advocating: the reconstruction, institution by institution, of our global decision-making system.

And, if leading US voices now seek reform, so do Chinese leaders. President Xi insists that China has no desire to dismantle, only to reform, the multilateral system and that the country's goal is to safeguard the global free trade system and an open world economy. Of course, no one should underestimate the difficulties. One school of thought, represented by Chinese academic J. C. Liow, is pessimistic, fearing that a 'one world, two systems' future is now a real possibility, as 'it is unlikely the World Bank or IMF will remain the primary ports of call in future storms, internal reforms of these institutions notwithstanding'. Perhaps more worrying is the view from another Chinese academic, Rebecca Liao, who sets down a difficult marker for the West to meet, as we are at odds with his argument that 'the Bretton Woods system cannot continue its promulgation of liberal democracy, free markets, and Western governance institutions if it wants to effectively head the economic world order'. However, now that we, in the West, are revisiting the role of markets and governments, there is some common ground for us to concede when Liao says that the US's 'leadership of the global economy' must 'stop being partial to Western neoliberal orthodoxy'. And, if the most important of these voices from China, that of Zheng Bijian, is calling for 'a multipolar system with a strong Sinocentric component', there may be a basis for some understanding on the future role of the premier global institutions.[27]

The question for me is: how do we find a way forward that upholds the principles underlying a liberal, rules-based order, but takes us beyond the Washington Consensus, which for too long has defined this order in a neoliberal way?

I believe that, just as we can chart a route for international cooperation *issue by issue* – for health, climate change, nuclear non-proliferation and the other great global challenges – we can also show *institution by institution*, and perhaps *network by network* the future contribution that a reformed international system can make to building a more prosperous, more stable and fairer world. Multilateral institutions should provide benefits that are underprovided or simply not available if countries act bilaterally. The success of such institutions should dissuade states from defining their national interests too narrowly or in ways that make them reluctant to ever share decision-making authority with other countries.

All our multilateral institutions – some born in a wave of optimism in 1945, other creatures of the Cold War – have been slow to adapt to the spread of globalisation. When created in 1945, the IMF was named a 'fund', but, as we have suggested earlier, its future remit should be much closer to that of a bank. Established to deal with the balance-of-payments problems of ailing but sheltered national economies, the IMF has focused its past seventy-five years of activity on restructuring at a national level.

We now have an open international economy and yet, while flows of capital are predominantly global, financial supervision remains predominantly local. The IMF's primary function should be to do what no one else today is yet doing successfully: monitor the international economy and on the basis of its global surveillance provide early warning of any risks ahead. Moreover, in order to make crisis prevention and crisis resolution work effectively, the IMF must closely coordinate the many financial supervisory organisations that already exist but all too often work in silos.

When the constitution of the IMF was being negotiated in 1944, there was some dispute as to whether the new body should be housed in Europe or the US. But the agreement reached by the drafters seventy-five years ago was not as some imagine. A widely misconceived notion is that the authors of the IMF's constitution agreed to locate the fund in Washington in perpetuity. However, the actual agreement was that the headquarters would be in the capital city of the country that has the largest share of voting rights, which would almost certainly be the country that accounts for the largest share of the world economy. What would more vividly illustrate an epochal change than an assertion by China, as potentially the biggest economy and biggest shareholder a decade or so from now, that Beijing be the new home of the IMF? Of course, the US would leave the IMF before the IMF ever left the US, but this prospect gives China greater negotiating power than before to push for a more balanced representation of emerging markets on the board and in the shareholdings of the fund.

Table 7: Unbalanced World? IMF and World Bank Voting Rights

Country	Share of Global Population (%)	IMF Voting Share (%)	World Bank Voting (%)
USA	4.4	16.74 (Veto)	15.89
Europe	7.0	31.06	26.50
Japan	1.7	6.01	6.85
Advanced Economies	13.1	53.81	49.24
China	19.1	3.65	4.43

Country	Share of Global Population (%)	IMF Voting Share (%)	World Bank Voting (%)
India	17.9	2.34	2.91
Russia	2.0	2.69	2.77
South Africa	0.8	0.64	0.76
Brazil	2.8	1.38	2.24
The BRICS five	42.6	10.70	13.10
Indonesia	3.5	0.95	0.98

For the IMF will only be able to enjoy the legitimacy it ought to have if the emerging markets are given their proper place. Today, Europe, the US and Japan comprise only 13 per cent of the world's population, but together control around 55 per cent of IMF votes. EU countries had, in 2020, a disproportionate level of control, too, comprising 7 per cent of the population, but holding 31 per cent of the votes. On the other hand: the BRICS, with 43 per cent of the world's population, have just 11 per cent of the voting power; China, with 19 per cent of the global population, has only 3.65 per cent of the votes; and India, with 18 per cent of the population, holds a mere 2.34 per cent of votes. A rising country like Indonesia has less than 1 per cent of the votes, but Saudi Arabia, with a tenth of Indonesia's population, has twice Indonesia's share of votes. That cannot continue for ever. Nor can the US continue to enjoy the veto that is provided for under the constitution, whereby, in most decisions, its 15 per cent share of the vote constitutes a blocking minority.

The World Bank must also become more representative of our changing world and more open to adaptation and new ideas. I have suggested how it can generate more resources for global public goods and, with the gap between the resources the UN needs for humanitarian work and the resources available greater than ever, proposed a closer working relationship between the two agencies. I have also suggested the use of single-purpose vehicles, modelled on the vaccination facility GAVI and the refugee fund Education Cannot Wait, to deliver specified social, economic and environmental objectives.

Just as the IMF and the World Bank must improve their early warning systems to deal with potential economic crises, so, too, must the UN improve its capacity to respond in emergencies. For a long time many observers like me have favoured a broader, more representative Security Council through the expansion of the Security Council's permanent membership and by agreement of the current five – all nuclear weapons powers – to renounce their right to unrestrained use of the veto.

China's 2019 UN reform paper pushed for practical changes that few could oppose – a more transparent process, a stronger peace and security pillar, and the streamlining of internal man-agement – and the paper reiterated China's previous 2015 proposal to create a designated 8,000-member standby force. Already the Security Council's biggest contributor to peacekeeping, China is also a proponent of greater geographic diversity in the hiring practices of UN peacekeeping forces, as well as of more 'explicit, feasible and focused mandates' tailored to the particular requirements of specific missions. Furthermore, to support con-flict prevention and conflict resolution, China wants a stronger UN Secretariat that will work more closely in partnership with regional organisations. Additionally, with China's nominee as the head of the UN Department of Economic and Social Affairs, a think tank with an annual budget of just $80 million, China wants the UN to have a greater say in global economic policy and thus a bigger voice given to developing countries.

So could revitalised US engagement with other countries and with the UN itself allow us to find common ground on a UN reform programme? Under President Biden, the US could re-establish its political and moral leadership by re-entering the Human Rights Council, signing up to the UN Convention of the Rights of the

Child and the International Criminal Court, and as the President has done rejoining the WHO, reengaging with UNESCO, the UN's Population Fund, Relief and Works Agency and the Global Compact for Migration. This would strengthen a UN already committed to the 'responsibility to protect' in its resolve to defend human rights and broker an end to at least some of the forty-nine civil wars and conflicts disfiguring the world. The UN should also become a stronger force in preventing nuclear proliferation and reducing all weapons of mass destruction. And we have suggested it should take a new lead in ending global tax abuse. A reformed and more inclusive UN Security Council might also be well placed to take the lead in pioneering a global digital highway by promoting interoperability and common rules for both digital software and hardware in fields like machine learning and 5G.

Debt relief – and debt restructuring – for poor countries is another area where there is insufficient international coordination. It is unlikely that China will want to join the Paris Club of official creditors, not least because it would have to be fully transparent about the conditions it attaches to its lending. However, given the scale of China's recent lending to poorer countries ($150 billion to Africa alone) and the debt-servicing problems that countries are already encountering, it makes sense for all creditor countries to work together to negotiate what ought to be a globally coordinated response. There ought to be greater coordination too among aid donors and while China may object to the transparency – and common standards – demanded in the OECD process for reporting aid contributions, it is clear that the modern Marshall Plan now urgently needed for Africa's development requires China, Europe and the US to work together.

Some see the G20 as no more than the 'rich countries club' – a cartel that strongarms the poorer and weaker economies – but the G20 is the only world leaders economic forum big enough to span 80 per cent of the world's economic activity but small and manageable enough to conduct business around one table and get things done. Of course, a G20 that truly reflects the size of national economies would now have to admit Taiwan and Thailand, as well as offering seats over the next thirty years to Vietnam, Nigeria, Pakistan and the Philippines. By 2050, Bangladesh would be the world's twenty-third largest economy and also knocking on the G20's door. All this means that, with Indonesia, China, India, South Korea and Japan already in the group, a representative G20 could, by 2040 or 2050, have an Asian majority, with the US the sole non-Asian country in the top five.[28] Of course, a scenario like this, which would see a number of smaller European and Latin American countries removed from the group, would see their larger compatriots like Brazil and Germany resist their exclusion and perhaps break with the G20 itself. What makes greater sense is to bring more countries within the G20's ambit, possibly through the same kind of constituency system that the IMF has evolved. This would offer one seat to a group of countries, with each group then selecting one of its members every year, on a revolving basis, to be its G20 representative.

But, if the G20 is to be effective, it needs its own secretariat and an executive committee – perhaps of current, past and future chairs – as well as a long-term agenda that reflects more than just the host country's favoured themes of the year. No one should want to repeat the fiasco of 2020 when, despite entering the biggest health and economic crisis of the past century, eight months passed before the G20 met.

Populist nationalism, and all the chaos and danger it brings, can be disarmed and defeated if we are able to show that international cooperation can deliver shared solutions to shared problems and practical benefits in the form of peace, stability, social justice and a clean environment. Such reforms do not set out to stop the nation state, but to connect nations together in practical, workable arrangements that will ensure security in the face of a series of global challenges that no nation, however great, can conquer alone.

In short, the four measures that will start to erode the appeal of populist nationalism involve us acting locally, nationally and internationally; committing ourselves to tackling the corrosive effects of economic insecurity on families and communities; upholding our need for belonging and – in Orwell's words – the value of place; standing up for an enlightened patriotism that will dispose of obsolete notions of absolute national sovereignty; and restructuring our global institutions to help bring our troubled world back together.

For the last several centuries, national leaders have failed by regarding war as an extension of politics by other means, and simply an unavoidable part of history – bringing the death of many millions. In our nuclear age, and as more and more nations threaten to acquire nuclear weapons, the costs of conflict will be immeasurably greater. International cooperation is our best chance.

A more connected world is not a guarantee against 'us versus them' nationalism. The COVID-19 pandemic provided stark evidence of what happens when we fail to respond quickly and collectively to a hideous threat affecting our whole world and the global economy. And as we have seen to our cost over this past decade, the fact of our connectedness can be used just as easily by nationalists to divide people as others wish to unite them.

I am, however, certain that alongside the many we already know of, fresh global challenges will follow, be that a new pandemic, another financial crash, a solar storm or an unpredictable nuclear crisis. So we must learn to anticipate rather than react, and we must do so as one. 'United we stand, divided we fall' are words thought to first appear in *Aesop's Fables*. They reappear in the Bible, were mobilised for the independence cause of America's founding fathers, and have never been far from the lips of crusaders for change ever since. They are more relevant than ever as we deal with shared global challenges today. Up against waves of nationalist sectarianism, we will find strength in unity.

CONCLUSION
THE POWER OF HOPE

I have tried in this book to describe the world we are heading towards and the world I think we can build, each chapter setting out concrete deliverable changes that could, in my view, make for a fairer and more sustainable and peaceful future.

The year 2020 will be remembered for our collective failure as an international community to come together and manage the most severe global health and economic crises we have faced in peacetime. It is a tale of a world managed badly that needlessly destroyed hundreds of thousands of lives and livelihoods.

I want 2021 – and the 2020s – remembered not just for the triumph of science over disease but also for building a better future: in other words, for a world managed well.

For if, in 2020, our very openness as a world – our interdependence and connectivity – accelerated the spread of both the virus and the economic recession, the 2020s can be the decade where that same interdependence and connectivity is mobilised for good: through enhanced international cooperation which can eliminate not just the pandemic but the worst of global poverty, pollution and the ever-present threats to peace.

So while some view politics as the art of the possible, I prefer to see it as making the desirable possible, and the seven proposals I have made and summarise below are not just at the radical end of the possible but at the credible end of the desirable.

- A new and equitable system of burden-sharing to finance global health can help tackle the epidemics and chronic diseases now cutting short human lives and end the lottery of provision between and within countries that determines who lives and who dies.
- A reformed set of international institutions – a revamped IMF and a global early warning system – can address the ever-present threat of financial instability and create a global safety net that avoids the chaos and disruption to lives and livelihoods caused by economic crises and spreads prosperity to those currently excluded from it.
- A practical plan to cut emissions, green the environment, expand renewables, encourage innovative energy-saving technology and repair our forest and farmlands to create a net carbon-free world by 2050, and to coordinate what is as yet a disorganised push to the goal of a sustainable environment.
- A radically different relationship between the two great global institutions of our post-1945 world – the United Nations and the World Bank – that can free millions from never-ending humanitarian crises, and finally turn the SDGs from mere aspiration into solid achievements.
- Our shared goals of universal education and an end to extreme poverty finally attained by mobilising the necessary finance. Ours can be the first generation in history where every child goes to school and every family is free from famine and destitution.
- And to help fund this progress, an intergovernmental agreement can be reached to isolate and then close down those tax havens that siphon off $400 billion every year, money which, if taxed fairly, could radically improve healthcare and public services that both advanced and developing countries need.

- Nuclear proliferation is not a phenomenon relegated to the second half of the last century when nine countries joined the nuclear arms race: it remains a real and present threat as many non-nuclear countries contemplate a nuclear future. Preventing a 21st-century nuclear arms race will not be easy, but there is a process by which we can make nuclear weapons a thing of the past. Declarations by nuclear weapon states that they will never be the first to use such weapons will downgrade the role of nuclear weapons and by banning both the testing of such weapons and the enrichment of uranium and plutonium in their production we can take the first significant step on the road to their elimination.

And so, how do we make what is both desirable and possible happen? Globalisation has made the world flatter and the world wide web has made it possible for millions of us – and soon, hopefully all of us – to connect to just about anyone in any continent in any place and at any time and to know more about each other than ever before.

And this opening up of the world through technology and communications should be empowering: bringing into being a new generation of global citizens who understand each other's concerns and can work together. But the opposite seems to be the case: decisions which directly affect our lives being made at such a distance from us that we feel out of the loop, as if the world is divided into 8 billion pieces separated off from one another. Not only have many concluded that there is nothing we can do to make a positive difference by coming together but they have embraced extreme nationalist solutions.

Indeed, when we look at military-led repression in Myanmar, religious bigotry in India, Al-Qaeda actions in the Middle East, the role the Taliban still play in Afghanistan and authoritarian leaderships engaged in the repression of dissent in every continent, adding to the intolerance and xenophobia that comes from the rise of populist nationalisms, the reader may be tempted to think the tide of history is against us. Even those who believe that history goes in cycles may fear that the collectivist spirit we saw when international cooperation was at its height has given way, at least for a long time to come, to a new individualism at home and isolationism abroad.

The situation is perilous, but we are anything but powerless if can bring together our galaxy of 8 billion individuals, 8 billion different people with different interests and passions, recognising that they have much more in common than they have that separates them. This is not to advocate a world government or some post-national future, but simply to recognise the value and importance of us coming together to build a fairer and better world.

But the reader will rightly ask: what role can I play in shaping the story that is being told, when elites with money seem to exercise so much more political power than I do, when political parties seem to be less effective than ever in bringing people together and performing their traditional function of aggregating opinion, when the institutions of our democracy seem so tarnished and unfit for purpose and opportunities for – and gains from – participation seem so limited. And of course when, as we discussed in the last chapter, strong-arm dictators are in vogue and demagogues can manipulate democratic institutions to preach messages of hate and 'divide and rule'.

But distrust of the actions of leaders should not lead us to withdraw from acting ourselves. We should not allow the public square to be colonised by leaders whose talk of a 'silent majority' – or, as ex-President Trump put it, the 'real people' – is to ascribe views to people that they have never expressed, and to act as if the natural reticence of people gives demagogues permission to speak on their behalf.

'Silent majority' is a term popularised in its post-1945 form by the disgraced US president Richard Nixon to distinguish the vast mass of people from anti-government demonstrators whom he portrayed as an angry and villainous anti-social mob; but his summoning up of the 'silent majority' was not a call to empower the mass of people and to invite them on to the public stage. Rather it was an attempt to co-opt their support for his own personal prejudices, irrespective of what their views really were. And the lesson is clear: if we fail to make our views known, others will define them for us.

So we must not resign ourselves to a world where we, as citizens, allow ourselves to act as if we are powerless. Quite the opposite. My answer is that progress is possible. Progress in history – to eradicate slavery, to counter gender, sexual and racial discrimination, to win the right to vote, to access decent working conditions and universal healthcare – happened because of the inspiration of social movements that were built on strong ethical foundations. And so too progress can, in future, come from sustained movements of people imbued with a strong sense of what is just and fair, who see the bigger picture, can explain and motivate people through telling a story that captures their passions and who can bend what Martin Luther King called 'the arc of the moral universe' in favour of change.

Despite the chaos and setbacks of the last year there are grounds for optimism. Often going unreported, and often in the remotest and least advantaged parts of the world, new voices, most of them young, are speaking out for change, and the demand for a different world is rising.

Black Lives Matter, Extinction Rebellion, #MeToo, Girls Not Brides and the Global March Against Child Labour are just a few of the recently formed global social movements for change that sit alongside thousands of already existing campaigning pressure groups and non-governmental organisations.

These social movements are, of course, creatures of their times, born of inherited circumstances that are not necessarily of their choosing, and, on occasion, they will reflect our worst tendencies and impulses – like the cancel culture that freezes out opponents. But the world's successful movements are drivers of change. Invariably they will start small, their voices barely audible above the noise around us, but just as a handful of single voices can grow into a loud and harmonious chorus, so too a cause can spring from inauspicious beginnings and become an unstoppable force.

One death, that of George Floyd, suffocated at the hands – and under the knee – of a brutal police officer, provided the spark that ignited a movement long in the making and in urgent need of being heard; a demand that black lives cannot be valued less than white lives. But BLM did not fall out of the sky: the 'Black Lives Matter' hashtag had started after the death of 17-year-old Trayvon Martin in Florida eight years before in 2012 and in demonstrations one year later in response to the acquittal of his killer. But today, with its immediate demands for police reform, and with its long-term objective, an end to systemic racism, Black Lives Matter's message, has gone global, altering the way we do sport, music and the arts; and while there will always be questions around how much gestures change actions and how much actions change attitudes, a cultural shift is definitely under way.

This year Greenpeace celebrates fifty years of action in the cause of saving our planet, and this half-century has seen a groundswell of support, handed on from generation to generation, and growing each decade. At the same time we see the planet's leading environmentalist, Sir David Attenborough, more influential than ever, though only five years away from his hundredth birthday. We also see young school pupils moving centre stage, most notably Greta Thunberg, who went from protesting outside her school gates to addressing political leaders across the globe. Recent years have also seen those demands for environmental change pervade every sphere, from the more radical climate activists demonstrating outside company offices to the corporate executives working inside the very same offices to deliver climate 'mission statements' for their firms, and all reflecting a bigger truth that

COVID-19 has also exposed: that we are one humanity facing common existential challenges and that we cannot run away from the responsibility we share for the one planet we occupy.

Observers have counted 230 significant protest movements, covering 100 countries that have sprung to life in the last three years, one hundred of them in the last year alone. They range from the anti-rape demonstrators in India, to democracy demonstrators furious at the fixing of elections in places like Belarus and Uganda and the restrictions on free speech in Russia and elsewhere, to mass gatherings demanding the removal of corrupt elites from Latin America to Lebanon to Myanmar and Thailand.

Not all demonstrations are as memorable as the coup d'état that brought down the Estrada government in the Philippines in 2001: a protest that was the first 'e-revolution' and 'a coup de text',[1] because thousands of protestors were mobilised through modern ways of communicating. And few recent uprisings are as dramatic as the popular rebellion that brought down Haiti's Jean-Bertrand Aristide in 2004, the mass occupations in Kiev during the Ukrainian Revolution in 2014 and the Venezuelans' numerous attempts to dislodge the Maduro regime. And, of course, not all progressive movements for change have been successful – some of the most popular and vibrant have been brutally suppressed with huge loss of life, as in the wake of the Arab Spring, despite its hopeful beginnings. But some recent movements like the protests in Sudan over the price of food in 2018 grew strong enough to overthrow a government, in this case the three-decade-old authoritarian regime of President Omar al-Bashir.

Some protests work to shock us through the outlandishness and sometimes extremism of their actions – naked bike rides through Lima and other cities of Peru to highlight environmental concerns; the 'union of clowns' marching in Mexico to call for an end to the violence of gangs and drug cartels; migrants on the border of Greece and Macedonia sewing their mouths shut to protest at their squalid conditions; and some protests have been as basic as

Brazilians banging pots and pans and their kitchen utensils from their windows to call for the removal of their populist president because of his handling of the COVID-19 pandemic.[2]

But, of course, not all demands for change are progressive and we should be aware of just how badly wrong organisations – even those that start with the best of intentions – can go. As we can see from the anti-Muslim violence in India to the attacks on the Rohingya communities in Myanmar, populist nationalists can mobilise people by conjuring up enemies as punchbags for prejudice. If we want to live in something resembling a global community, we have to be prepared for – and be tolerant of – dissenting voices. Unless we see evidence of discriminatory behaviour systemically targeted against groups of people or the blatant dissemination of lies, prejudice and hate, we have to defend the right to free speech. But the anti-progressive movements remind us that at all times we have to challenge the power that authoritarian and populist nationalist leaders can mobilise for ill.

As I write, there are thousands of young people out on the street in a score of countries round the world from Africa to Asia, from Latin America to Eastern Europe, protesting about the way they have been treated and demanding their rights be taken seriously. In Nigeria, young people have recently led protests that were initially sparked by rises in bus fares. But their more fundamental complaint is that they are not being listened to and even that their demonstrations are being suppressed. They complain of the insidious role played by Nigerian secret state police in the intimidation of – and suspected murder of – young protestors. In Chile, protests, again led by young people, are calling for a new democratic constitution that overturns the current settlement designed by the Chilean dictator General Pinochet fifty years ago. In Thailand, protesting under the 'Free Youth' umbrella and with their 'three fingered' salute, students have led the calls for an end to a monarchical despotism.

In all these countries, young people have registered successes against the odds: in Nigeria, the abolition of the hated secret police; and in Chile and Thailand agreements, if only partial, to consider new constitutions. Inevitably these youthful demonstrators are mocked and written off as radical and extreme; and their detractors, who invariably mouth all too familiar platitudes that they too think discrimination is bad but that great progress has been made, ask why Black Lives Matter don't behave with the dignity and nobility of Martin Luther King and the civil rights movement of the 1960s, and why the #MeToo movement does not demonstrate the same grace and poise that some critics of #MeToo ascribe to the Suffragettes. But these critics do not know, or choose not to tell us, that in their own times these early women's rights protestors were labelled in exactly the same way as dangerous extremists who broke laws and windows, and as a result endured imprisonment and cat-and-mouse intermittent forced tube-feeding; and were dismissed as rebels without a cause, and hounded out of public life.

While many of today's movements declare that their aims are limited and purely defensive – to stop a detention, or a censorship, or to fight one unjust law – most also raise fundamental questions about the kind of society we want to create. And the best social movements are unremittingly positive. Objections without objectives incite fury. Objections with objectives force change. And I would single out a new dimension to recent protests: the mounting pressure from a new generation of young people despairing of the injustices that continue to scar our world and what they see as our ageing generation's abysmal failure to come together to address them, but nonetheless determined to champion positive ideas for change.

At this time of crisis we need to take firm and effective action to shape what that future will be. Persuading people to volunteer will of course change lives, but may not in itself change structural injustices. Through individual empowerment we can make a difference – but collective action can make *all* the difference, because failing institutions and previously unaccountable vested interests come under sustained pressure to change. And just as I have suggested seven policies that can help improve our world, I want to close with seven practical ways that each of us, as individuals, can play our part.

1. Movements matter

The people who are having the greatest impact today understand the power we can exercise when we think of ourselves as part of social movements for change and we form communities committed to acting upon shared ideals.

I witnessed at first hand the rise of Live Aid in the 1980s and Make Poverty History at the turn of the century, and each were far too broad-based and ambitious for social advancement to be pigeon-holed as mere 'organisations' or just 'campaigns': they were social purpose movements. Such movements make people aware of a great injustice; bring about changes in attitudes, usually as the impetus for changes in laws; create the space for things to happen without which political leaders may be unable or unwilling to act, and thus make possible the conditions in which reform can take place. But these earlier causes were often one-off explosions of compassion, anger, hope and possibility that, having appeared to arrive out of thin air, faded – like the famous American Occupy 'we are the 99 per cent' Movement of 2011 – almost as quickly as they rose to prominence. And they also tended to replicate an all too familiar pattern of organisation – of leaders and followers – and seemed to perpetuate a myth that all you need is a few exceptional people like rock stars to mobilise millions.

These moments are no substitute for a sustained commitment of people organised over a period of time; for unless social movements can maintain their momentum, like a permanent drumbeat, even an unanswerable case for change can be neutralised by powerful vested interests or by political leaders who make commitments they do not honour. Only through continuous and sustained action can progress be guaranteed and rendered irreversible, and so a successful movement is one that not only opens the door to change but ensures that that door can never be locked shut again.

So recent years have seen a new determination to create movements that are not just creatures of a particular moment in time but represent an ongoing and sustained engagement. This manifests in two ways: they have a long-term agenda for social change, and they are focused on building support from the ground up – 'no base, no movement' as Black Lives Matter puts it – and making it easier for people and communities to hold power to account. This latter point requires a new understanding of the role of both leaders and the rank and file, and foregrounds the importance of grass roots organising.

Watching an old film of a mass demonstration organised by the American civil rights movement challenged me to rethink the role of leaders and what we so often call 'followers'. On this occasion, the cameras were pointed not towards the platform and its speakers but towards the crowd. This film director was trying to capture what he saw as the real power behind the push for civil rights. The protestors were not only flag wavers and placard carriers. They were not just spectators, not present there as passive bystanders but active protagonists and change makers in their own right. This filmmaker understood that the future lay not in all-powerful leaders instructing a passive rank and file. He was showing us that there is no road to sustainable change, no way of embedding change, that does not travel through a more participatory form of social action.

So we should think of change happening not to people but with people, for it is only sustainable when this is the case. It is a 21st-century model of social change that has learned from what has been the great success of the women's liberation movement over many years: to create a movement that is driven forward through dialogue and deliberation, and through respect for each other, and thus from building relationships across nationalities and generations. It is by doing so that people discover enough in common to come to a shared view of the way forward.

But saying this, we should not fall into the trap that snared the Occupy Movement of 2011, which designated itself as leaderless, and having said everyone was a leader – and you should just show up to have a say – found that no one was a leader and things fell apart. Social movements on both the right and left describe themselves as not leader-less but leader-full, meaning not one leader but many and that leadership is not conferred on anyone but identified and singled out through the effort that is applied. And it is, indeed, empowering to reject the idea that the only leadership that matters is of the heroic, charismatic top-down, almost always male and heterosexual, and focused on command and control rather than consultation and collaboration.

In *The Purpose of Power*, her account of the history of Black Lives Matter, Alicia Garza dispels the notion that BLM is a movement with no leaders. It has a collegiate leadership – not one leader but many – with power dispersed and not central-ised, or as she puts it: 'Distributing leadership throughout the organisation rather than concentrating it in one place or in one person or even a few people'.[3] And indeed this is the strategy that has had, by necessity, to be employed by the leaders of protests in Hong Kong. If they had acted differently, each new leader, once appointed, would immediately have been arrested and imprisoned. They knew that if their leader disappeared so too would their movement.

Because of their significant social support as movements that belong to the wider populace, Black Lives Matter, #MeToo and the various environmental movements have been and continue to be hugely successful in bringing about change. They work, and become powers in the land, not by preaching to the converted, nor by retreating into their own silos and talking only to each other or to likeminded allies, but by reaching out beyond their own bubbles and tribal cliques to a wider audience than the traditional single-issue pressure groups ever did.

And they reach the political leaders too. I admit to being brought up in the social democratic tradition: I am one of those who in Robert Kennedy's words, 'see an injustice and want to end it', usually by mobilising the power of government, and so my primary concern has been to develop and deliver the public reforms that can make an immediate difference to people's conditions. In so many situations the material need is, in my view, so immediate, the suffering so acute, the case so compelling, the response that is required so urgent that getting things done – progress on the road to securing equal access to the material underpinnings essential for a dignified life – always seemed to matter most. And the way I have sought to see this happen was through government.

But that is not the way I should be thinking today, and certainly not the way of the future. Governments and political leaders may lay claim to making change happen, but it is social movements that not only make progress possible but also make progress sustainable and irreversible.

In 2005 as we prepared for the successful Make Poverty History marches, the renowned British filmmaker Richard Curtis made a moving account of a fictional finance minister and how he had to be pushed by 'the girl in the café' into doing anything for the world's poor. The film suggested that the mass movement she was part of was everything – and that political leaders were well behind the curve. Without the push from the crowds, these leaders would have done nothing. The reality was somewhat different. In 2005, our government worked with the NGOs to build a mass movement. To encourage more and more to join our campaign it was important, we thought, to reinforce the idea that leaders needed a rank and file movement pushing us. In fact, leaders and demonstrators worked together in a partnership that made Make Poverty History the success it was.

New initiatives like the Civic Power Fund in Britain and the appropriately named 'Sumofus' in the United States are intent on empowering a new generation of community activists. New ways of communicating that emphasise the importance of 'deep canvassing', an effort to have meaningful conversations with people who disagree with you, could, over time, revivify political parties in the local communities they exist to serve.[4]

A participatory politics is essential if we are to deliver sustainable change, but we should not undervalue the importance of a strong, accountable, representative democracy. No movement, however broadly based – neither a national nor international NGO – can be fully representative of the people or claim to speak for everyone. A participatory democracy can bring the widest group of individuals into the process of deliberation, but of course such a plebiscite democracy in which the population as a whole are expected to make all the key decisions, however complex, is a technical impossibility. Our democracy, imperfect as it is, requires representative government where leaders who are accountable to the entire population agree, disagree and debate decisions that when implemented can change lives for the better. So movements cannot simply replace government ministers and elective representatives. Both participation and representation must work together in balance towards a shared aim. This must happen: the stakes – for our lives and livelihoods – are high.

2. Never lose sight of the bigger picture

We must never lose sight of the big picture. Justice is the connecting tissue for the concerns most of us feel strongly about. 'Learn how to see,' the great artist and polymath Leonardo da Vinci once wrote. 'Realize that everything connects to everything else,'[5] and, indeed, almost every social issue people care about deeply comes down to what we think of as 'just' and what is 'fair', whether it be social justice, economic justice, environmental justice, racial justice or gender justice.

So it is important to see and make the connections between the different concerns people raise. Climate change is at its most devastating where poverty is at its worst and the threat of war, nuclear or otherwise, is at its most dangerous where conflict over resources is at its most acute. Failing to vaccinate and deliver our commitments on development compounds – and then entrenches – already deep inequalities, just as failing to take head on a nationalism that sees life as a struggle between 'us and them' creates a barrier to all kinds of social progress.

Seeing the big picture is also understanding the thread that connects us together across the generations, for there is a tendency to think that all the great causes were the causes of centuries past and to fall for the cynical view that there are no great causes left and nothing out there really worth fighting for.

But history has not ended. Just as the anti-slavery, anti-colonialist, anti-apartheid and anti-imperialist movements were transformational in their times, so are the pro-women's rights, pro-black rights, pro-LGBT movement, pro-disability rights and more generally all the pro-equality and pro-justice movements of our times.

Of course history has not yet conferred on today's movements the status, legitimacy and authority that time and distance can – and will – eventually provide, but these new movements have already lit a candle that no matter how dimly it burns cannot easily be extinguished. And these movements have a right to be considered part of that halting and oft-interrupted but, in the end, unstoppable journey to expand civil, social and economic rights – part of a long revolution that is liberating humanity by rectifying and removing the terrible truncation of opportunities people face because of race, religion, gender or social class. Seeing the big picture is especially important when we are up against an out-of-date world view embedded and reproduced across our culture and which has for too long accepted these injustices as natural and irreversible.

Nor should we be distracted or divided by those wanting to turn every issue into a culture war, which would in the end weaken and fragment. We should deny the culture warriors the fight they want and which would destroy the bonds of solidarity we need if we are to meet and master the challenges of our times. I don't want to see a racialised world in any form and we must reject the idea we have to choose between 'justice' issues and 'identity' issues. We should, instead, be building movements that unite us across all lines of difference.

This also means resisting the idea that campaigning can ever be a zero-sum exercise, meaning that for my campaign to succeed, other campaigns, even like-minded campaigns, must fail. We cannot talk of 'success' if we simply stop climate change in one part of the world but everyone goes hungry in another. For I have found that even those campaigns that define themselves as single-issue initiatives – on homelessness, drugs, nutrition, cancer – come down in the end to justice for all and the dignity of all. Oxfam was started to deal with an African famine but its basic objective is 'a just world without poverty'. Save the Children started off as a fundraiser for refugee children left behind in Eastern Europe after the First World War but its inspiration was always – and is still – a desire, and a demand, that every child can realise their potential.

And so it's not just a commendable willingness to work together that marks out successful movements: we should not think of ourselves coming together simply for instrumental reasons or in a transactional way that suggests expediency rather than principle: we connect because we want to emphasise the ties that bind us not the differences that divide us and because out of challenges we have in common can come a shared vision of what's possible.

Avaaz, a non-profit online platform, was inspired by one committed individual, Ricken Patel, but operates as a members' collective, masterminding global campaigns on a wide-ranging number of issues. One day Avaaz will campaign on the threat to whales in our oceans, the next day against racial violence in

Myanmar, the day after that the denial of educational opportunities in Africa and the day after that ask for support for the million struggling farmers of India. But not only does Avaaz make connections between people but they make the connections between the causes they take up and the underlying injustices that inspire them; and so when we talk of the big picture, we mean mobilising people around a shared vision of the better world we are trying to create. It was once said that if you want to persuade people to help you build a ship, you don't talk about the different parts you need them to assemble. You keep the main objective at the front of people's minds: 'Don't drum up the men to gather wood, divide the work, and give orders. Instead teach them to yearn for the vast and endless sea,'[6] all the time raising people's sights as to what is possible.

3. Build upon what's best in people

We are more likely to succeed when we build upon what is best in people, and appeal to what one respected campaigner, Alex Evans, has called 'the larger us', our common humanity, our better instincts, without ever falling into the trap of believing that human values have somehow magically been reset. For while in the wake of COVID-19 people don't want to get back to a normal where the accepted normal was the problem, we should not assume that human nature has suddenly and miraculously been rewired. People are nostalgic, too, for what was good about the past, and we should not confuse a public appetite to build back better with one that is to bring everything down.

But change is in the air. I've noticed that men and women everywhere now have a stronger sense than ever before of their own rights – an observation that is also brought out in the detailed conclusions of a worldwide study organised by the philosopher Michael Ignatieff. He found that even in the least prosperous and most desperately depressed communities that he visited, the world's poorest citizens no longer see themselves as subjects with no rights and with no choice but to be deferential or subservient. The first step is being taken: for everyone to recognise their individual rights. The next stage has not, he said, been reached: where we have a strong sense, not just of our own rights but of everyone else's rights too and understand that these rights are completely interdependent.

'Everyone has a right not to suffer', people do affirm when asked, but we do need to do more to convince people that the maintenance of all our own civil, social and economic rights depends on defending the rights of others and that our collective life is best organised around a social contract in which the rights we have and the responsibilities we share go hand in hand. Or better still we agree a covenant based on what we believe are the values we share in common with each other and agree to uphold.

In Chapter 2 I argued that funding global health – and supporting the poorest countries – is a matter of enlightened self-interest because we all benefit from eradicating infectious diseases like COVID-19. But instead of spending all our energies persuading each other to fight for change by talking in purely material terms about what is of benefit to our own self-interest, we should also appeal to our common humanity. And here change is already afoot. A major study of the advertising and marketing industry, a profession whose very success depends on an in-depth understanding of the people it seeks to influence, reveals that, for decades, most of their appeals to us have been founded on an over-pessimistic assumption about human nature: of individuals obsessed by the desire for money and possessions, and perhaps also the lure of fame and status. And so not surprisingly a highly individualist view of the world is pumped into us through TV and social media advertising. Historically, mass media has underplayed the importance of ordinary people's generosity and their benevolence – and the empathy we are capable of showing that allows us to put ourselves in other people's shoes and identify with their plight.[7] However of late, the more enlightened advertising agencies are starting to recognise that instead of always focusing on 'I', on a 'me first, me now' world of instant gratification, they should not underestimate the power of 'we', and we are seeing a resultant shift in emphasis.

So while we should not deny that each of us is as capable of being appetitive, aggressive and competitive as we are of being altruistic, empathetic and cooperative, what Lincoln called the 'better angels of our nature' can rise above the more selfish inclinations. Indeed, we have found during the COVID-19 crisis that people want 'to tend and befriend'. And we can all identify millions of acts of kindness to neighbours that have distinguished every community's response to the COVID-19 crisis.

Appeals for justice that start from empathy and ideas of solidarity and the cooperation and reciprocity that follow on from this, can and do succeed. When we seek help to eradicate poverty and injustices, appeals to our wider humanity resonate. This can be seen in the way countries are responding to the demand to end centuries of discrimination against the LGBT community and in particular to legalise same-sex partnerships. When we were in the process of reforming the laws in the UK, my first instinct was to see the issue as a fight for equality, about rights, and to cite the clear grounds for change as the right to be free from discrimination. But it was not an appeal to human rights but an appeal to shared values, indeed to family values, that won the public.

Gay rights advocates in the US were devastated when they lost the Californian referendum of 2008 and shocked because their cause had fallen victim to a deadly ad campaign that played on lingering fears that gay marriage threatened the safety of children.[8] They found that while they had called for support for their human rights, those who opposed the change spoke of marriage in terms of love, commitment, responsibility and family – exactly what the gay rights group had wanted to say of their own aspirations, but had not done so.

I remember an event I hosted in No 10 Downing Street in 2009 in celebration of LGBT rights month. The night of the reception happened also to be the eve of a same-sex partnership ceremony. There, in No 10, the couple spoke publicly of the love they had for each other, the commitment they wanted to make to each other, the family they wanted to create with each other. And so it was when the equal marriage campaign focused on love – appealing to the best in human nature and our shared experiences – and introduced the world to gay families – and not just gay rights – the legal change that for centuries had seemed impossible became unstoppable.

A similar message was at the centre of the unique and successful election campaign run by Ekrem İmamoğlu, who was installed as mayor of Istanbul before he was ousted by the increasingly authoritarian Turkish President Erdoğan. He described himself as the 'radical love' candidate and 'the love your enemies' candidate and campaigned under the optimistic slogan 'everything will be fine'. His masterplan, the 'Radical Love Book', called on his supporters to talk less and listen more, to abandon the usual political tit-for-tat of fighting 'polarising populists with polarising responses', and instead to 'find a neighbour who doesn't think like you and just give them a hug'. Rather than fight culture wars, his supporters should 'show that walls can be torn down with love'.

The mayor's manifesto was inspired by religious thinking. And between faiths that have for centuries been at odds with each other and whose internecine fights made us doubt whether coexistence was ever possible, we can and do find common ground in our shared humanity. When Christians say: 'do to others what you would have them do to you'; Muslims say: 'no one of you is a believer until he desires for his brother that which he desires for himself'; Jews say: 'what is hateful to you, do not to your fellow man'; Hindus say: 'this is the sum of duty: do naught unto others which would cause pain if done to you'; Sikhs say: 'treat others as you would be treated yourself'; and Buddhists say: 'hurt not others in ways that you yourself would find hurtful'. Of course this 'golden rule', common to all faiths, can be criticised for giving us an incomplete and partial view of our duties and rights – but I suspect if we had to come together to agree an ethical code for our shared global society, the golden rule would be at its core, and in addition to stating how each of us can and should help each other, we would set out how much each of us depend on each other. The African term Ubuntu – 'I am because you are' – sums that up. Derived from the Zulu phrase 'Umuntu ngumuntu ngabantu', its literal meaning is that a person is someone who comes alive through other people.

4. Tell a story: the narrative that matters

Experience has taught me that movements will succeed only if they explain what needs to be done – not in slogans and sound-bites we endlessly regurgitate or in stereotyped scripts but through stories that inspire. It is important to communicate in everyday language that people can understand, using narrative to take people on a journey that helps them see how an existing problem can be addressed and provides a vision for change.

On 22 July 2011, sixty-seven Norwegian young people and older volunteers attending a summer school conference on an island were brutally shot dead by an extreme right-wing terrorist disguised as a policeman, with another two dying indirectly – one falling from a cliff trying to escape, one drowning trying to swim away – and eight had already died in a preceding bombing in the middle of Oslo, leading a shocked country into mourning. But the country's prime minister, Jens Stoltenberg, captured the defiant mood of a whole nation by the way he paid tribute to the dead. He recounted to a shocked Norwegian people the appeal made to him by one young girl who had lost many friends: 'If one man can display so much hate', she told the Prime Minister, 'you can imagine how much love that coming together we can create.' 'We will answer hatred with love,' Stoltenberg told the country. And with his promise that 'we will never give up on our values', he showed the world that the Norwegian response would not be vengeful but champion the best of humanitarian values: 'more democracy, more openness, and more humanity'.[9]

Nearly ten years later when a white supremacist shot dead Muslim worshipers at prayer in their mosques, it was New Zealand prime minister Jacinda Ardern who in that moment of grief appealed to the best in human nature and told a story that united her country in solidarity across religions.

In her speech to the nation she quoted the words of Muslims who, mourning for friends and loved ones, had whispered from their hospital beds and from their mosques. 'As-salamu Alaykum,' she said. 'Peace be upon you.' By identifying with that heart-warming demonstration of resilience and courage shown by the bereaved, she was persuasively summoning all New Zealanders to discharge what she called 'a responsibility to be the place that we wish to be. A place that is diverse, that is welcoming, that is kind and compassionate.'[10]

As Stoltenberg and Ardern showed, a positive and optimistic narrative – even amid tragedy and disaster – will achieve more impact than a doom-laden narrative that assumes that everything is out of kilter. Such a narrative will encourage people to respond, to do more and to share with others what they've heard.

And there are good British examples of getting things right. In 2015, Save the Children and others launched a campaign to per-suade the then government that Britain should invite in hundreds of unaccompanied refugee children who were wandering through Europe without a home and without hope.

In past times, the temptation would have been to home in on a campaign that showed the public how terrible the suffering of the child refugees was (and it was), and with a narrative that demonstrated how unique a problem this was (and it was) and how if we did not help no one would (and this was true). But the organisers of the campaign quickly realised that a narrative that emphasised the enormity of the problem would frighten potential supporters off. It would deter rather than encourage donations and indeed if they kept talking of the scale of the problem – one of the biggest movements of people since 1945 – even sympathetic supporters would consider it was almost impossible to solve – and certainly beyond their capacity to do much about it.

Instead, those most dedicated to the relocation of the refugees explained to the British people why helping child refugees today was important in a very different way. They dug deep into British values and traditions and explained that helping child refugees was not an aberration but in the best of British traditions. They reminded the public of the Kindertransport of the late 1930s when one British hero, Sir Nicholas Winton, had brought hundreds of Jewish refugees from Central and Eastern Europe, saving them from Nazi persecution and Hitler's gas chambers by offering them a new life in Britain.

These refugees, now in their 70s and 80s like Alf Dubs, a refugee now in the House of Lords, became the moral leaders of the campaign to resettle the unaccompanied children of Syria. The British people persuaded a reluctant government that we could resettle refugee children because we had resettled refugee children before. The narrative that worked was one that recalled our successes as a country. A narrative that 'we can do this because we've already done it'.

Fundraising charities that once launched campaigns to persuade people to donate by saying how desperate and terrible things were, and often did so to the point at which people felt pressured, almost mugged, into giving – and usually handed over as little as they could get away with – have thought twice. They now focus on all that is good, and not all that is bad: they do not want to leave people so pessimistic that they conclude that things are so difficult and so out of control and unmanageable that there is nothing they can do and perhaps no point in even trying.

Save the Children captured the mood of the nation in a crisis in a way I did not manage to do during an earlier crisis, one that affected millions of lives and livelihoods, the global financial crisis of 2009. Indeed I know from the lessons I learned from my own failure to communicate in a way that connected with people that we must have stories that SHOW rather than TELL if you are to take people with you.

During that crisis when people feared for the loss of their jobs and savings, I should have gone out of my way to explain what was happening before our eyes: how and why the financial collapse had started, what had gone wrong, who was to blame, and what the repercussions would be if we failed to act. In particular I should have told the story of why we needed to run a fiscal deficit and to borrow, and how it was the only possible way to get the economy moving forward again, people back to work and living standards on the rise again.

Instead, my political opponents seized the moment to insinuate that government deficits were always bad and any debt always evil, and that I was responsible. They told a story that was simple, obvious and dead wrong: drawing an analogy to family budgets – the kind of reasoning best expressed by Micawber in Dickens' *David Copperfield* when he talked of 'annual income, twenty pounds; annual expenditure, nineteen nineteen and six, result, happiness. Annual income, twenty pounds; annual expenditure, twenty pounds ought and six; result misery'.[11]

I should have shared the poignant letters that had come to me from mothers and fathers, sick with worry about where the next meal for their children would come from, and explained that the most important thing any leader had to do at this time of crisis was not to balance the books – as if I were a corporate chief accountant – but to save livelihoods and lives, as anyone with an ounce of humanity would want to do. And I should have explained the deficit as akin to another sensible everyday form of family budgeting. It was like taking out a mortgage on your home, on the basis that the best way to provide for your family is to think long term and, where necessary, borrow to pay for an asset that is essential to your family's future and an investment that will over the years to come rise in value.

But I was so busy working out the technical solutions to the crisis that I lost sight of the need to explain to people what we were trying to achieve. And soon I fell victim to the power of other people's stories. So while I knew the recession had caused the deficit, my opponents twisted the truth to claim the deficit had caused the recession, and that I was personally to blame.

I learned a lot through this experience about the importance of having a narrative and owning it. Because the stories we tell, and the way we tell them and the words we use, are matters of huge importance, as is the question of who is the storyteller. This is particularly important when sharing the stories of others; if we want to help people, we should share their narrative, but we should not write it for them.

5. Big lies need to be exposed

If we are to discuss and agree a better way to come to decisions, we must find it in reason not in threats, aggression, bullying or any resort to violence in words or in action.

The career of Donald Trump is characterised by the use of violent dehumanising language, personalised attacks on opponents, the dissemination of conspiracy theories, the manufacturing of insults and the manipulation of statistics.

But he is not only a demagogue but a truth denier, and it is the falsification of the truth, and the devaluing of science and reason, taking the 'big lie' to a point not previously witnessed among democratically elected leaders, that should worry us most.

For no lasting consensus can be built other than around

reasoned arguments. If the public square is dominated by claims which no one can ever substantiate, or even agree any basis for doing so, we have abandoned any appeal to reason and we will not be able to understand or relate to each other.

And the lesson of history is that if you make an accommodation with a lie it will catch up with you later. 'Nane ever fear'd that the truth should be heard, But they whom the truth would indite,' wrote the Scottish poet Robert Burns.[12] And it is a lesson that perhaps President Trump should have learned from the story of a predecessor as US president, and of a US Army commander trying to displace him.

In the late 1940s and early 1950s General Douglas MacArthur thought that his much-celebrated status as an outstanding military commander who had liberated much of Asia gave him the right to disobey presidential orders. He started to believe he could displace the sitting president, Harry Truman, and he planned to do so by alleging that Truman was soft on communism and supine in his prosecution of the Cold War.

Sacked by Truman for insubordination, the much-decorated general returned to the US to a hero's reception, feted everywhere, with millions cheering him in cavalcades through the major cities. But faced with a direct challenge to his leadership, Truman and his supporters in the US senate adopted a strategy that would in the end expose MacArthur's true objectives: they would not shout out the truth. Instead they would allow the general to set out his views in an extended set of hearings which interrogated his claims, and challenged him on the quality of his evidence and on the logic of his assertions. In this way they would lay bare his real views and his true intentions.

Under questioning and proper scrutiny, MacArthur was exposed: it soon became clear that his policies would risk peace and stability and, if pursued to their logical conclusion, would provoke a Third World War. The sunlight that exposed his views was the great disinfectant. Once the truth was known, people started to desert him. MacArthur's gymnastics in propagating the big lie contained the seeds – as it has for ex-President Trump – of his own destruction.

We must never run from reason, science, evidence and facts. Indeed we must heed Thomas Jefferson's warnings two and a half centuries ago that we should be 'not afraid to follow truth wherever it may lead, nor to tolerate any error so long as reason is left free to combat it'.[13] And elevating the importance of rational thinking and reasoned argument is precisely what Open Mind, an initiative by Professor Jonathan Haidt to raise the quality of public interaction and debate, seeks to do. All of us make assumptions and come to judgements about people and events, he argues, that would, if closely examined, not stand up to the facts. As a result Open Mind offers a course of studies that teaches us to be aware of our own prejudices and to challenge often unconscious biases and how they influence not just what we think about individual issues but the way we actually see the world.

6. Social media matters, but we must make the message matter more

No one can discount the explosive impact of social media – and the digital technology that underpins it – that is changing not just how we communicate with each other and receive and share knowledge but also how we relate to each other. And it is not an exaggeration to say that social media is a new sphere of our very existence that does not only *reflect* what we think but in fact *shapes* it, affecting how – and whether – we can deliver change.

Heard from outer space the Internet will sound like a modern Tower of Babel – a shouting match without an umpire – and if we are not careful in our use of it, it can be exactly the opposite of what it purports to be: unsocial media.

Someone once said of television, it brings voices into your front room that you would never allow through your front door. Partly because the Internet thrives on instantaneous responses, many people end up communicating what they would never say face to face, and so develops a 'call-out' or 'cancel' culture of often unrestrained vitriol where individuals are publicly shamed. And while the Internet can help us hear each other, it is also prone to filtering out the opinions that the service provider concerned has detected we avoid, and thus creates in effect an echo-chamber, and provides a facility in which extremists confirm and amplify their prejudices. Hence our society can be further polarised into warring online tribes never challenged by those opposing their views.

The social media companies talk of a Twitter democracy and a Facebook community, but in practice this can prove to be a dangerous fallacy. Twitter feeds, Facebook posts and Instagram pictures may give the impression that each of us can have a direct relationship with – and can influence – the powers that be. But the supposed two-way traffic between leaders and followers is not, as the Trump Twitter experience shows, always what it seems. Unofficial outside agencies – as recent examples from Cambridge Analytica to the two Russian 'Bears' demonstrate – have shown the ability to manipulate data, to intrude in the political processes of nations via false material as seen in the run-up to US and other elections, and private companies can be literally held to ransom by threats to destroy, publish or otherwise misuse their data. Perhaps, more worryingly, the algorithms that rank and order vast quantities of content and information based on clicks and 'likes' rather than on accuracy or any measure of quality and linked to advertisers' needs, as opposed to a desire to inform, have themselves become a dangerous way of determining reality: one with no regard for truth but with endless efforts to influence. So, however challenging it might be, society has a role – via legislation or the breaking up of the major players – to reduce such damage: such measures are already under discussion in Europe, Australia and the USA.

Social media – and its reform – must itself now become a target for social action. We need, as the founder of the world wide web, Tim Berners-Lee, has argued, to recapture the idea of the web as a democratising force that genuinely opens up new possibilities for a more collegiate global society. Algorithms will need to be rewritten to counter hate speech, harassment and social bias. Treating these Internet companies as regulated media utilities – and not just as the private empires of a few tech conglomerates – would help us develop what has been called a 'call-in' culture where people invite each other to discuss their views and usher in new ways of running our democracy and ensuring the collective judgement of citizens is fairly expressed.

7. The power of hope

To sum up, successful movements for change need the same combination of mission, urgency and vision that inspired Martin Luther King's memorable 'I have a dream' speech that helped turned the tide in favour of civil rights in America in the mid-1960s. In it, he sought to 'hew out of the mountain of despair a stone of hope' and create a world where children of all races and religions would, one day, live in harmony.

Surprisingly, as we now know, King had not intended to refer to 'the dream' and it was not in his written notes. He had rejected the words as too cliched and too difficult to explain in a short five-minute oration. But as he struggled to enthuse his audience, his friend the gospel singer Mahalia Jackson shouted out: 'Tell them about the dream, Martin, tell them about the dream.'

And a few moments later as he took her advice and articulated his vision of a new world, King had elevated his campaign from a single-issue protest – to deliver the Civil Rights Act of 1964 – into an appeal to the best in human nature that transcended the generations, and, in doing so, he recorded a moral victory that established a consensus on civil rights that has endured.

Movements succeed, we have suggested, by demonstrating the power of possibility and by painting the bigger picture and illustrating what change should take place and why and how.

Indeed what successful movements have in common is that they expose what is fundamentally wrong and show that the old order not only cannot last but is breaking down.

They show the why: the injustice that has to be urgently rectified. And they show how, by our coming together and choosing to act, we find the power within ourselves to change the status quo.

And it is this idea that something new is being born and that a world that has been tearing itself apart can be made whole that does more to capture people's imagination than any recitation of facts or figures.

And so when we call for action on pollution, poverty, taxation and on public health and security, we gain our strength and hasten change by connecting these just demands to a wider purpose; the dream of building the world anew.

And successful movements need to be powered forward by something even bigger than themselves — the power of hope. It is ultimately through generating and spreading hope that we will convince people of the need for change. Hope is more than the absence of despair. It is hope that provides us as human beings with a sense of direction and the energy to get things done. Hope is more than 'a wing and a prayer' and more than wishful thinking — a statement that something might change — and it is more than optimism — that something could change, such as a policy announcement with no commitment to follow through.

Hope is an affirmation that things must change and will change. That is because hope inhabits the space between what we have been told is possible and our desire and determination to create something better. For an individual, hope can provide the inspiration to take you from what you are to what you have it in yourself to become; and for a society hope is the bridge between what is and what can be, making what seems impossible in one generation possible in the next – as a number of striking examples that follow will show.

I do not think you can begin to build for the future without hope. The first two questions the philosopher Immanuel Kant set down for anyone seeking a meaningful life were, perhaps unsurprisingly, 'to know who I am' and 'to know what I can do'. But his third question was: 'for what may I hope?'

I think of what influenced me growing up in a small industrial town in Fife, Scotland. As the son of a Presbyterian minister I was taught early on the words of one Biblical text, and soon knew it off by heart: 'Those that have hope shall renew their strength. They shall take wings as eagles. They shall run and not be weary: they shall walk and not faint.' Words that have stayed with me ever since.

I think of coming of age in the 1960s when the world feared nuclear catastrophe and John F. Kennedy talked of 'the torch passing to a new generation', and of 'never negotiating from fear but never fearing to negotiate', and issued a challenge to the entire world when he said: 'My fellow citizens of the world: ask not what America will do for you, but what together we can do for the freedom of man.' And he issued an equally demanding challenge just over a year before he was assassinated, when in a speech in Philadelphia in the very hall in which the founding fathers had agreed the American constitution, he said that while in the 1770s the US had issued its Declaration of Independence, now was the time for the world to issue a Declaration of Interdependence.[14]

Like so many others of my generation, in a 1960s dominated by protests over war, racial discrimination and social injustice, I found hope reignited yet again in the energising appeal for radical change that came from Martin Luther King and Robert Kennedy; and then again nearly three decades later in Nelson Mandela, who after twenty-seven long years in prison forgave his enemies, declaring that – even after torture and a show trial, imprisonment, threatened execution and enduring tuberculosis in jail – he felt no bitterness to anyone. And I found hope revived during the 1980s in the idealism of young people who tore down the Berlin Wall – an event so memorable that in 2009 when speaking with Angela Merkel, Nicolas Sarkozy and Mikhail Gorbachev at the Wall at the twentieth anniversary of its fall, I ventured to remind Berliners of their historic promise that the Germany that had been the cause of so many of the world's problems in one century could be a solution for them in the next, as has been the case for thirty years.

Across the decades our world has often had its hope renewed. And throughout my time in politics, I and others have found inspiration not just from speeches by leaders but from our wider culture, our arts and our literature in stories we find memorable. Consider what has been called the most patriotic scene ever played out in any film, and its impact. The script writer of *Casablanca* felt challenged to deliver what he saw as an anti-Nazi filmscript by his pre-war visit to Austria. There, he had seen at first hand the intimidation and fear spread by fascist gangs and militias and, as he recalled, he felt 'the white heat of anger' over the persecution of his fellow Jews. He was determined to show in dramatic form that hope can win out when the cause is just – and this he does as *Casablanca* nears its end. One by one, the diners in Rick's Café take on their fascist overlords that are seated next to them. Defiantly standing up, and first softly and then less softly and then loudly and triumphantly at full voice, they sing the words of the French national anthem, La Marseillaise. They turn the song into a call to arms and make it a symbol of what would from now on, the film suggests, will be undying resistance to Nazi rule.

Hope that as individuals we can make progress together is also to be found not just in popular films but in popular music which can inspire people, not least in that famous song that is now an anthem across the world, 'You'll Never Walk Alone'. First sung on stage in the 1945 Rogers and Hammerstein musical *Carousel* its optimistic message that we should 'walk on with hope in your heart' was the call to arms that wartime America needed. And its message of unity and hope is still heard in football stadiums in every continent today. Of course, we cannot live by hope alone – but we cannot live without hope.

Men and women can be held back from fulfilling their potential by poverty in their earliest years and by lack of opportunity in their youth, but they can also be held back by the absence of hope. For, as Noam Chomsky wrote, 'If you assume there is no hope you guarantee that there is no hope.'[15] Or as put by a French writer: an individual 'can survive for forty days without food, eight days without water, eight minutes without air, but not for a second without hope'. For it is the capacity to yearn for, and look forward to, better things that makes us truly human, it is the belief that we can create a more hopeful future that should encourage us to establish better ways of cooperating across borders as a way of overruling those cynics who believe little or nothing can ever improve.

In 1947, as the Cold War got under way, Anthony Eden, who had been British foreign secretary during the Second World War and was later to become prime minister, said that the world could be united only when we 'find someone in Mars to get mad against'.[16] Eden's dyspeptic comment may have arisen from Churchill's perhaps wise refusal to resign in his favour. But it also articulates the world-weary cynicism of global leaders throughout history who have long felt global cooperation was always doomed to fail.

Nearly forty years later, in 1985, at a pre-meeting on Lake Geneva in advance of the famous Reykjavík summit which ended the nuclear arms race, Ronald Reagan – the president who had talked of the Soviet Union as the evil empire – asked Mikhail Gorbachev: 'What would you do if the United States were suddenly attacked by someone from outer space? Would you help us?'

'No doubt about it,' Gorbachev replied.

There was laughter as Reagan added, 'We too.' And so, between a humorist and a realist, a world-changing bond was formed.[17]

It is in that spirit of 'we too' that the case for international cooperation and the benefits it can bring needs to be explored.

For thirty years before the Gorbachev–Reagan meetings the world had been locked in a space race, the Soviet Union and the US competing for dominance. The Russians were first to fly to space; the Americans the first to reach the moon. Then a few years after the Gorbachev–Reagan meetings, Russia and the US – to be joined later by a score of other nations – abandoned their war for complete dominance in space and came together to create the International Space Station. So dependent on each other did the Russians and Americans become that until recently, when private companies entered the space race, no space probe could happen without both working together. The US could not reach the space station on its own without the use of Russian launchers and Russia could not man the space station itself without reliance on American technology. In each space mission a Russian cosmonaut joins an American astronaut.

It is commented on little, but it is remarkable that what was unthinkable in the first thirty years after 1945 has become commonplace in the last thirty years. In every other sphere, Russia and the US may be at daggers drawn, but, until 2025 at least, every few hours the International Space Station that passes above our heads, with Russian and American astronauts sharing the controls, is a tribute to the idea of cooperation. This joint enterprise makes us think that if in the 1980s we could find a new a way to cooperate in outer space in what was once the scene of one of the most hotly contested conflicts of the Cold War years, we can surely find new ways today to cooperate on earth.

And as we live through this unprecedented pandemic and its economic consequences what Aleksandr Solzhenitsyn called an all-important 'bridgehead of good' is found in those who are now determined 'to build back better'. Indeed, you can find hope almost everywhere once you start to look. Ernest Bloch argued that hope weaves its dreams, often unnoticed, in everyday life.

We can see it in how people have helped each other to avoid infection; in workers from hospitals to care homes who have added to their shifts to save the lives of people who might otherwise have died; in teenagers who have donated computers to fellow pupils so that they too can join in school studies online from home; and in the philanthropy of struggling shopkeepers who, despite the pressure on them to balance their books, have delivered supplies free to infirm and housebound customers: all individuals who set out to do good and in the end have done so much better than that.

The year 2020 was when, just at the moment people wanted us all to pull together against a common enemy, the world struggled to establish the cooperation and solidarity needed to fight the pandemic and a concomitant global economic downturn. But everywhere caring and compassionate men and women achieved what politicians did not: we saw scientists cooperating across borders to contain and cure disease; aid workers moving heaven and earth to get protective equipment to the poorest corners of the world; nurses and doctors in Médecins Sans Frontières and other international charities risking their lives to save lives; the vaccinated in rich countries donating money to help the unvaccinated in poor countries, offering help to men, women and children they would never meet and whose names they would never know – all proving by their actions a basic truth about human solidarity. Yes, we cooperate out of need, but yes, too, there is a human need to cooperate.

The future that we shape together out of the tribulations of 2020 can be one that builds on that spirit of cooperation. Together we can ensure that it is made up of more than fleeting moments of hope that turn to despair when, as so often happens, we move one step forward only to be pushed two steps back. Instead we can come together to push for lasting social change that no one, no matter how powerful, can reverse and no setback, however painful, can undo. 'You cannot uneducate the person who has learned to read,' proclaimed Cesar Chavez, the 1960s leader of the American farm workers' union. 'You cannot oppress the people who are not afraid anymore.'[18]

Enduring and irreversible progress must be our aim coming out of this crisis. We must make a promise to future generations that this planet will be a home for everyone without being harmful to anyone.[19] Where battles are fought with arguments not armaments, and at no point do we have to count the minutes to a nuclear midnight. Where we will never again turn a blind eye to poverty or inequality – because we now know it is within our power to overcome injustice with justice, oppression with opportunity and hate with hope.

This book has highlighted seven proposals for lasting change, and my hope is these ideas will resonate with you, and joined with your ideas, will add to the debate, and, in due course, bring social progress. My aim has been to convey a renewed sense of hope for the future, and the part you can play in it. There are many reasons to act decisively and together, and the time to act is now.

ACKNOWLEDGEMENTS

My public image as a Finance Minister was one of the sombre, perhaps verging on the gloomy. Writing this book was a journey, an exploration of masses of data and opinion on many and various subjects, and an attempt to convey details to make credible and realistic the pursuit of a small number of straightforward and well-defined goals. The work involved in writing it was long and hard, but it has left me with a sense of hope greater than before – and that is something I hope you will share.

What you gain in breadth in a multi-subject book like this, you may lose in depth. To try to avoid this fate, I have not only read widely but sought the advice and drawn on the expertise of many people much wiser than me and in my search for answers, in late night and early morning phone calls with people I respect, I have perhaps stretched friendships to the limit.

I have benefited from hearing, watching and evaluating the evolution of global networks in health, and from the insights of respected international leaders like Tharman Shanmugaratnam, Jeremy Farrar, Larry Summers, Ricken Patel, Jim O'Neill, John-Arne Røttingen and Ed Balls, who share my view that we need to find better ways to fund what are global public goods. I have also drawn on research carried out by Daniel Susskind and Evie Robertson.

My chapter on the economy has benefited from many conversations, and I have talked at some length with Mohamed El-Erian,

Shriti Vadera, Hiro Mizuno, Gene Frieda, Erik Berglöf of the LSE, now the chief economist at the AIIB, and Alison McGovern MP. Help with research has come from Cormac Hollingsworth, Iain Begg, Ross Christie and Holly Higgins. I am grateful for conversations with Joe Burns and to David Sainsbury, whose insights in his book *Windows of Opportunity* have informed my thoughts on the components of a new growth agenda.

In examining climate change, I had the benefit of the advice of Andrew Steer, whose enthusiasm for environmental progress I have long admired and who created from scratch the hugely successful World Resources Institute, which plays a huge part in forging the new international agreements on climate change. I am also grateful for the advice of my erstwhile Treasury and No 10 Downing Street policy adviser on energy and climate change matters, Michael Jacobs, now Professor of Political Economy at the University of Sheffield. Here, too, I have also benefited from the insights of Mark Carney, former governor of the Bank of England, John Studzinski of PIMCO, and Urs Wietlisbach and Kevin Lu of Partners Group, who are among those championing a new era of social responsibility in business.

I'm grateful to Nathan Small for early research he did on tax havens and other issues and to Daniella Lock, Clare Rewcastle Brown, Nyasha Weinberg and, in particular, Alex Cobham, who has been the driving force behind the success of the Tax Justice Network.

For my chapter on nationalism I have had the benefit of conversations, on various occasions, with Andreas Willner, Branko Milanović, Michael Wills, Professor Jim Gallagher, Heather McGregor and Henry Stannard but also from friends locally, Marilyn and Peter Livingstone. David Muir and Eddie Barnes have helped me increase my knowledge of both nationalism and the China–US relationship, and I thank the Berggruen Institute and the Twenty-First Century Council for convening a seminar which discussed a paper they commissioned on this issue.

My chapters on the SDGs and on education were inspired by

my work as a special envoy on global education for UN Secretary-General António Guterres and his deputy Amina Mohammed. In examining the SDGs I have drawn on the research of Kevin Watkins, currently head of Save the Children UK, and his deputy Kirsty McNeill, who, as one of our most impressive thinkers on social movements, also opened my eyes to the role that they can play in delivering change. I have benefited greatly from conversations with Christian Lackner, 'Chico' Francisco Ferreira, Branko Milanović, Nick Vaughan and Pedro Alba, and I want to thank Raj Shah, president of the Rockefeller Foundation, and Masood Ahmed, head of the Center for Global Development, for sharing their thinking with me. Ricken Patel, Alex Evans and Carmel Nolan have provided me with valuable insights into social movements past and present. For many years I have had the benefit of conversations with Asad Jamal, chairman and founder of ePlanet Capital, and I want to thank him for his charitable work in support of global education and human rights.

I have been able to draw on the excellent research done for the Global Education Commission on educational opportunity whose two brilliant recent directors, Justin van Fleet until 2018 and Liesbet Steer, have commissioned and overseen path-breaking studies of educational inequality that have enhanced my knowledge and guided my thinking. I have enjoyed and greatly benefited from seminars organised by President Emeritus of New York University John Sexton, who I cannot thank enough for opening the door to many conversations with his colleagues which have influenced me greatly.

Bringing this together, I have benefited hugely from the comments of and improvements made by Dr Colin Currie CBE, a friend from university days who worked with me in Downing Street and who is an accomplished writer with many books to his name. I have also been able to draw on his special expertise in health policy.

Thanks also go to Dr Hector Chawla, OBE, Dr Jas Singh and Dr Rick Gold.

From the other side of the Atlantic, as the prospects of a new American presidency grew, Bob Shrum has often had to adjust to British time as I drew on his knowledge and insights. I have benefited from a close association with friends at the University of Southern California and am particularly grateful to Steve Lamy and Jacob Soll and to their dean, Amber Miller. Philip Revzin and Reid Lidow have added valuable insights that have helped me order my thoughts.

Jayne Baxter has been a constant source of support in correcting, recorrecting and then re-recorrecting the many drafts of my chapters. These have required constant updating as events have unfolded. I owe a huge debt to Bill Taylor who has given me consistently good and expert advice on all matters economic and environmental over nearly forty years since we first met when I became an MP in 1983. Special thanks are owed also to each member of our office team for their work in coordinating this project and many others: Mary Bailey, Patrick Brown, Ross Christie, Alex Fincham, and Gil McNeil. I cannot begin to thank them and Bruce Waddell, Alex Rowley, David Robson, Stachu and Lesley McEwan for the help they have given me. Once again I have benefited from help from those who organise my day and keep our family safe.

Undoubtedly in the rush to publish I will have glossed over important points, drawn on information which is now out of date, and misunderstood some of what I have been told. All mistakes are mine.

I am grateful to Simon & Schuster, who published my book on the global financial crisis, *Beyond the Crash*, and could not have done more to help me as I have completed this one. I want to thank Ian Marshall for his supervision of the project and I am especially grateful to Kat Ailes for her skills as an editor and as a writer. Both have been patient and accommodating as my 'updating' took us beyond December, January and February deadlines! Melissa Bond's excellent copy-editing of the manuscript is much appreciated. And, once again, I am grateful to Jonny Geller and to his assistant Viola, who have been a constant and dependable source of advice and support.

Previous books have been dedicated to my wife Sarah and to my sons, John and Fraser. The encouragement and forbearance of the three who are closest to me makes it possible to undertake a book such as this and deserves my continuing gratitude. This book is written for my brothers, John and Andrew. For as long as I can remember, right back to our teenage years, whether over breakfast, lunch or dinner, John, Andrew and I have discussed the themes I am now exploring in print. They have had to listen to me, humour me and put up with me longer than anyone else I know. And they have never once complained about the demands that I made on them and their families during my time in politics. I owe them a huge and lasting debt of gratitude.

NOTES

INTRODUCTION

1   Galbraith, J. K. (1958), *The Affluent Society* (Houghton Mifflin)

2   Speech by Martin Luther King, 'Beyond Vietnam: A Time to Break Silence' (4 April 1967)

3   Carson, R. (2000), *Silent Spring* (Penguin Classics). Originally published in 1962, Carson dedicated her book to Albert Schweitzer, writing in her dedication: 'Man has lost the capacity to foresee and to forestall. He will end by destroying the Earth' – which was part of a letter that Schweitzer wrote in the 1950s to a beekeeper whose bees were destroyed by pesticide

4   'Climbing Mount Everest is Work for Supermen' (*New York Times*, 19 March 1923). See: https://www.nytimes.com/1923/03/18/archives/climbing-mount-everest-is-work-for-supermen-a-member-of-former.html

5   Olivia Solon, 'Elon Musk: we must colonise Mars to preserve our species in a third world war' (*Guardian*, 11 March 2018). See: https://www.theguardian.com/technology/2018/mar/11/elon-musk-colonise-mars-third-world-war

6   Pallab Ghosh, 'Hawking urges Moon landing to "elevate humanity"' (BBC News, 20 June 2017). See: https://www.bbc.co.uk/news/science-environment-40345048

7   Ian Goldin, 'Rethinking Global Resilience' (International Monetary Fund, September 2020), p. 7. See: https://www.imf.org/external/pubs/ft/fandd/2020/09/rethinking-global-resilience-ian-goldin.htm

8   James Manyika, Jacques Bughin, Susan Lund, Olivia Nottebohm, David Poulter, Sebastian Jauch and Sree Ramaswamy, 'Global flows in a digital age' (McKinsey & Company, April 2014), p. 4. See: https://www.mckinsey.com/business-functions/strategy-and-corporate-finance/our-insights/global-flows-in-a-digital-age

9   See: https://data.worldbank.org/indicator/IS.AIR.PSGR

10   Source: UNESCO Institute for Statistics, http://data.uis.unesco.org/Index.aspx

11   Thomas L. Friedman, 'How We Broke the World' (*New York Times*, 30
     May 2020). See: https://www.nytimes.com/2020/05/30/opinion/sunday/
     coronavirus-globalization.html
12   See: https://www.wto.org/english/news_e/sppl_e/sppl142_e.htm
13   Gramsci, A., Hoare, Q. and Nowell-Smith, G. (1998), *Selections from the Prison
     Notebooks of Antonio Gramsci* (Lawrence & Wishart)

CHAPTER 1: THE 'BC' WORLD

1   Cristina O'Callaghan-Gordo and Josep M. Antó, 'COVID-19: The disease
     of the anthropocene' (*Environmental Research*, 187:109683, August 2020). See:
     https://doi.org/10.1016/j.envres.2020.109683
2   Robert D. Putnam, 'Bowling Alone: America's Declining Social Capital'
     (*Journal of Democracy*, 6:1, January 1995), pp. 65–78. See: https://doi.
     org/10.1353/jod.1995.0002
3   'Margaret Thatcher: a life in quotes' (*Guardian*, 8 April 2013). See: https://
     www.theguardian.com/politics/2013/apr/08/margaret-thatcher-quotes
4   Beck, U. (1992), *Risk Society: Towards a New Modernity* (Sage Publications)
5   'Bouncing back: a safety net for the post-covid world' (*The Economist,* 6 March
     2021). See: https://www.economist.com/weeklyedition/2021-03-06
6   'Thatcher's quest left "lasting scar" on economy' (*Financial Times*, 8 April 2013).
     See: https://www.ft.com/content/7c3d0cee-a06c-11e2-88b6-00144feabdc0
7   Piketty, T. (2014), *Capital in the Twenty-First Century* (Harvard University
     Press)
8   Milanović, B. (2019), *Capitalism, Alone: The Future of the System That Rules the
     World* (Harvard University Press)
9   'The "Marshall Plan" speech at Harvard University, 5 June 1947'. See: https://
     www.oecd.org/general/themarshallplanspeechatharvarduniversity5june1947.
     htm
10   Acheson, D. (1987), *Present at the Creation* (W. W. Norton & Company)
11   Franklin D. Roosevelt, 'Fourth Inaugural Address of Franklin D. Roosevelt'
     (20 January 1945)
12   Harry S. Truman, 'Address at the Closing Session of the United Nations
     Conference' (26 June 1945)
13   Galbraith, J. K. (1955), *The Great Crash, 1929* (Houghton Mifflin)
14   Donald J. Trump, 'Remarks by President Trump to the 74th Session of the
     United Nations General Assembly' (25 September 2019)
15   Henry Kissinger, 'The Coronavirus Pandemic Will Forever Alter the World
     Order' (*Wall Street Journal*, 3 April 2020). See: https://www.wsj.com/articles/
     the-coronavirus-pandemic-will-forever-alter-the-world-order-11585953005
16   See: http://www.historyhome.co.uk/polspeech/portugal.htm
17   James Baldwin, 'As Much Truth As One Can Bear' (*New York Times Book Review*,

14 January 1962), republished in Kenan, R., ed. (2011), *The Cross of Redemption: Uncollected Writings* (Vintage International)

18   Kasparov, G. (2017), *Deep Thinking* (John Murray), p. 10

19   MacMillan, M. (2010), *The Uses and Abuses of History* (Profile Books)

20   Gilbert Shapiro and John Markoff, 'Officially Solicited Petitions: The "Cahiers de Doléances" as a Historical Source' (*International Review of Social History*, 46, 2001), pp. 79–106. See: www.jstor.org/stable/44735333

21   William Darby Templeman, 'A Consideration of the Fame of "Locksley Hall"' (*Victorian Poetry*, 1:2, 1963), pp. 81–103. See: www.jstor.org/stable/40001204.

22   Winston Churchill, 'Nations on the Loose' (*Collier's*, May 1935), as stated in Michael Richards, 'Churchill and Tennyson' (The Churchill Project, 17 July 2015). See: https://winstonchurchill.hillsdale.edu/churchill-and-tennyson/

CHAPTER 2: PREVENTING PANDEMICS

1   Richard N. Cooper, Barry Eichengreen, Gerald Holtham, Robert D. Putnam and C. Randall Henning, 'Can Nations Agree? Issues in International Economic Cooperation' (Brookings Institution, 1 June 1989), p. 181

2   *Scott Barrett Discusses Coronavirus, International Cooperation, And What's Ahead* (Columbia SIPA, 2 April 2020). See: https://www.sipa.columbia.edu/news/scott-barrett-discusses-coronavirus-international-cooperation-and-what%E2%80%99s-ahead

3   'International Health Regulations (2005): Second Edition' (WHO, 2008), p. 12. See: https://www.globalhealthrights.org/wp-content/uploads/2013/10/International-Health-Regulations-2005.pdf

4   'Jeremy Farrar: Make vaccine available to other countries as soon as our most vulnerable people have received it' (*BMJ* 2021; 372). See: https://doi.org/10.1136/bmj.n459

5   See: https://blogs.bmj.com/bmj/2020/12/11/covid-19-has-turned-the-spotlight-on-the-uneven-provision-of-oxygen-a-stark-health-inequity/; https://www.thelancet.com/journals/lanres/article/PIIS2213-2600(21)00087-4/fulltext#%20

6   'G20 Leaders' Statement' (26 March 2020). See: https://www.gov.uk/government/news/g20-leaders-summit-statement-on-covid-19-26-march-2020

7   Patrick Wintour, Fiona Harvey and Peter Beaumont, 'US scuppers G20 coronavirus statement on strengthening WHO' (*The Guardian*, 20 April 2020). See: https://www.theguardian.com/world/2020/apr/20/us-scuppers-g20-coronavirus-statement-on-strengthening-who

8   Josh Lederman, 'U.S. insisting that the U.N. call out Chinese origins of coronavirus' (NBC News, 26 March 2020). See: https://www.nbcnews.com/politics/national-security/u-s-insisting-u-n-call-out-chinese-origins-coronavirus-n1169111

9   Resolution 1308, UN. See: https://www.un.org/press/en/2000/20000717.
    sc6890.doc.html

10 Resolution 2177, UN. See: https://www.un.org/press/en/2014/sc11566.doc.
    htm

11 Edith M. Lederer, 'US objects to UN resolution on virus in dispute
    with China' (Associated Press, 9 May 2020). See: https://apnews.com/
    article/36a2ff24d9d19f22a67aed6418db0629

12 See: https://www.gavi.org/investing-gavi/innovative-financing/iffim

13 See: https://www.gavi.org/news/media-room/
    g7-backs-gavis-covid-amc-boost-covid-19-vaccines-worlds-poorest-countries

14 See: https://www.who.int/publications/m/item/
    access-to-covid-19-tools-tracker

15 Marco Hafner et al., 'The global economic cost of COVID-19 vaccine
    nationalism' (RAND Corporation, 2020). See: https://www.rand.org/
    randeurope/research/projects/cost-of-covid19-vaccine-nationalism.html,
    accessed March 3 2021

16 'The Economic Case for Global Vaccinations', The International
    Chamber of Commerce, 2021. See: https://iccwbo.org/publication/
    the-economic-case-for-global-vaccinations

17 Note this excludes $1.5 billion promised by the US for further COVAX
    funding to be provided between 2021-22. See: https://www.who.int/
    publications/m/item/access-to-covid-19-tools-tracker

18 'Covid vaccines: Boris Johnson pledges surplus to poorer countries at
    G7' (BBC News, 19 February 2021). See: https://www.bbc.co.uk/news/
    uk-politics-56117120; from Duke Global Health Innovation Centre

19 Our World in Data COVID-19 cumulative vaccines as of 2 March 2021

20 'COVID-19: Which countries are receiving vaccines in WHO-backed
    COVAX programme – and how many doses each?' (Sky News, 3 March
    2021). See: https://news.sky.com/story/which-countries-are-getting-covid-
    vaccines-in-who-backed-programme-and-how-many-12233880

21 Taken from interview and private conversation with Professor Thomas Pogge

22 'US law may hit export of raw materials for COVID vaccines: Poonawalla'
    (The Federal, 5 March 2021). See: https://thefederal.com/covid-19/
    us-law-may-affect-export-of-raw-materials-for-covid-vaccines-poonawalla/

23 Katherine F. Smith et al., 'Global rise in human infectious disease outbreaks'
    (Journal of the Royal Society Interface, 11:20140950, 6 December 2014). See:
    https://doi.org/10.1098/rsif.2014.0950

24 Nick Watts et al., 'Health and climate change: policy responses to protect
    public health' (The Lancet, 386:10006, pp. 1861–1914, 22 June 2015). See:
    https://doi.org/10.1016/S0140-6736(15)60854-6

25 Barrett, S. (2007), Why Cooperate? The Incentive to Supply Global Public Goods
    (Oxford University Press), p. 125

26 Ali Maow Maalin, a Somali hospital worker, was the last member of the

general public to catch smallpox – worldwide. Once recovered, he worked for years to wipe out polio in Somalia

27 Scott Barrett, 'The Smallpox Eradication Game' (*Public Choice*, 130, pp. 179–207, 2007), p. 189. See: https://doi.org/10.1007/s11127-006-9079-z

28 F. Fenner, D. Henderson, I. Arita, Z. Jezek and I. Ladnyi, 'Smallpox and its Eradication' (World Health Organization, 1988), p. 1364

29 Nicholas Jackson, 'A Conversation with Scott Barrett, Professor at the Earth Institute' (*The Atlantic*, 5 December 2011). See: https://www.theatlantic.com/national/archive/2011/12/a-conversation-with-scott-barrett-professor-at-the-earth-institute/249065/

30 From: Levine. R and What Works Working Group (2007), *Case Studies in Global Health: Millions Saved* (Jones & Bartlett Publishers), p. 20. Originally from: Mark A. Miller et al., 'A model to estimate the potential economic benefits of measles eradication for the United States' (*Vaccine*, 16:20, pp. 1917–1922, 1998); H. Carabin and J. Edmunds, 'Future savings from measles eradication in industrialised countries' (*Journal of Infectious Diseases*, 187:1, pp. S29–S35, 2003)

31 Quote from: Thomas Gokey, 'I volunteered to be a human guinea pig for a Covid vaccine. Now I'm having second thoughts' (*The Guardian*, 17 September 2020). See: https://www.theguardian.com/commentisfree/2020/sep/17/covid-vaccine-trial-coronavirus

32 Global Polio Eradication Initiative, World Health Organization & United Nations Children's Fund (UNICEF) (2001). 'Global Polio Eradication Initiative: estimated external financial resource requirements 2002–2005, as of 1 September 2001' (World Health Organization), p. 1. See: https://apps.who.int/iris/handle/10665/66960

33 Gavin Yamey et al., 'Financing Global Common Goods for Health: When the World is a Country' (*Health Systems & Reform*, 5:4, pp. 334–349, 20 December 2019). See: https://doi.org/10.1080/23288604.2019.1663118

34 Berkeley Lovelace Jr, 'Top WHO official warns world may be "dangerously unprepared" for next pandemic as coronavirus outbreak spreads' (CNBC, 3 February 2020). See: https://www.cnbc.com/2020/02/03/top-who-officials-world-is-unprepared-for-next-pandemic-as-coronavirus-spreads.html

35 Elizabeth Fee, Marcu Cueto and Theodore M. Brown, 'At the Roots of The World Health Organization's Challenges: Politics and Regionalization' (*American Journal of Public Health*, 106:11, pp. 1912–1917, November 2016), p. 1912. See: https://doi.org/10.2105/AJPH.2016.303480

36 Andrew Lakoff, 'Why the WHO, often under fire, has a tough balance to strike in its efforts to address health emergencies' (*The Conversation*, 1 May 2020). See https://theconversation.com/why-the-who-often-under-fire-has-a-tough-balance-to-strike-in-its-efforts-to-address-health-emergencies-137464

37 Lakoff, A. (2017), *Unprepared: Global Health in a Time of Emergency* (University of California Press), pp. 7–8

38 Barrett, S. (2007), *Why Cooperate? The Incentive to Supply Global Public Goods* (Oxford University Press), p. 19

39 Barrett, S. (2003), *Environment and Statecraft: The Strategy of Environmental Treaty-Making* (Oxford University Press), p. 33

40 'Global health 2035: a world converging within a generation' (*The Lancet*, 3 December 2013). See: https://www.thelancet.com/commissions/global-health-2035

41 GNI Data from the World Bank, UN Contributions based on www.un.org/en/ga/contributions/scale.html

42 Max Bearak and Danielle Paquette, 'Africa's most vulnerable countries have few ventilators – or none at all' (*Washington Post*, 18 April 2020). See: https://www.washingtonpost.com/world/africa/africa-coronavirus-ventilators/2020/04/17/903163a4-7f3e-11ea-84c2-0792d8591911_story.html

43 Abdi Sheikh, 'Doctor's self-funded test lab leads way in Somalia's COVID fight' (Reuters, 5 November 2020). See: https://www.reuters.com/article/uk-health-coronavirus-somalia-doctor/doctors-self-funded-test-lab-leads-way-in-somalias-covid-fight-idUKKBN27L1EO?edition-redirect=uk

44 Larry Brilliant, 'Sometimes Brilliant in Conversation with Stewart Brand', (*The Interval*, 21 February 2017) See: https://theinterval.org/salon-talks/02017/feb/21/sometimes-brilliant-conversation-stewart-brand

CHAPTER 3: A NEW KIND OF ECONOMY

1 See: https://blogs.imf.org/2021/02/24/the-great-divergence-a-fork-in-the-road-for-the-global-economy/

2 See: https://www.imf.org/en/Publications/WEO/Issues/2021/01/26/2021-world-economic-outlook-update

3 All estimates for 2021 and 2022 are based on IMF modelling. See: https://www.imf.org/external/np/g20/pdf/2021/022421.pdf

4 See: https://www.imf.org/external/np/g20/pdf/2021/022421.pdf

5 Kristalina Georgieva, 'Continued Strong Policy Action to Combat Uncertainty' (IMF Blog, 19 November 2020). See: https://blogs.imf.org/2020/11/19/continued-strong-policy-action-to-combat-uncertainty/

6 Gita Gopinath, 'A Long, Uneven and Uncertain Ascent' (IMF Blog, 13 October 2020). See: https://blogs.imf.org/2020/10/13/a-long-uneven-and-uncertain-ascent/

7 For facts in this paragraph, see: Valentina Romei, 'How the pandemic is worsening inequality' (*Financial Times*, 31 December 2020). See: https://www.ft.com/content/cd075d91-fafa-47c8-a295-85bbd7a36b50

8 For further information, see: https://www.mckinsey.com/business-functions/strategy-and-corporate-finance/our-insights/how-covid-19-has-pushed-companies-over-the-technology-tipping-point-and-transformed-business-forever

9   See: https://www.mckinsey.com/business-functions/operations/our-insights/
     risk-resilience-and-rebalancing-in-global-value-chains

10   Richard E. Baldwin and Simon J. Evenett, 'COVID-19 and Trade Policy: Why
     Turning Inward Won't Work' (Centre for Economic Policy Research, 29 April
     2020)

11   Brown, G. (2010), *Beyond the Crash: Overcoming the First Crisis of Globalisation*
     (Simon & Schuster, 2010), Chapter 3

12   Ibid.

13   Taleb, N., *The Black Swan* (Random House, 2009)

14   Jose De Gregorio, Barry Eichengreen, Takatoshi Ito and Charles Wyplosz,
     'IMF Reform: The Unfinished Agenda' (CEPR, 11 September 2018), p. 8. See:
     https://cepr.org/sites/default/files/events/Geneva20.pdf

15   Willem Buiter, 'What has changed since the crisis?', in *New
     Approaches to Economic Challenges: The Financial System* (OECD, 2020),
     p. 77. See: https://www.oecd-ilibrary.org/finance-and-investment/
     the-financial-system_d45f979e-en

16   Board of Governors, 'December 2020 Stress Test Results' (Federal Reserve,
     2020), p. 2. See: https://www.federalreserve.gov/publications/files/2020-dec-
     stress-test-results-20201218.pdf

17   'Global Financial Stability Report: Markets in the Time of COVID-
     19' (International Monetary Fund, April 2020), p. 17. See: https://
     www.imf.org/en/Publications/GFSR/Issues/2020/04/14/
     global-financial-stability-report-april-2020

18   Jean-Claude Trichet, 'The crisis, finance and central banking', John Vickers,
     'Regulatory reform and equity', and Willem Buiter, 'What has changed
     since the crisis?', in *New Approaches to Economic Challenges: The Financial
     System* (OECD, 2020), pp. 46, 73, 77. See: https://www.oecd-ilibrary.org/
     finance-and-investment/the-financial-system_d45f979e-en

19   Trichet, ibid., p. 45

20   'Global Monitoring Report on Non-Bank Financial Intermediation 2019'
     (Financial Stability Board, 19 January 2020), p. 84. See: https://www.fsb.org/
     wp-content/uploads/P190120.pdf

21   Ibid., p. 4

22   Martin Wolf, 'Coronavirus crisis lays bare the risks of financial leverage,
     again' (*Financial Times*, 28 April 2020). See https://www.ft.com/
     content/098dcd60-8880-11ea-a01c-a28a3e3fbd33. See also: https://www.
     imf.org/en/Publications/GFSR/Issues/2020/10/13/global-financial-
     stability-report-october-2020. And: https://www.ecb.europa.eu/pub/
     financial-stability/fsr/html/ecb.fsr202011~b7be9ae1f1.en.html

23   Andy Haldane, 'From economic crisis to crisis in economics', and John
     Llewellyn, 'Lessons from the financial crisis', in *New Approaches to Economic
     Challenges: The Financial System* (OECD, 2020), pp. 18, 60. See: https://www.
     oecd-ilibrary.org/finance-and-investment/the-financial-system_d45f979e-en

24 Some of these proposals are contained in the important report of Tharman Shanmugaratnam's commission to the G20 on global financial governance: 'Report of the G20 Eminent Persons Group on Global Financial Governance', in *Making the Global Financial System Work for All* (October 2018). See: https://www.globalfinancialgovernance.org/assets/pdf/G20EPG-Full%20Report.pdf

25 Ibid., p. 21

26 Ricardo Hausmann, 'Opponents of more IMF lending may have blood on their hands' (*Financial Times*, 18 June 2020). See: https://www.ft.com/content/351f5a02-4ba9-454b-ba42-83a6b662c665

27 Frieden, J. et al., 'After the Fall: The Future of Global Cooperation', in *Geneva Reports on the World Economy* (Centre for Economic Policy Research, 2012), p. 62. See: https://j.mp/2nTbuH5

28 Ibid., p. 61

29 'G20: Leaders' statement from Seoul summit' (BBC News, 12 November 2010). See: https://www.bbc.co.uk/news/business-11741674

30 Isabel Ortiz and Matthew Cummins, 'Austerity: The New Normal – A Renewed Washing Consensus 2010–24' (1 October 2019). Available at SSRN: https://ssrn.com/abstract=3523562

31 Frieden, J. et al., 'After the Fall: The Future of Global Cooperation', in *Geneva Reports on the World Economy* (Centre for Economic Policy Research, 2012), p. 69. See: https://j.mp/2nTbuH5

32 'Brisbane Action Plan' (G20, November 2014), p. 1. See: http://www.g20.utoronto.ca/2014/brisbane_action_plan.pdf

33 Lawrence Summers has set out his theory of secular stagnation in a series of forums, starting with a speech in 2013 to the IMF: Lawrence Summers, 'IMF Fourteenth Annual Research Conference in Honor of Stanley Fischer' (8 November 2013). See: http://larrysummers.com/imf-fourteenth-annual-research-conference-in-honor-of-stanley-fischer/

34 See Sainsbury, D. (2020), *Windows of Opportunity* (Profile Books)

35 'Fiscal Monitor: Policies for the Recovery' (International Monetary Fund, October 2020), p. x. See: https://www.imf.org/en/Publications/FM/Issues/2020/09/30/october-2020-fiscal-monitor#Full%20Report%20and%20Executive%20Summary

36 For Olivier Blanchard quote: 'The Covid-19 pandemic is forcing a rethink in macroeconomics' (*The Economist*, 25 July 2020). See: https://www.economist.com/briefing/2020/07/25/the-covid-19-pandemic-is-forcing-a-rethink-in-macroeconomics

37 Paul Krugman, 'The Case for Permanent Stimulus (Wonkish)' (*New York Times*, 7 March 2020). See: https://www.nytimes.com/2020/03/07/opinion/the-case-for-permanent-stimulus-wonkish.html

38 'Full Employment and Balanced Growth Act (Humphrey–Hawkins Act)', p. 16. See: https://fraser.stlouisfed.org/title/full-employment-balanced-growth-act-humphrey-hawkins-act-1034

39 Robert Skidelsky has been the strongest advocate of such action. His two most recent books are *Keynes: The Return of the Master* (Allen Lane, 2009) and *Money and Government* (Yale University Press, 2018). Also, a joint article with him appears in *Project Syndicate* 2020. See: https://www.project-syndicate.org/commentary/united-kingdom-fiscal-monetary-policy-full-employment-by-gordon-brown-and-robert-skidelsky-2020-11

40 See: https://www.piie.com/publications/policy-briefs/fiscal-resiliency-deeply-uncertain-world-role-semiautonomous-discretion

41 'G-20 Surveillance Note' (International Monetary Fund, 21–22 November 2020), p. 11. See: https://www.imf.org/external/np/g20/111920.htm

42 UNCTAD, 'COVID-19's economic fallout will long outlive the health crisis, UNCTAD warns' (Press release, 19 November 2019). See: https://unctad.org/press-material/covid-19s-economic-fallout-will-long-outlive-health-crisis-unctad-warns

43 I am grateful for the compilation of these figures to the Center for Global Development and in particular to Masood Ahmed for conversations with him

44 Rebecca Henderson, 'Reimagining Capitalism in a World on Fire', (*Public Affairs*, 28 April 2020), Chapter 1, pp. 1–2

45 Olivier J. Blanchard and Lawrence H. Summers, 'Rethinking Stabilization Policy: Evolution or Revolution?' (National Bureau of Economic Research, Working Paper 24179, December 2017), p. 39. See: https://www.nber.org/papers/w24179

CHAPTER 4: A GLOBAL GREEN NEW DEAL

1 Jamie Hannaford, 'Guest post: Are UK floods becoming worse due to climate change?' (Carbon Brief, 20 February 2020). See: https://www.carbonbrief.org/guest-post-are-uk-floods-becoming-worse-due-to-climate-change

2 Eleanor Ainge Roy, '"One day we'll disappear": Tuvalu's sinking islands' (*Guardian*, 16 May 2019). See: https://www.theguardian.com/global-development/2019/may/16/one-day-disappear-tuvalu-sinking-islands-rising-seas-climate-change

3 'Global Warming of 1.5°C' (Intergovernmental Panel on Climate Change, October 2018). See: https://www.ipcc.ch/sr15/download/#full. And: Jonathan Watts, 'Arctic methane deposits "starting to release", scientists say' (*Guardian*, 27 October 2020). See: https://www.theguardian.com/science/2020/oct/27/sleeping-giant-arctic-methane-deposits-starting-to-release-scientists-find. And: 'Arctic wildfires: How bad are they and what caused them?' (BBC News, 2 August 2019). See: https://www.bbc.co.uk/news/world-europe-49125391. And: Rebecca Lindsey, 'Climate Change: Atmospheric Carbon Dioxide' (Climate.gov, 14 August 2020). See: https://www.climate.gov/news-features/understanding-climate/climate-change-atmospheric-carbon-dioxide

4   Matt McGrath, 'Climate change: Last decade confirmed as warmest on record' (BBC News, 15 January 2020). See: https://www.bbc.co.uk/news/science-environment-51111176

5   Gaia Vince, 'The heat is on over the climate crisis. Only radical measures will work' (*Observer*, 18 May 2019). See: https://www.theguardian.com/environment/2019/may/18/climate-crisis-heat-is-on-global-heating-four-degrees-2100-change-way-we-live

6   'UK weather: Hottest late August Bank Holiday Monday on record' (BBC News, 26 August 2019). See: https://www.bbc.co.uk/news/uk-49471053

7   Chi Xu, Timothy A. Kohler, Timothy M. Lenton, Jens-Christian Svenning and Marten Scheffer, 'Future of the human climate niche' (*Proceedings of the National Academy of Sciences*, 117:21, pp. 11350–11355, May 2020). See: https://doi.org/10.1073/pnas.1910114117

8   Wallace-Wells, D. (2019), *The Uninhabitable Earth: Life after Warming* (Tim Duggan Books)

9   Bill Gates, 'COVID-19 is awful. Climate change could be worse' (GatesNotes, 4 August 2020). See: https://www.gatesnotes.com/Energy/Climate-and-COVID-19

10 'Global Warming of 1.5°C' (Intergovernmental Panel on Climate Change, October 2018), p. 12. See: https://www.ipcc.ch/sr15/download/#full

11 Severn Cullis-Suzuki, 'Speech at UN Conference on Environment and Development' (1992). See: https://www.americanrhetoric.com/speeches/severnsuzukiunearthsummit.htm

12 'Adapt Now: A Global Call for Leadership on Climate Resilience' (Global Commission on Adaptation, 2019), p. 54. See: https://gca.org/reports/adapt-now-a-global-call-for-leadership-on-climate-resilience/. And: Sophie Yeo, 'Green Climate Fund attracts record US$9.8 billion for developing nations' (*Nature*, 1 November 2019). See: https://www.nature.com/articles/d41586-019-03330-9

13 Kerry, J. (2019), *Every Day is Extra* (Simon & Schuster)

14 Stern, N. (2007), *The Economics of Climate Change: The Stern Review* (Cambridge University Press). See: https://doi.org/10.1017/CBO9780511817434

15 'Unlocking the Inclusive Growth Story of the 21st Century' (New Climate Economy, 5 September 2018), p. 8. See: https://newclimateeconomy.report/2018/wp-content/uploads/sites/6/2019/04/NCE_2018Report_Full_FINAL.pdf

16 Paris Agreement, p. 3. See: https://unfccc.int/process-and-meetings/the-paris-agreement/the-paris-agreement

17 'Emissions Gap Report' (United Nations Environment Programme, 2020), p. ix. See: https://wedocs.unep.org/bitstream/handle/20.500.11822/34438/EGR20ESE.pdf?sequence=25

18 'About Montreal Protocol' (United Nations Environmental Programme). See: https://www.unenvironment.org/ozonaction/who-we-are/about-montreal-protocol

19   Ibid.

20   Chen, S. et al., 'The Potential Photovoltaics to Power the Belt and
     Road Initiative' (*Joule*, 3:8, pp. 1795–2052, 21 August 2019), p.
     1904. See: https://doi.org/10.1016/j.joule.2019.06.006. Also, Adam
     Tooze, 'Welcome to the Final Battle for the Climate' (*Foreign Policy*,
     17 October 2020). See: https://foreignpolicy.com/2020/10/17/
     great-power-competition-climate-china-europe-japan/

21   This table has been compiled from many separate but official sources based on
     reports from the IMF World Bank and the UN. See: Table 3

22   See: https://www.climatewatchdata.org/ghg-emissions?calculation=PER_
     CAPITA&end_year=2017&regions=TOP&start_year=1990

23   'The European Green Deal sets out how to make Europe the first climate-
     neutral continent by 2050, boosting the economy, improving people's health
     and quality of life, caring for nature, and leaving no one behind' (European
     Commission, 11 December 2019). See: https://ec.europa.eu/commission/
     presscorner/detail/en/IP_19_6691

24   'South Korea follows Japan and China in carbon neutral pledge'
     (*Financial Times*, 27 October 2020). See: https://www.ft.com/
     content/185e5043-fd72-4fef-a05c-f2a5001c7f4b

25   Branko Milanovic, review of *Doughnut Economics: Seven Ways to Think Like a
     21st-Century Economist* by Kate Raworth, (*Brave New Europe*, 25 June 2018);
     https://braveneweurope.com/doughnut-economics-seven-ways-to-think-
     like-a-21st-century-economist-by-kate-raworth#comment-373" https://
     braveneweurope.com/doughnut-economics-seven-ways-to-think-like-a-21st-
     century-economist-by-kate-raworth#comment-373

26   'Sustainable Recovery: World Energy Outlook Special Report in collaboration
     with the International Monetary Fund' (International Energy Agency, June
     2020), p. 14. See: https://www.iea.org/reports/sustainable-recovery

27   'Greenness of Stimulus Index' (vivideconomics, February 2021). See: https://
     www.vivideconomics.com/casestudy/greenness-for-stimulus-index/

28   See: https://www.energypolicytracker.org/region/g20/

29   Hepburn, C. et al., 'Will COVID-19 fiscal recovery packages accelerate or
     retard progress on climate change?' (*Oxford Review of Economic Policy*, 36:1,
     pp. S359–S381, 8 May 2020). See: https://doi.org/10.1093/oxrep/graa015.
     And: Unsworth, S. et al., 'Jobs for a strong and sustainable recovery from
     Covid-19' (Centre for Economic Performance, 10 October 2020). See:
     https://www.lse.ac.uk/granthaminstitute/wp-content/uploads/2020/10/
     Jobs_for_a_strong_and_sustainable_recovery_from_Covid19.pdf. And: Dr
     María Mendiluce, 'COVID-19 stimulus should address health, economy and
     climate together' (We Mean Business, 20 March 2020). See: https://www.
     wemeanbusinesscoalition.org/blog/covid-19-stimulus/

30   Heidi Garrett-Peltier, 'Green versus brown: Comparing the employment
     impacts of energy efficiency, renewable energy, and fossil fuels using an

input-output model' (*Economic Modelling*, 61, pp. 439–447, February 2017).
See: https://doi.org/10.1016/j.econmod.2016.11.012

31 'Unlocking the Inclusive Growth Story of the 21st Century' (New Climate
Economy, 5 September 2018), p. 12. See: https://newclimateeconomy.
report/2018/wp-content/uploads/sites/6/2019/04/NCE_2018Report_Full_
FINAL.pdf

32 'The Case for a Green and Just Recovery' (C40, October
2020). See: https://www.c40knowledgehub.org/s/article/
The-Case-for-a-Green-and-Just-Recovery?language=en_US

33 'Maximising the benefits: Economic, employment and emissions
impacts of green recovery stimulus in Europe' (We Mean Business, 22
October 2020). See: https://www.wemeanbusinesscoalition.org/blog/
maximising-the-benefits-economic-employment-and-emissions-impacts-of-
green-recovery-stimulus-in-europe/

34 Alberto Carrillo Pineda et al., 'The new normal: 1,000 companies are now
setting science-based climate targets' (Science Based Targets, 8 October 2020).
See: https://sciencebasedtargets.org/blog/the-new-normal-1-000-companies-
are-now-setting-science-based-climate-targets

35 Mark Carney, 'Speech: The Road to Glasgow' (27 February 2020), p. 4. See:
https://www.bankofengland.co.uk/-/media/boe/files/speech/2020/the-road-
to-glasgow-speech-by-mark-carney.pdf

36 'Mainstreaming the Transition to a Net-Zero Economy' (Group of Thirty,
October 2020), p. xvi. See: https://group30.org/publications/detail/4791

37 Ibid., p. xii

38 Cohen, R. (2020), *Impact* (Ebury Digital)

39 See: https://climateprinciplesforenterprises.org/

40 'Mainstreaming the Transition to a Net-Zero Economy' (Group of Thirty,
October 2020), p. 6. See: https://group30.org/publications/detail/4791

41 Ian Parry, 'Putting a Price on Pollution', in *The Economics of Climate*
(International Monetary Fund, December 2019), p. 16. See: https://www.imf.
org/external/pubs/ft/fandd/2019/12/index.htm

42 'The world urgently needs to expand its use of carbon prices' (*The Economist*,
23 May 2020). See: https://www.economist.com/briefing/2020/05/23/
the-world-urgently-needs-to-expand-its-use-of-carbon-prices

43 Leslie Hook and Patrick Temple-West, 'Carney calls for global carbon offset
market' (*Financial Times*, 2 December 2020). See: https://www.ft.com/
content/8ed608b2-25c8-48d2-9653-c447adbd538f

44 Janet L. Yellen and Ted Haldstead, 'The Most Ambitious Climate Plan In
History' (*Fortune*, 10 September 2018). See: https://fortune.com/2018/09/10/
baker-shultz-climate-plan/

45 Ian Parry, 'Putting a Price on Pollution', in *The Economics of Climate*
(International Monetary Fund, December 2019), p. 18. See: https://www.imf.
org/external/pubs/ft/fandd/2019/12/index.htm

46 Larsen, J. et al., 'Energy and Environmental Implications of a Carbon Tax in the United States' (July 2018), p. 19. See: https://www.energypolicy.columbia.edu/research/report/energy-and-environmental-implications-carbon-tax-united-states

47 'Mainstreaming the Transition to a Net-Zero Economy' (Group of Thirty, October 2020), p. 16. See: https://group30.org/publications/detail/4791

48 Grant Smith, 'Global Oil Demand to Hit a Plateau Around 2030, IEA Predicts' (Bloomberg, 13 November 2019). See: https://www.bloomberg.com/news/articles/2019-11-13/global-oil-demand-to-hit-a-plateau-around-2030-iea-predicts

49 Coady, D. et al., 'Global Fossil Fuel Subsidies Remain Large: An update Based on Country-Level Estimates' (International Monetary Fund, 2 May 2019), p. 5. See: https://www.imf.org/en/Publications/WP/Issues/2019/05/02/Global-Fossil-Fuel-Subsidies-Remain-Large-An-Update-Based-on-Country-Level-Estimates-46509

50 'Mainstreaming the Transition to a Net-Zero Economy' (Group of Thirty, October 2020), p. 5. See: https://group30.org/publications/detail/4791

51 Adela Suliman, 'World's forests "in emergency room" after years of losses' (Reuters, 25 April 2019). See: https://www.reuters.com/article/global-environment-climatechange/worlds-forests-in-emergency-room-after-years-of-losses-idUKL5N2254HP?edition-redirect=uk. And: https://www.wri.org/our-work/topics/forests

52 Susan Minnemeyer et al., 'Atlas of Forest and Landscape Restoration Opportunities' (World Resources Institute, May 2014). See: https://www.wri.org/resources/maps/atlas-forest-and-landscape-restoration-opportunities

53 See: https://www.bonnchallenge.org/

54 René Zamora Cristales, Salima Mahamoudou, Ruchika Singh, Will Anderson, Peter Ndunda, Mariana Oliveira, Katie Reytar, John Brandt and Marcelo Matsumoto, 'The Road to Restoration: 3 Steps For Transforming Landscapes' (World Resources Institute, 1 October 2020). See: https://www.wri.org/blog/2020/10/3-steps-for-land-restoration

55 James Mulligan et al., '6 Ways to Remove Carbon Pollution from the Sky' (World Resources Institute, 9 June 2020). See: https://www.wri.org/blog/2020/06/6-ways-remove-carbon-pollution-sky

56 Tom Heap, 'Why I'm feeling hopeful about the environment in 2021' (BBC News, 4 January 2021). See: https://www.bbc.co.uk/news/science-environment-55429607

57 Katie Lebling and Eliza Northrop, 'Leveraging the Ocean's Carbon Removal Potential' (World Resources Institute, 8 October 2020). See: https://www.wri.org/blog/2020/10/ocean-carbon-dioxide-sequestration

58 https://www.oxfam.org/en/press-releases/carbon-emissions-richest-1-percent-more-double-emissions-poorest-half-humanity

CHAPTER 5: UNLOCKING THE WORLD'S POTENTIAL

1 I have relied on comments and research help given by Dr Liesbet Steer, director of the Education Commission – I am very grateful to her for her expert support

2 David Istance, 'Learning in the 21st Century: Research, Innovation and Policy' (Organisation for Economic Co-operation and Development, 15 May 2008)

3 There are many calculations from as early as 1997: each additional year of education is associated with about 30 per cent higher GDP per capita (Heckman and Klenow, 1997); a one-year increase of years in education is associated with 0.3 per cent per year faster growth (Bils and Klenow, 2000); a one-year increase in average education raises per-capita income by 3–6 per cent (Bassanini and Scarpetta, 2001); a one-year increase in the mean years of education is associated with a rise in per-capita income by 3–6 per cent or a higher growth rate of 1 percentage point (Sianesi and Van Reenen, 2003); the macro-estimated rate of return to education is 18–30 per cent (Krueger and Lindahl, 2001); the macro-estimated rate of return to education is 27 per cent (de la Fuente and Doménech, 2006); the macro-estimated rate of return to education is 9–12.3 per cent (Hanushek and Woessmann, 2008); controlling for physical capital stock, the rate of return to the average year of education is 12.1 per cent (Barro and Lee, 2010); each additional year of education is associated with 18 per cent higher GDP per capita (Crespo Cuaresma, Lutz and Sanderson, 2012); each additional year of education is associated with 13 per cent higher GDP per capita (Thomas and Burnett, 2013); each additional year of education is associated with 35 per cent higher GDP per capita (Patrinos and Psacharopoulos, 2013)

4 Maria Quattri and Kevin Watkins, 'Child labour and education: a survey of slum settlements in Dhaka' (Overseas Development Institute, December 2016). See: https://www.odi.org/publications/10654-child-labour-and-education-survey-slum-settlements-dhaka

5 'Save Our Future: Averting an Education Catastrophe for the World's Children' (OCHA, 22 October 2020). See: https://reliefweb.int/report/world/save-our-future-averting-education-catastrophe-world-s-children. And: Kevin Watkins and Maria Quattri, 'Child poverty in Africa' (ODI, August 2019). See: https://www.odi.org/sites/odi.org.uk/files/resource-documents/12863.pdf

6 'Education Finance Watch 2021' (UNESCO, 23 February 2021). See: https://reliefweb.int/report/world/education-finance-watch-2021

7 Ibid.

8 'COVID-19: Are children able to continue learning during school closures?' (UNICEF, August 2020). See: https://data.unicef.org/resources/remote-learning-reachability-factsheet/

9   'TV-Based Learning in Bangladesh: Is it Reaching Students?' (World Bank, 16 July 2020). See: https://openknowledge.worldbank.org/bitstream/ handle/10986/34138/TV-Based-Learning-in-Bangladesh-Is-it-Reaching- Students.pdf

10 'Students, computers and learning' (Organisation for Economic Co-operation and Development, 14 September 2015). See: https://www.oecd.org/ education/students-computers-and-learning-9789264239555-en.htm

11 The concept of 'High-Touch, High-Tech' learning was a direct result of the recommendations of the Education Commission as set out in its report 'The Learning Generation: Investing in Education for a Changing World'. The concept was further developed in a follow-up report, 'Transforming the Education Workforce'. A brief description can also be found here: https://www.theewf.org/research/2019/ combining-high-tech-and-high-touch-to-personalize-learning-for-every- child

12 Pauline Rose and Benjamin Alcott, 'Assignment Report: How can education systems become equitable by 2030? (Health and Education Advice and Resource Team (HEART), 1 January 2015). See: https://www. gov.uk/research-for-development-outputs/assignment-report-how-can- education-systems-become-equitable-by-2030. See also: 'Addressing the learning crisis: An urgent need to better finance education for the poorest children' (UNICEF, January 2020). See: https://www.unicef.org/reports/ addressing-learning-crisis-2020

13 International Institute for Applied Systems Analysis (IIASA). The researchers who created this projection describe it as their 'middle of the road scenario that can also be seen as the most likely path'.

14 Lange, Glenn-Marie; Wodon, Quentin; Carey, Kevin. 2018. 'The Changing Wealth of Nations 2018: Building a Sustainable Future.' Washington, DC: World Bank. © World Bank. See: https://openknowledge.worldbank.org/ handle/10986/29001 License: CC BY 3.0 IGO.

15 Markovits, D. (2019), *The Meritocracy Trap: How America's Foundational Myth Feeds Inequality, Dismantles the Middle Class, and Devours the Elite* (Penguin Random House); Sandel, M. (2020), *The Tyranny of Merit: What's Become of the Common Good?* (Allen Lane)

16 Goldin, C. and Katz, L. (2009), *The Race Between Education and Technology* (Harvard University Press)

17 Kaushik Basu, 'The World Economy's Labor Pains' (Project Syndicate, 4 January 2016). See: https://www.project-syndicate.org/onpoint/ labor-automation-slow-global-growth-by-kaushik-basu-2016-01

18 David Autor and Anna Salomons, 'Does Productivity Growth Threaten Employment? "Robocalyspe Now?"' (European Central Bank, 27 June 2017). See: https://www.ecb.europa.eu/pub/conferences/shared/pdf/20170626_ ecb_forum/Autor-Salomons-Productivity-Presentation.pdf

19   Noshir Kaka et al., 'Digital India: Technology to transform a connected
     nation' (McKinsey Global Institute, March 2019). See: https://www.
     mckinsey.com/business-functions/mckinsey-digital/our-insights/
     digital-india-technology-to-transform-a-connected-nation

20   Anton Korinek and Joseph E. Stiglitz, 'Artificial Intelligence and Its
     Implications for Income Distribution and Unemployment', in *The Economics of
     Artificial Intelligence: An Agenda* (University of Chicago Press, 2019), p. 352

21   The 2050 figures come from a number of sources, including Max Roser and
     Mohamed Nagdy, 'Projections of Future Education' (Our World in Data,
     2013). See: https://ourworldindata.org/projections-of-future-education

22   EdX founder Anant Agarwal has laid out his visions of how online education
     can multiply choice in post-school education in 'A Conversation with Anant
     Agarwal: Online Education in the New Normal' (Columbia Center for
     Teaching and Learning, 20 April 2020). See: https://ctl.columbia.edu/
     announcements/pcool-anant-agarwal/

23   Data on financing were drawn from the Education Commission model used as
     a basis for this report: 'The Learning Generation: Investing in Education for a
     Changing World' (Education Commission, 2016)

24   Interview with Walter Scheidel, 'Can inequality only be fixed by
     war, revolution or plague?' (*The Economist*, 10 September 2018).
     See: https://www.economist.com/open-future/2018/09/10/
     can-inequality-only-be-fixed-by-war-revolution-or-plague

CHAPTER 6: THE HUMANITARIAN CHALLENGE

1   Dag Hammarskjöld, 'Address at University of California Convocation' (United
     Nations, 13 May 1954). See: https://ask.un.org/faq/14623

2   'Global Humanitarian Overview 2021' (OCHA, 1 December 2020). See:
     https://gho.unocha.org/

3   The best summary of the condition of refugees and displaced persons is
     Collier, P. and Betts, A. (2018), *Refuge: Transforming a Broken Refugee System*
     (Penguin)

4   'More Than 750 Million Worldwide Would Migrate If They Could' (Gallup,
     10 December 2018). See: https://news.gallup.com/poll/245255/750-million-
     worldwide-migrate.aspx

5   'U.N. Food Program Is The First Line Against Terrorism, Beasley Says' (NPR,
     24 July 2017). See: https://www.npr.org/2017/07/24/538970963/u-n-food-
     program-is-the-first-line-against-terrorism-beasley-says?t=1606398938066

6   Collier P. and Betts A. (2018), *Refuge: Transforming a Broken Refugee System* (Penguin)

7   'Appeals and response plans 2020' (OCHA). See: https://fts.unocha.org/
     appeals/overview/2020. And: Watkins, K. and Sridhar, D. (2018), 'Pneumonia: a
     global cause without champions'. *The Lancet*, 392 (10149), 718–719)

8   'Global Humanitarian Overview 2021' (OCHA, 1 December 2020). See:
    https://gho.unocha.org/

9   'Cerf Funding' (OCHA). See: https://fts.unocha.org/pooled-funds/cerf/
    summary/2020

10 Skidelsky, R. (2000), *John Maynard Keynes: Fighting for Britain 1937–1946 (Vol. 3)*
    (Macmillan)

11 Kapur, D., Lewis, J. P. and Webb, R. C. (1997), *The World Bank: Its First Half
    Century, Volume 1* (Brookings Institution Press), p. 130

12 Ibid., p. 140

13 Colin Scott and Ian Bannon. 2003. ''Mind the Gap': The World Bank,
    Humanitarian Action and Development—A Personal Account.' (Social
    Development Notes; No. 10. World Bank, Washington, DC. © World Bank.).
    See: https://openknowledge.worldbank.org/handle/10986/11306 License: CC
    BY 3.0 IGO

14 Wolfensohn, J. D. (2008), *My Global Life: My Journey Among Rich and Poor, from
    Sydney to Wall Street to the World Bank* (PublicAffairs)

15 For further information on data, see: https://ourworldindata.org/grapher/
    world-population-in-extreme-poverty-absolute

16 Martin Ravallion, 'A Comparative Perspective on Poverty Reduction in Brazil,
    China and India' (*World Bank Research Observer*, vol. 26, no. 1, 2011, pp. 71–104)
    See: www.jstor.org/stable/41261423

17 Homi Kharas and Kristofer Hamel, 'A global tipping point: Half the world is
    now middle class or wealthier' (Brookings Institute, 27 September 2018). See:
    https://www.brookings.edu/blog/future-development/2018/09/27/a-global-
    tipping-point-half-the-world-is-now-middle-class-or-wealthier/

18 Homi Kharas and Meagan Dooley, 'China's Influence on the Global Middle
    Class' (Brooking's Institution, October 2020). See: https://www.brookings.
    edu/wp-content/uploads/2020/10/FP_20201012_china_middle_class_
    kharas_dooley.pdf

19 Rosling, H., Rosling, O. and Rosling Rönnlund, A. (2019), *Factfulness: Ten
    Reasons We're Wrong About the World – And Why Things Are Better Than You Think*
    (Hodder & Stoughton)

20 Steven Pinker, 'Steven Pinker: what can we expect from the 2020s?'
    (*Financial Times*, 27 December 2019). See: https://www.ft.com/content/
    e448f4ae-224e-11ea-92da-f0c92e957a96

21 Chris Weller, 'Barack Obama has a one-question test that
    proves how good the world is today' (*Business Insider*, 20
    September 2017). See: https://www.businessinsider.com/
    president-barack-obama-speech-goalkeepers-2017-9?r=US&IR=T

22 Steven Pinker, 'Steven Pinker: what can we expect from the 2020s?'
    (*Financial Times*, 27 December 2019). See: https://www.ft.com/content/
    e448f4ae-224e-11ea-92da-f0c92e957a96

23 Ibid.

24 'Save Our Future: Averting an Education Catastrophe for the World's Children' (OCHA, 22 October 2020). See: https://reliefweb.int/report/world/save-our-future-averting-education-catastrophe-world-s-children

25 See the World Poverty Clock: https://worldpoverty.io/

26 Kristofer Hamel, Baldwin Tong and Martin Hofer, 'Poverty in Africa is now falling – but not fast enough' (Brookings Institution, 28 March 2019). See: https://www.brookings.edu/blog/future-development/2019/03/28/poverty-in-africa-is-now-falling-but-not-fast-enough/

27 Kevin Watkins and Maria Quattri, 'Child poverty in Africa' (ODI, August 2019). See: https://www.odi.org/sites/odi.org.uk/files/resource-documents/12863.pdf

28 'The State of Food Security and Nutrition in the World' (Food and Agriculture Organization, 2020). See: http://www.fao.org/3/ca9692en/CA9692EN.pdf

29 Some also argue that the World Bank method that calculated poverty at $1.90 a day is also wrong . See critique from Reddy, Sanjay G. and Lahoti, Rahul, '$1.90 Per Day: What Does it Say?' (October 27, 2015), http://dx.doi.org/10.2139/ssrn.2685096; and Allen, Robert C. 'Absolute Poverty: When Necessity Displaces Desire.' (*American Economic Review*, 107 (12): 3690–3721. 12 December 2017). https://www.aeaweb.org/articles?id=10.1257/aer.20161080

30 Roge Karma, '5 Myths about Global Poverty' (*Current Affairs*, 26 July 2019). See: https://www.currentaffairs.org/2019/07/5-myths-about-global-poverty

31 Jason Hickel, 'A Letter to Steven Pinker (and Bill Gates, for that matter) About Global Poverty' (*Class, Race and Corporate Power*, 7:1, 2019). See: https://core.ac.uk/download/pdf/212915314.pdf

32 Nicholas Kristof, 'The Mistakes That Will Haunt Our Legacy' (*New York Times*, 11 July 2020). See: https://www.nytimes.com/2020/07/11/opinion/sunday/animal-rights-cruelty.html

33 'The State of the Social Safety Nets 2018' (World Bank, 14 March 2018), p. 18. See: https://openknowledge.worldbank.org/handle/10986/29115

34 'World Social Protection Report 2017–19' (International Labour Office, 2017) p. 155. See: http://www.ilo.org/wcmsp5/groups/public/---dgreports/---dcomm/---publ/documents/publication/wcms_604882.pdf

35 Kevin Watkins, 'Opinion: How to prevent the 2020s from becoming a lost decade for children' (Devex, 12 May 2020). See: https://www.devex.com/news/opinion-how-to-prevent-the-2020s-from-becoming-a-lost-decade-for-children-97211

36 JP O'Malley, '"Solutions exist, and we can find better ones": Q&A with linguist and cognitive scientist Steven Pinker' (*New Humanist*, 27 February 2018). See: https://newhumanist.org.uk/articles/5293/solutions-exist-and-we-can-find-better-ones

37 Branko Milanović, 'Global Inequality: From Class to Location, from Proletarians to Migrants' (World Bank, September 2011)

38 'Impact of the COVID-19 Pandemic on Trade and Development' (United Nations, 19 November 2020), pp. 54, 58. See: https://unctad.org/webflyer/impact-covid-19-pandemic-trade-and-development-transitioning-new-normal

39 Ibid., p. 54

40 'Aid to the rescue' (*The Economist*, 14 August 2014). See: https://www.economist.com/finance-and-economics/2014/08/14/aid-to-the-rescue

41 'Mobilizing Tax Resources to Boost Growth and Prosperity in Sub-Saharan Africa' (World Bank, 9 September 2019). See: https://www.worldbank.org/en/results/2019/09/09/mobilizing-tax-resources-to-boost-growth-and-prosperity-in-sub-saharan-africa

42 My estimates from published studies

43 'Corruption Perceptions Index 2018' (Transparency International). See: https://www.transparency.org/files/content/pages/2018_CPI_Executive_Summary.pdf

44 Consolate K. Rusagara, 'Francophone Africa has the most promising tech startups and they are looking for investors' (*World Bank Blogs*, 6 May 2019). See: https://blogs.worldbank.org/psd/francophone-africa-has-most-promising-tech-startups-and-they-are-looking-investors

45 Aubrey Hruby, 'Tap creative industries to boost Africa's economic growth' (*Financial Times*, 22 March 2018). See: https://www.ft.com/content/9807a468-2ddc-11e8-9b4b-bc4b9f08f381

46 John F. Kennedy, 'Inaugural Address of John F. Kennedy' (20 January 1961)

CHAPTER 7: ABOLISHING TAX HAVENS

1 The OECD report reads: 'Excluding the Special Administrative Regions, which have committed to implement the internationally agreed tax standard.' We understand this to relate to Macau and also Hong Kong. See: https://www.oecd.org/ctp/42497950.pdf

2 'G20 Draft Communiqué' (*Financial Times*, 29 March 2009). See: https://www.ft.com/content/f6f30eaa-1c88-11de-977c-00144feabdc0

3 See: https://www.imf.org/external/np/sec/pr/2009/pdf/g20_040209.pdf

4 Ed Pilkington, 'Farewell to the woman they called the Queen of Mean: Leona Helmsley dies at 87' (*Guardian*, 21 August 2007). See: https://www.theguardian.com/business/2007/aug/21/usnews

5 Alex Cobham, Javier Garcia-Bernardo, Miroslav Palansky and Mark Bou Mansour, 'The State of Tax Justice 2020' (Tax Justice Network, 20 November 2020), p. 4. See: https://www.taxjustice.net/reports/the-state-of-tax-justice-2020/

6 Zucman, G. (2015), *The Hidden Wealth of Nations* (University of Chicago Press, translated by Teresa Lavender Fagan)

7 Anna Zakrzewski, Brent Beardsley, Daniel Kessler, Martin Mende, Federico

Muxí, Matthias Naumann, Jürgen Rogg, Tjun Tang, Tyler Woulfe and André Xavier, 'Global Wealth 2018: Seizing the Analytics Advantage' (Boston Consulting Group, 14 June 2018), p. 12. See: https://www.bcg.com/en-gb/publications/2018/global-wealth-seizing-analytics-advantage

8   Alex Cobham, Javier Garcia-Bernardo, Miroslav Palansky and Mark Bou Mansour, 'The State of Tax Justice 2020' (Tax Justice Network, 20 November 2020), p. 40. See: https://www.taxjustice.net/reports/the-state-of-tax-justice-2020/

9   Ibid., p. 4

10   Zucman, G. (2015), *The Hidden Wealth of Nations* (University of Chicago Press, translated by Teresa Lavender Fagan), p. 104

11   Ernesto Crivelli, Ruud De Mooij and Michael Keen, 'Base Erosion, Profit Shifting and Developing Countries' (International Monetary Fund, May 2015), p. 21. See: https://www.imf.org/external/pubs/ft/wp/2015/wp15118.pdf

12   Thomas Tørsløv, Ludvig Wier and Gabriel Zucman, *The Missing Profits of Nations* (NBER Working Paper 24701, June 2018, revised April 2020). See: http://www.nber.org/papers/w24701. There are different calculations, all of them large. Using foreign direct investment data, it is estimated that, as long ago as 2012, $700 billion in profits were relocated to tax havens: Richard Bolwijn, Bruno Casella and Davided Rigo, 'An Fdi-Driven Approach to Measuring the Scale and Economic Impact of BEPS' (*Transnational Corporations*, 25:2, 2018). See: https://papers.ssrn.com/sol3/papers.cfm?abstract_id=3422774. But, using data from the *Forbes* Global 2000 list of the world's largest corporations, the figure for 2012 was assessed to be more than $1 trillion ($1,076 billion in relocated profits): Kimberly A. Clausing, 'The Effect of Profit Shifting on the Corporate Tax Base in the United States and Beyond' (17 June 2016). See: https://papers.ssrn.com/sol3/papers.cfm?abstract_id=2685442

13   Alex Cobham, Javier Garcia-Bernardo, Miroslav Palansky and Mark Bou Mansour, 'The State of Tax Justice 2020' (Tax Justice Network, 20 November 2020), p. 14. See: https://www.taxjustice.net/reports/the-state-of-tax-justice-2020/

14   Paul Sweeney, 'An effective corporation-tax system for the EU' (Social Europe, 4 November 2020). See: https://www.socialeurope.eu/an-effective-corporation-tax-system-for-the-eu

15   See: https://fsi.taxjustice.net/en/

16   Heather Chen, Kevin Ponniah and Mayuri Mei Lin, '1MDB: The playboys, PMs and partygoers around a global financial scandal' (BBC News, 9 August 2019). See: https://www.bbc.co.uk/news/world-asia-46341603

17   Alex Cobham, Javier Garcia-Bernardo, Miroslav Palansky and Mark Bou Mansour, 'The State of Tax Justice 2020' (Tax Justice Network, 20 November 2020), p. 14. See: https://www.taxjustice.net/reports/the-state-of-tax-justice-2020/

18 Harrington, B. (2016), *Capital Without Borders: Wealth Managers and the One Percent* (Harvard University Press)

19 Ibid., p. 162

20 Brown, G. (2010), *Beyond the Crash: Overcoming the First Crisis of Globalization* (Free Press)

21 'Narrative Report on the Cayman Islands' (Tax Justice Network, 2020), p. 8. See: https://fsi.taxjustice.net/PDF/CaymanIslands.pdf

22 Charles Levinson, 'How Wall Street captured Washington's effort to rein in banks' (Reuters, 9 April 2015). See: https://www.reuters.com/investigates/special-report/usa-bankrules-weakening/

23 See: https://www.icij.org/investigations/panama-papers/pages/panama-papers-about-the-investigation/

24 Ibid. Also: Mike McIntire, Sasha Chavkin and Martha M. Hamilton, 'Commerce Secretary's Offshore Ties to Putin "Cronies"' (*New York Times*, 5 November 2017). See: https://www.nytimes.com/2017/11/05/world/wilbur-ross-russia.html

25 'Improving Access to Bank Information for Tax Purposes' (Organisation for Economic Co-operation and Development, 24 March 2000), p. 3. See: http://www.oecd.org/tax/exchange-of-tax-information/2497487.pdf

26 'Model Agreement on Exchange of Information in Tax Matters (Model TIEA)', (Organisation for Economic Co-operation and Development, April 2002). See: https://www.oecd.org/tax/exchange-of-tax-information/taxinformationexchangeagreementstieas.htm

27 'G20 Leaders' Declaration'. See: http://www.g20.utoronto.ca/2013/2013-0906-declaration.html

28 'International community continues making progress against offshore tax evasion' (Organisation for Economic Co-operation and Development, 30 June 2020). See: https://www.oecd.org/ctp/exchange-of-tax-information/international-community-continues-making-progress-against-offshore-tax-evasion.htm

29 Milanović, B. (2019), *Capitalism, Alone: The Future of the System That Rules the World* (Harvard University Press), p. 29

30 See: https://www.factipanel.org/documents/facti-panel-interim-report

31 FACTI Panel, 'Financial Integrity for Sustainable Development: Report of the High Level Panel on International Financial Accountability, Transparency and Integrity for Achieving the 2030 Agenda', February 2021, p. 17. See: https://www.factipanel.org/report.

32 Following a two-year process with a multi-stakeholder technical committee, pilot work with reporter companies and various rounds of public consultation, the Global Reporting Initiative – the leading setter of global sustainability standards – launched its technical standard for tax, including the most robust international standard for country-by-country reporting, GRI 207: Tax 2019. In 2021, the first full year for adoption of the standard,

there is growing uptake. Investors and civil society groups are calling for the OECD standard to be enhanced, so that it converges to the GRI standard. Full details of GRI 207 and the consultation process can be found at: https://www.globalreporting.org/standards/standards-development/topic-standard-project-for-tax/

33 See: https://www.theguardian.com/world/2021/feb/26/eu-states-back-plan-to-expose-big-companies-tax-avoidance

34 See: https://uk.ambafrance.org/COVID-19-Europe-will-weather-this-crisis-together

35 Paul Sweeney, 'An effective corporation-tax system for the EU' (Social Europe, 4 November 2020). See: https://www.socialeurope.eu/an-effective-corporation-tax-system-for-the-eu

36 Natasha Sarin and Lawrence H. Summers, 'Increasing tax compliance in the United States' (VoxEU & CEPR), 24 April 2020. See: https://voxeu.org/article/increasing-tax-compliance-united-states

37 The METR proposal for a minimum effective tax rate, for example, is both much less complex than the current OECD proposals, and unlike the latter does not require changes to international tax treaties. Economic modelling shows that the revenue gains would be much higher for the METR both for non-haven OECD members and for lower-income countries. See: Sol Picciotto, Jeffery M. Kadet, Alex Cobham, Tommaso Faccio, Javier Garcia-Bernardo and Petr Janský, 'For a Better GLOBE: A Minimum Effective Tax Rate for Multinationals', Tax Notes International, February 15, 2021, p. 863.

38 Zucman, G. (2015), The Hidden Wealth of Nations (University of Chicago Press, translated by Teresa Lavender Fagan), p. 84

39 Joseph R. Biden, Jr, 'Why America Must Lead Again' (Foreign Affairs, March/April 2020). See: https://www.foreignaffairs.com/articles/united-states/2020-01-23/why-america-must-lead-again

40 'A Practical Proposal to End Corporate Tax Abuse', Institute of Economic Studies: https://ies.fsv.cuni.cz/sci/publication/show/id/6412/lang/en

41 'Polling shows near total public support for measures to end corporate tax haven use' (Tax Justice Network, 17 September 2020). See: https://www.taxjustice.net/press/polling-shows-near-total-public-support-for-measures-to-end-corporate-tax-haven-use

CHAPTER 8: ELIMINATING NUCLEAR WEAPONS

1 The Syrian bombing has now been publicly seen
2 See: 'On the Brink: The Cuban Missile Crisis', Interview with Arthur M. Schlesinger, Jr, (20 October 2002), https://www.jfklibrary.org/events-and-awards/forums/past-forums/transcripts/on-the-brink-the-cuban-missile-crisis

3   John F. Kennedy, 'Address before the General Assembly of the United
     Nations' (25 September 1961). See: https://www.jfklibrary.org/archives/
     other-resources/john-f-kennedy-speeches/united-nations-19610925

4   The story of Khan is written up in International Institute for Strategic
     Studies, *Nuclear Black Markets: Pakistan, A. Q. Khan and the Rise of Proliferation*
     (International Institute for Strategic Studies, 2007)

5   Robert Einhorn and Richard Nephew, 'The Iran nuclear deal:
     Prelude to proliferation in the Middle East?' (Brookings Institution,
     31 May 2016). See: https://www.brookings.edu/research/
     the-iran-nuclear-deal-prelude-to-proliferation-in-the-middle-east/

6   See: https://www.cbsnews.com/news/mohammad-bin-salman-denies-
     ordering-khashoggi-murder-but-says-he-takes-responsibility-for-it-60-
     minutes-2019-09-29/

7   Leaked by WikiLeaks: 'Speech by Hillary Clinton to Goldman Sachs, 2013
     IBD Ceo Annual Conference, 6/4/13'. See for further information: https://
     www.wikileaks.org/

8   Paul Dorfman, 'Opinion: Why is UAE about to open four nuclear reactors?'
     (*The Conversation*, 13 March 2020). See: https://www.ucl.ac.uk/news/2020/
     mar/opinion-why-uae-about-open-four-nuclear-reactors

9   Geert De Clercq, 'Qatar says UAE nuclear plant is threat to regional
     stability' (Reuters, 20 March 2019). See: https://www.reuters.com/article/
     qatar-emirates-nuclearpower-idUSL8N2175GH

10   David E. Sanger and William J. Broad, 'Erdoğan's Ambitions Go Beyond
     Syria. He Says He Wants Nuclear Weapons' (*New York Times*, 20 October 2019).
     See: https://www.nytimes.com/2019/10/20/world/middleeast/erdogan-
     turkey-nuclear-weapons-trump.html

11   Ibid.

12   Thomas Jonter, 'Sweden and the Bomb: The Swedish Plans to Acquire
     Nuclear Weapons, 1945–1972' (Uppsala University, September 2001). See:
     https://inis.iaea.org/collection/NCLCollectionStore/
     _Public/32/056/32056064.pdf

13   Uri Friedman, 'Why One President Gave Up His Country's Nukes' (*The
     Atlantic*, 9 September 2017). See: https://www.theatlantic.com/international/
     archive/2017/09/north-korea-south-africa/539265/

14   Judith Miller, 'How Gadhafi Lost His Groove' (*Wall Street Journal*, 16 May
     2006). See https://www.wsj.com/articles/SB114773941211953610

15   Busch, N. and Pilat, J. (2017), *The Politics of Weapons Inspections: Assessing WMD
     Monitoring and Verification Regimes* (Stanford University Press), p. 113

16   Statement by Gaddafi's son Saif of the September 11 attacks, in Judith Miller,
     'How Gadhafi Lost His Groove' (*Wall Street Journal*, 16 May 2006). See:
     https://www.wsj.com/articles/SB114773941211953610

17   Ibid.

18   For further details, see Bruce W. Jentleson and Christopher A. Whytock,

'Who "Won" Libya? The Force-Diplomacy Debate and Its Implications for Theory and Policy' (*International Security*, 30:3, 2005), pp. 47–86

19   'Nuclear Proliferation and Safeguards' (Congress of the United Sates, Office of Technology Assessment, 1977) Chapter IV, p. 97. See: https://books.google.co.uk/books?id=53AWfnJCorYC&printsec=frontcover#v=onepage&q&f=false

20   Secretary of Defence Robert McNamara told President Kennedy, in 1963 –Andrew Buncombe, 'JFK was ready to use nuclear bomb on China, tapes reveal' (*The Independent*, 12 July 2013). See: https://www.independent.co.uk/news/world/americas/jfk-was-ready-to-use-nuclear-bomb-on-china-tapes-reveal-308341.html

21   Bajwa, F. (2013), *From Kutch to Tashkent: The Indo-Pakistan War of 1965* (Hurst), p. 368

22   Graham Allison, 'Nuclear Disorder: Surveying Atomic Threats' (*Foreign Affairs*, January/February 2010). See: https://www.foreignaffairs.com/articles/pakistan/2010-01-01/nuclear-disorder

23   Harry S. Truman, 'Statement by the President Reviewing Two Years of Experience With the Atomic Energy Act'. See: https://www.presidency.ucsb.edu/documents/statement-the-president-reviewing-two-years-experience-with-the-atomic-energy-act

24   Ronald Reagan, 'Speech by Ronald Reagan to the National Association of Evangelicals in March 1983'. See: https://web.archive.org/web/20040609055415/http://www.presidentreagan.info/speeches/empire.cfm

25   Nicole Winfield, 'Pope Francis warns nuclear deterrence offers only a false sense of security' (*America: The Jesuit Review*, 10 November 2017). See: https://www.americamagazine.org/politics-society/2017/11/10/pope-francis-warns-nuclear-deterrence-offers-only-false-sense-security

26   'Joint Soviet–United States Statement on the Summit Meeting in Geneva' (Reagan Library, 21 November 1985). See: https://www.reaganlibrary.gov/archives/speech/joint-soviet-united-states-statement-summit-meeting-geneva

27   George P. Shultz, William J. Perry, Henry A. Kissinger and Sam Nunn, 'A World Free of Nuclear Weapons' (*Wall Street Journal*, 4 January 2007). See: https://www.wsj.com/articles/SB116787515251566636

28   Barack Obama, 'Remarks By President Barack Obama In Prague As Delivered' (Obama White House, April 5 2009). See: https://obamawhitehouse.archives.gov/the-press-office/remarks-president-barack-obama-prague-delivered

29   See 'Nuclear Posture Review Report' (Department of Defense, April 2010). See: https://dod.defense.gov/Portals/1/features/defenseReviews/NPR/2010_Nuclear_Posture_Review_Report.pdf

30   Eric Levitz, 'In Hiroshima, President Obama Calls for "Moral Revolution" to End Threat of Nuclear War' (*New York Magazine*, 27 May 2016). See: https://nymag.com/intelligencer/2016/05/hiroshima-obama-proposes-moral-revolution.html

31 Michael E. O'Hanlon, 'Is a World Without Nuclear Weapons Really Possible?' (Brookings Institution, 4 May 2010). See: https://www.brookings.edu/opinions/is-a-world-without-nuclear-weapons-really-possible/

32 George P. Shultz, William J. Perry, Henry A. Kissinger and Sam Nunn, 'A World Free of Nuclear Weapons' (*Wall Street Journal*, 4 January 2007) See: https://www.wsj.com/articles/SB116787515251566636

33 Perry, W. and Collina, T. (2020), *The Button: The New Nuclear Arms Race and Presidential Power from Truman to Trump* (BenBella Books)

34 Joe Biden, 'Remarks by the Vice President on Nuclear Security' (Obama White House, 12 January 2017). See: https://obamawhitehouse.archives.gov/the-press-office/2017/01/12/remarks-vice-president-nuclear-security

35 Joe Biden, 'Presidential Candidates: Joe Biden' (Council For a Livable World). See: https://livableworld.org/presidential-candidates-joe-biden/

36 Megan Messerly, 'Resuming U.S. nuclear testing, as Trump administration officials have reportedly discussed, would be 'as reckless as it is dangerous,' Biden says' (*Nevada Independent*, 22 February 2020). See: https://thenevadaindependent.com/article/resuming-u-s-nuclear-testing-as-trump-administration-officials-have-reportedly-discussed-would-be-as-reckless-as-it-is-dangerous-biden-says

37 'Fissile Material' (United Nations Office for Disarmament Affairs). See: https://www.un.org/disarmament/fissile-material/

38 David E. Sanger and William J. Broad, 'Pentagon Suggests Countering Devastating Cyberattacks With Nuclear Arms' (*New York Times,* 16 January 2018). See: https://www.nytimes.com/2018/01/16/us/politics/pentagon-nuclear-review-cyberattack-trump.html

39 'Interim National Security Strategic Guidance' (The White House, March 2021). See: https://www.whitehouse.gov/wp-content/uploads/2021/03/NSC-1v2.pdf

40 Kennan, G. (1967), *Memoirs: 1925–1950* (Little, Brown)

41 Liping Xia, 'China's Nuclear Doctrine: Debates and Evolution' (Carnegie Endowment, 30 June 2016). See: https://carnegieendowment.org/2016/06/30/china-s-nuclear-doctrine-debates-and-evolution-pub-63967

42 'National Security Strategy and Strategic Defence and Security Review 2015' (HM Government), pp. 34–35. See: https://www.gov.uk/government/publications/national-security-strategy-and-strategic-defence-and-security-review-2015

43 See 'Select Committee on International Relations' (*House of Lords*, March 6 2019) – see http://data.parliament.uk/writtenevidence/committeeevidence.svc/evidencedocument/international-relations-committee/the-nuclear-nonproliferation-treaty-and-nuclear-disarmament/oral/97600.html

44 'Defence and National Security Strategic Review 2017' (French Government), p. 69. See: https://otan.delegfrance.org/2017-Strategic-Review-of-Defence-and-National-Security

45 Cynthia Roberts, 'Revelations About Russia's Nuclear Deterrence Policy' (*War on the Rocks,* 19 June 2020). See: https://warontherocks.com/2020/06/revelations-about-russias-nuclear-deterrence-policy/

46 'Basic Principles of State Policy of the Russian Federation on Nuclear Deterrence' (MFA Russia, 8 June 2020). See: https://www.mid.ru/en/foreign_policy/international_safety/disarmament/-/asset_publisher/rpofiUBmANaH/content/id/4152094

47 Joe Biden, 'Presidential Candidates: Joe Biden' (Council For a Livable World). See: https://livableworld.org/presidential-candidates-joe-biden/

48 Robert Burns, 'Biden would push for less US reliance on nukes for defense' (Associated Press, 21 September 2020). See: https://apnews.com/article/election-2020-nuclear-weapons-elections-joe-biden-russia-1299ae16f3f21db12e4a41ce2392a0f7

49 Joe Biden, 'Remarks by the Vice President on Nuclear Security' (Obama White House, 12 January 2017). See: https://obamawhitehouse.archives.gov/the-press-office/2017/01/12/remarks-vice-president-nuclear-security

50 Stephen Dziedzic, 'Australia's new defence strategy unveils a significant strategic shift in foreign policy to meet new threats from China' (ABC News, 1 July 2020). See: https://www.abc.net.au/news/2020-07-02/australias-new-defence-strategy-strategic-shift-foreign-policy/12412650

51 Eisenhower, D., *Mandate for Change, 1953–56* (Doubleday & Company, 1963), p. 180

52 Dwight D. Eisenhower, 'Atoms for Peace Speech' (8 December 1953). See: https://www.iaea.org/about/history/atoms-for-peace-speech

53 Dulles–Eisenhower conversations contained in Thomas C. Shelling, 'The Nuclear Taboo' (*MIT International Review,* 2007). See: http://web.mit.edu/mitir/2007/spring/taboo.html

54 Jonathan Baron and Stephen Herzog, 'Poll: What the American public likes and hates about Trump's nuclear policies' (*The Bulletin,* 27 April 2020). See: https://thebulletin.org/2020/04/poll-what-the-american-public-likes-and-hates-about-trumps-nuclear-policies/

55 'Building on George Shultz's Vision of a World Without Nukes' (*Wall Street Journal,* 23 March 2021) Perry, Kissinger, Nunn op-ed.

CHAPTER 9: 'ONE WORLD, TWO SYSTEMS'

1 See: https://www.bloomberg.com/news/articles/2019-11-21/kissinger-says-u-s-and-china-in-foothills-of-a-cold-war. Also: https://www.newsweek.com/listen-henry-kissinger-china-state-media-chief-warns-joe-biden-1548023

2 'Xi warns Biden and EU not to reignite Cold War' (*Politico,* 25 January 2021). See: https://www.politico.eu/article/xi-warns-biden-and-eu-not-to-reignite-cold-war/

3 In Article I it mentions 'the principle of equal rights and self-determination of peoples'. See: https://www.un.org/en/about-us/un-charter/full-text

4 Eleanor Albert, 'Which Countries Support the New Hong Kong National Security Law?' (*The Diplomat*, 6 July 2020). See: https://thediplomat.com/2020/07/which-countries-support-the-new-hong-kong-national-security-law/

5 For the most recent examination of the relationship, see Hamilton, N. (2019), *War and Peace, Volume 3: FDR's Final Odyssey: D-Day to Yalta, 1943–1945* (Houghton Mifflin Harcourt)

6 See: https://web.archive.org/web/20131006055540/http://www.newamericancentury.org/aboutpnac.htm

7 See: https://2001-2009.state.gov/s/d/former/zoellick/rem/53682.htm

8 See: https://trumpwhitehouse.archives.gov/briefings-statements/remarks-president-trump-75th-session-united-nations-general-assembly/

9 See: https://www.fmprc.gov.cn/mfa_eng/zxxx_662805/t1817098.shtml

10 António Guterres, 'Secretary-General's address to the Opening of the General Debate of the 75th Session of the General Assembly' (22 September 2020). See: https://www.un.org/sg/en/content/sg/statement/2020-09-22/secretary-generals-address-the-opening-of-the-general-debate-of-the-75th-session-of-the-general-assembly

11 'Trump's unilateralism challenges global rules: China Daily editorial' (*China Daily*, 10 June 2018). See: http://www.chinadaily.com.cn/a/201806/10/WS5b1d274fa31001b82571f28a.html

12 'President Xi hosts welcoming dinner for SCO guests' (*China Daily*, 9 June 2018). See: https://global.chinadaily.com.cn/a/201806/09/WS5b1bc3f5a31001b82571f183.html

13 Branko Milanović, 'The World Is Becoming More Equal: Even as Globalization Hurts Middle-Class Westerners' (*Majalla*, 4 September 2020). See: https://eng.majalla.com/node/101761/the-world-is-becoming-more-equal

14 Ibid.

15 Li Yang, Filip Novokmet and Branko Milanović, 'From workers to capitalists in less than two generations: Chinese urban elite transformation between 1988 and 2013' (*Vox*, 9 October 2020). See: https://voxeu.org/article/chinese-urban-elite-transformation-between-1988-and-2013

16 These figures are based on original calculations made by Cambridge Econometrics, to whom I am very grateful

17 See: https://www.pewresearch.org/global/2020/10/06/unfavorable-views-of-china-reach-historic-highs-in-many-countries/

18 Daniel Lippman and Nahal Toosi, 'Trump administration weighs accusing China of "genocide" over Uighurs' (*Politico*, 25 August 2020). See: https://www.politico.com/news/2020/08/25/trump-administration-china-genocide-uighurs-401581

19 Mark Scott, 'The Internet is broken. Can this group fix it?' (*Politico*, 25 February 2018). See: https://www.politico.eu/article/internet-governance-ottawa-regulation-balkanization-splinternet-global-jurisdiction-policy-network/

20   See: https://www.bbc.co.uk/news/business-50570838

21   See: https://www.reuters.com/article/us-southchinasea-usa-china-navy/
china-naval-chief-says-minor-incident-could-spark-war-in-south-china-sea-
idUSKCN0SO05320151030

22   Michèle Flournoy and Gabrielle Chefitz, 'Sharpening the U.S. Military's
Edge: Critical Steps for the Next Administration' (Center for New American
Security, 13 July 2020). See: https://www.cnas.org/publications/commentary/
sharpening-the-u-s-militarys-edge-critical-steps-for-the-next-administration

23   Hank Paulson, 'Remarks by Henry M. Paulson, Jr., on the Delusions of
Decoupling' (21 November 2019). See: https://www.paulsoninstitute.org/
press_release/remarks-by-henry-m-paulson-jr-on-the-delusions-of-decoupling/

24   Kissinger, H. (2011), On China (Allen Lane), Chapter 18

25   Zhou Xiaochuan, 'Reform the international monetary system' (23 March
2009), p. 2. See: https://www.bis.org/review/r090402c.pdf

26   Anne-Marie Slaughter, 'The three pillars of US foreign policy under
Biden' (Financial Times, 19 October 2020). See: https://www.ft.com/
content/6f85ae61-2e16-4272-8974-a38123ed994f

27   Allison, G. (2017), Destined for War: Can America and China Escape Thucydides's
Trap? (Mariner Books)

28   Fareed Zakaria, 'The New China Scare' (Foreign Affairs, 99:1, January–
February 2020). See: https://www.foreignaffairs.com/articles/
china/2019-12-06/new-china-scare

29   Hank Paulson, 'Remarks by Henry M. Paulson, Jr., on the Delusions of
Decoupling' (21 November 2019). See: https://www.paulsoninstitute.org/
press_release/remarks-by-henry-m-paulson-jr-on-the-delusions-of-decoupling/

30   'US v China: A new Cold War?' (The Real Story, 30 October 2020). See:
https://www.bbc.co.uk/programmes/w3cszcns

31   James Crabtree, 'China's Radical New Vision of Globalization' (Noema,
10 December 2020). See: https://www.noemamag.com/chinas-radical-
new-vision-of-globalization/

32   Winston Churchill, 'The Sinews of Peace ("Iron Curtain Speech")' (5 March
1946). For further information, see: https://winstonchurchill.org/resources/
speeches/1946-1963-elder-statesman/the-sinews-of-peace/

33   See: https://www.washingtonpost.com/news/theworldpost/wp/2017/10/27/
china-party-congress-west/

34   Milanović, B. (2019), Capitalism, Alone: The Future of the System That Rules the
World (Harvard University Press)

35   'China to build high-level socialist market economy' (China Daily, 29
October 2020). See: https://www.chinadaily.com.cn/a/202010/29/
WS5f9acaf3a31024adoba81fb6.html

36   James Crabtree, 'China's Radical New Vision of Globalization'
(Noema, 10 December 2020). See: https://www.noemamag.com/
chinas-radical-new-vision-of-globalization/

37 'Chinese Communist Party to mark 100th anniversary in isolation' (*NIKKEIAsia*, 7 January 2021). See: https://asia.nikkei.com/Spotlight/Comment/Chinese-Communist-Party-to-mark-100th-anniversary-in-isolation

38 'Full Text: Xi Jinping's keynote speech at the World Economic Forum' (17 January 2017). See: http://www.china.org.cn/node_7247529/content_40569136.htm

39 'The Longer Telegram: Toward a new American China strategy' (*Atlantic Council,* 2021). See: https://www.atlanticcouncil.org/content-series/atlantic-council-strategy-paper-series/the-longer-telegram/#foreword

40 Nathan Gardels, 'Planetary Realism: Global warming may prevent a new Cold War' (*Noema*, 16 October 2020). See: https://www.noemamag.com/planetary-realism/

41 Ibid.

42 Joe Biden, 'Remarks by President Biden at the 2021 Virtual Munich Security Conference' (The White House, 19 February 2021). See: https://whitehouse.gov/briefing-room/speeches-remarks/2021/02/19/remarks-by-president-biden-at-the-2021-virtual-munich-security-conference.

43 Nathan Gardels, 'The World Doesn't Wait' (*Noema*, 20 November 2020). See: https://www.noemamag.com/the-world-doesnt-wait/

44 Statement from China Securities Regulatory Commission. For further information, see: http://www.china.org.cn/china/Off_the_Wire/2020-04/01/content_75886235.htm

45 Klein, M. and Pettis, M. (2020), *Trade Wars Are Class Wars: How Rising Inequality Distorts the Global Economy and Threatens International Peace* (Yale University Press)

46 'China issues guideline for enhancing IPR protection' (24 November 2019). See: http://english.www.gov.cn/policies/latestreleases/201911/24/content_WS5dda789bc6d0bcf8c4c17bd4.html

CHAPTER 10: TACKLING POPULIST NATIONALISM HEAD ON

1 Marshall, T. (2018), *Divided: Why We're Living in an Age of Walls* (Elliott & Thompson)

2 Orwell, G. (2018), *Notes on Nationalism* (Penguin)

3 Deutsch, K. (1953), *Nationalism and Social Communication: An Inquiry into the Foundation of Nationality* (Wiley), p. 232

4 Viroli, M. (1995), *For Love of Country: An Essay on Patriotism and Nationalism* (Oxford University Press)

5 Huizinga, J. (1984), *Men and Ideas: History, the Middle Ages, the Renaissance* (Princeton University Press), p. 97

6 Orwell, G. (2018), *Notes on Nationalism* (Penguin)

7 Wimmer, A. (2018), *Nation Building: Why Some Countries Come Together While Others Fall Apart* (Princeton University Press)

8   Jamie Smyth, 'Crosby backs Johnson to neuter EU with a "bit of crazy"'
     negotiation' (Financial Times, 20 September 2020). See: https://www.ft.com/
     content/2cfe0519-2ca0-401f-bb73-7045e564605c

9   Thorsten Benner, 'Merkel's next successor might be a bust'
     (Politico, 11 February 2020). See: https://www.politico.eu/article/
     german-cdu-afd-center-rights-crisis-is-kramp-karrenbauer-angela-merkel/

10   See: https://audiovisual.ec.europa.eu/en/video/I-181518

11   See: https://www.pewresearch.org/global/2020/02/09/
     nato-seen-favorably-across-member-states/pg_2020-02-09_nato_0-18/

12   Cathy Adams, 'Popular Japanese Sites are Refusing Entry to Tourists' (The
     Independent, 7 March 2019). See: https://www.independent.co.uk/travel/
     news-and-advice/japan-kyoto-overtourism-tourists-travel-tax-a8812311.html

13   David Autor, David Dorn and Gordon Hanson, 'The China syndrome: Local
     labor market effects of import competition in the United States' (American
     Economic Review, 103:6, 2013), pp. 2121–2168; David Autor, David Dorn,
     Gordon Hanson and Kaveh Majlesi, 'Importing Political Polarization? The
     Electoral Consequences of Rising Trade Exposure' (National Bureau of
     Economic Research, 2016); David Autor, David Dorn, Gordon Hanson and
     Kaveh Majlesi, 'A Note on the Effect of Rising Trade Exposure on the 2016
     Presidential Election' (MIT, 2016)

14   See: https://blogs.lse.ac.uk/europpblog/2018/01/16/
     we-dont-exist-to-them-do-we-why-working-class-people-voted-for-brexit/

15   See: Arlie R. Hochschild, Strangers in their Own Land: Anger
     and Mourning on the American Right, (New Press, 2016).
     Also see: https://www.davisvanguard.org/2016/09/
     arlie-russell-hochschild-strangers-land-anger-mourning-american-right/

16   See: http://eprints.lse.ac.uk/106530/1/Paper_14_golfing_with_trump.
     pdf. These ideas are also developed in Andrés Rodríguez-Pose, 'The revenge
     of the places that don't matter (and what to do about it)' (Cambridge Journal of
     Regions, Economy and Society, 11:1, March 2018), pp. 189–209). See: https://
     doi.org/10.1093/cjres/rsx024. The author's Twitter feed contains his initial
     comment on the US election of November 2020.

17   'Mistrust of politicians haunts France's Fifth Republic'
     (Financial Times, 5 March 2021) See: https://www.ft.com/
     content/7e422abf-5111-4444-835d-b87e16cd12f9

18   Kwame Anthony Appiah probes these ideas further in The Lies That Bind (2018)
     (Profile Books), which is based on the BBC Reith Lectures, 2016

19   Nathan Gardels' interview with Isaiah Berlin, conducted at the end of summer
     1991 in Portofino, Italy, was first published as 'The Ingathering Storm of
     Nationalism: The Return of the Volksgeist' (New Perspectives Quarterly, 8:4,
     1991), pp. 4–10. It was reprinted with amendments and additions as 'Two
     Concepts of Nationalism' (New York Review of Books, 21 November 1991), pp.
     19–23 (corrections 5 December 1991), and in its original form as 'Return

of the Volksgeist: Nationalism, Good and Bad' in Gardels, N. ed. (1997), *At Century's End: Great Minds Reflect on Our Times* (Wolfhound Press). A copy of the interview can be found here: http://berlin.wolf.ox.ac.uk/lists/interviews/gardels.pdf

20   Nussbaum, M. (1996), *For Love of Country: Debating the Limits of Patriotism* (Beacon Press), p. 50

21   Nussbaum, M. (2013), *Political Emotions: Why Love Matters for Justice* (Harvard University Press)

22   See Jürgen Habermas, 'The Inclusion of the Other' (MIT, 1998) and 'The European Nation-State: On the Past and Future of Sovereignty and Citizenship' (*Public Culture*, 10:2, 1998), pp. 397–416

23   D'Ancona, M. ed. (2009), *Being British: The Search for the Values that Bind the Nation*, (Mainstream)

24   Bolton, J. (2010), *How Barack Obama is Endangering Our National Sovereignty* (Encounter Books), p. 4

25   See: https://jamiemetzl.com/declaration-of-global-interdependence/

26   See: https://carnegieendowment.org/files/USFP_FinalReport_final1.pdf

27   Feng Zhang, 'China as a Global Force' (*Asia and the Pacific Policy Studies*, 3:1, 2016), pp. 120–128; J. C. Liow, 'Taking Shape: New Global Financial Architecture' (*RSIS Commentary*, 190, 2017); Rebecca Liao, 'Out of the Bretton Woods – How the AIIB is Different' (*Foreign Affairs*, 2015); Zheng Bijian, 'China's "Peaceful Rise" to Great-Power Status' (*Foreign Affairs*, 2005)

28   Figures compiled with the assistance of Cambridge Econometrics by assessing strength of major economies in 2030 and 2050

CONCLUSION: THE POWER OF HOPE

1   John Aglionby, 'Filipinos rally to oust the president' (*Guardian*, 20 January 2001). See: https://www.theguardian.com/world/2001/jan/20/johnaglionby1

2   See following articles: https://www.huffingtonpost.co.uk/entry/limas-naked-bike-ride-pro_n_4936197; https://mexiconewsdaily.com/news/clowns-get-together-to-have-a-few-laughs; https://www.bbc.co.uk/news/world-europe-34903677; https://www.theguardian.com/world/2020/mar/25/brazil-coronavirus-protests-get-out-bolsonaro

3   Garza A., (2020), The Purpose of Power: From the co-founder of Black Lives Matter (One World)

4   'How Do You Change Voters' Minds? Have a Conversation' (*New York Times*, 7 April 2016). See: https://www.nytimes.com/2016/04/10/magazine/how-do-you-change-voters-minds-have-a-conversation.html

5   See: https://www.goodreads.com/author/quotes/13560.Leonardo_da_Vinci

6   https://www.goodreads.com/quotes/384067-if-you-want-to-build-a-ship-don-t-drum-up

7   Andrew Tenzer and Ian Murray, 'The Empathy Delusion' (ReachSolutions, July 2019) See: https://www.reachsolutions.co.uk/sites/default/files/2019-07/Reach%20Solutions%20The%20Empathy%20Delusion%20V2.pdf

8   Jesse McKinley and Kirk Johnson, 'Mormons Tipped Scale in Ban on Gay Marriage' (*New York Times*, 14 November 2008) See: https://www.nytimes.com/2008/11/15/us/politics/15marriage.html

9   'Subtitled speech by Prime Minister Jens Stoltenberg to the victims of the 2011 Norway attacks' (YouTube, 24 July 2011) See: https://www.youtube.com/watch?v=80Pbd9UvZuY

10   'Jacinda Ardern's speech at Christchurch memorial – full transcript' (28 March 2019). See: https://www.theguardian.com/world/2019/mar/29/jacinda-arderns-speech-at-christchurch-memorial-full-transcript

11   Dickens, C. (1992), *David Copperfield* (Wordsworth Editions), p. 153

12   See: https://www.scottishpoetrylibrary.org.uk/poem/heres-health-them-thats-awa/

13   See: https://founders.archives.gov/documents/Jefferson/98-01-02-1712

14   See: John F. Kennedy, 'Inaugural Address' (20 January 1961), https://www.jfklibrary.org/learn/about-jfk/historic-speeches/inaugural-address. And: John F. Kennedy, 'Address to Independence Hall in Philadelphia', (4 July 1962), https://www.jfklibrary.org/learn/about-jfk/historic-speeches/address-at-independence-hall

15   See: https://www.goodreads.com/quotes/112259-if-you-assume-that-there-is-no-hope-you-guarantee

16   Speech by Anthony Eden at the United Nations Conference (1 March 1947)

17   Kaplan, F. (2020), *The Bomb: Presidents, Generals, and the Secret History of Nuclear War* (Simon & Schuster), pp. 165–166.

18   Speech by Cesar Chavez to the Commonwealth Club of California (9 November 1984). See: http://www.gvlibraries.org/content/1984-cesar-chavez-address-commonwealth-club-california

19   For a review of recent proposals for a new social contract, see excellent recent books by Minouche Shafik, *What we owe each other: A new social contract* (London, 2021); Raghuran Rajan, *The Third Pillar, The Revival of community in a Polarised World* (London, 2019); and Mark Carney, *Value(s)* (London, 2021).

INDEX